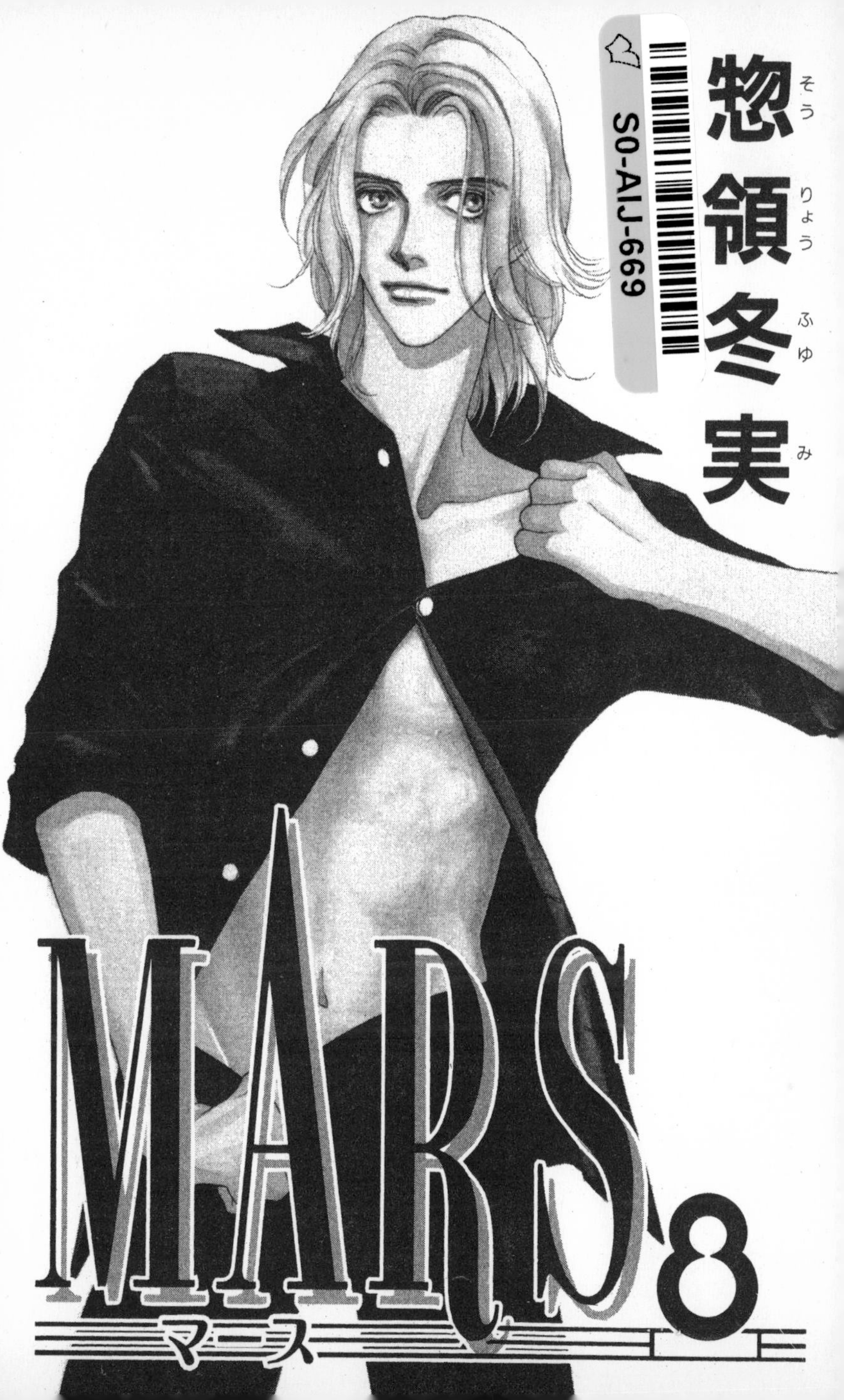
惣領冬実
そうりょうふゆみ
MARS
マース
8

ALSO AVAILABLE FROM ⊚TOKYOPOP®

MANGA

ACTION

ANGELIC LAYER*
CLAMP SCHOOL DETECTIVES* (April 2003)
DIGIMON (March 2003)
DUKLYON: CLAMP SCHOOL DEFENDERS* (September 2003)
GATEKEEPERS* (March 2003)
GTO*
HARLEM BEAT
INITIAL D*
ISLAND
JING: KING OF BANDITS* (June 2003)
JULINE*
LUPIN III*
MONSTERS, INC.
PRIEST
RAVE*
REAL BOUT HIGH SCHOOL*
REBOUND* (April 2003)
SAMURAI DEEPER KYO* (June 2003)
SCRYED* (March 2003)
SHAOLIN SISTERS* (February 2003)
THE SKULL MAN*

FANTASY

CHRONICLES OF THE CURSED SWORD (July 2003))
DEMON DIARY (May 2003)
DRAGON HUNTER (June 2003)
DRAGON KNIGHTS*
KING OF HELL (June 2003)
PLANET LADDER*
RAGNAROK
REBIRTH (March 2003)
SHIRAHIME:TALES OF THE SNOW PRINCESS* (December 2003)
SORCERER HUNTERS
WISH*

ROMANCE

HAPPY MANIA* (April 2003)
I.N.V.U. (February 2003)
LOVE HINA*
KARE KANO*
KODOCHA*
MAN OF MANY FACES* (May 2003)
MARMALADE BOY*
MARS*
PARADISE KISS*
PEACH GIRL
UNDER A GLASS MOON (June 2003)

SCIENCE FICTION

CHOBITS*
CLOVER
COWBOY BEBOP*
COWBOY BEBOP: SHOOTING STAR* (June 2003)
G-GUNDAM*
GUNDAM WING
GUNDAM WING: ENDLESS WALTZ*
GUNDAM: THE LAST OUTPOST*
PARASYTE
REALITY CHECK (March 2003)

MAGICAL GIRLS

CARDCAPTOR SAKURA
CARDCAPTOR SAKURA: MASTER OF THE CLOW*
CORRECTOR YUI
MAGIC KNIGHT RAYEARTH* (August 2003)
MIRACLE GIRLS
SAILOR MOON
SAINT TAIL
TOKYO MEW MEW* (April 2003)

CINE-MANGA™

AKIRA*
CARDCAPTORS
KIM POSSIBLE (March 2003)
LIZZIE McGUIRE (March 2003)
POWER RANGERS (May 2003)
SPY KIDS 2 (March 2003)

ANIME GUIDES

GUNDAM TECHNICAL MANUALS
COWBOY BEBOP
SAILOR MOON SCOUT GUIDES

NOVELS

SAILOR MOON
SUSHI SQUAD (April 2003)

ART BOOKS

CARDCAPTOR SAKURA*
MAGIC KNIGHT RAYEARTH*

TOKYOPOP KIDS

DISNEY CLASSICS (June 2003)
STRAY SHEEP (September 2003)

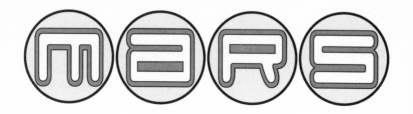

Volume 8
By Fuyumi Soryo

LOS ANGELES • TOKYO

Translator - Shirley Kubo
English Adaption - Elizabeth Hurchalla
Editor - Jodi Bryson
Associate Editor - Bryce P. Coleman
Retouch and Lettering - Songgu Kwan
Cover Layout - Anna Kernbaum

Senior Editor - Julie Taylor
Production Managers - Jennifer Miller and Jennifer Wagner
Art Director - Matthew Alford
VP of Production & Manufacturing - Ron Klamert
President & C.O.O. - John Parker
Publisher - Stuart Levy

Email: editor@TOKYOPOP.com
Come visit us online at www.TOKYOPOP.com

A  Manga
TOKYOPOP® is an imprint of Mixx Entertainment, Inc.
5900 Wilshire Blvd. Suite 2000, Los Angeles, CA 90036

ISBN: 1-59182-087-1

First TOKYOPOP® printing: December 2002

10 9 8 7 6 5 4 3 2 1
Printed in Canada

MARS

レジエンド　オブ　マース

LEGEND OF MARS

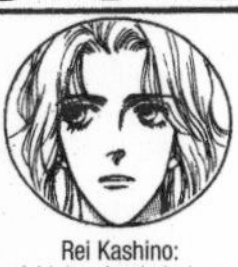

Rei Kashino:
A high school student who's into Kira's paintings. His twin brother Sei died recently.

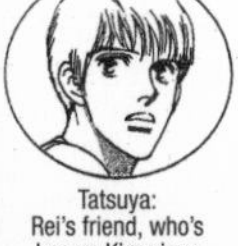

Tatsuya:
Rei's friend, who's known Kira since junior high.

The story until now:

Kira falls for Rei when she sees him kissing a statue of Mars in the art studio. Meanwhile, Rei finds himself drawn to Kira's sketch of a mother and child. Hoping to put aside the darkness in their hearts, they start dating. However, when Masao shows up, things start to feel darker than ever. Masao, who killed someone two years ago, was in love with Rei's reckless side, so when he finds out Kira is bringing light into Rei's life, he tries to kill her, too. Rei comes to her rescue, but in the process, he gets a little freaked about how much he and Masao are alike. Kira tries to reassure Rei that he and Masao are different and remind him of the strength of their love. But then the past she kept hidden for so long comes back to haunt her, and she warns Rei not to touch her...

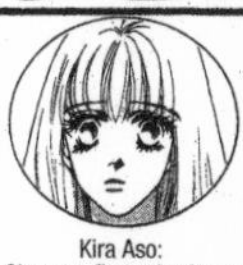

Kira Aso:
She won first prize in an art show for her painting of Rei, the guy she loves. Somehow, Masao knows about her secret past.

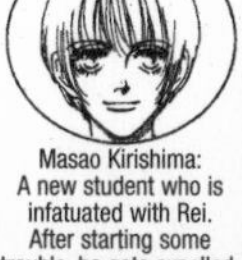

Masao Kirishima:
A new student who is infatuated with Rei. After starting some trouble, he gets expelled.

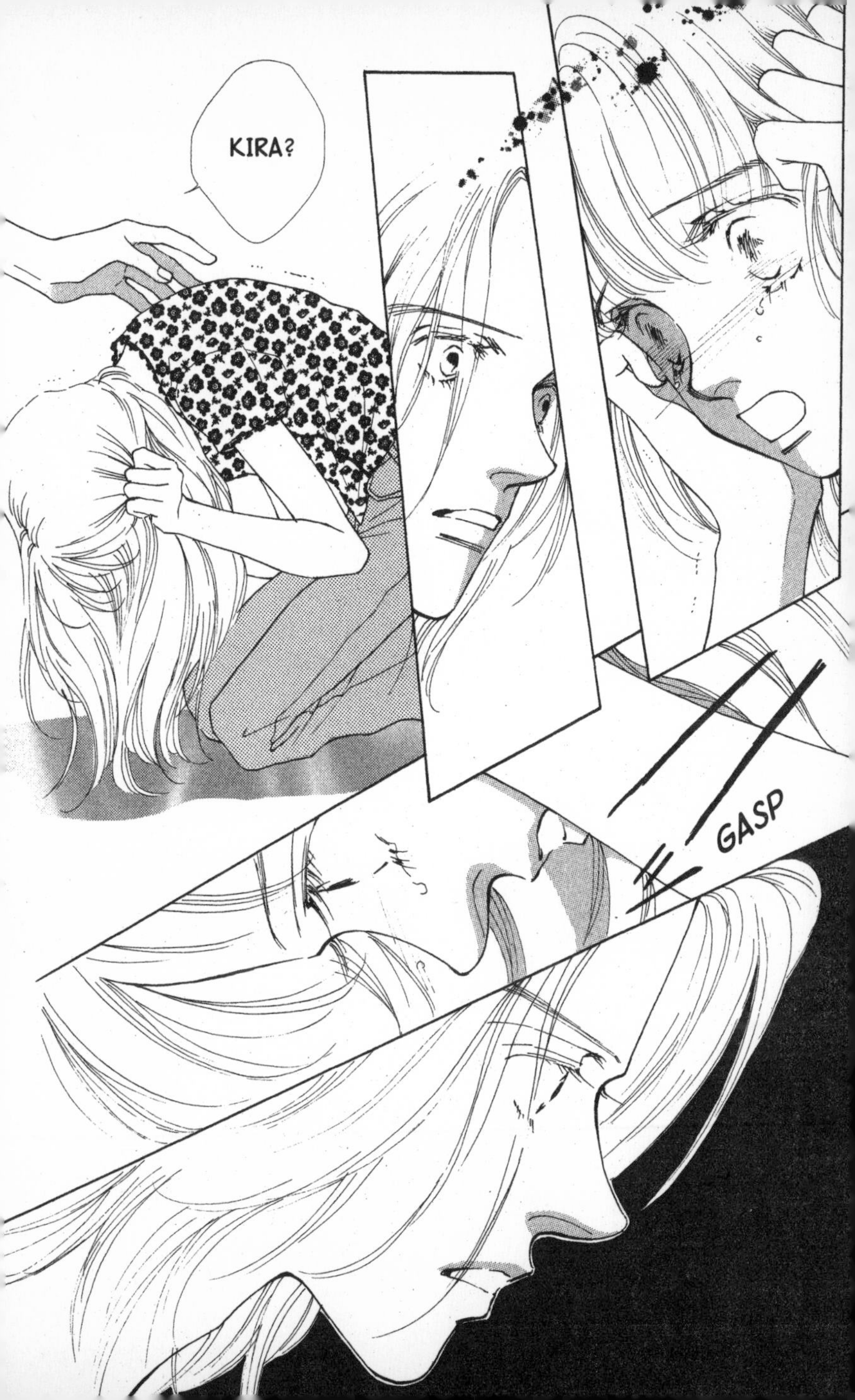
KIRA?
GASP

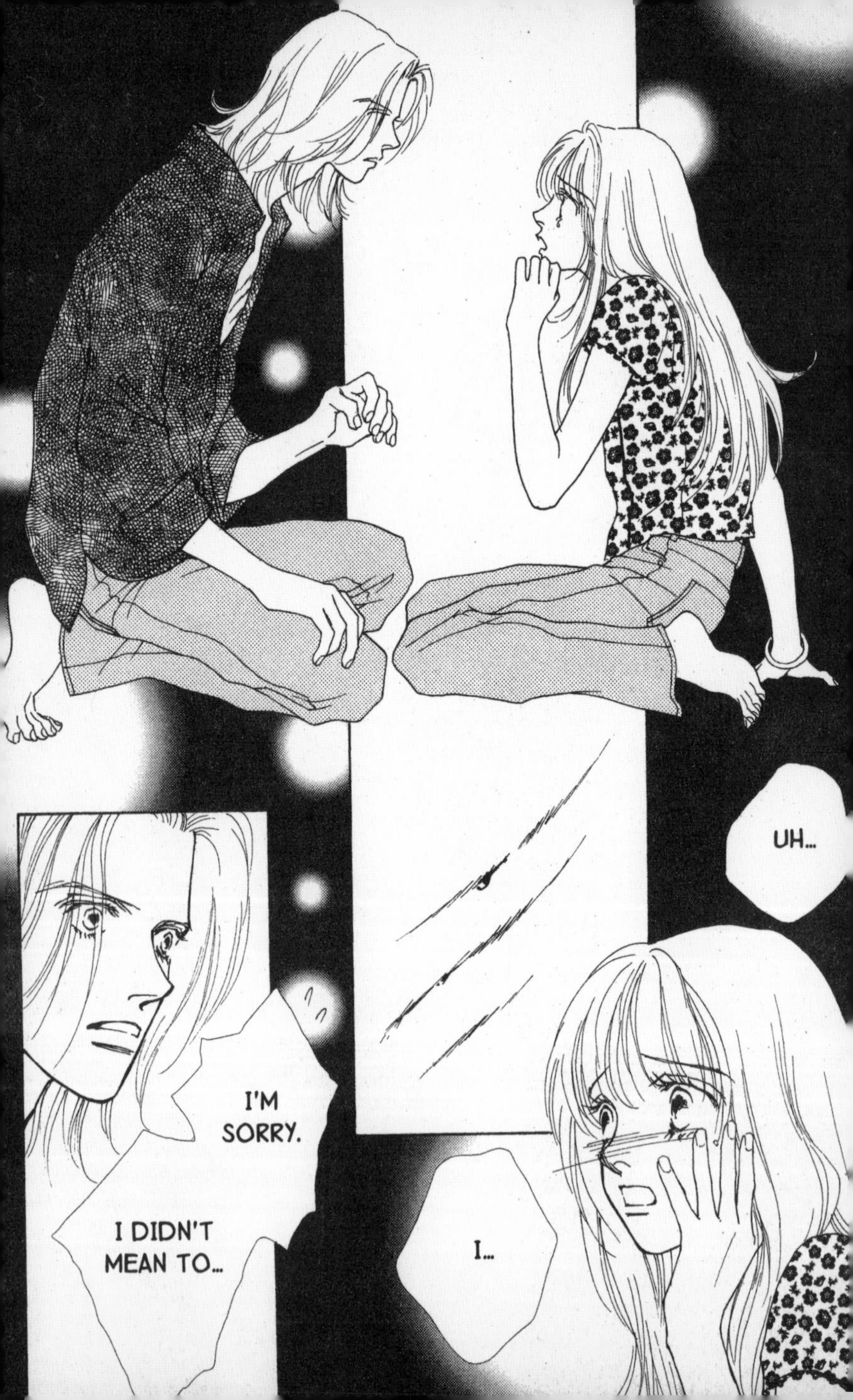
UH...
I...
I'M SORRY.
I DIDN'T MEAN TO...

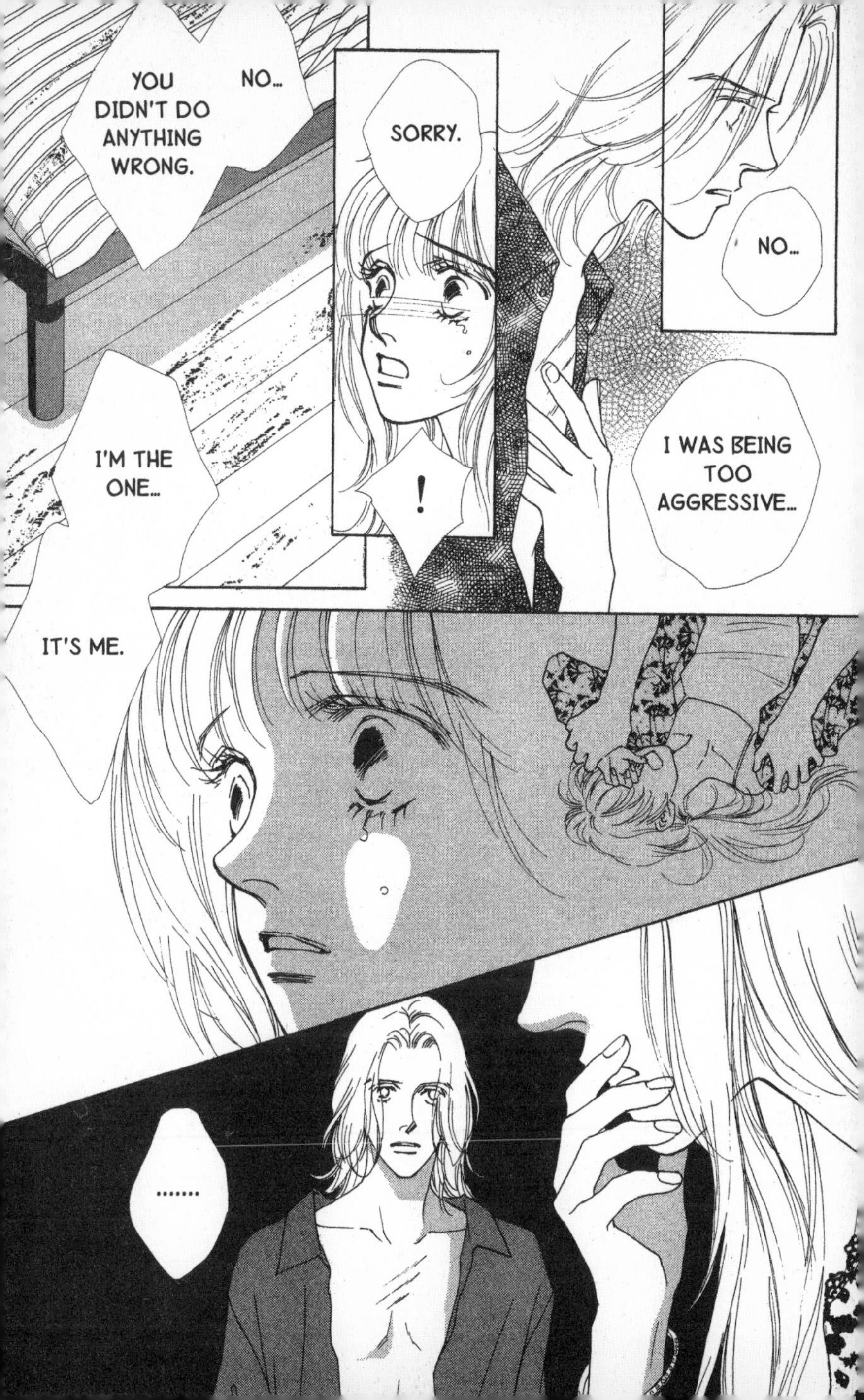
NO...
I WAS BEING TOO AGGRESSIVE...
SORRY.
!
NO...
YOU DIDN'T DO ANYTHING WRONG.
I'M THE ONE...
IT'S ME.
....

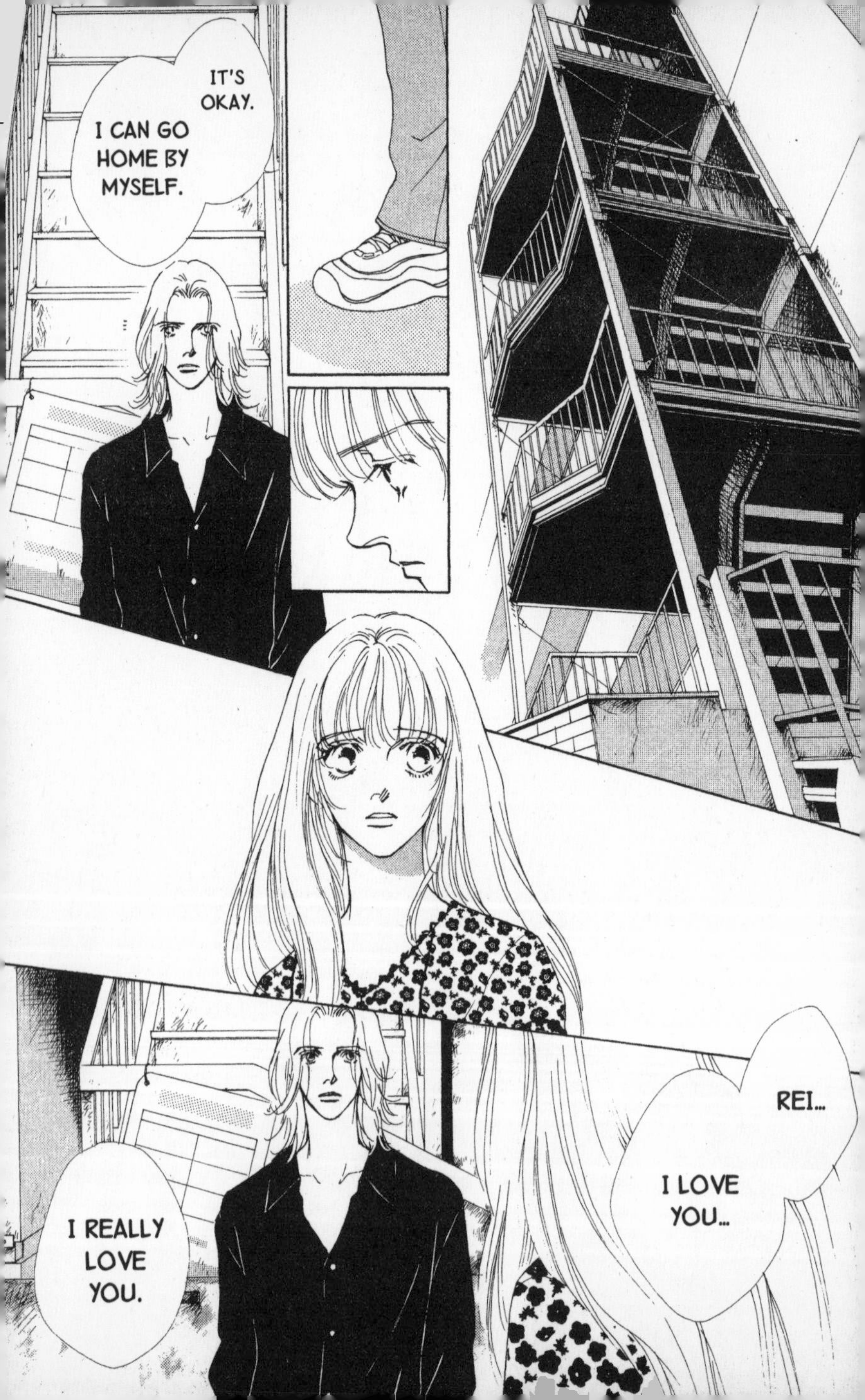
IT'S OKAY. I CAN GO HOME BY MYSELF.
REI...
I LOVE YOU...
I REALLY LOVE YOU.

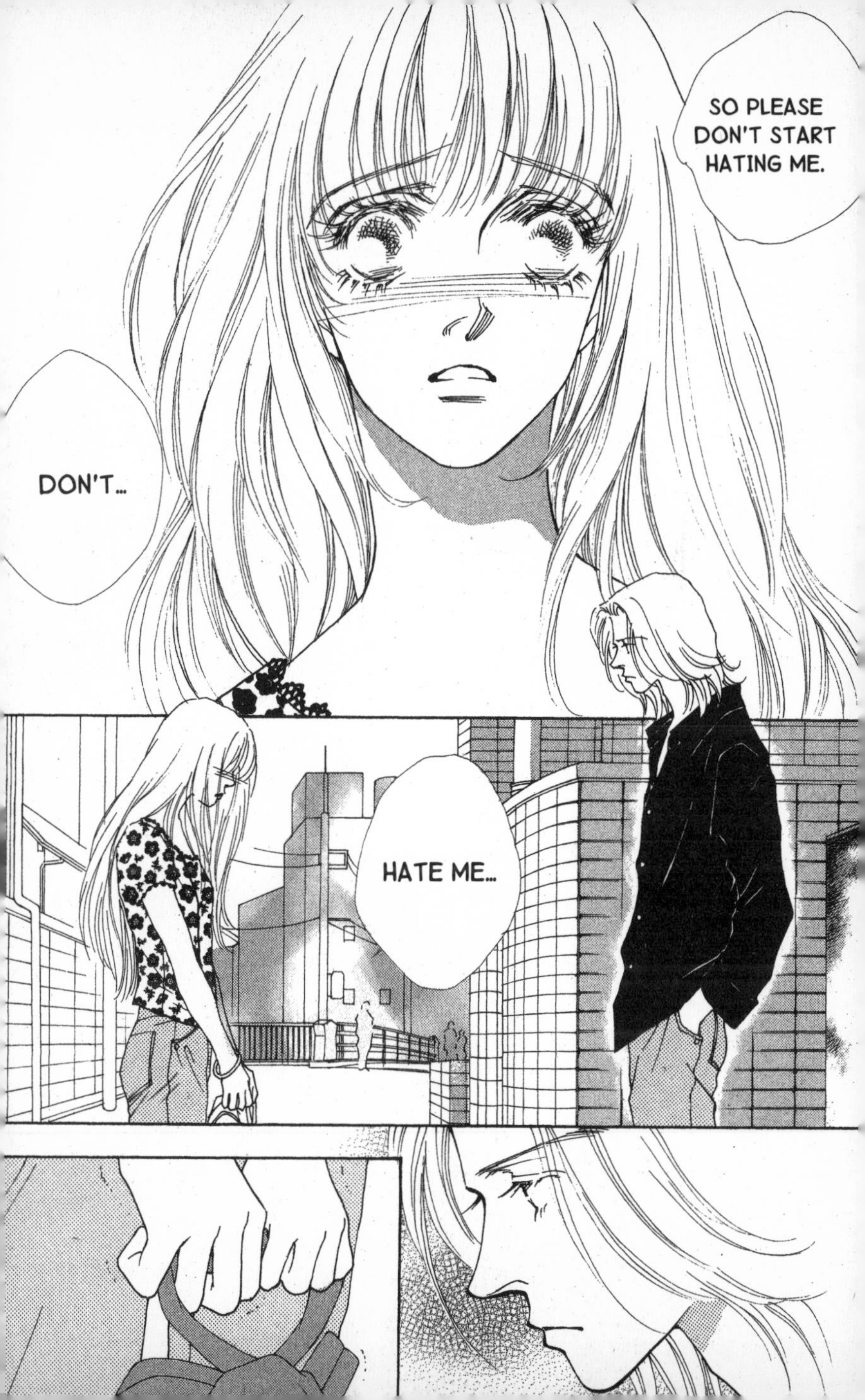
SO PLEASE DON'T START HATING ME.
DON'T...
HATE ME...

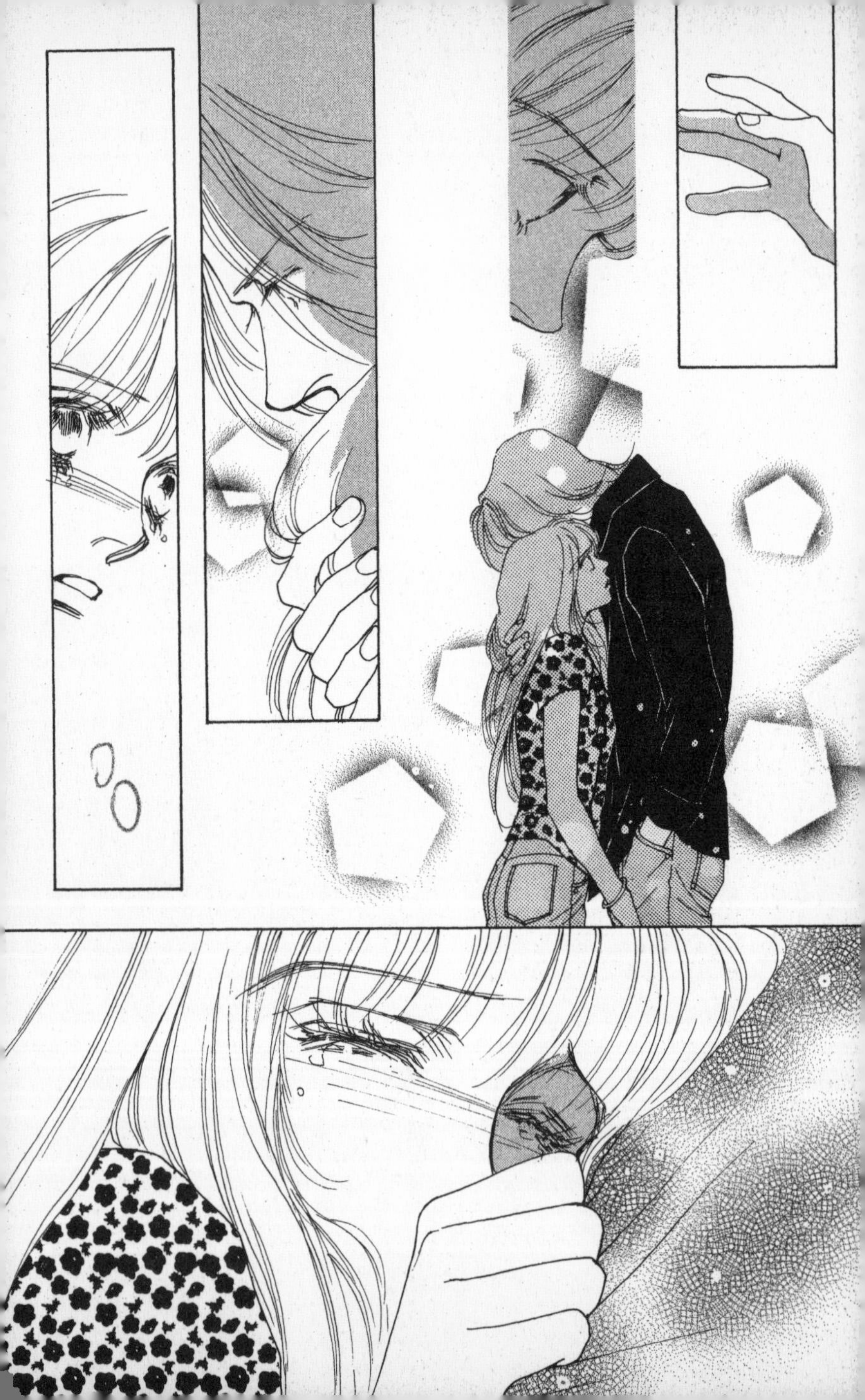

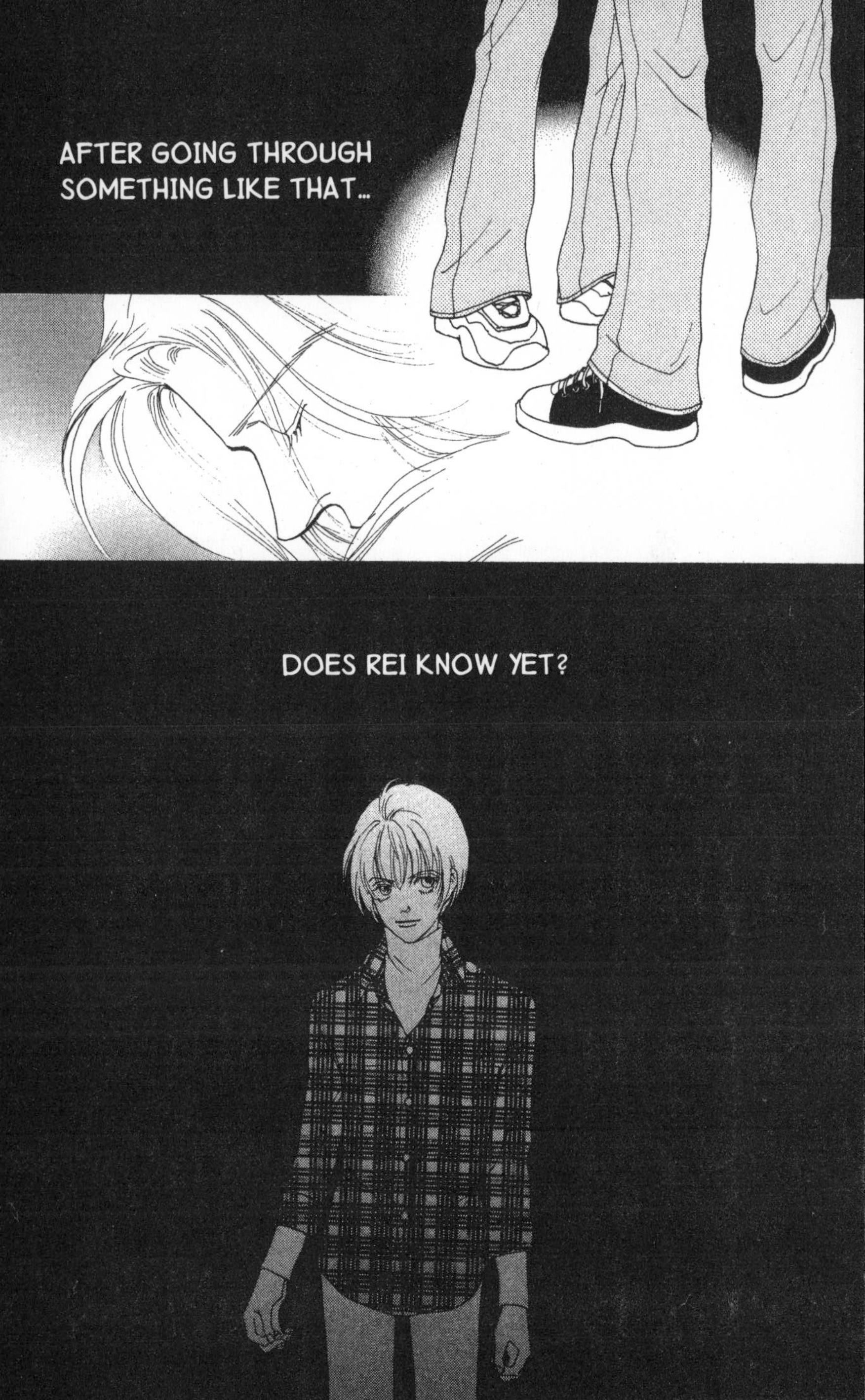
AFTER GOING THROUGH SOMETHING LIKE THAT...
DOES REI KNOW YET?

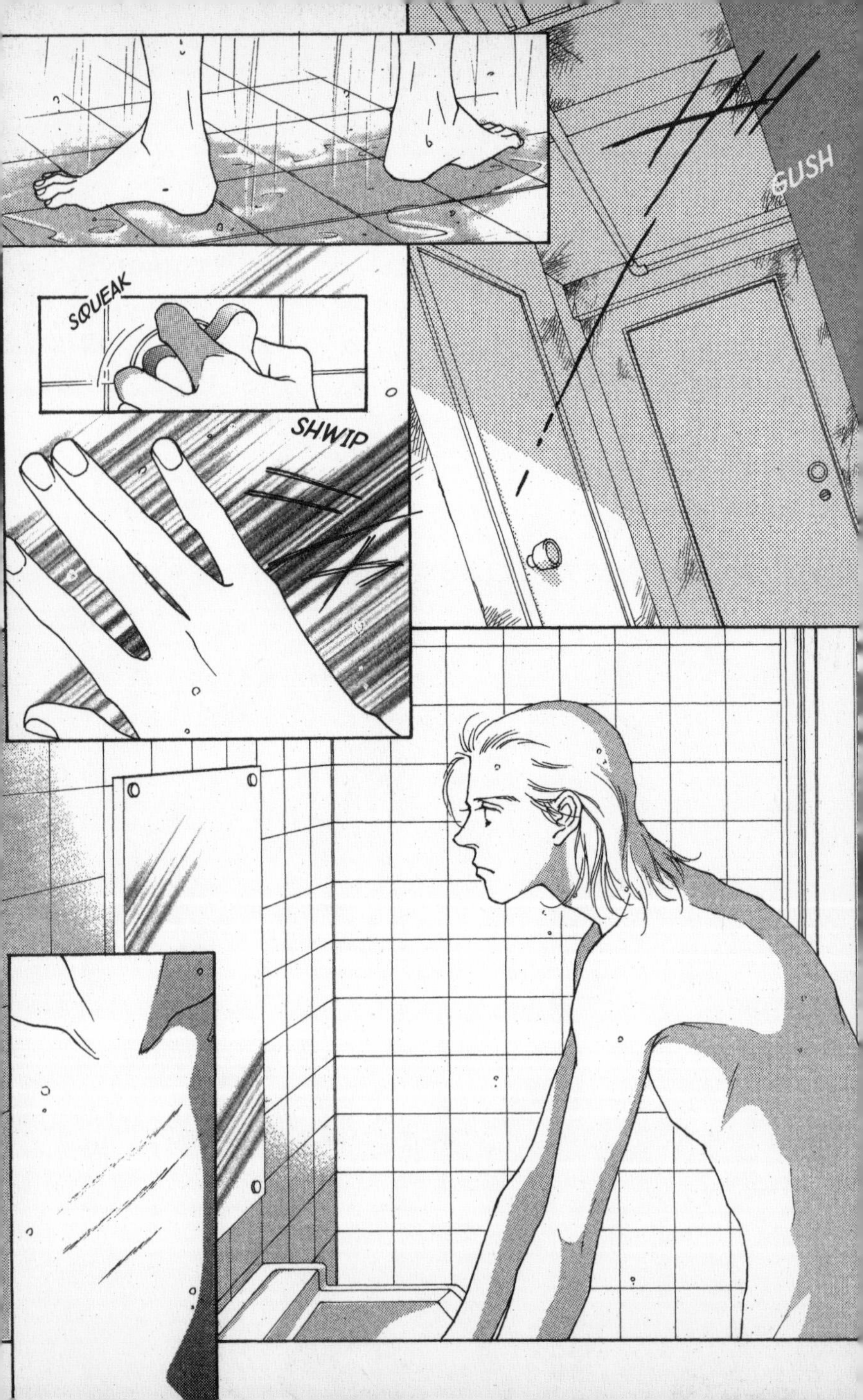
GUSH
SQUEAK
SHWIP

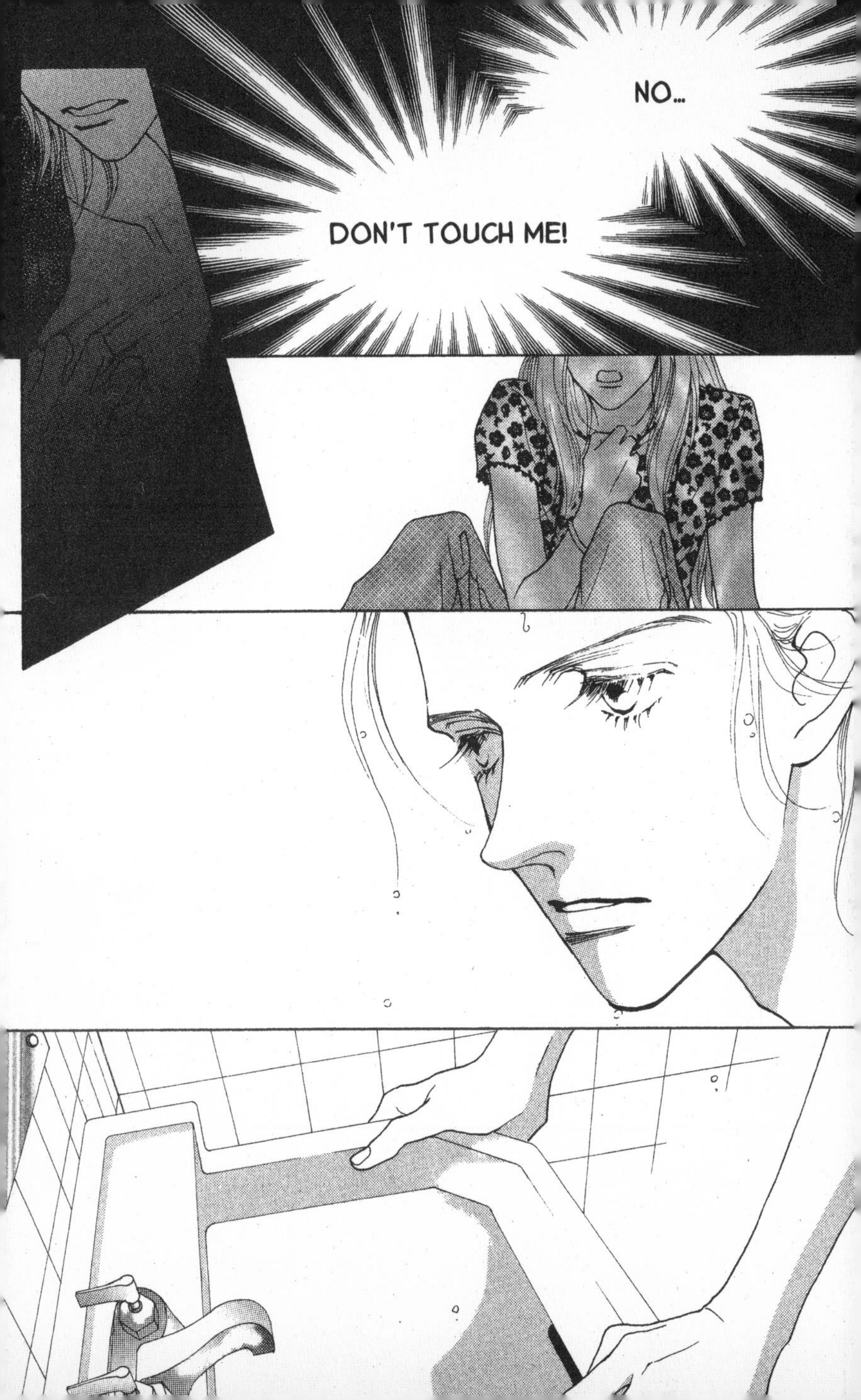
NO...
DON'T TOUCH ME!

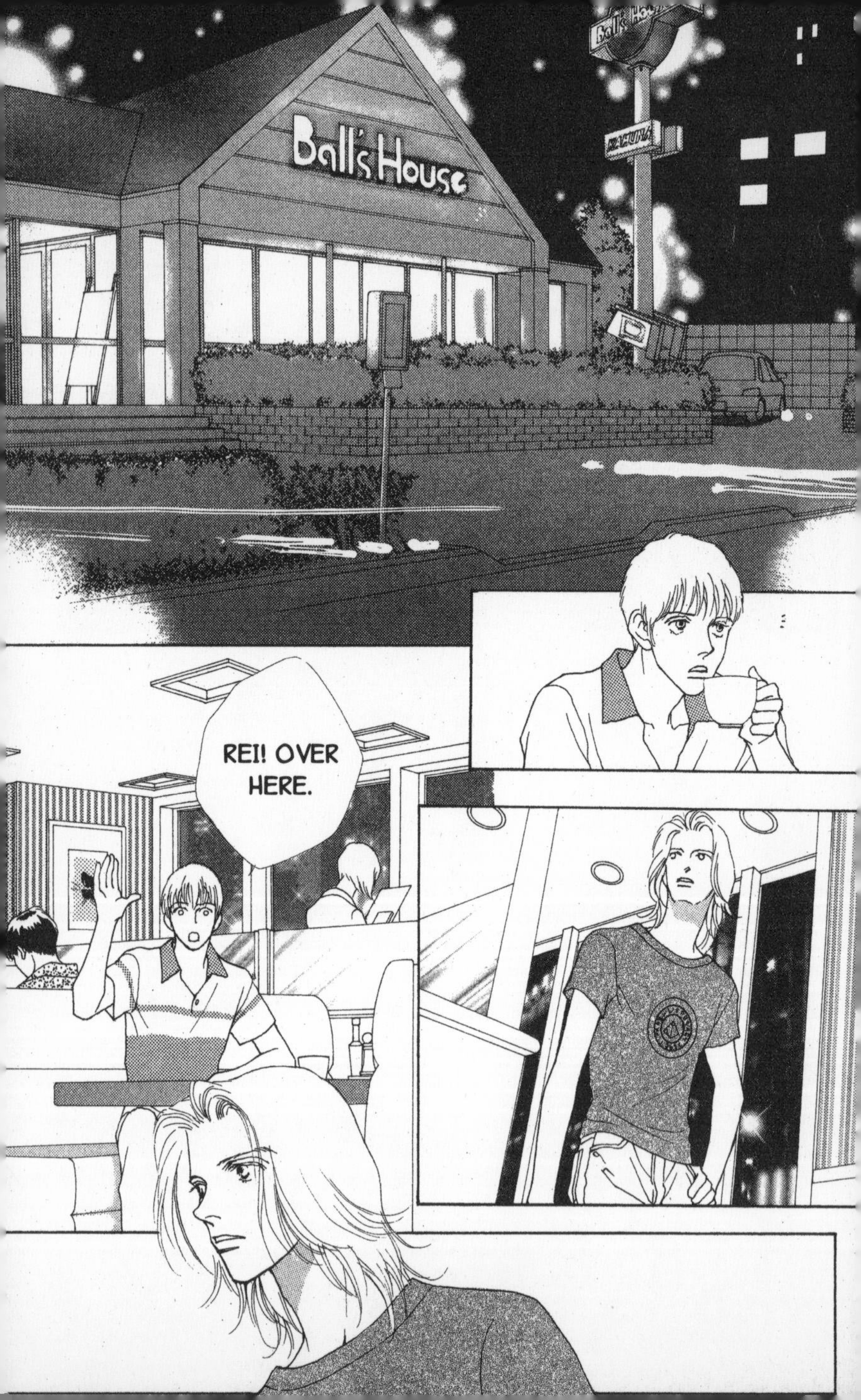
Ball's House
REI! OVER HERE.

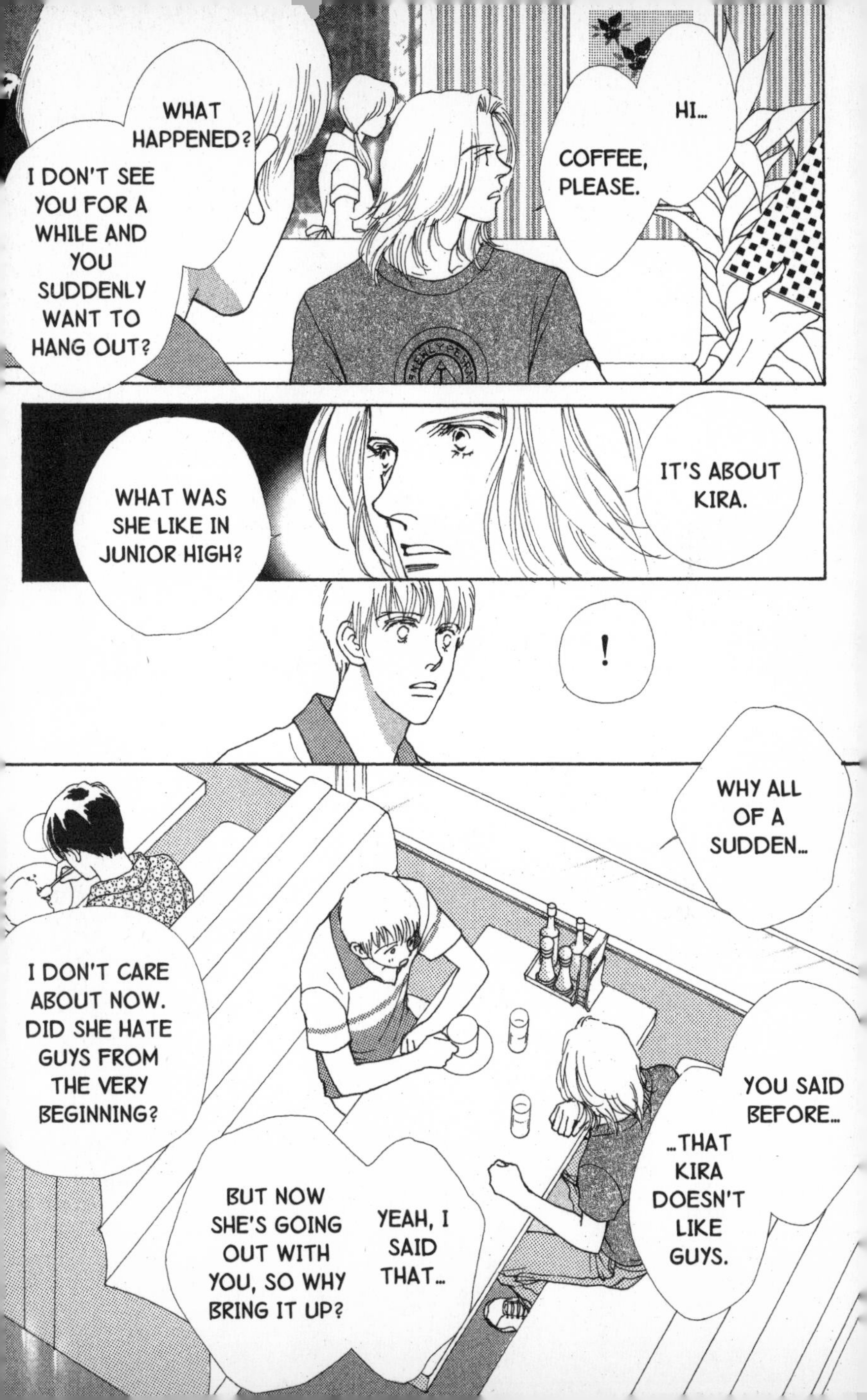
HI...
COFFEE, PLEASE.
WHAT HAPPENED?
I DON'T SEE YOU FOR A WHILE AND YOU SUDDENLY WANT TO HANG OUT?
IT'S ABOUT KIRA.
WHAT WAS SHE LIKE IN JUNIOR HIGH?
!
WHY ALL OF A SUDDEN...
YOU SAID BEFORE...
...THAT KIRA DOESN'T LIKE GUYS.
YEAH, I SAID THAT...
BUT NOW SHE'S GOING OUT WITH YOU, SO WHY BRING IT UP?
I DON'T CARE ABOUT NOW. DID SHE HATE GUYS FROM THE VERY BEGINNING?

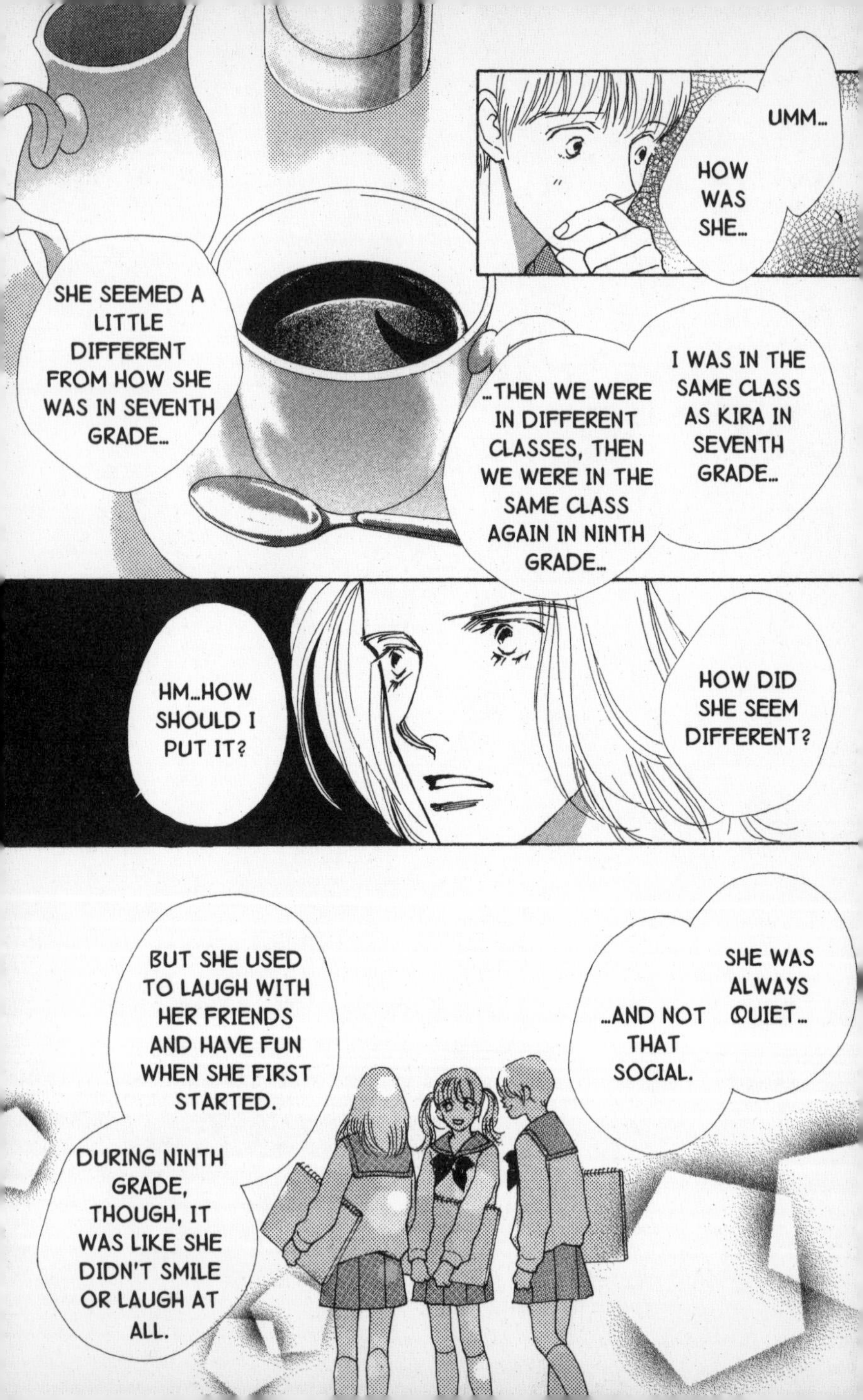
UMM...
HOW WAS SHE...
I WAS IN THE SAME CLASS AS KIRA IN SEVENTH GRADE...
...THEN WE WERE IN DIFFERENT CLASSES, THEN WE WERE IN THE SAME CLASS AGAIN IN NINTH GRADE...
SHE SEEMED A LITTLE DIFFERENT FROM HOW SHE WAS IN SEVENTH GRADE...
HOW DID SHE SEEM DIFFERENT?
HM...HOW SHOULD I PUT IT?
SHE WAS ALWAYS QUIET...
...AND NOT THAT SOCIAL.
BUT SHE USED TO LAUGH WITH HER FRIENDS AND HAVE FUN WHEN SHE FIRST STARTED.
DURING NINTH GRADE, THOUGH, IT WAS LIKE SHE DIDN'T SMILE OR LAUGH AT ALL.

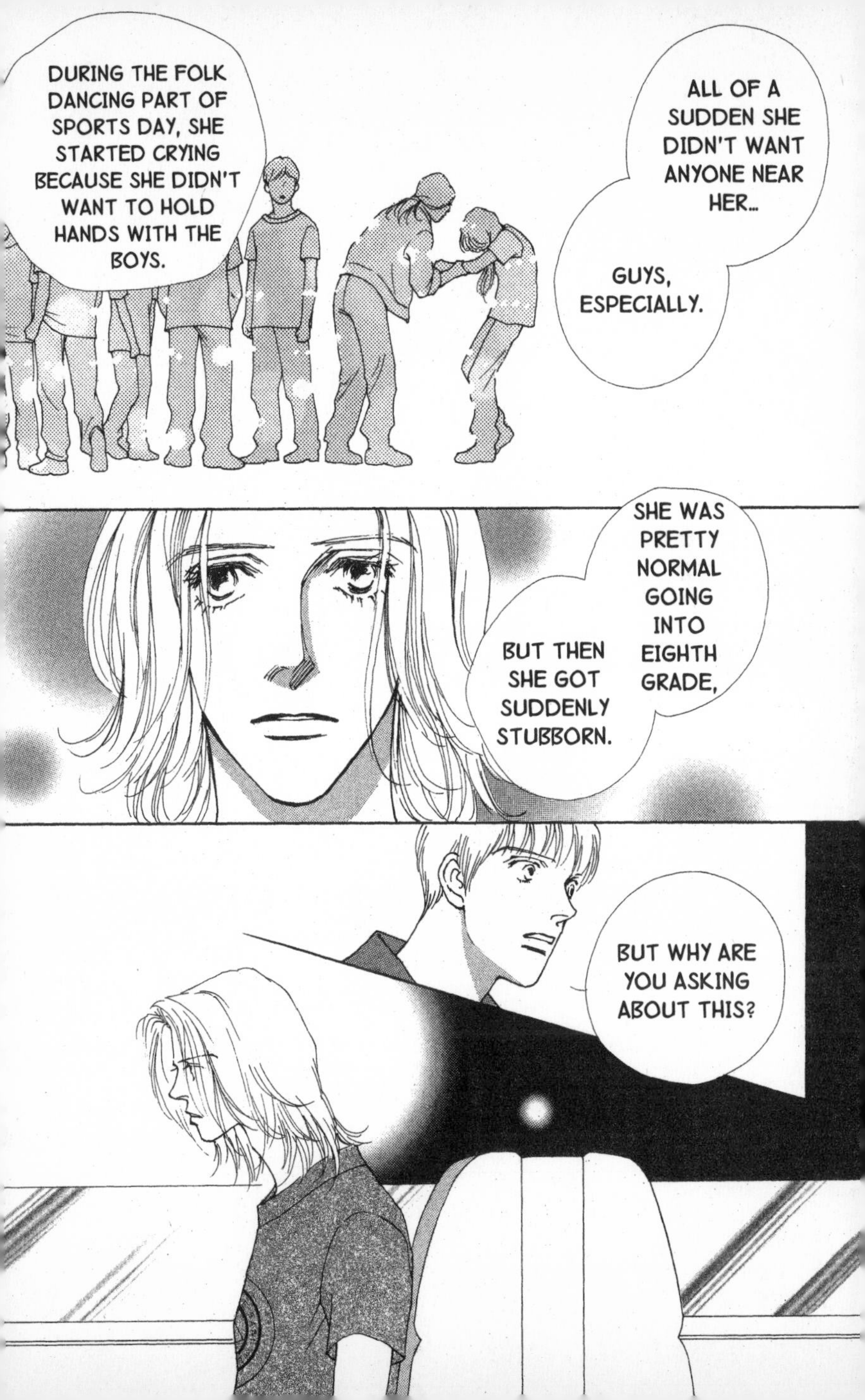
ALL OF A SUDDEN SHE DIDN'T WANT ANYONE NEAR HER...
GUYS, ESPECIALLY.
DURING THE FOLK DANCING PART OF SPORTS DAY, SHE STARTED CRYING BECAUSE SHE DIDN'T WANT TO HOLD HANDS WITH THE BOYS.
SHE WAS PRETTY NORMAL GOING INTO EIGHTH GRADE,
BUT THEN SHE GOT SUDDENLY STUBBORN.
BUT WHY ARE YOU ASKING ABOUT THIS?

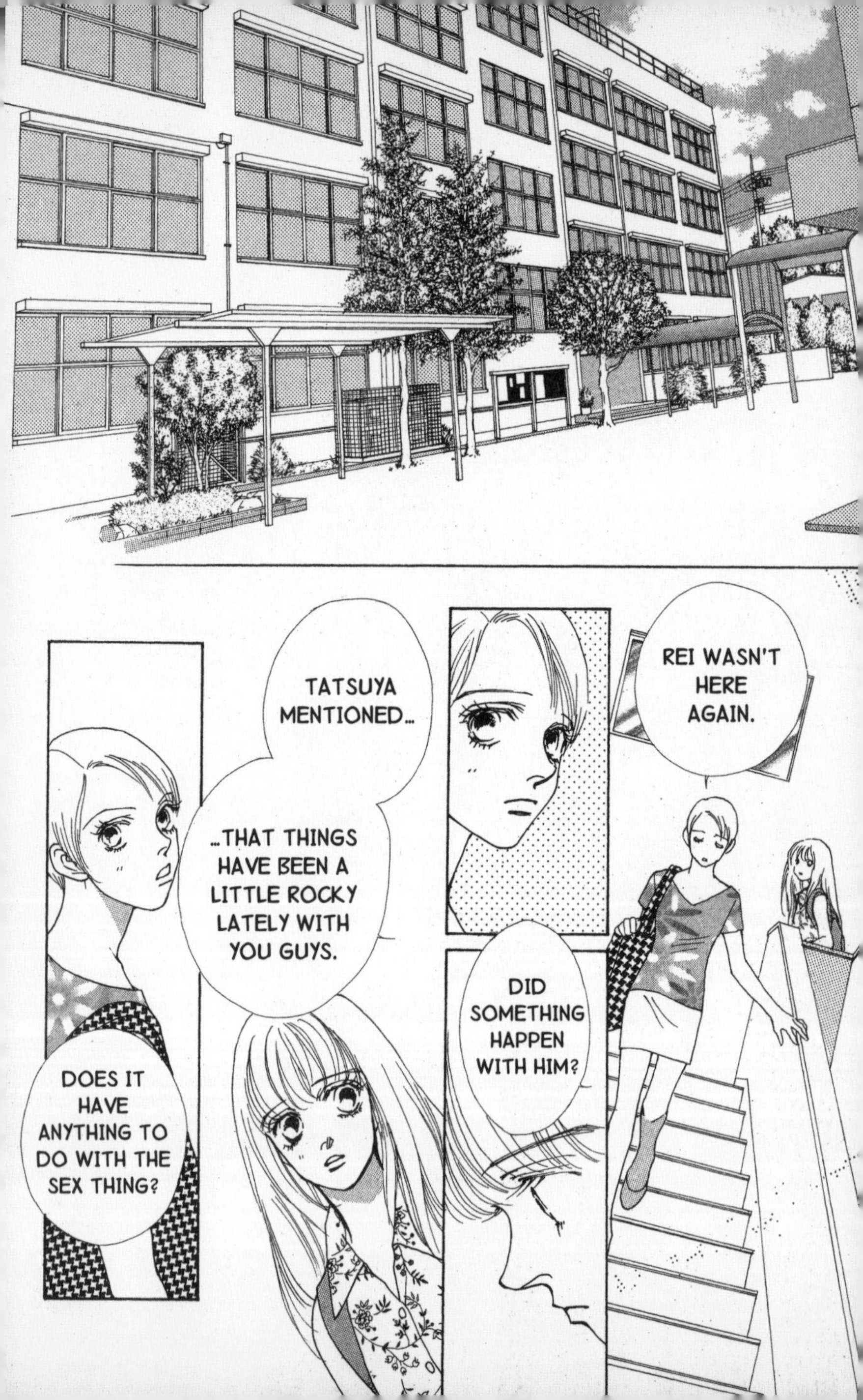
REI WASN'T HERE AGAIN.
DID SOMETHING HAPPEN WITH HIM?
TATSUYA MENTIONED...
...THAT THINGS HAVE BEEN A LITTLE ROCKY LATELY WITH YOU GUYS.
DOES IT HAVE ANYTHING TO DO WITH THE SEX THING?

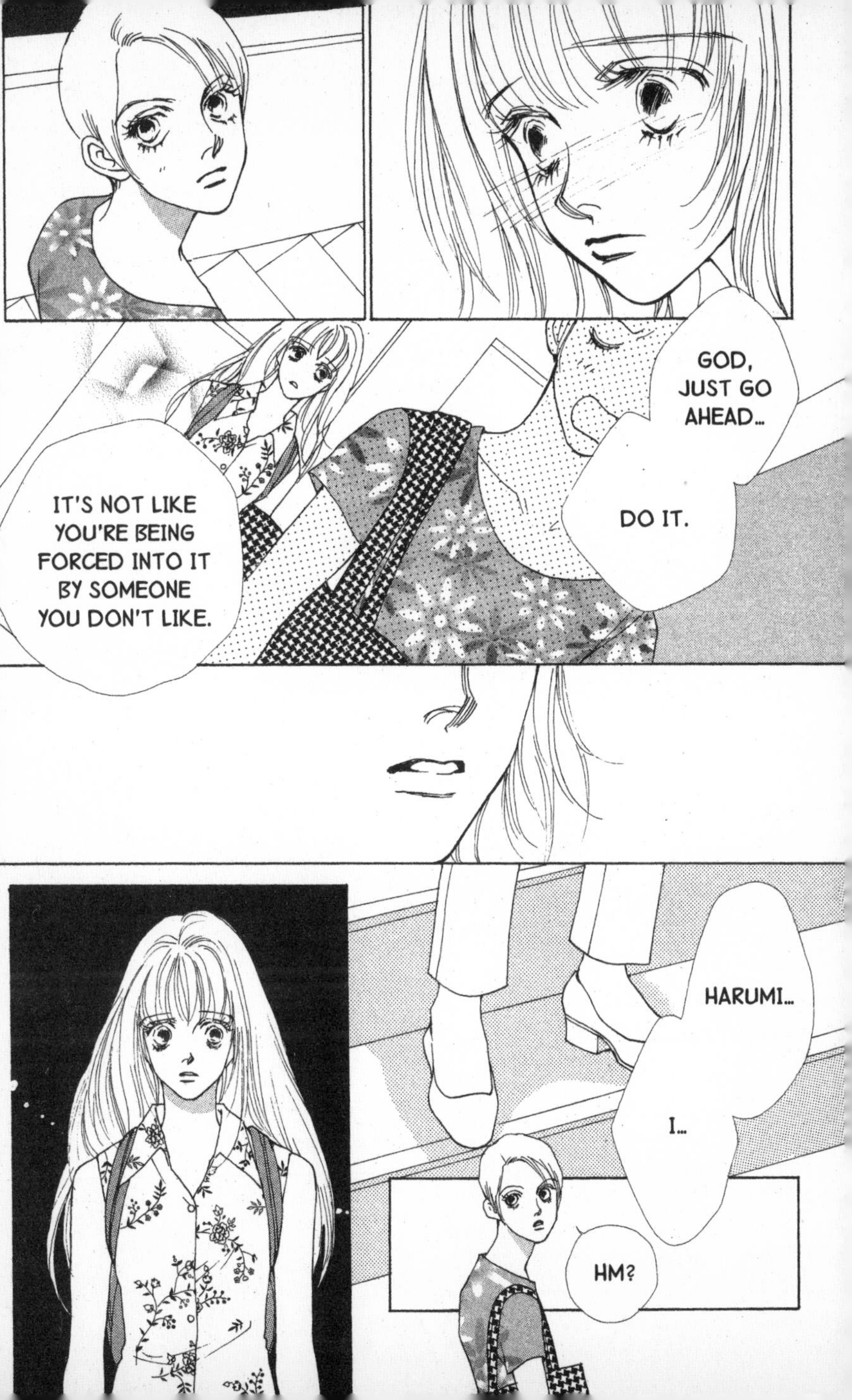
GOD, JUST GO AHEAD...
DO IT.
IT'S NOT LIKE YOU'RE BEING FORCED INTO IT BY SOMEONE YOU DON'T LIKE.
HARUMI...
I...
HM?

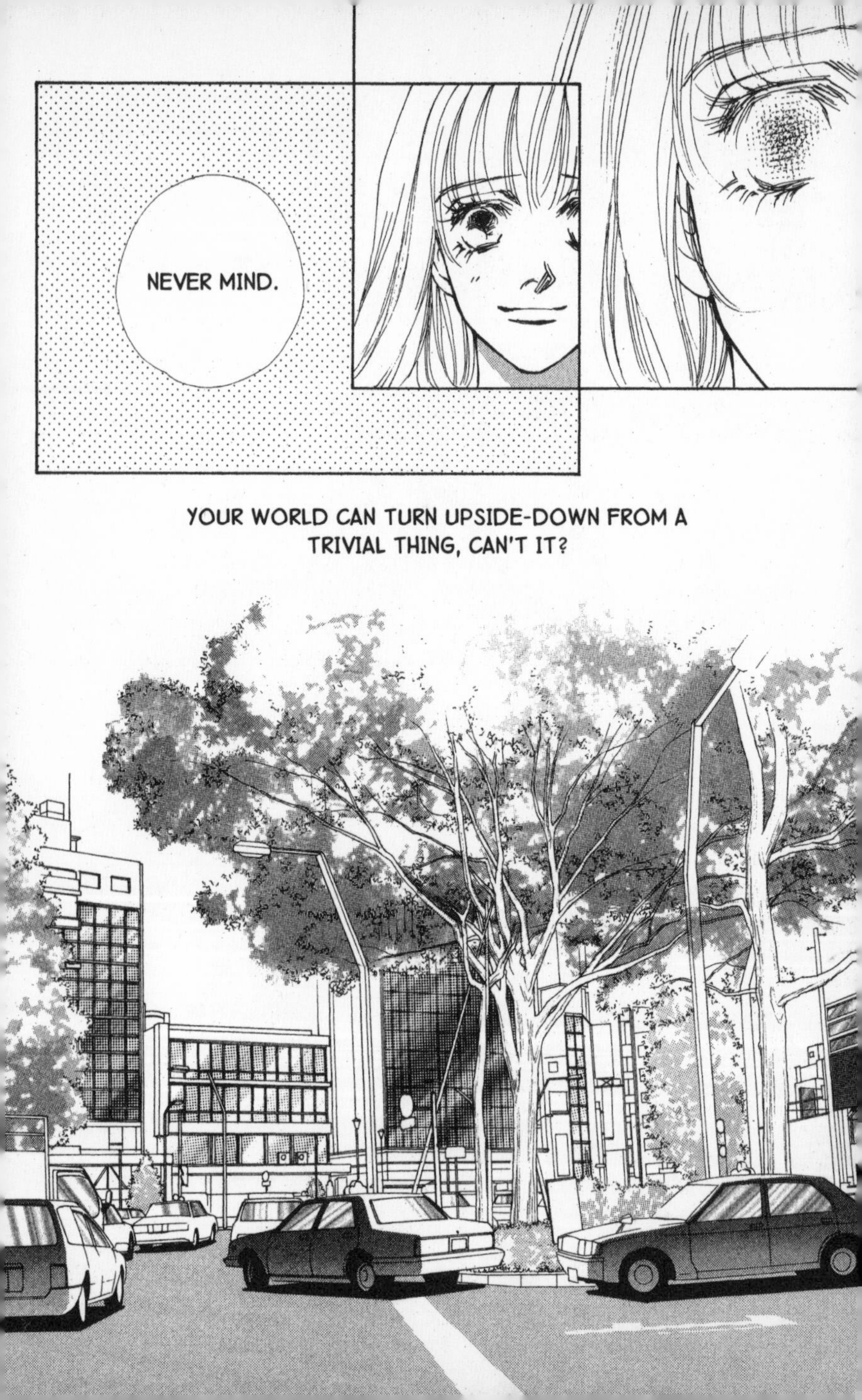
NEVER MIND.
YOUR WORLD CAN TURN UPSIDE-DOWN FROM A TRIVIAL THING, CAN'T IT?

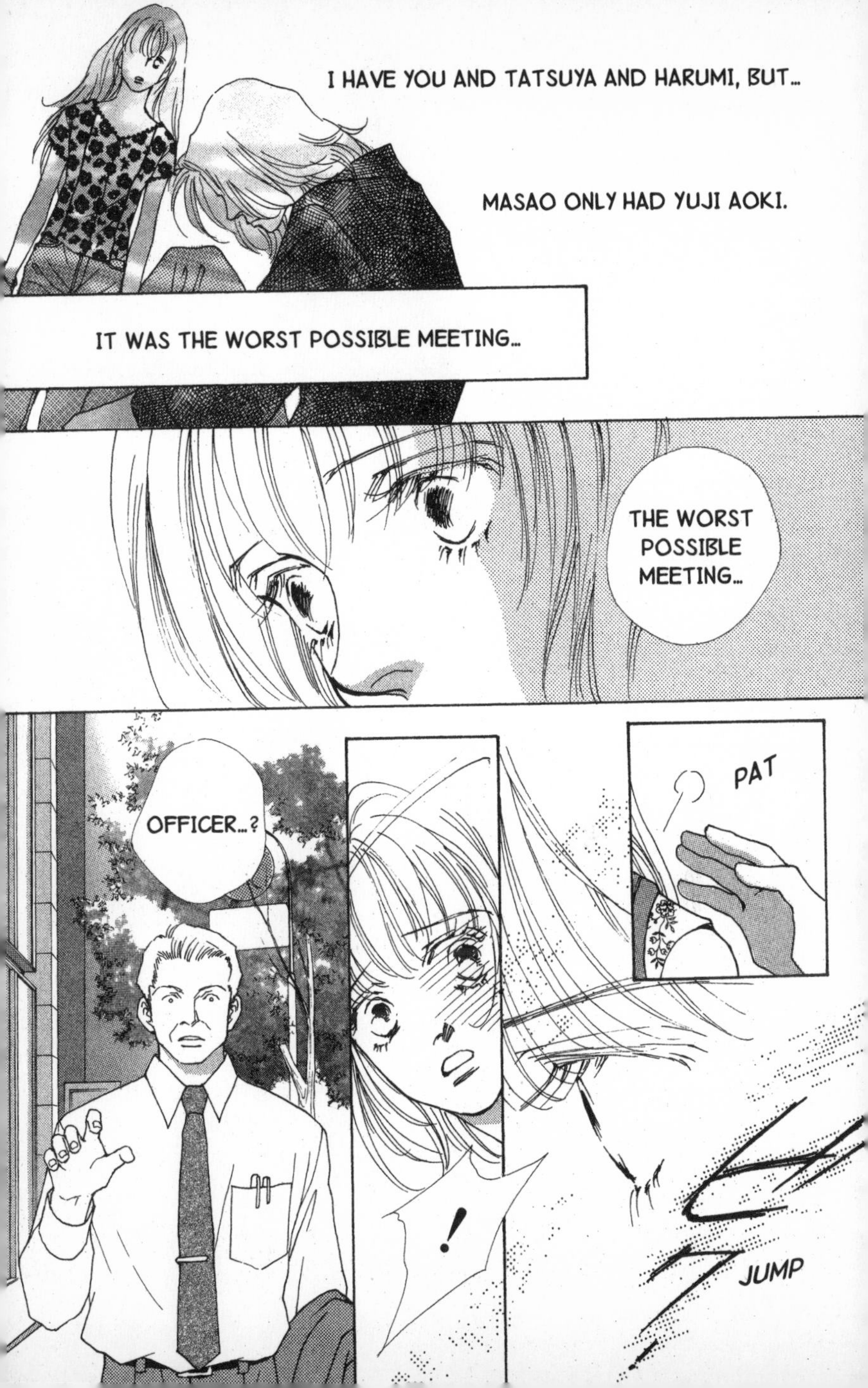
I HAVE YOU AND TATSUYA AND HARUMI, BUT...
MASAO ONLY HAD YUJI AOKI.
IT WAS THE WORST POSSIBLE MEETING...
THE WORST POSSIBLE MEETING...
PAT
JUMP
!
OFFICER...?

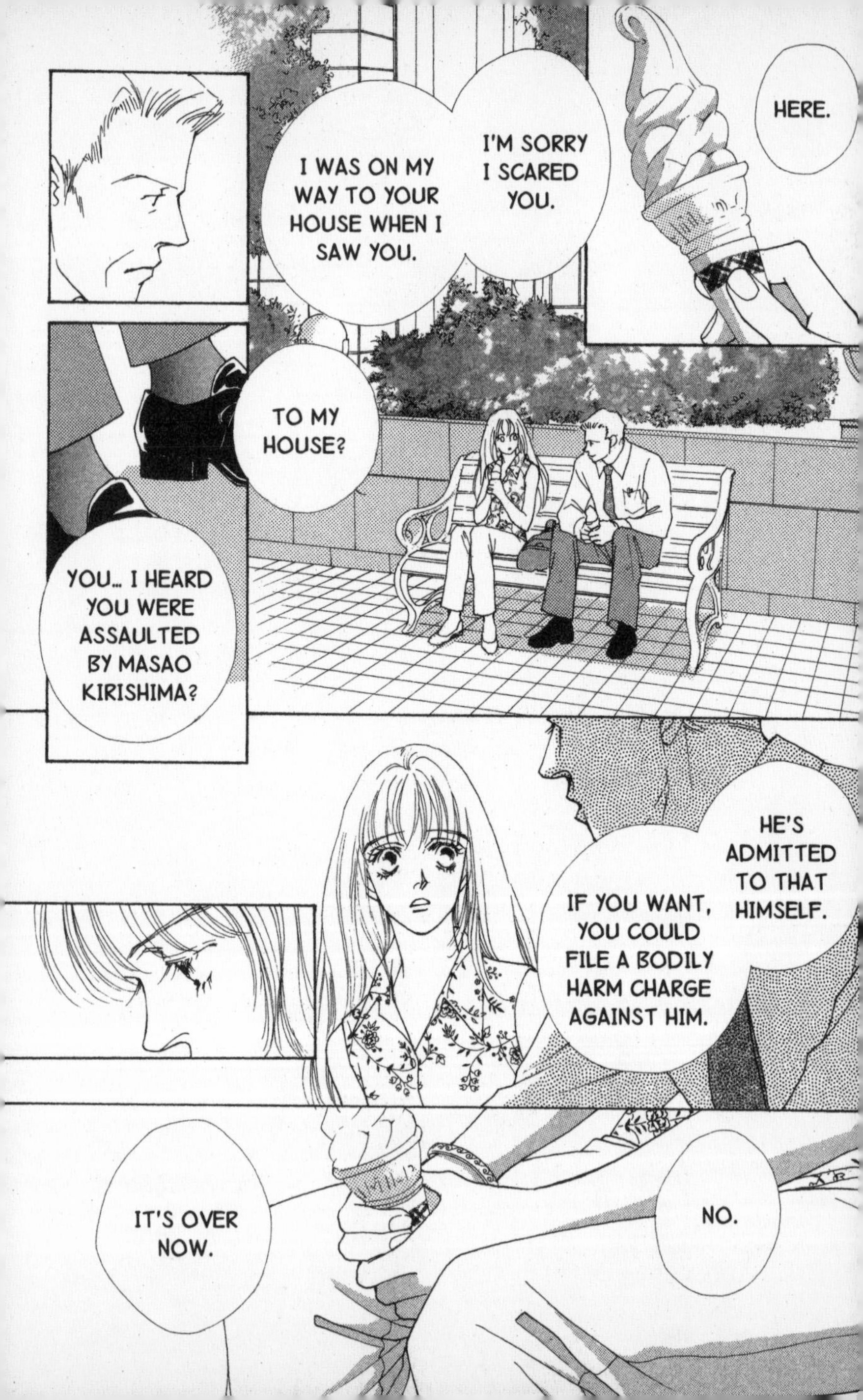
HERE.
I'M SORRY I SCARED YOU.
I WAS ON MY WAY TO YOUR HOUSE WHEN I SAW YOU.
TO MY HOUSE?
YOU... I HEARD YOU WERE ASSAULTED BY MASAO KIRISHIMA?
HE'S ADMITTED TO THAT HIMSELF.
IF YOU WANT, YOU COULD FILE A BODILY HARM CHARGE AGAINST HIM.
NO.
IT'S OVER NOW.

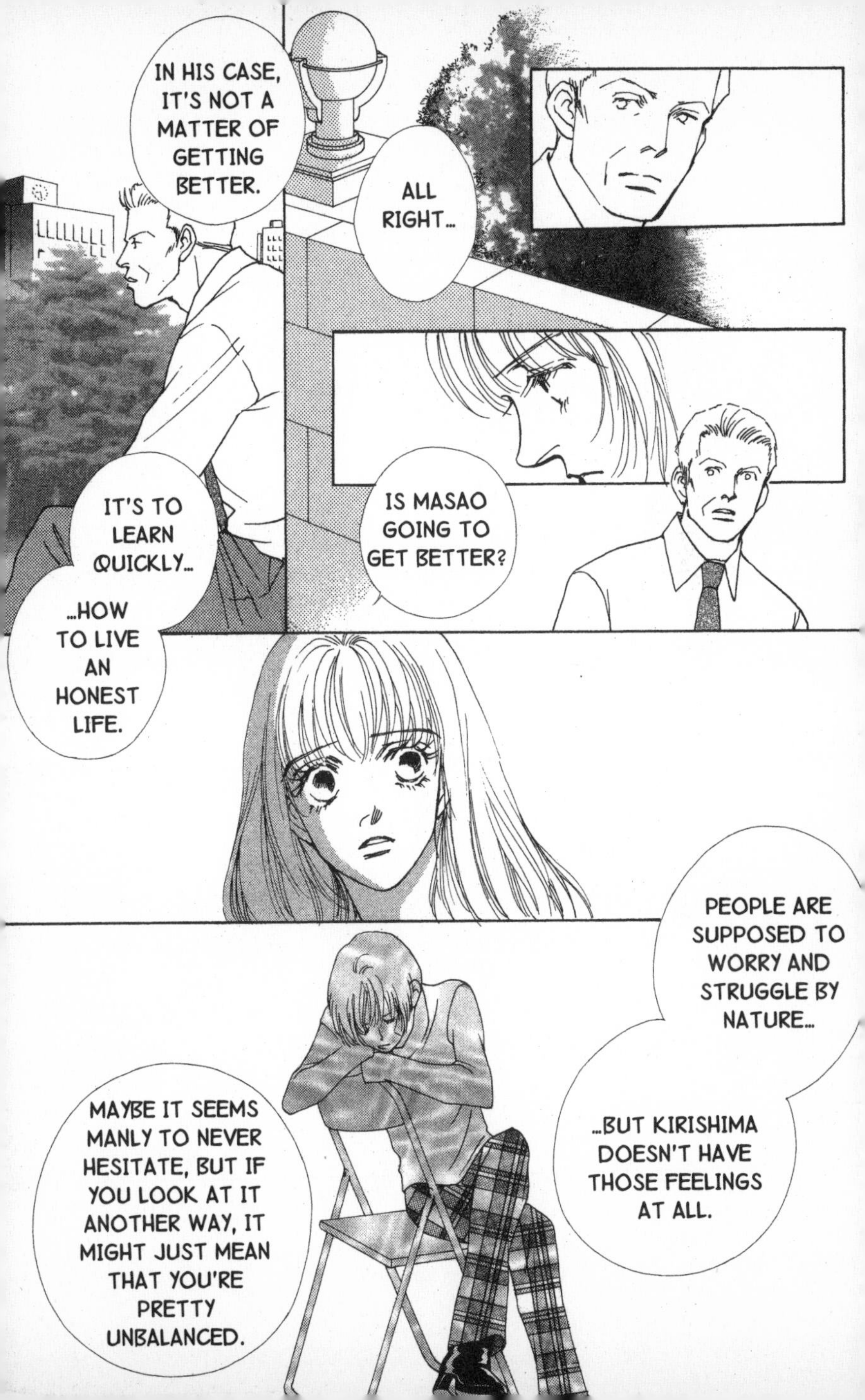
ALL RIGHT...
IS MASAO GOING TO GET BETTER?
IN HIS CASE, IT'S NOT A MATTER OF GETTING BETTER.
IT'S TO LEARN QUICKLY...
...HOW TO LIVE AN HONEST LIFE.
PEOPLE ARE SUPPOSED TO WORRY AND STRUGGLE BY NATURE...
...BUT KIRISHIMA DOESN'T HAVE THOSE FEELINGS AT ALL.
MAYBE IT SEEMS MANLY TO NEVER HESITATE, BUT IF YOU LOOK AT IT ANOTHER WAY, IT MIGHT JUST MEAN THAT YOU'RE PRETTY UNBALANCED.

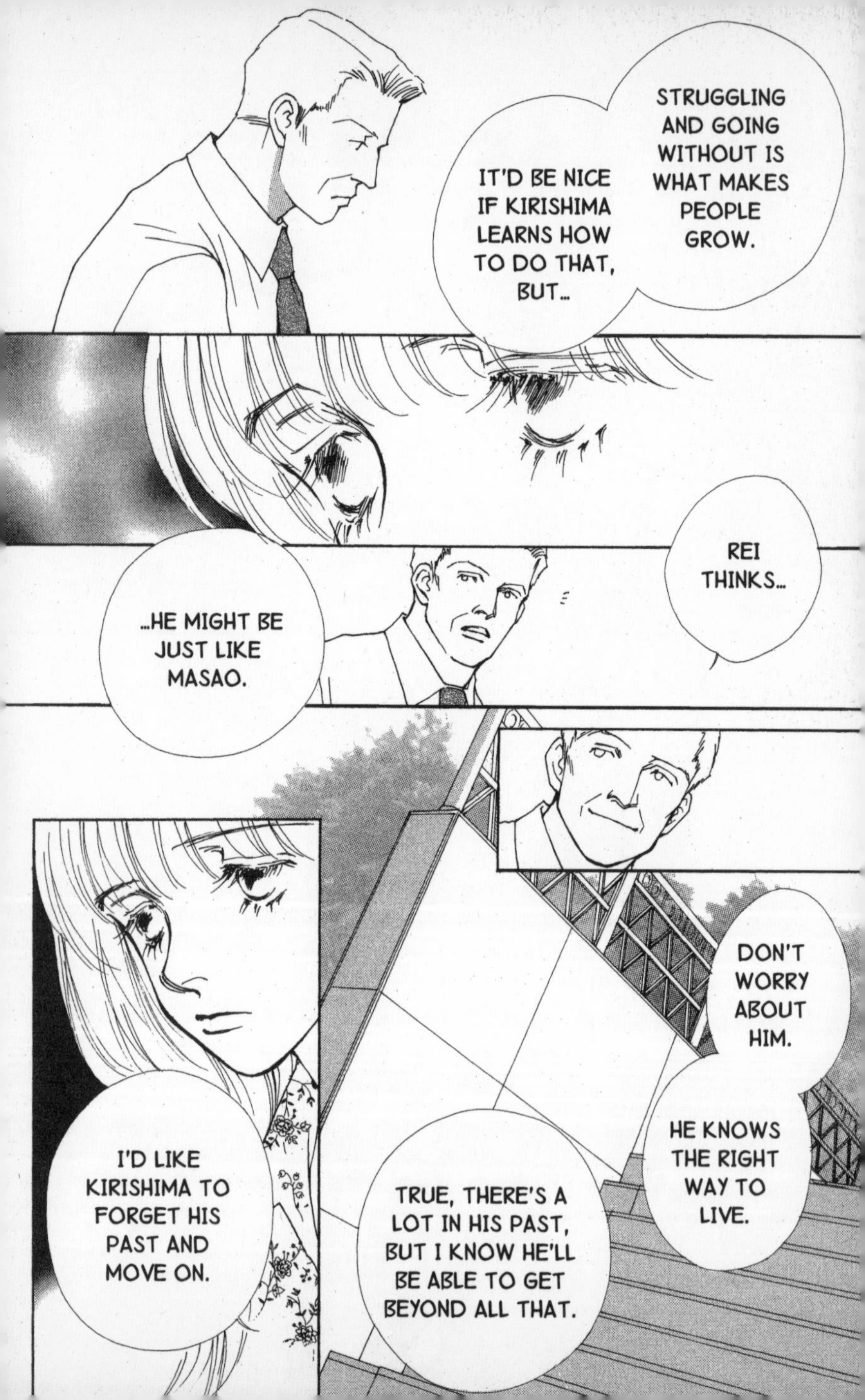
STRUGGLING AND GOING WITHOUT IS WHAT MAKES PEOPLE GROW.
IT'D BE NICE IF KIRISHIMA LEARNS HOW TO DO THAT, BUT...
REI THINKS...
...HE MIGHT BE JUST LIKE MASAO.
DON'T WORRY ABOUT HIM.
HE KNOWS THE RIGHT WAY TO LIVE.
TRUE, THERE'S A LOT IN HIS PAST, BUT I KNOW HE'LL BE ABLE TO GET BEYOND ALL THAT.
I'D LIKE KIRISHIMA TO FORGET HIS PAST AND MOVE ON.

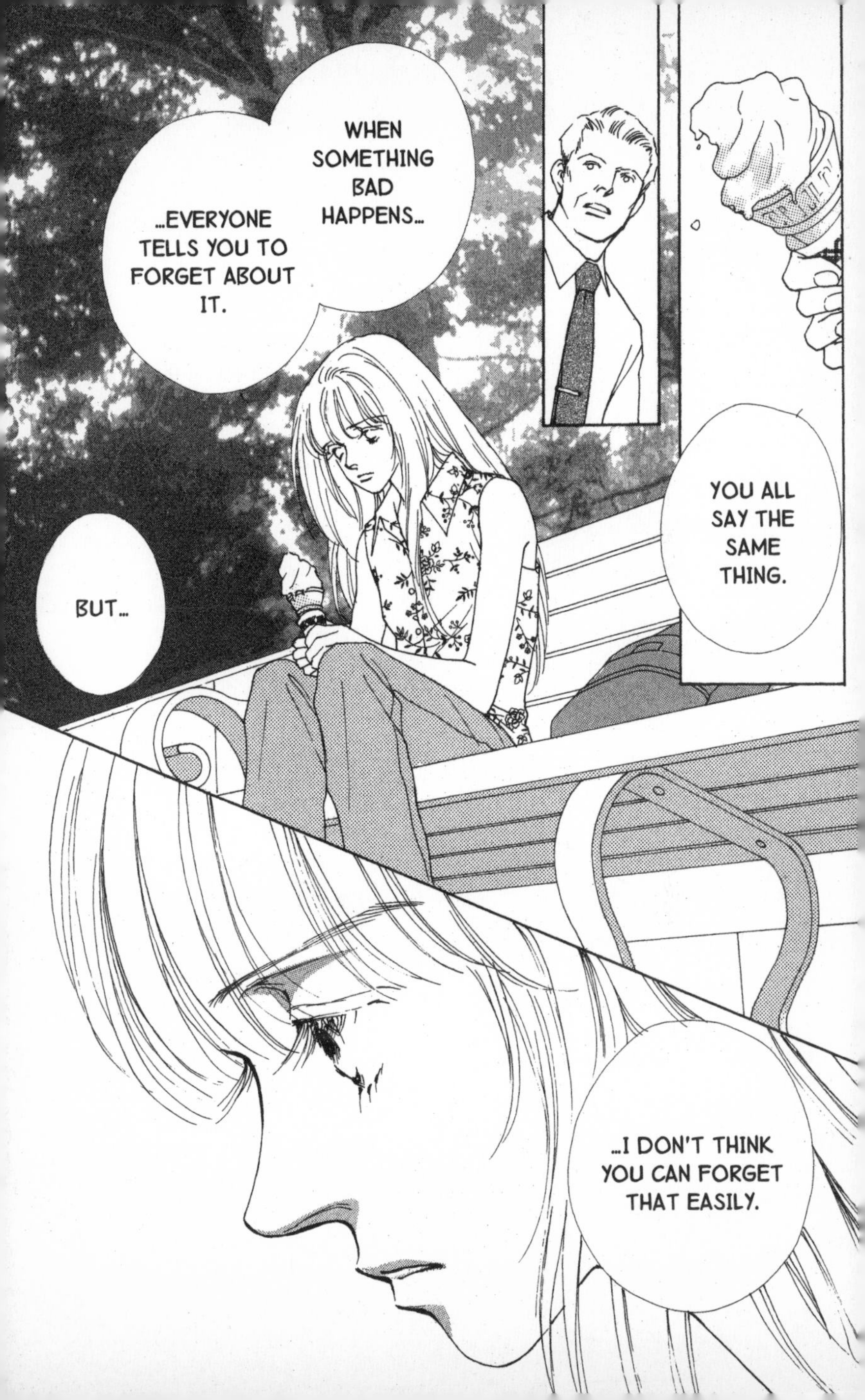
YOU ALL SAY THE SAME THING.
WHEN SOMETHING BAD HAPPENS...
...EVERYONE TELLS YOU TO FORGET ABOUT IT.
BUT...
...I DON'T THINK YOU CAN FORGET THAT EASILY.

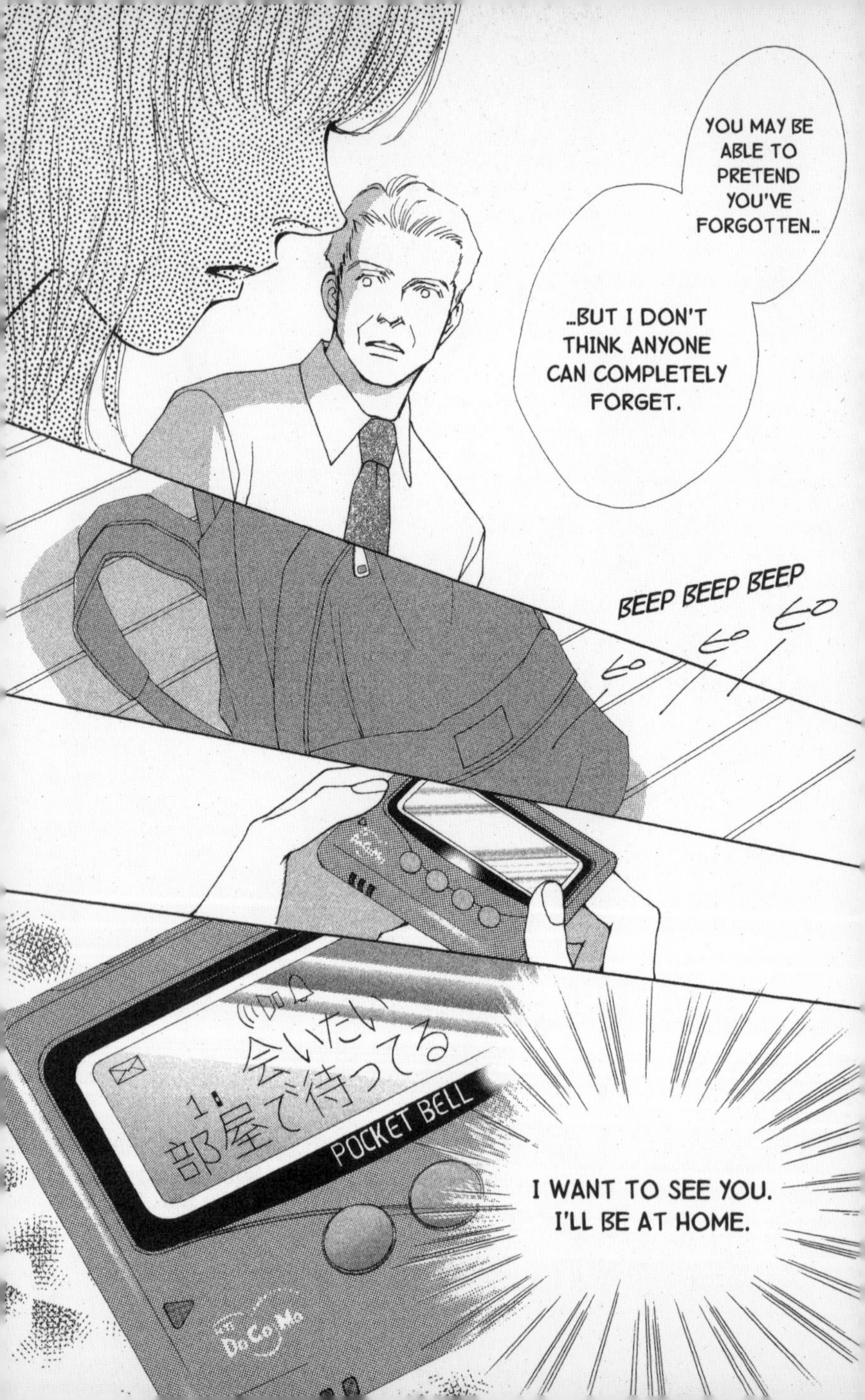
YOU MAY BE ABLE TO PRETEND YOU'VE FORGOTTEN...
...BUT I DON'T THINK ANYONE CAN COMPLETELY FORGET.
BEEP BEEP BEEP
会いたい
部屋で待ってる
POCKET BELL
I WANT TO SEE YOU. I'LL BE AT HOME.
DoCoMo

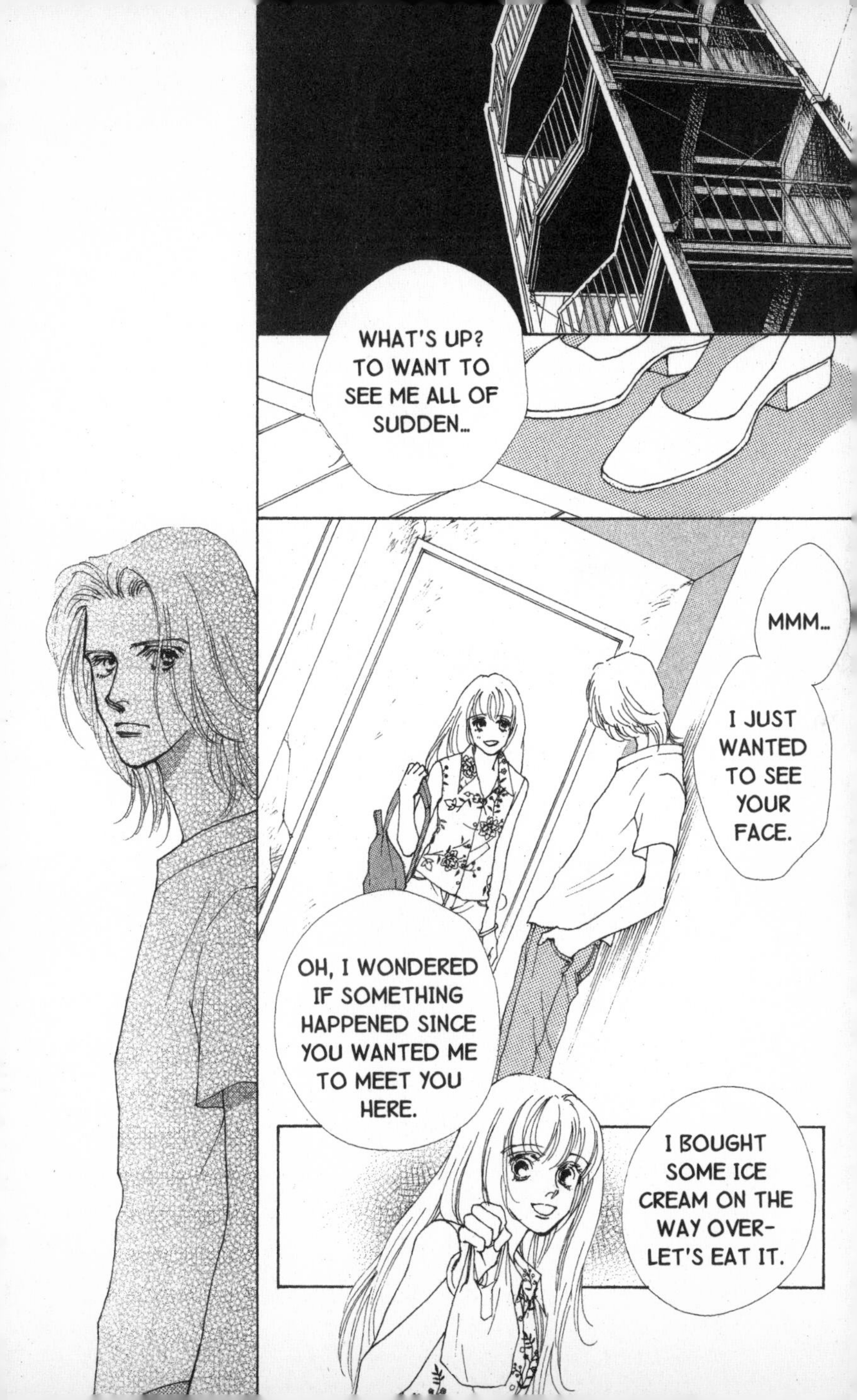
WHAT'S UP? TO WANT TO SEE ME ALL OF SUDDEN...
MMM...
I JUST WANTED TO SEE YOUR FACE.
OH, I WONDERED IF SOMETHING HAPPENED SINCE YOU WANTED ME TO MEET YOU HERE.
I BOUGHT SOME ICE CREAM ON THE WAY OVER-LET'S EAT IT.

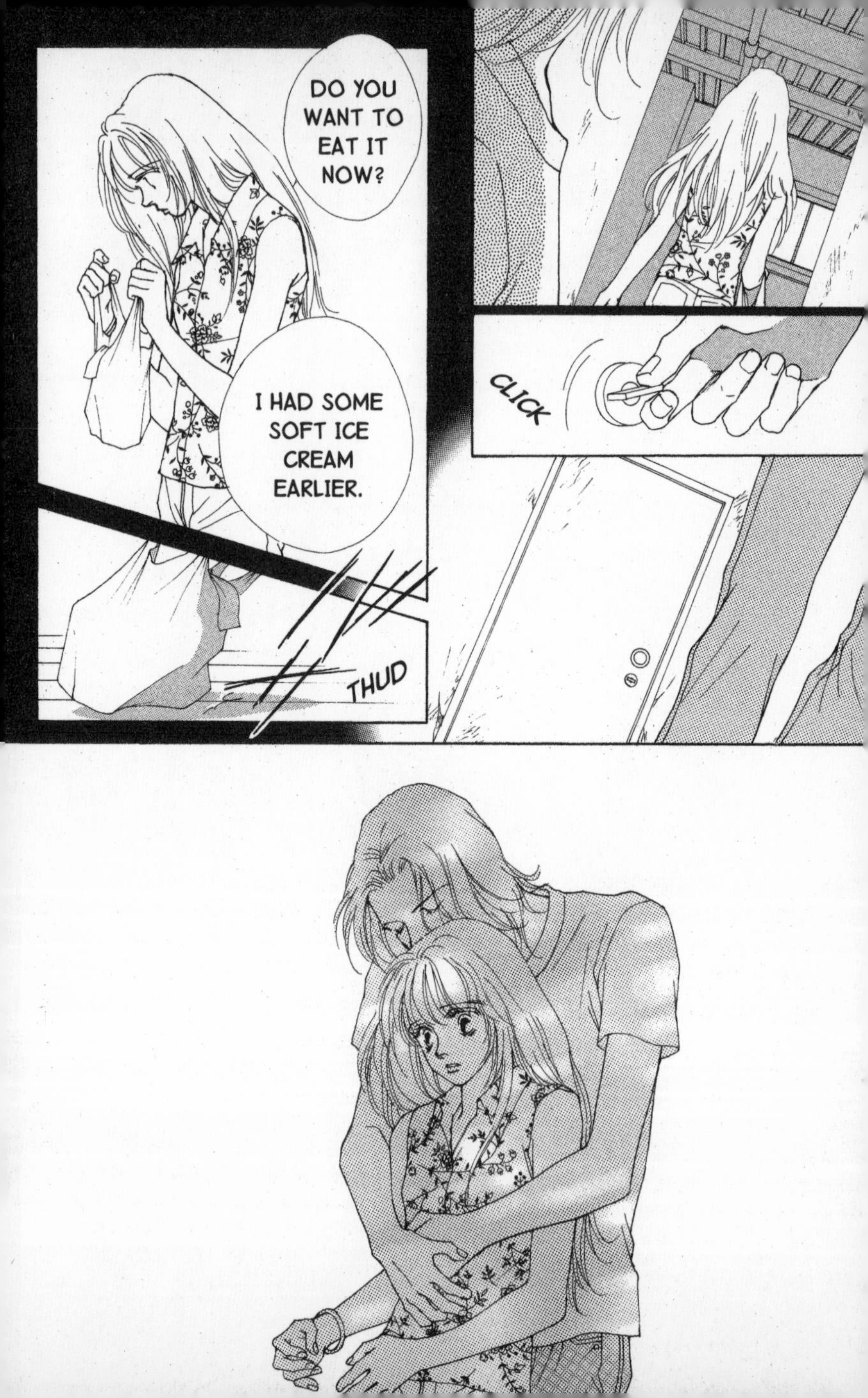
CLICK
DO YOU WANT TO EAT IT NOW?
I HAD SOME SOFT ICE CREAM EARLIER.
THUD

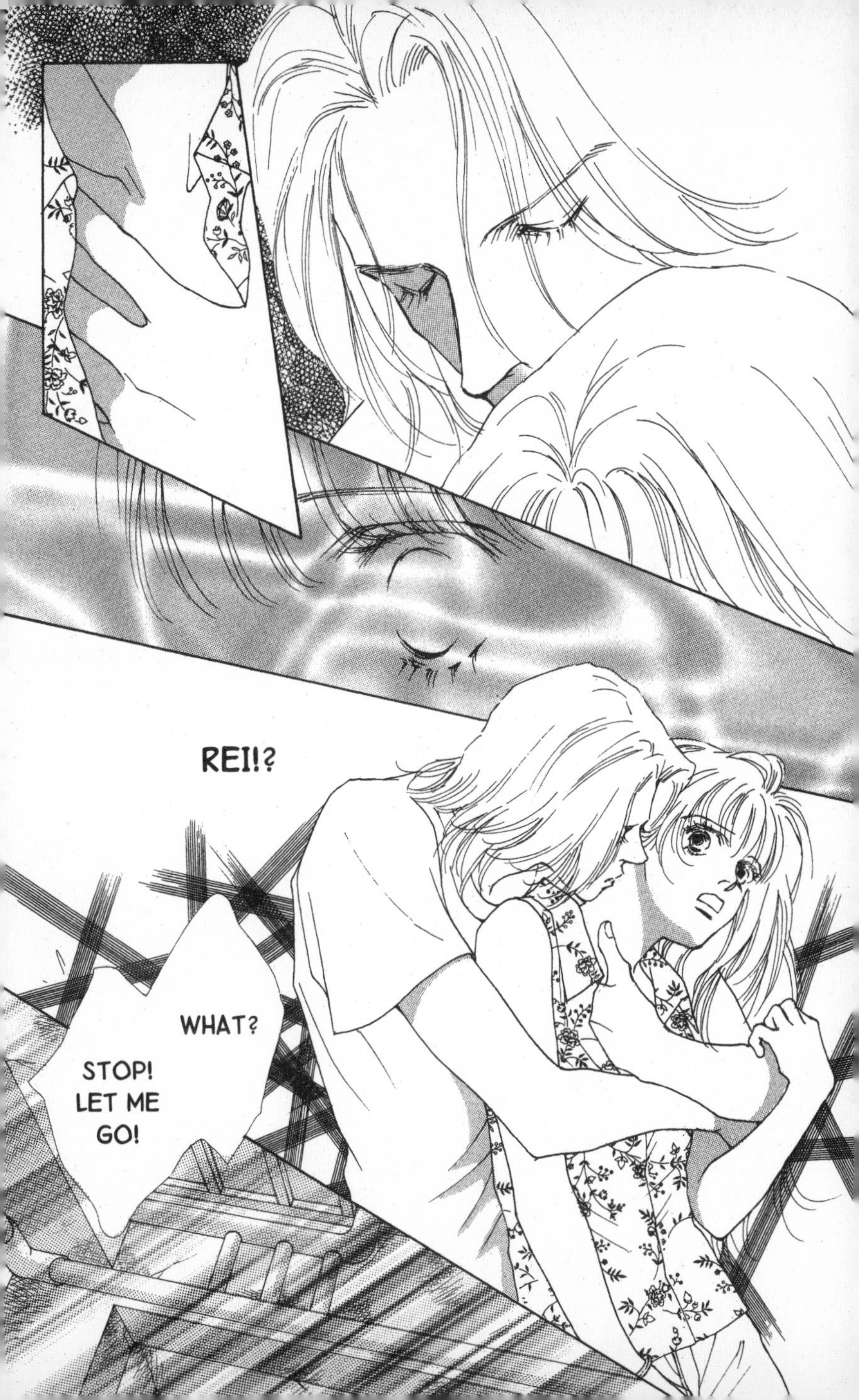

REI!?
WHAT?
STOP! LET ME GO!

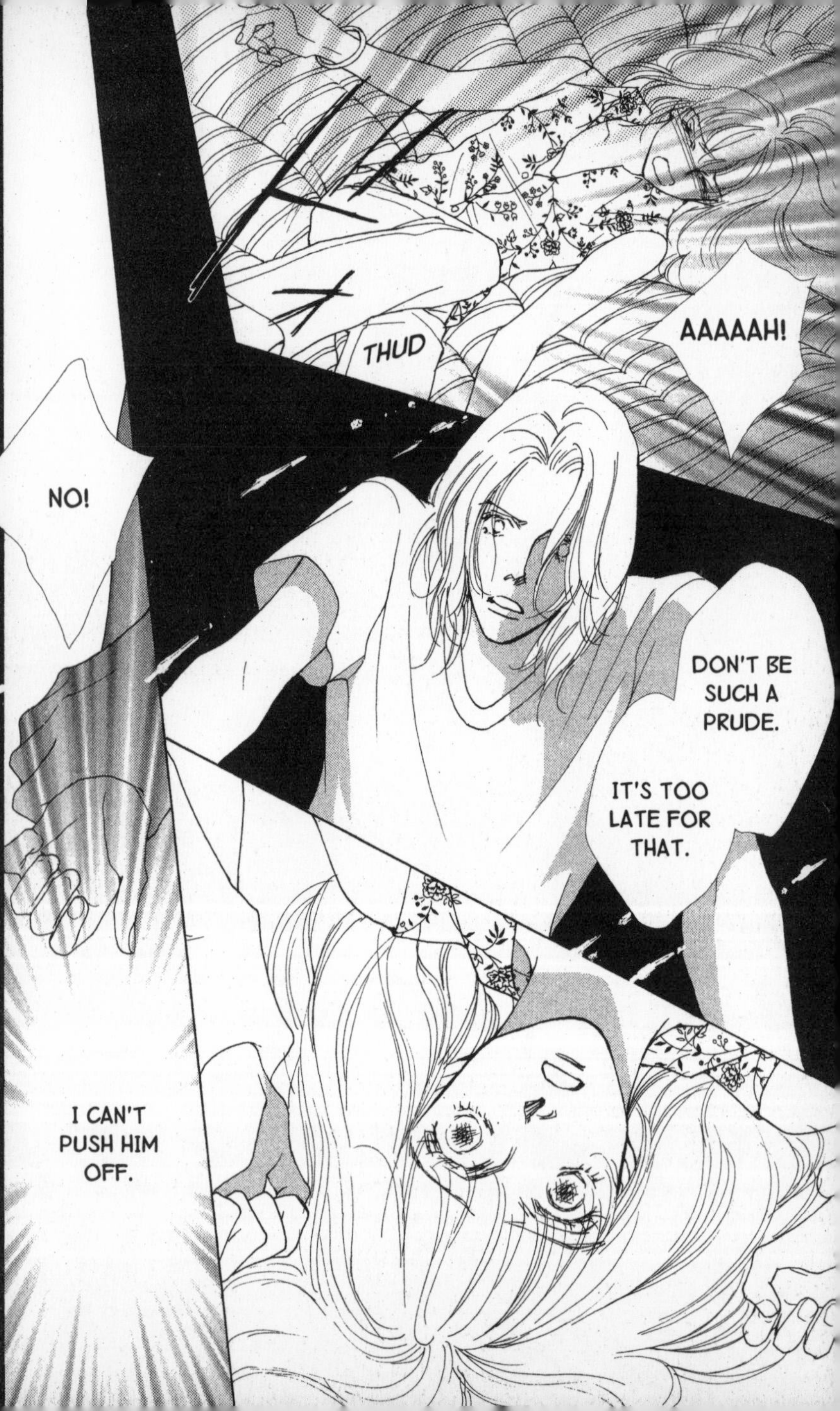
AAAAAH!
THUD
DON'T BE SUCH A PRUDE.
IT'S TOO LATE FOR THAT.
NO!
I CAN'T PUSH HIM OFF.

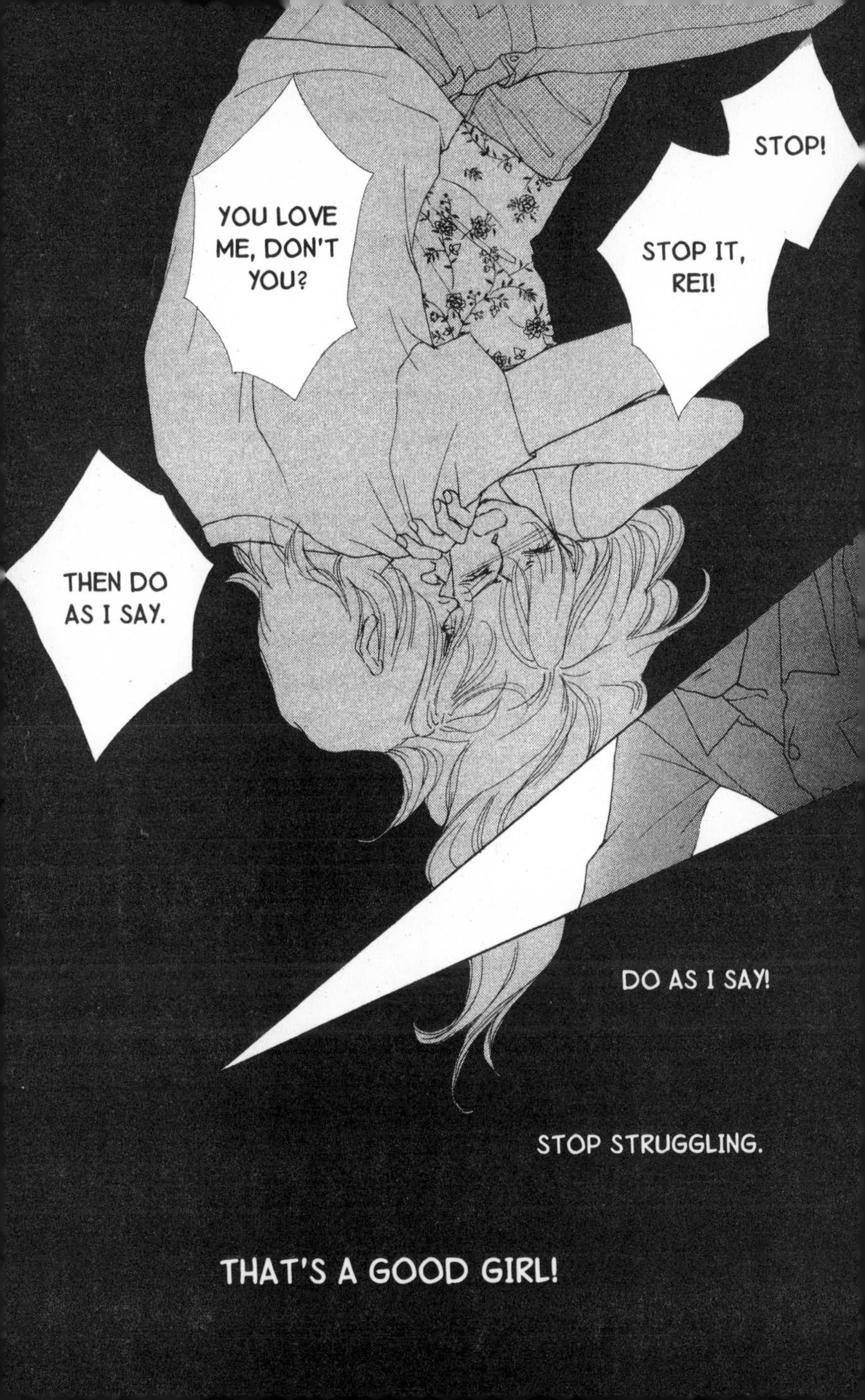
STOP!
STOP IT, REI!
YOU LOVE ME, DON'T YOU?
THEN DO AS I SAY.
DO AS I SAY!
STOP STRUGGLING.
THAT'S A GOOD GIRL!

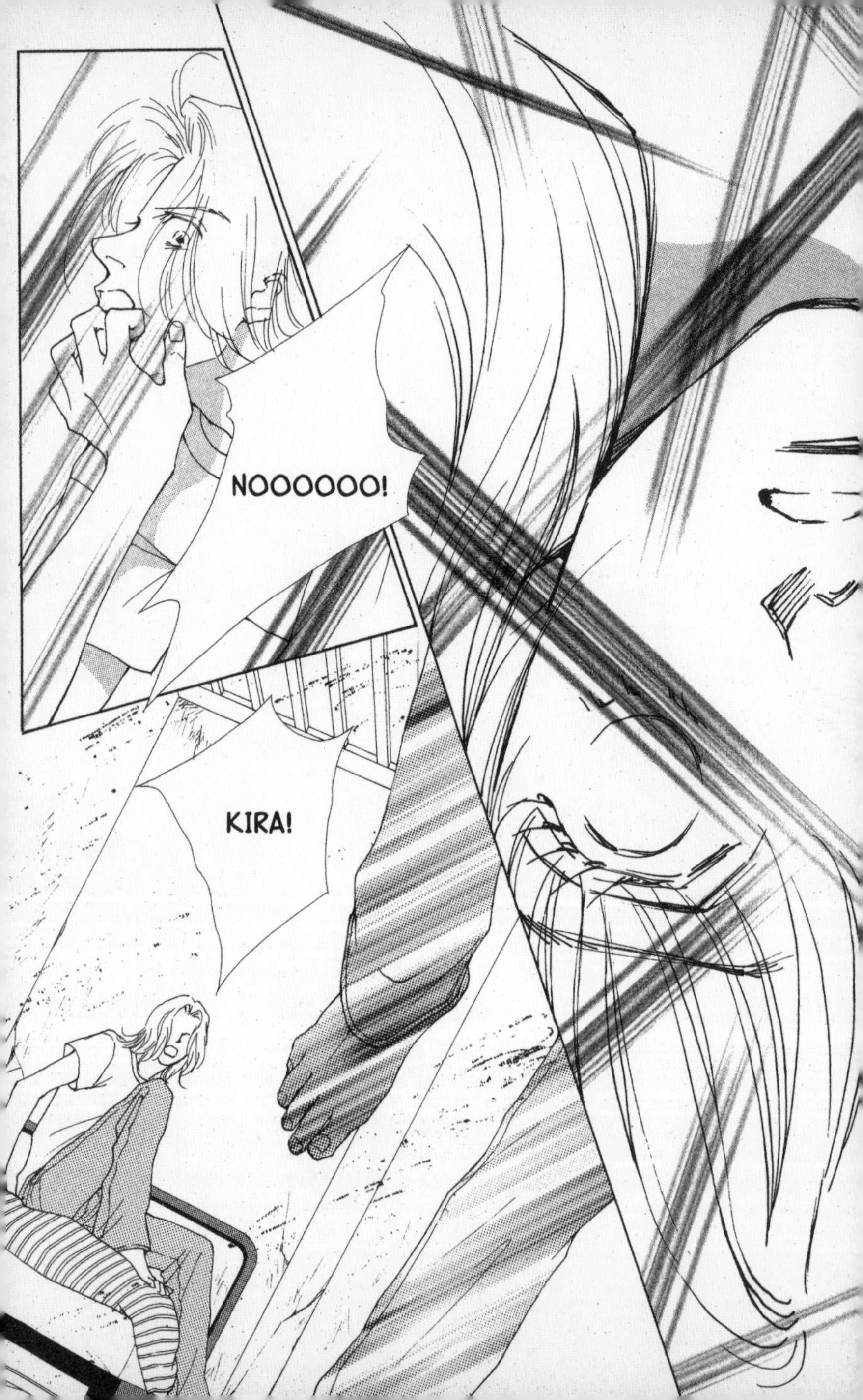
NOOOOOO!
KIRA!

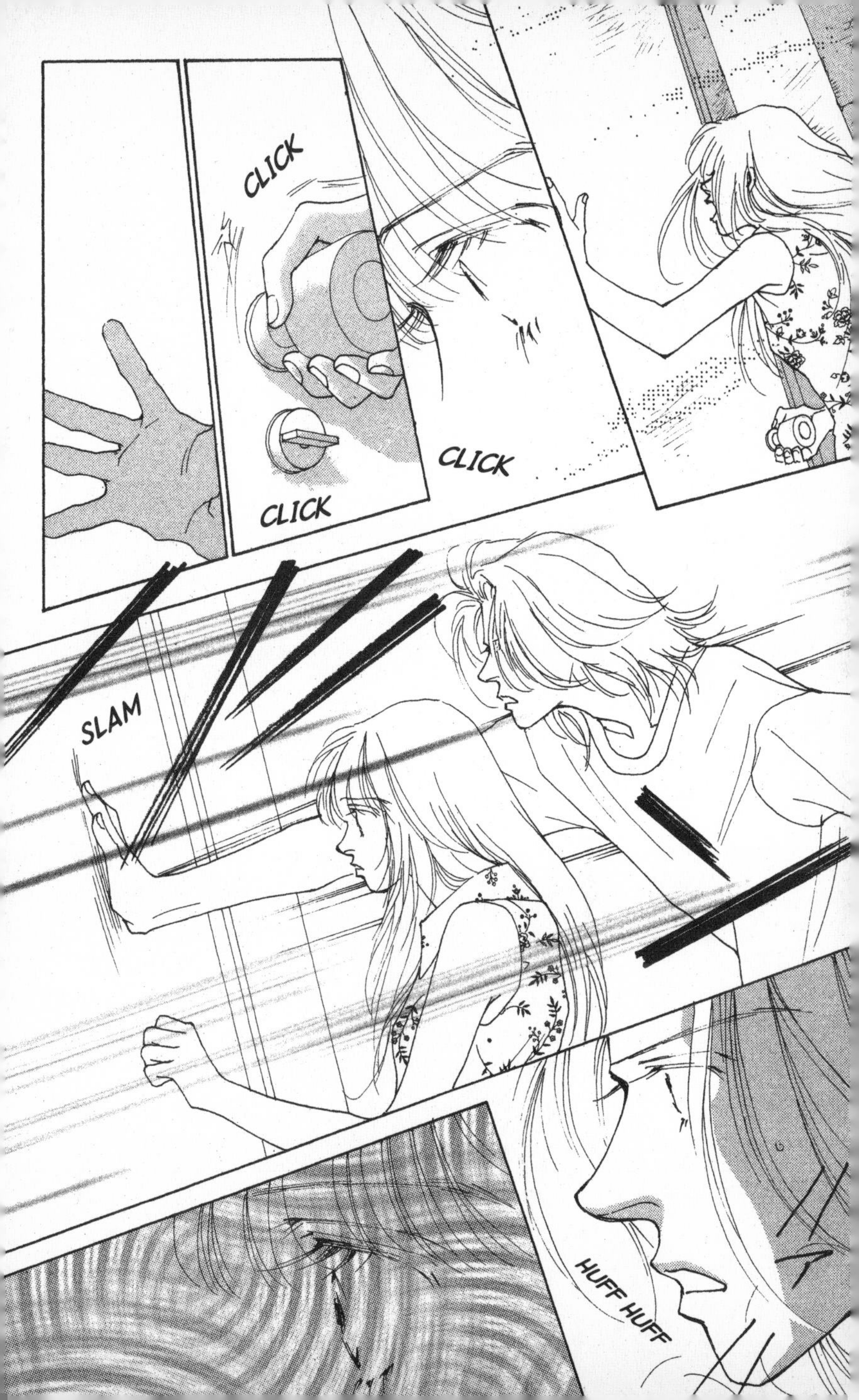
CLICK
CLICK
CLICK
SLAM
HUFF HUFF

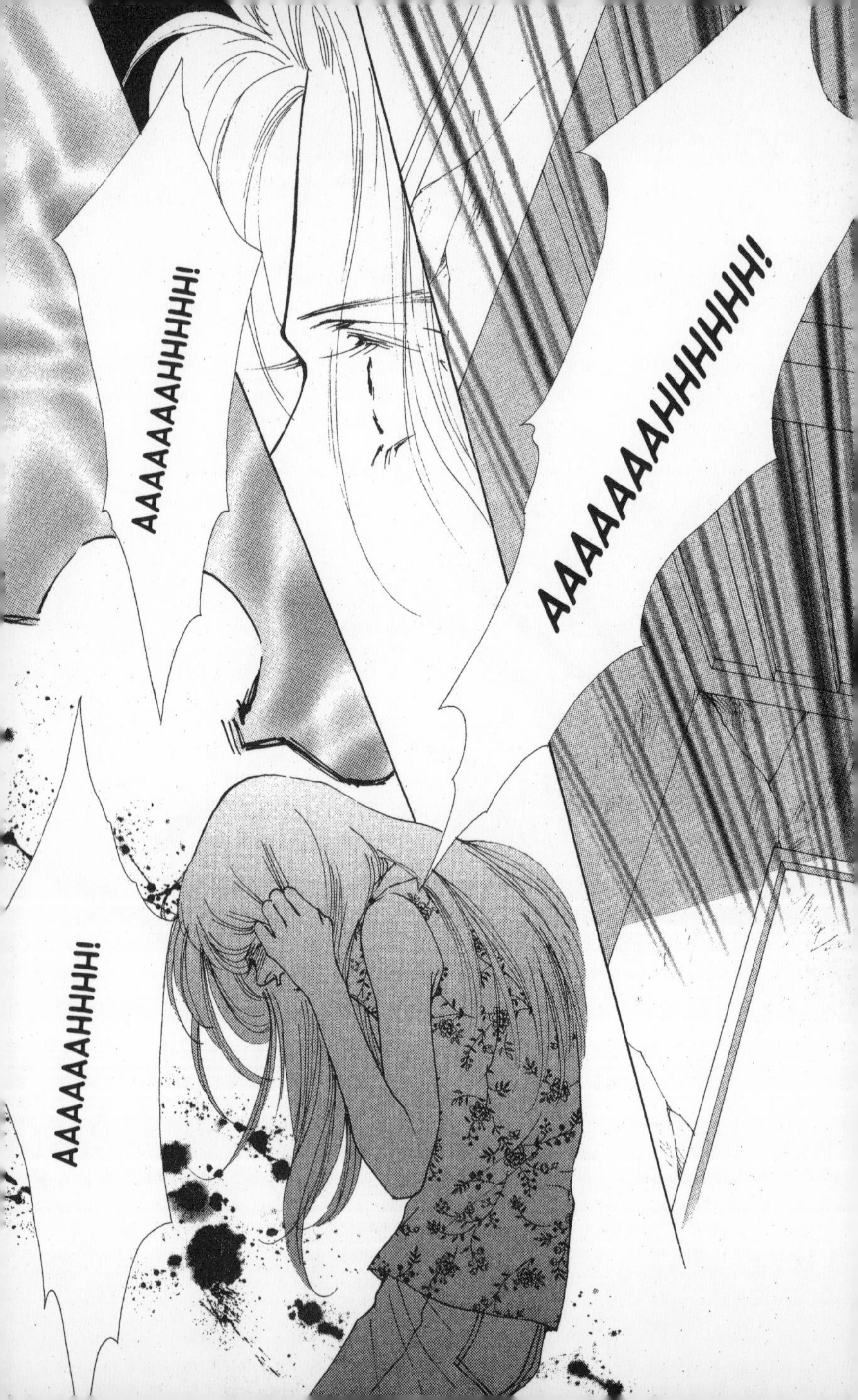
AAAAAAAHHHHHHHH!
AAAAAAAHHHHHH!
AAAAAAAHHHH!

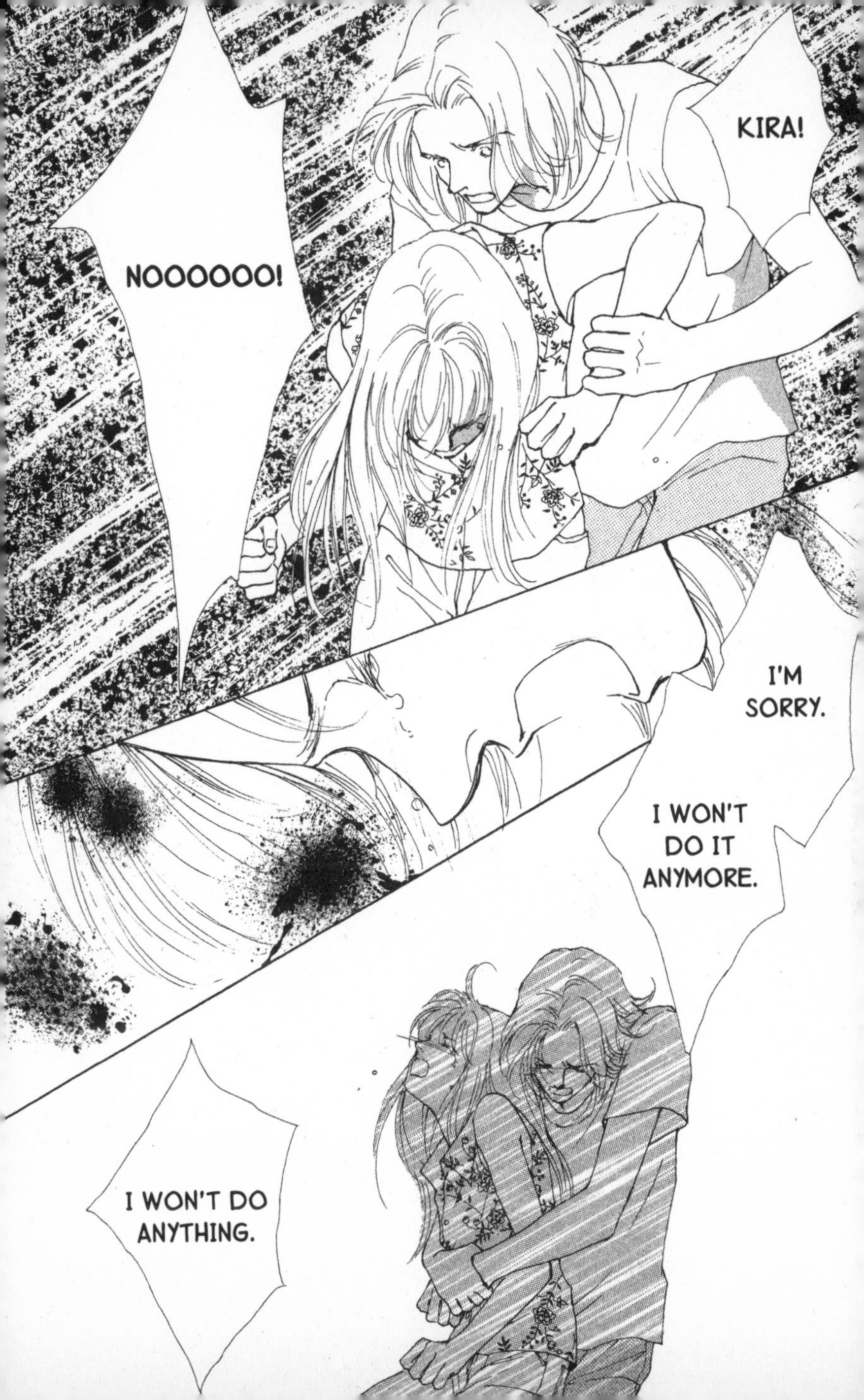
KIRA!
NOOOOOO!
I'M SORRY.
I WON'T DO IT ANYMORE.
I WON'T DO ANYTHING.

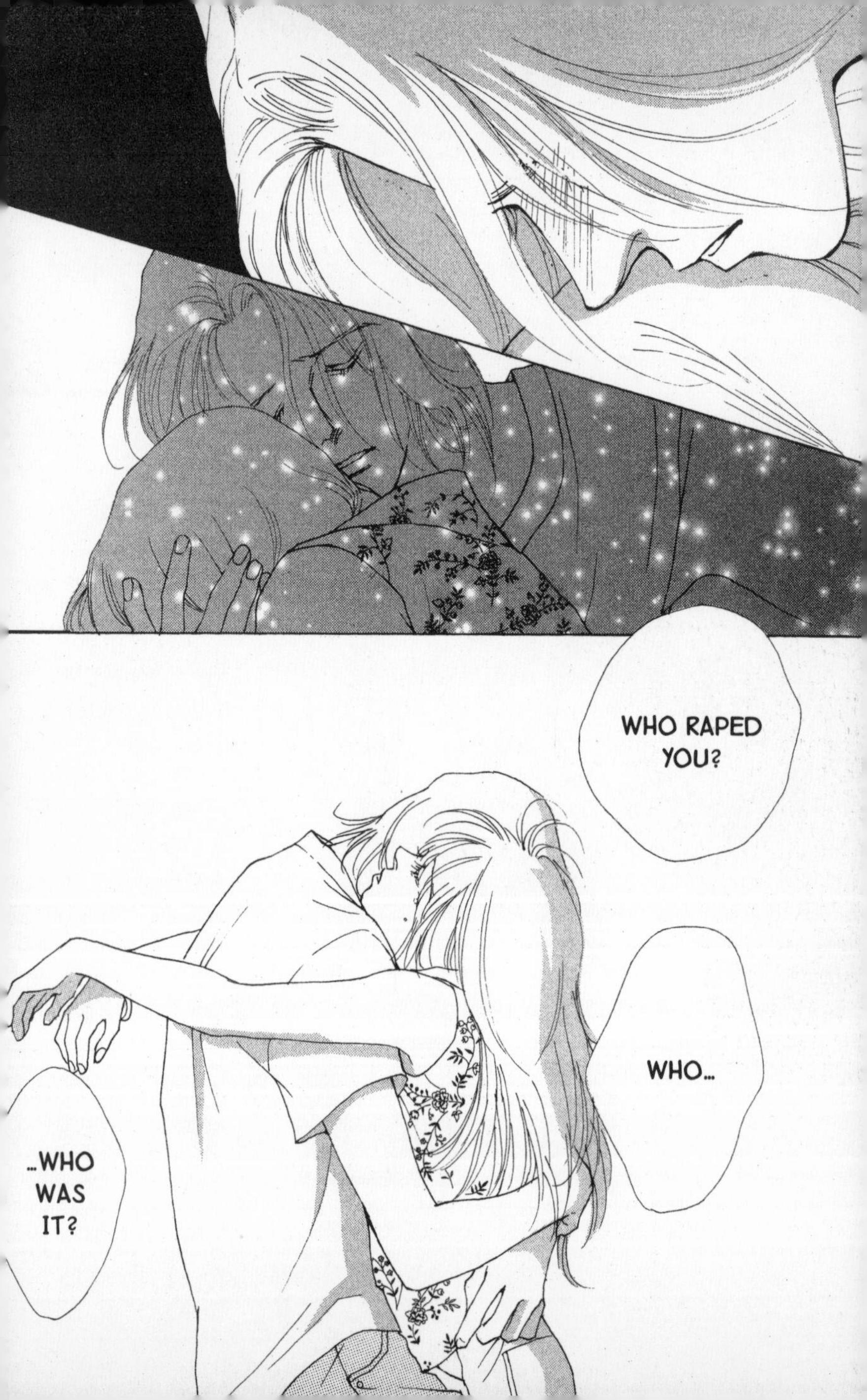
WHO RAPED YOU?
WHO...
...WHO WAS IT?

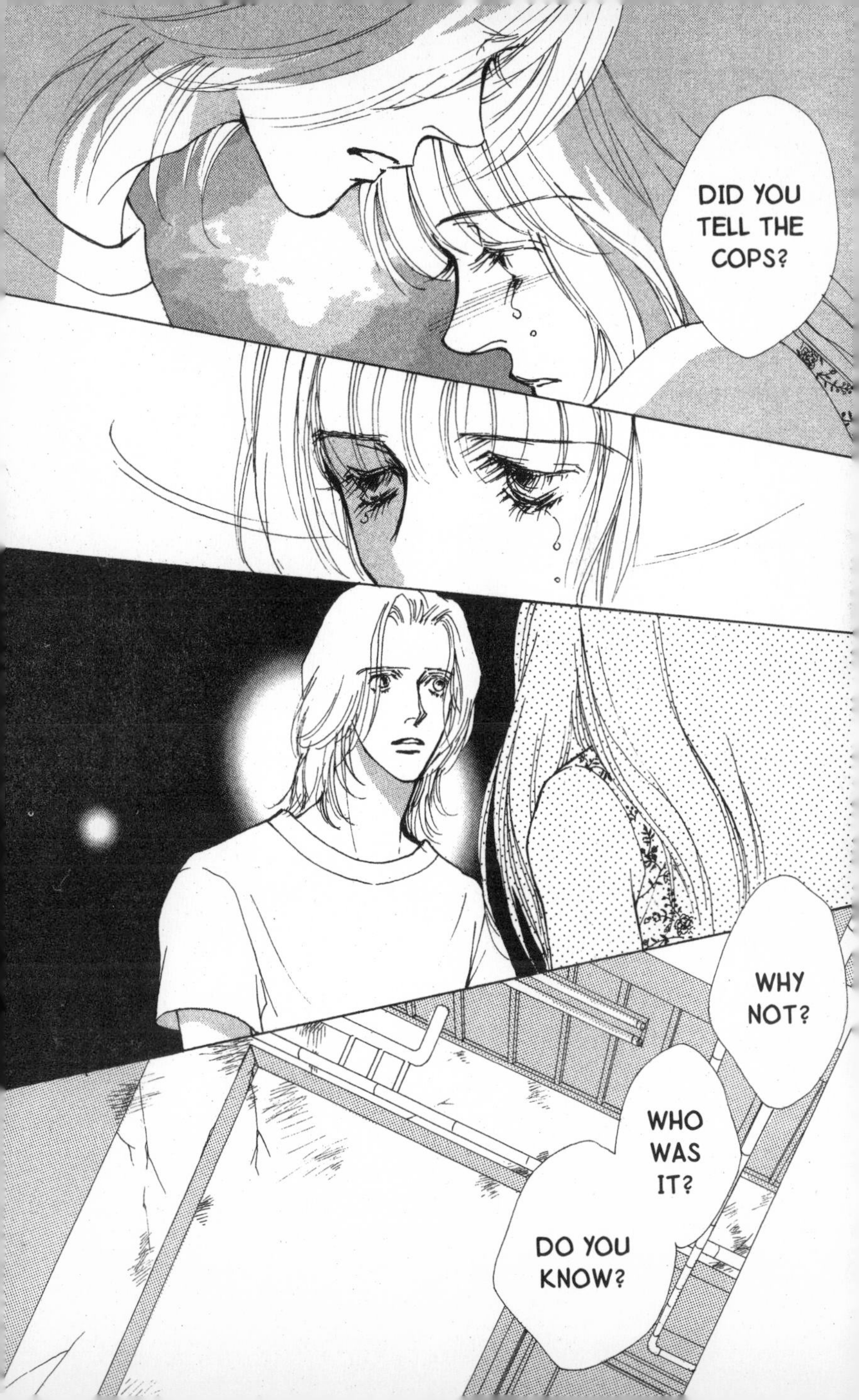
DID YOU TELL THE COPS?
WHY NOT?
WHO WAS IT?
DO YOU KNOW?

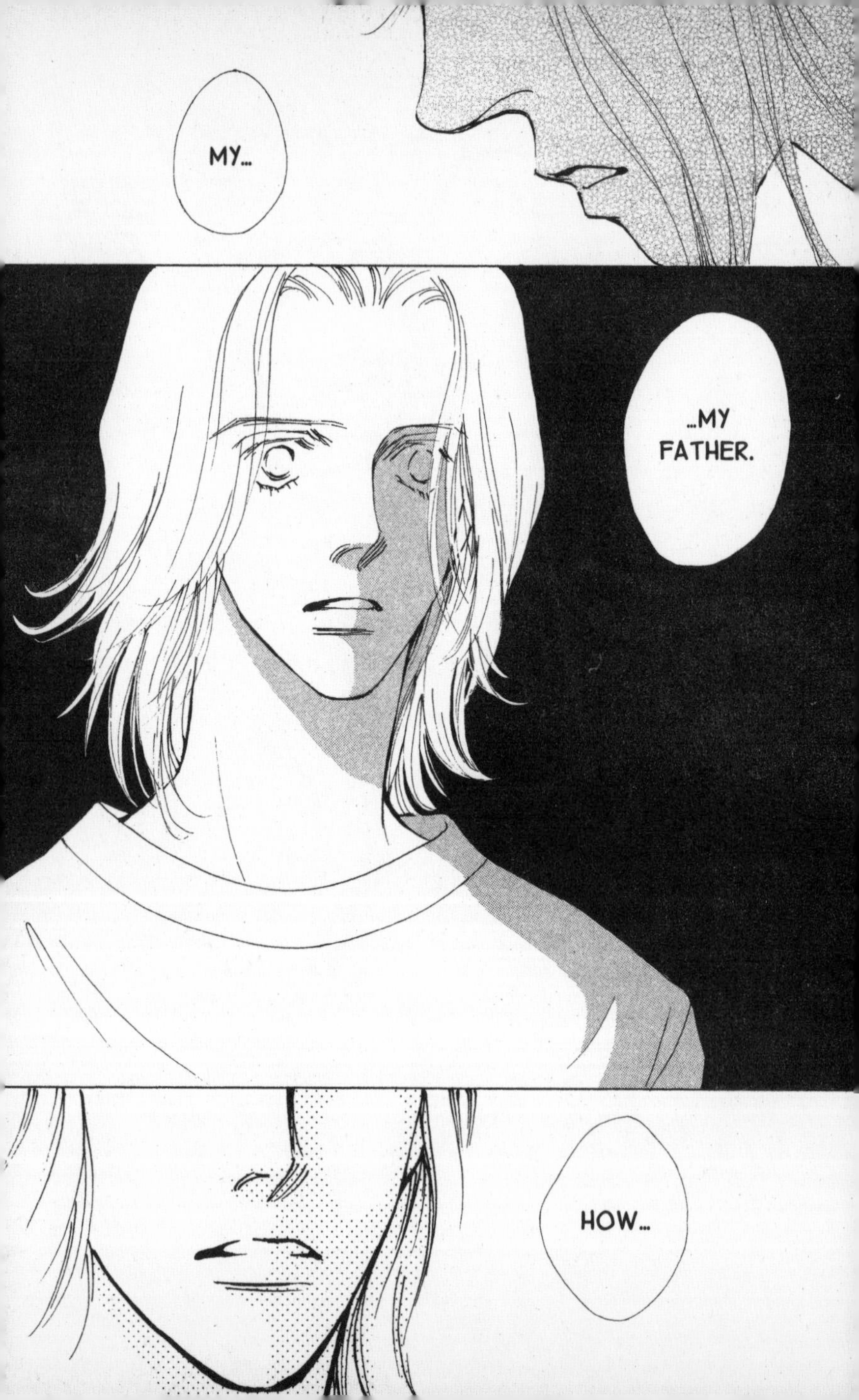
MY...
...MY FATHER.
HOW...

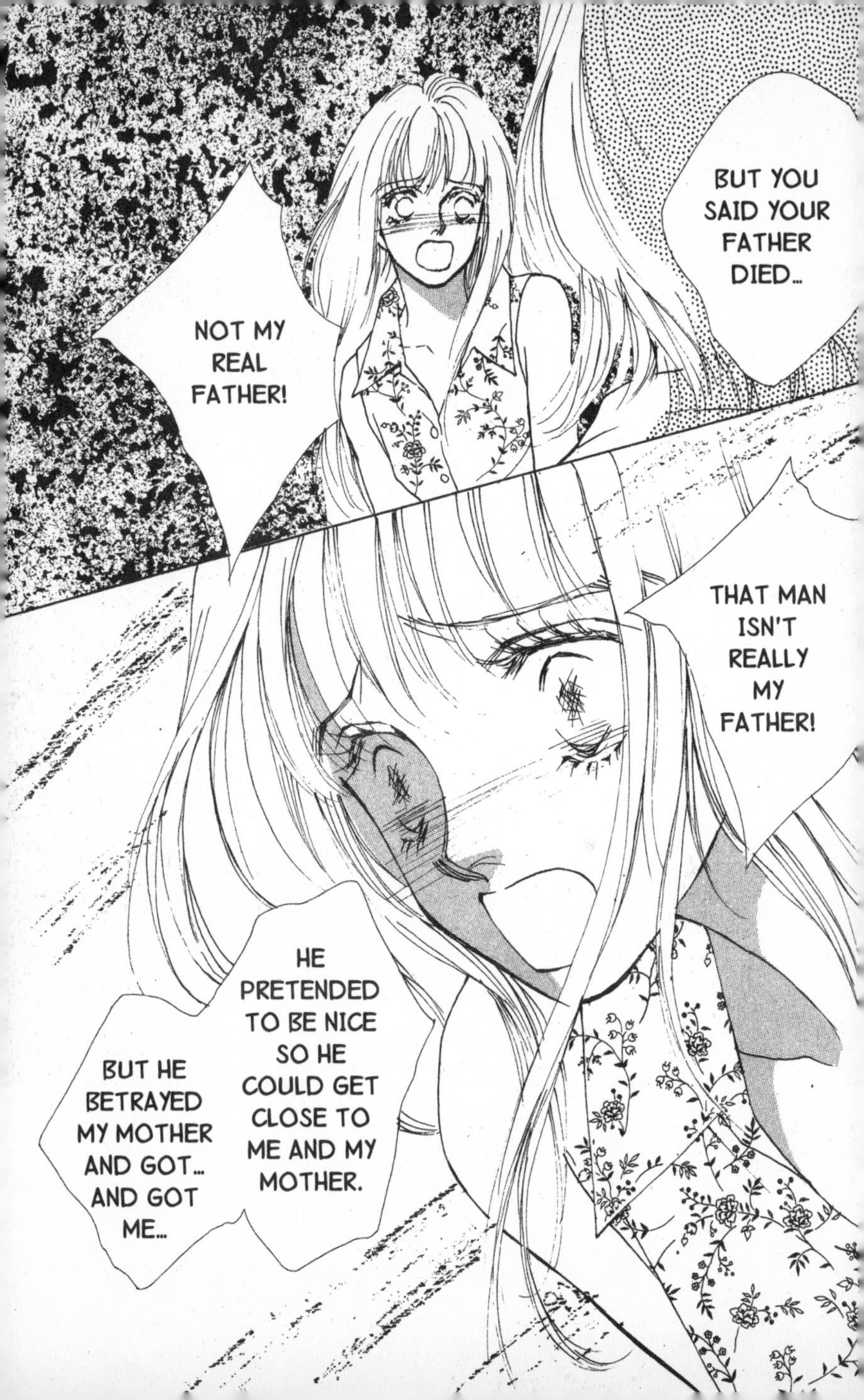
BUT YOU SAID YOUR FATHER DIED...
NOT MY REAL FATHER!
THAT MAN ISN'T REALLY MY FATHER!
HE PRETENDED TO BE NICE SO HE COULD GET CLOSE TO ME AND MY MOTHER.
BUT HE BETRAYED MY MOTHER AND GOT... AND GOT ME...

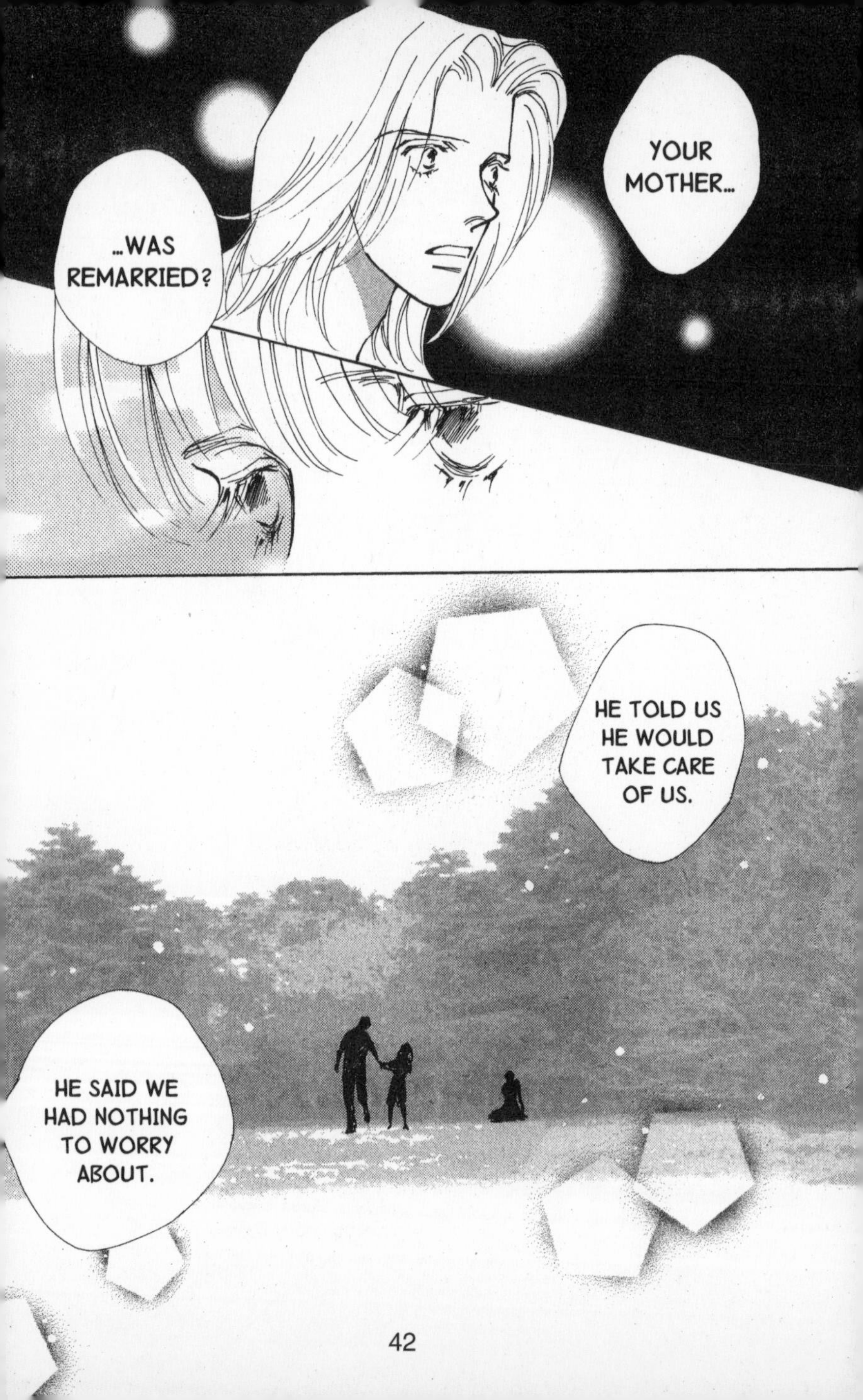
YOUR MOTHER...
...WAS REMARRIED?
HE TOLD US HE WOULD TAKE CARE OF US.
HE SAID WE HAD NOTHING TO WORRY ABOUT.

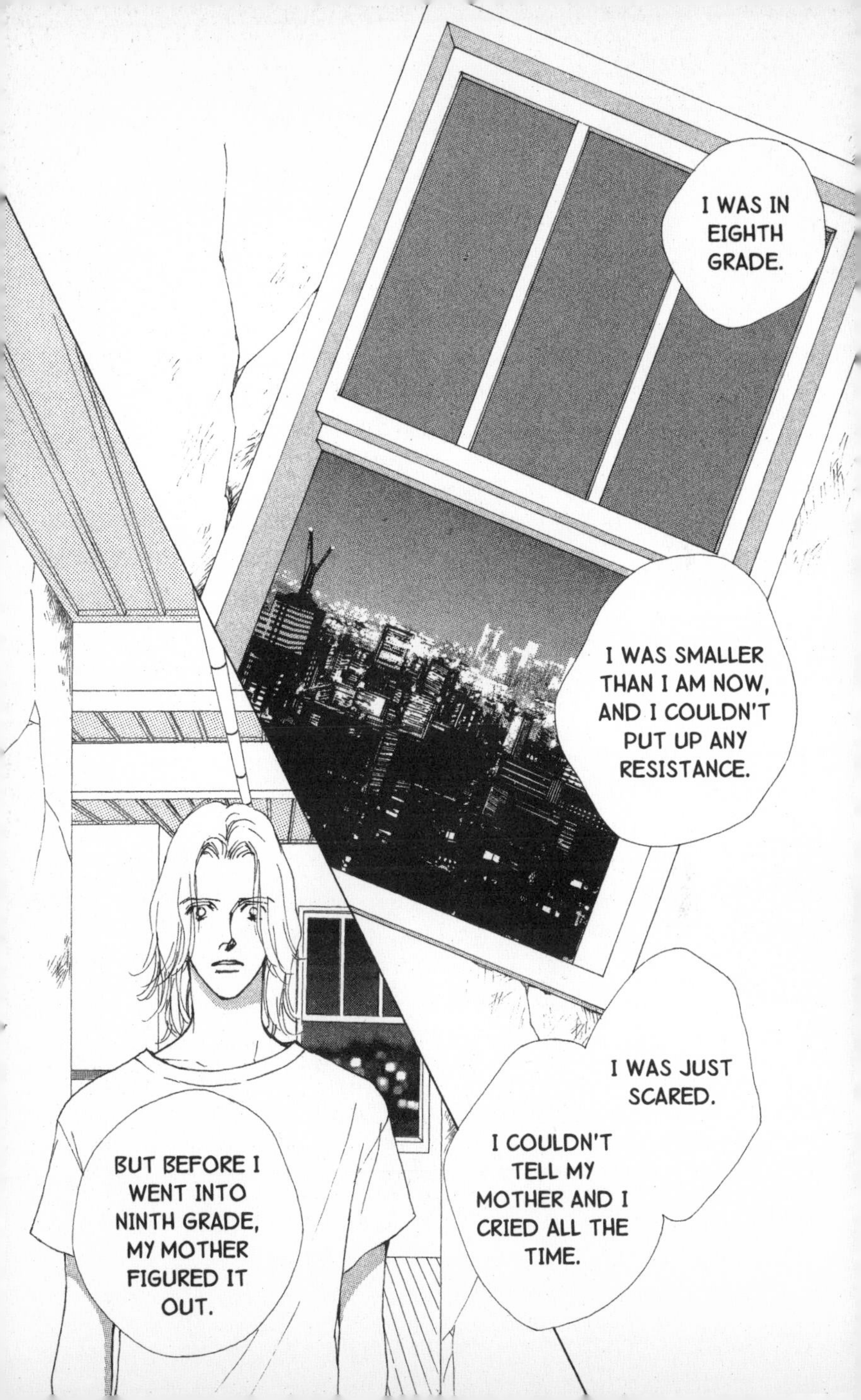
I WAS IN EIGHTH GRADE.
I WAS SMALLER THAN I AM NOW, AND I COULDN'T PUT UP ANY RESISTANCE.
I WAS JUST SCARED.
I COULDN'T TELL MY MOTHER AND I CRIED ALL THE TIME.
BUT BEFORE I WENT INTO NINTH GRADE, MY MOTHER FIGURED IT OUT.

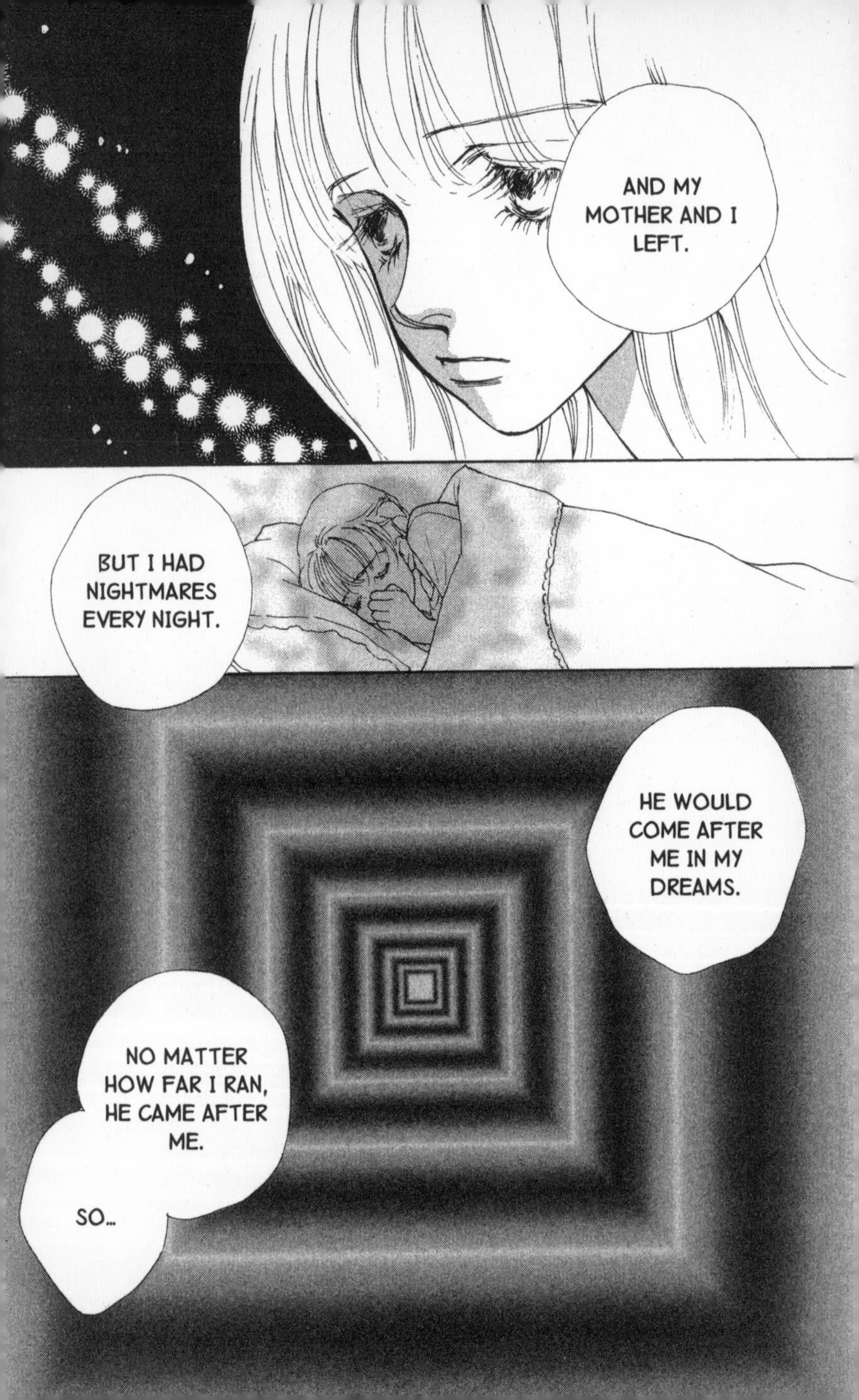
AND MY MOTHER AND I LEFT.
BUT I HAD NIGHTMARES EVERY NIGHT.
HE WOULD COME AFTER ME IN MY DREAMS.
NO MATTER HOW FAR I RAN, HE CAME AFTER ME.
SO...

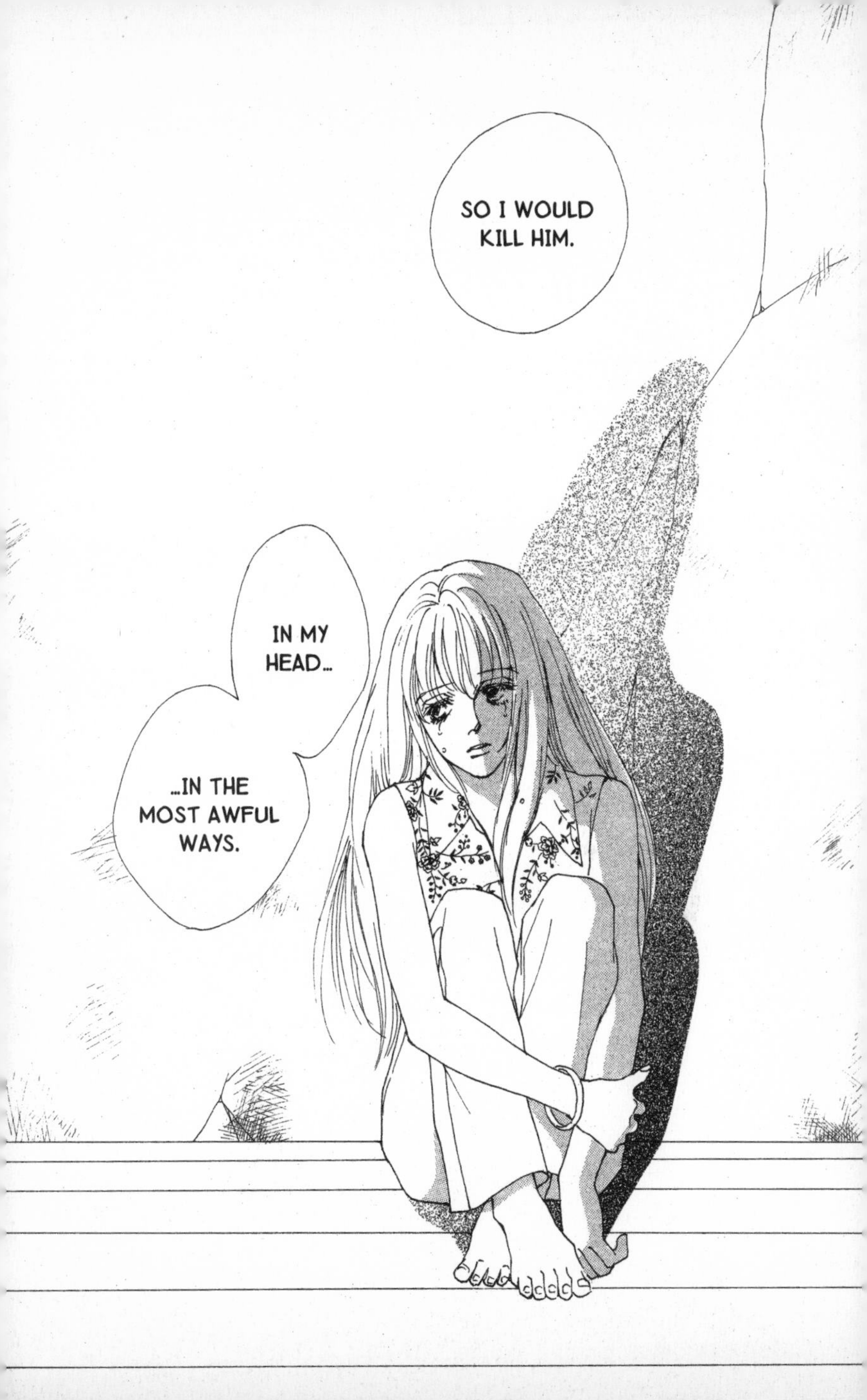
SO I WOULD KILL HIM.
IN MY HEAD...
...IN THE MOST AWFUL WAYS.

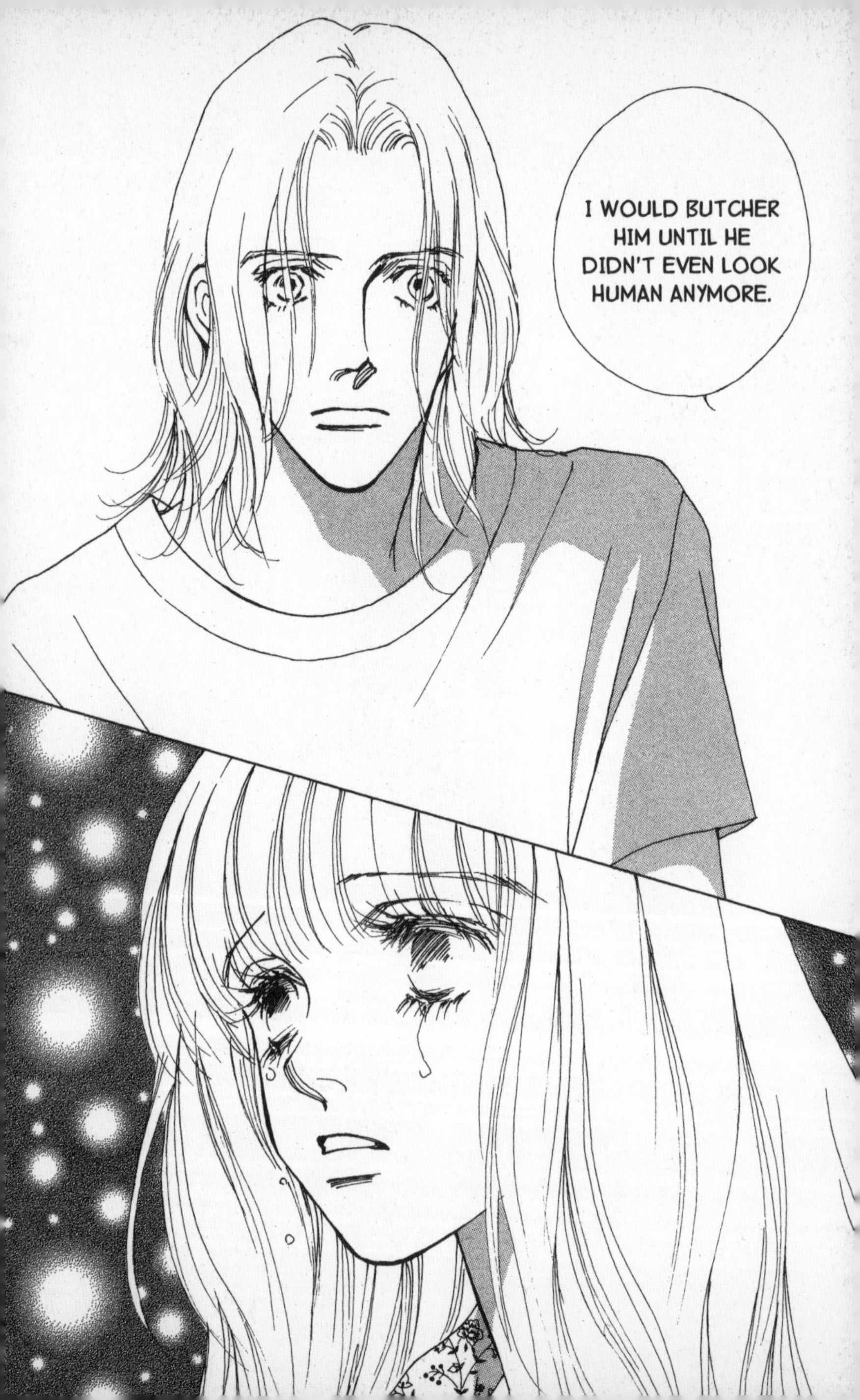
I WOULD BUTCHER HIM UNTIL HE DIDN'T EVEN LOOK HUMAN ANYMORE.

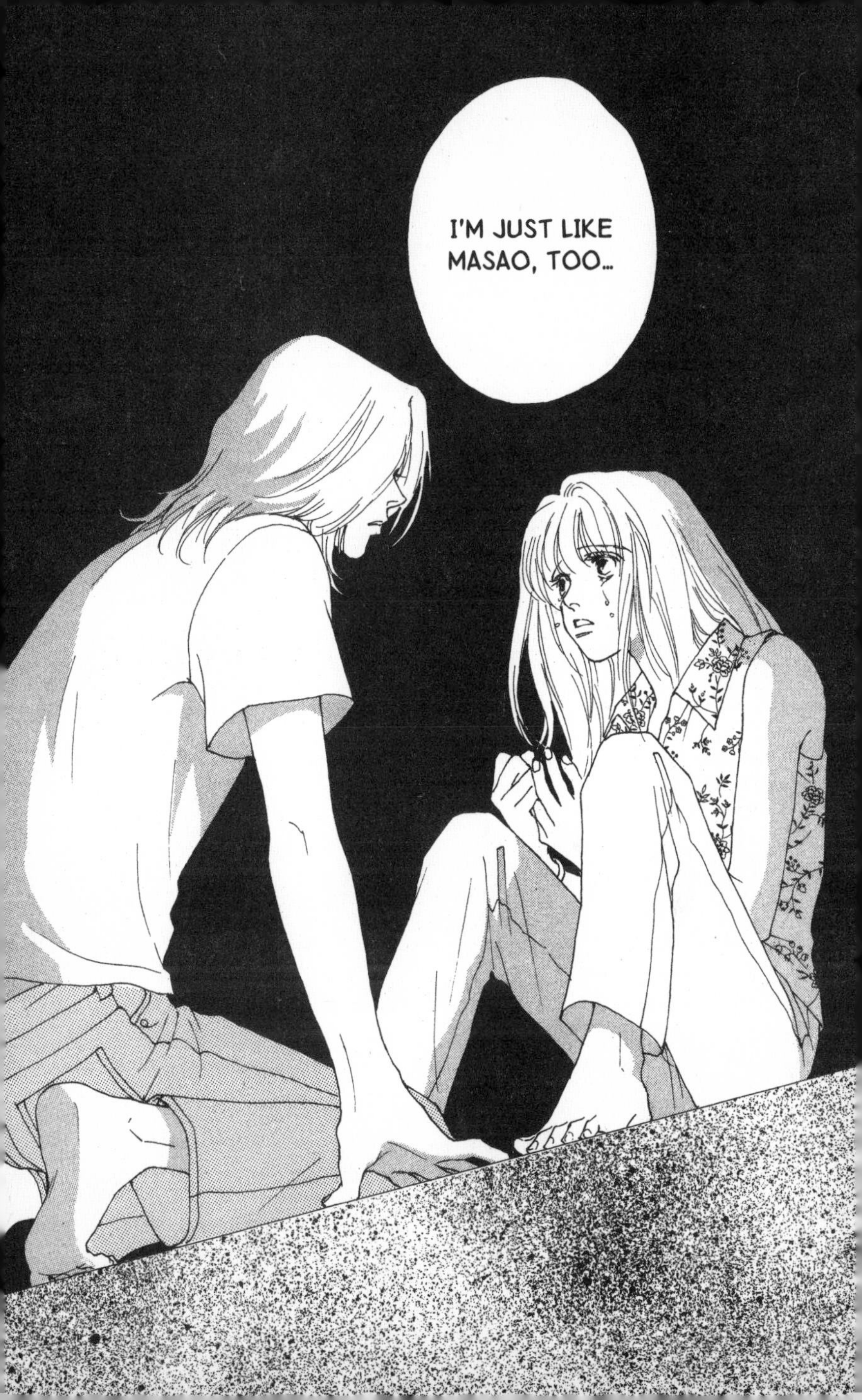
I'M JUST LIKE MASAO, TOO...

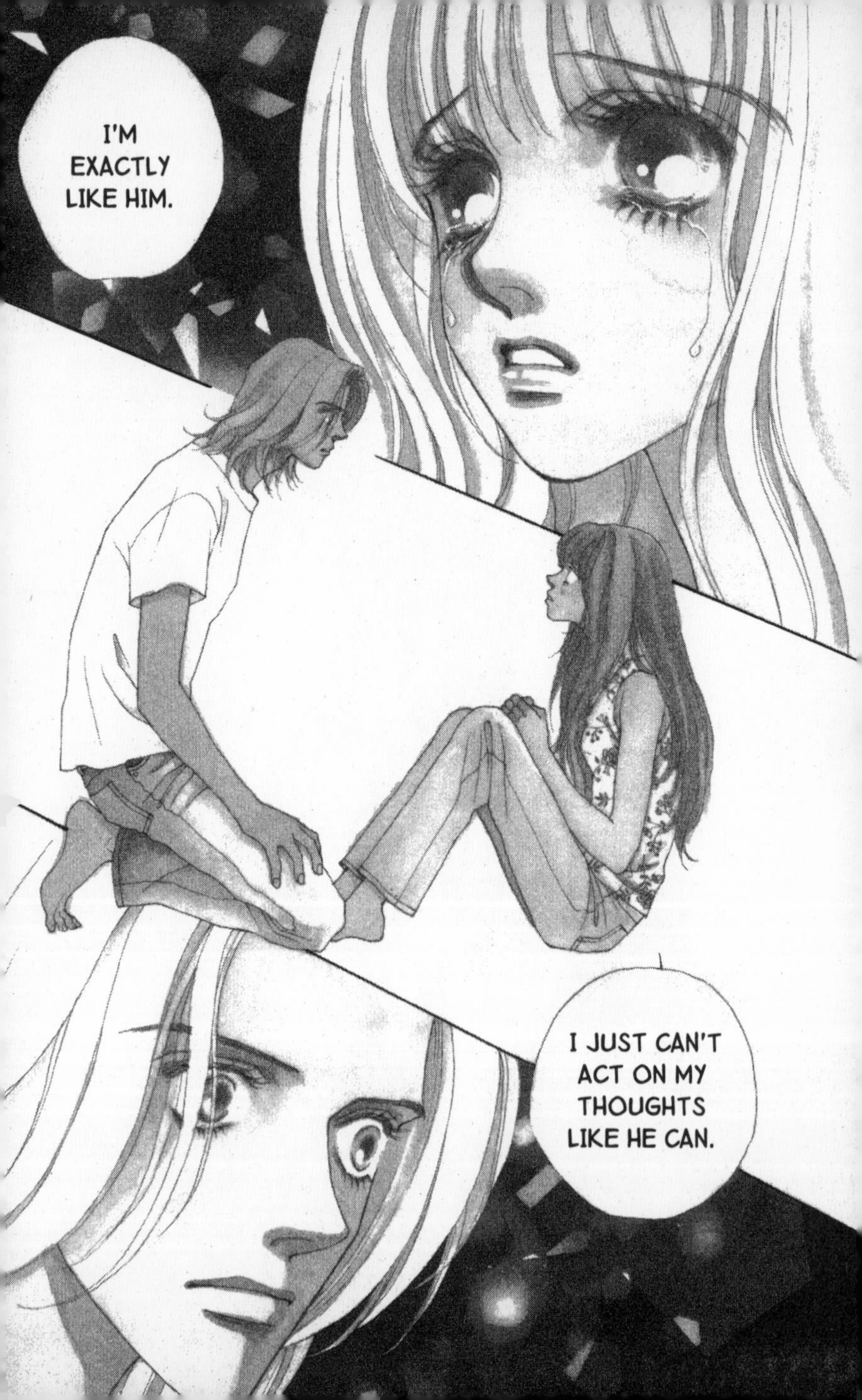
I'M EXACTLY LIKE HIM.
I JUST CAN'T ACT ON MY THOUGHTS LIKE HE CAN.

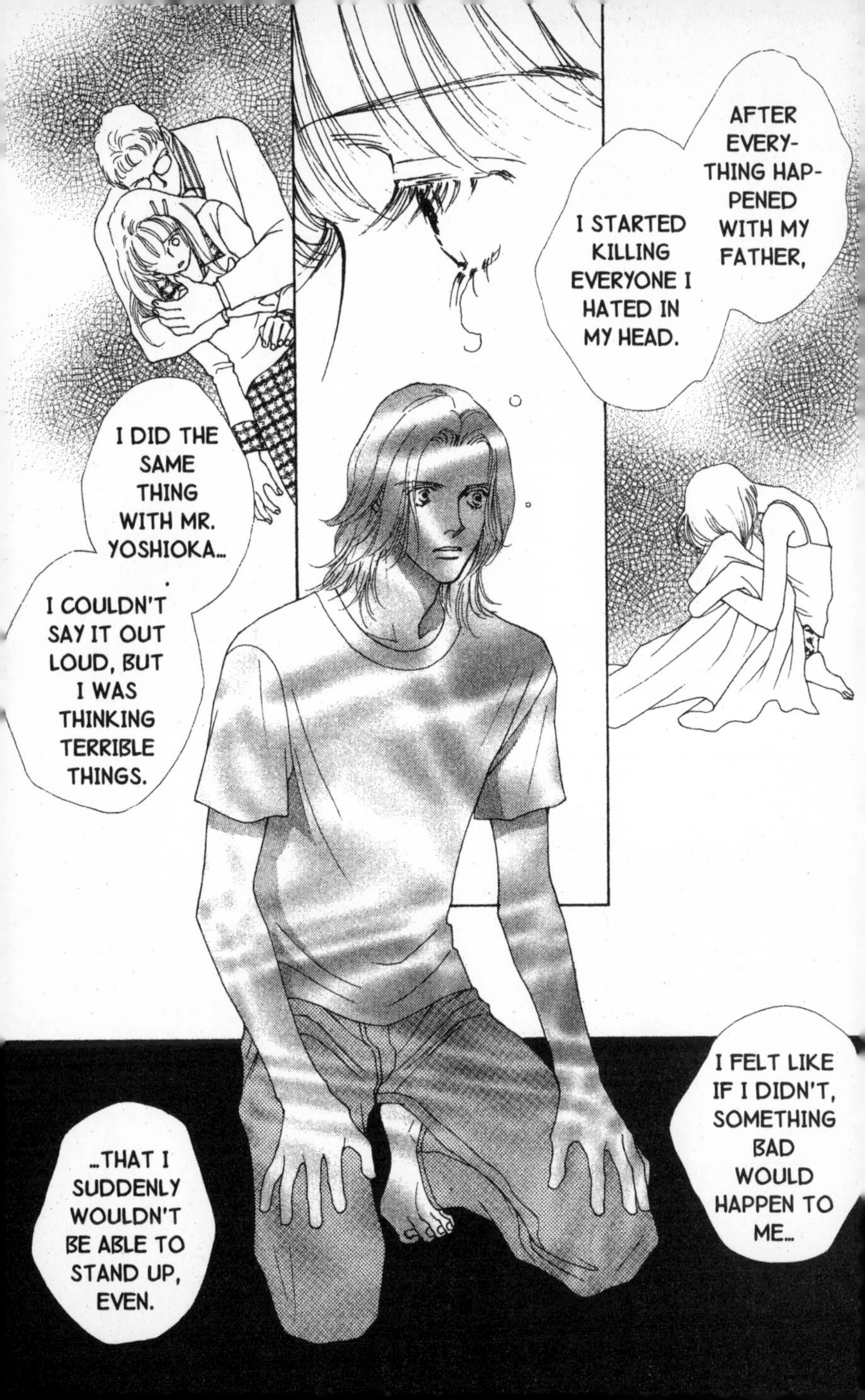
AFTER EVERYTHING HAPPENED WITH MY FATHER,
I STARTED KILLING EVERYONE I HATED IN MY HEAD.
I DID THE SAME THING WITH MR. YOSHIOKA....
I COULDN'T SAY IT OUT LOUD, BUT I WAS THINKING TERRIBLE THINGS.
I FELT LIKE IF I DIDN'T, SOMETHING BAD WOULD HAPPEN TO ME...
...THAT I SUDDENLY WOULDN'T BE ABLE TO STAND UP, EVEN.

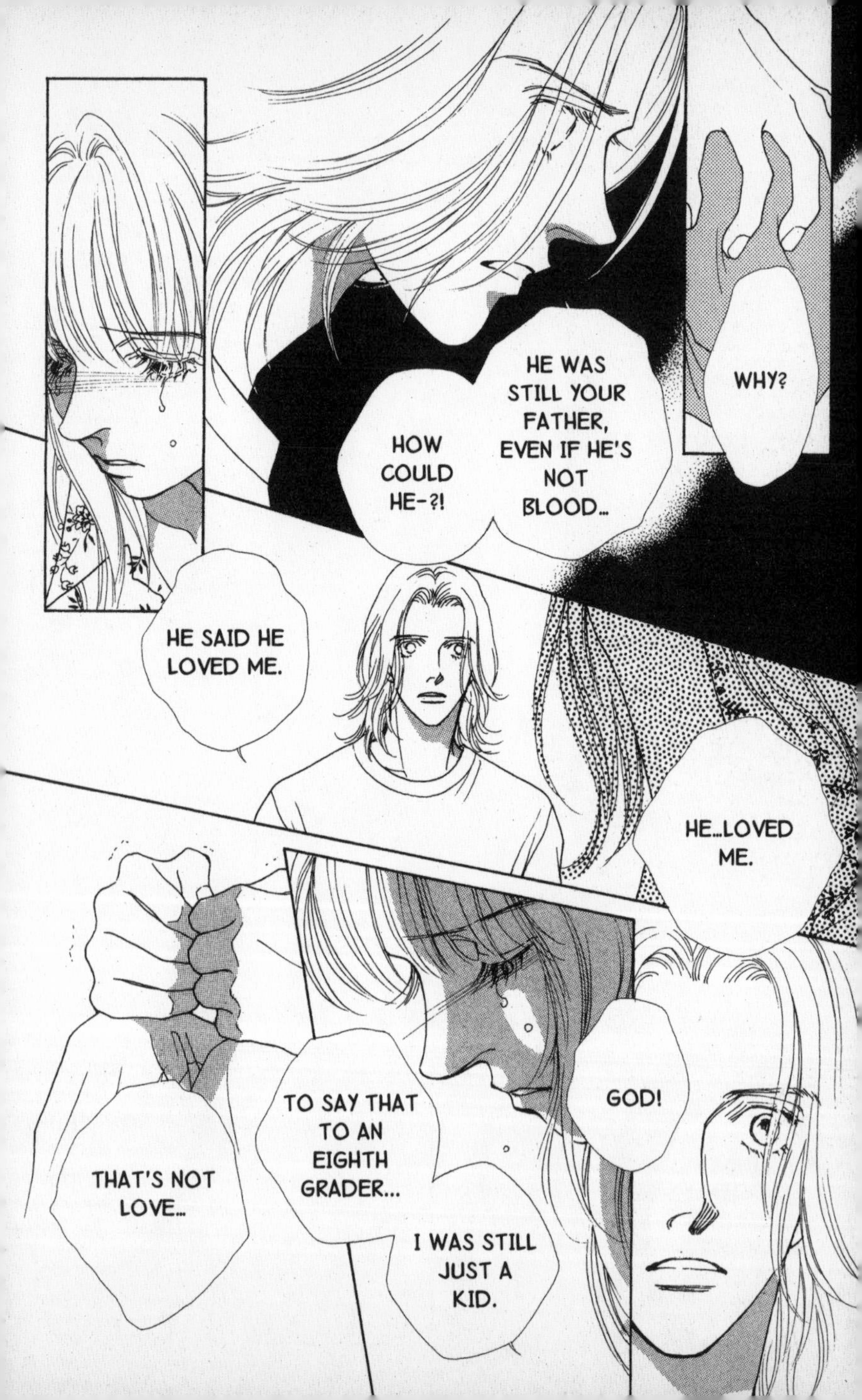
WHY?
HE WAS STILL YOUR FATHER, EVEN IF HE'S NOT BLOOD...
HOW COULD HE-?!
HE...LOVED ME.
HE SAID HE LOVED ME.
GOD!
TO SAY THAT TO AN EIGHTH GRADER...
I WAS STILL JUST A KID.
THAT'S NOT LOVE...

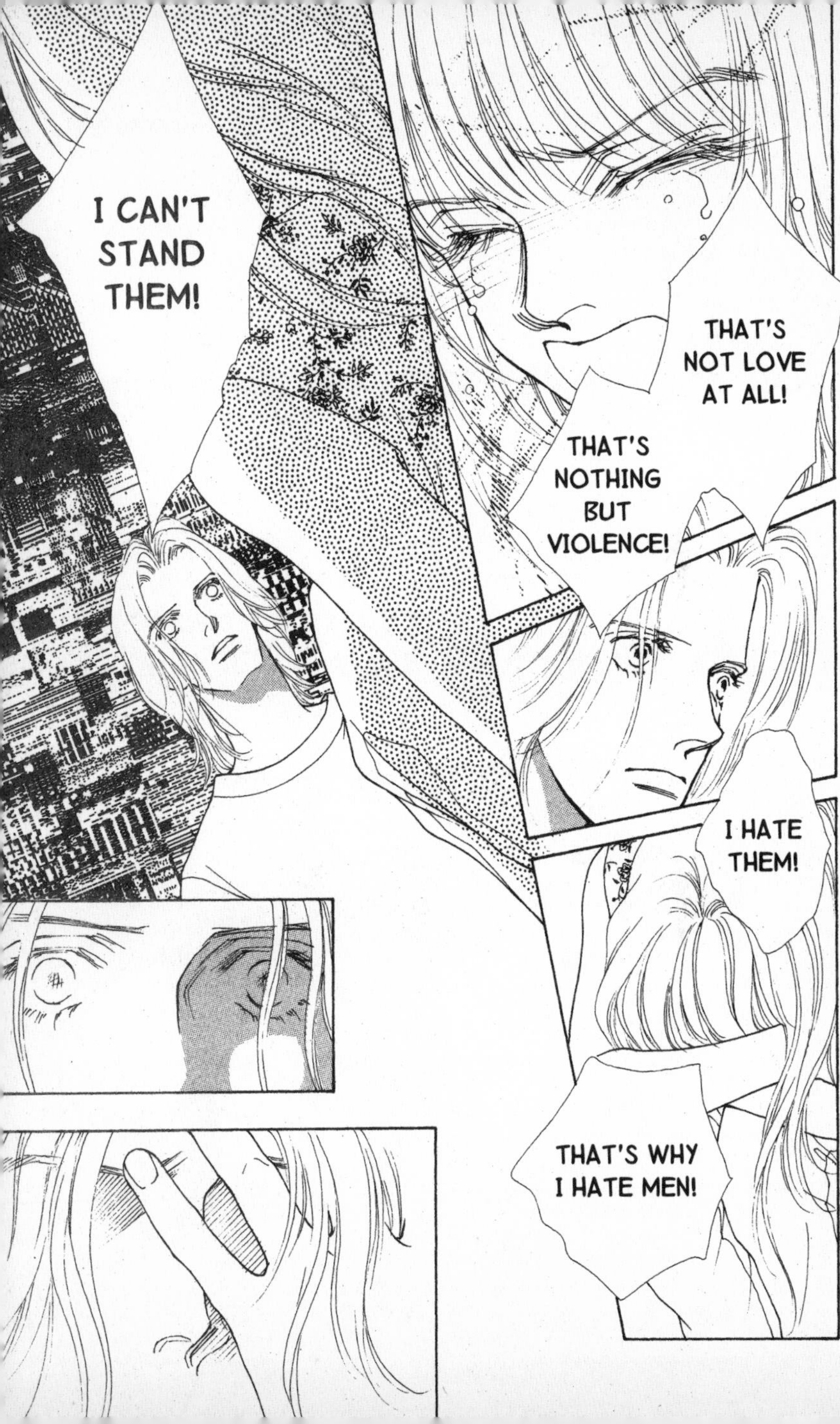
THAT'S NOT LOVE AT ALL!
THAT'S NOTHING BUT VIOLENCE!
I HATE THEM!
THAT'S WHY I HATE MEN!
I CAN'T STAND THEM!

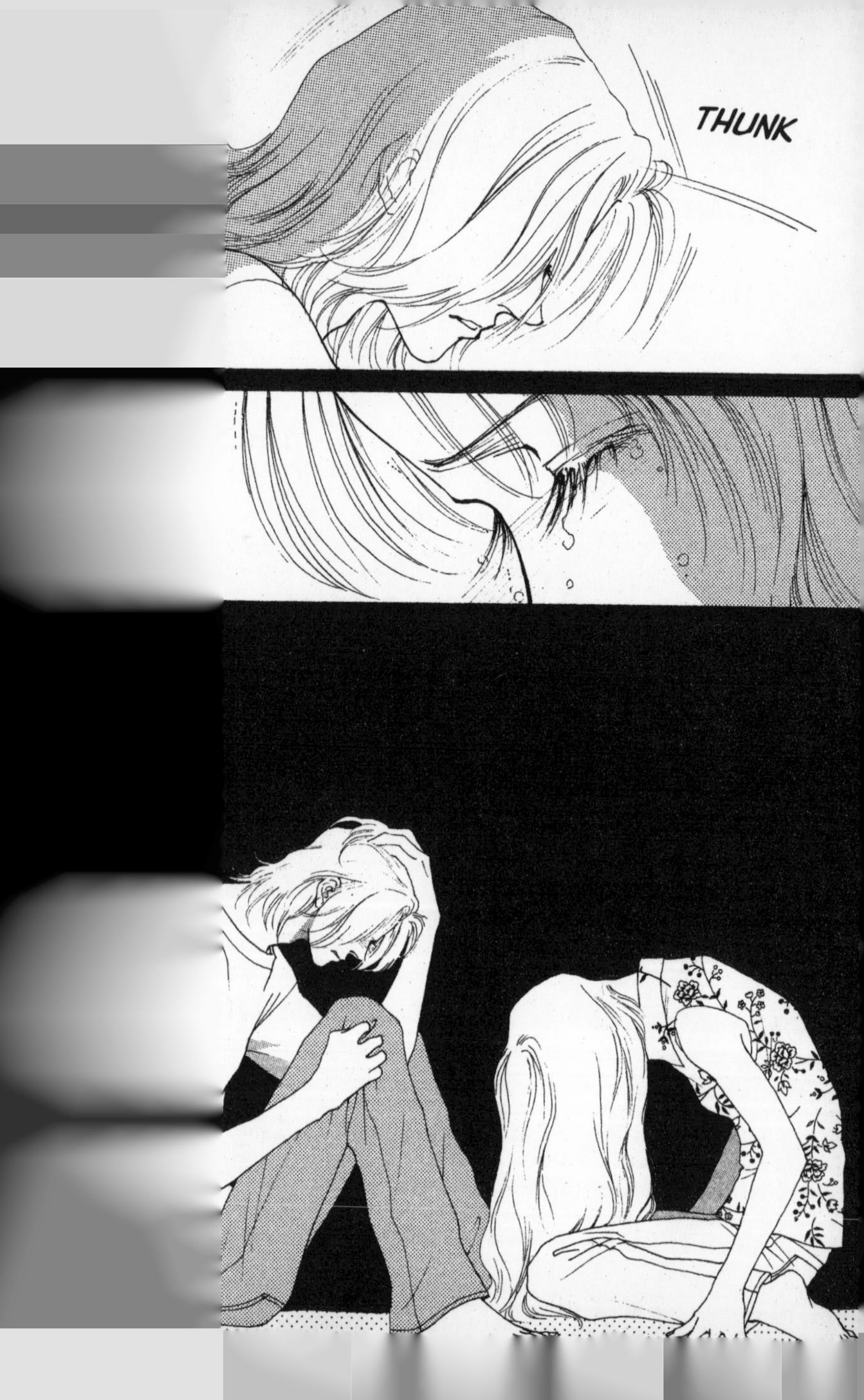
THUNK

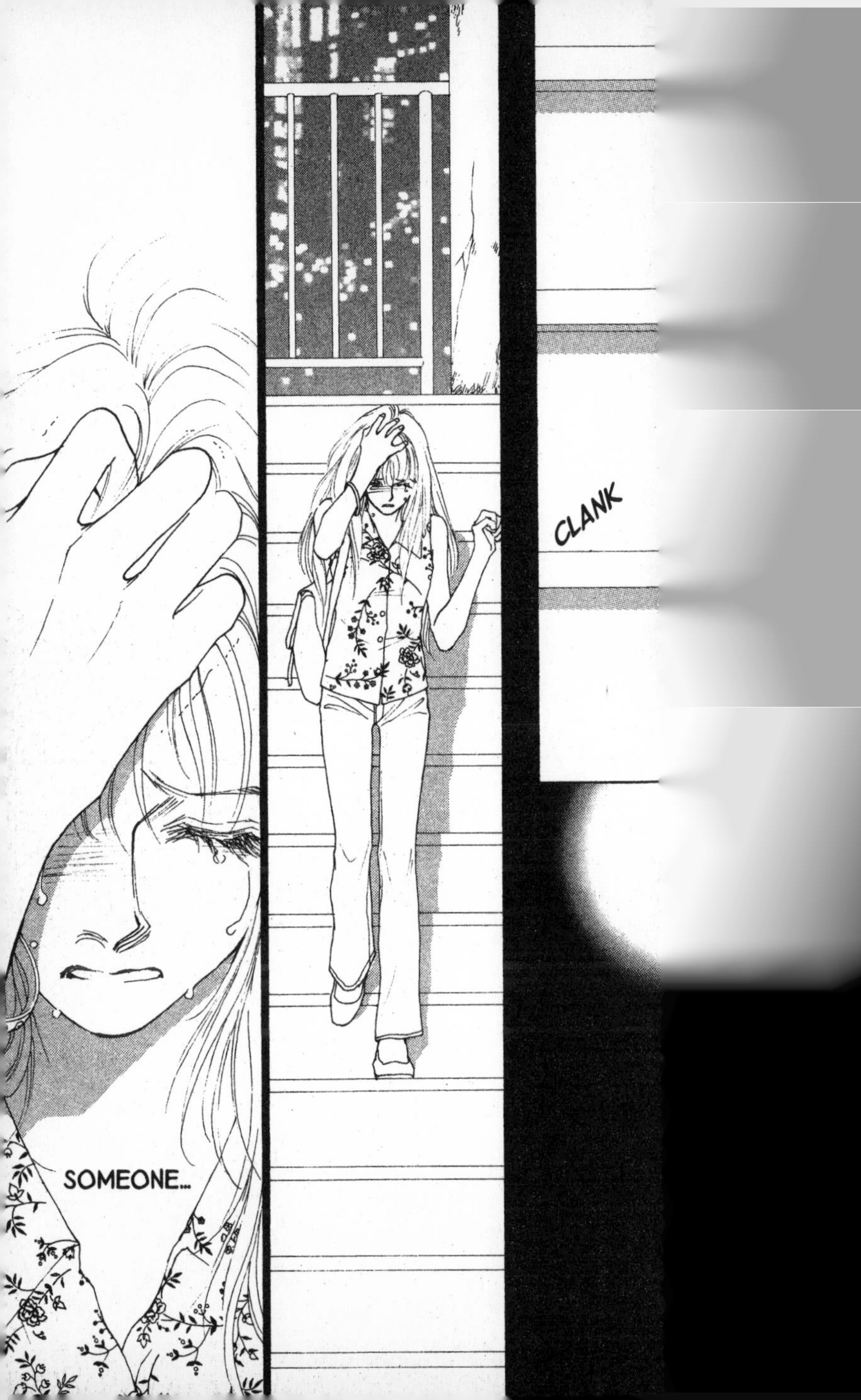
CLANK
SOMEONE...

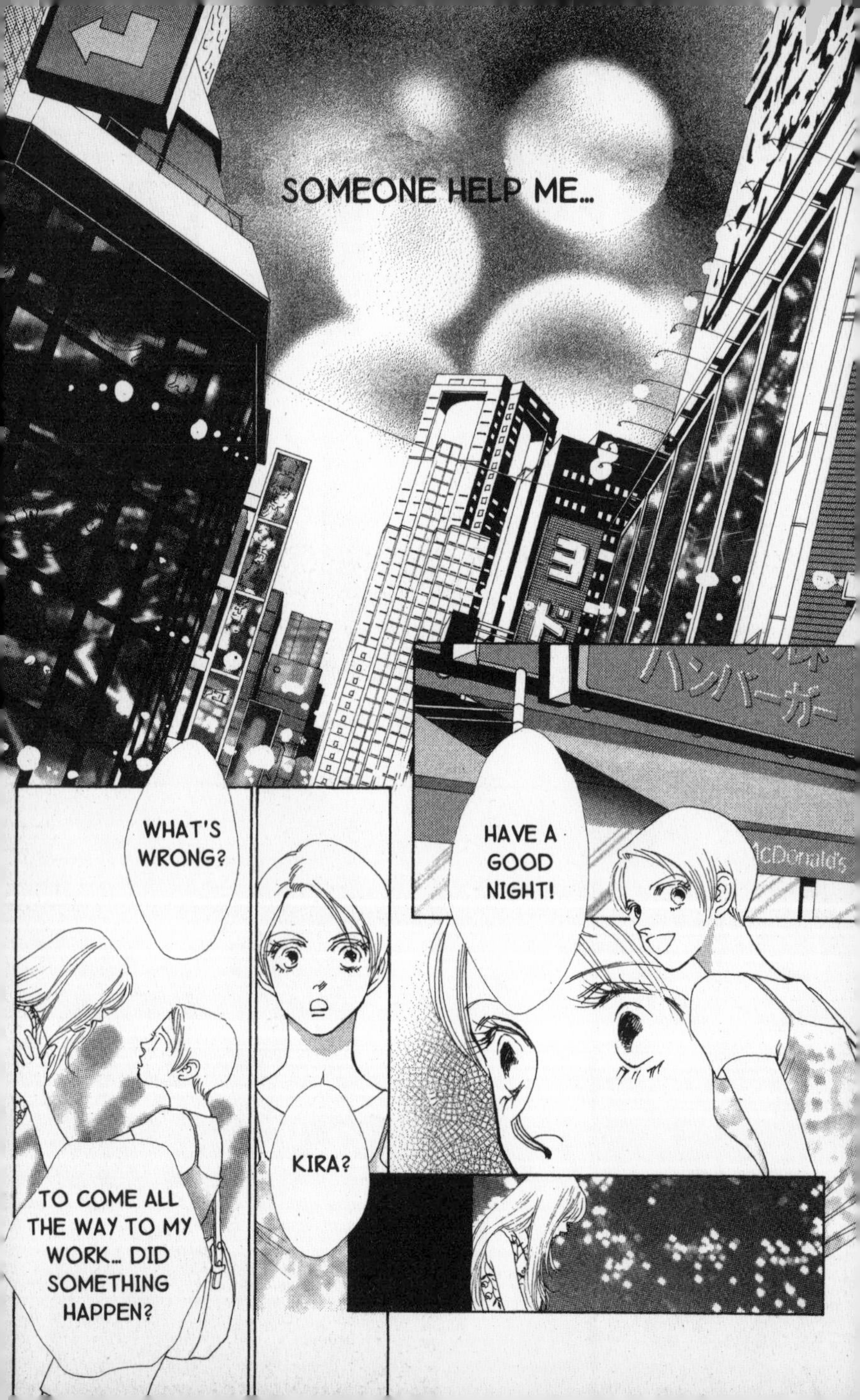
SOMEONE HELP ME...
ハンバーガー
McDonald's
HAVE A GOOD NIGHT!
KIRA?
WHAT'S WRONG?
TO COME ALL THE WAY TO MY WORK... DID SOMETHING HAPPEN?

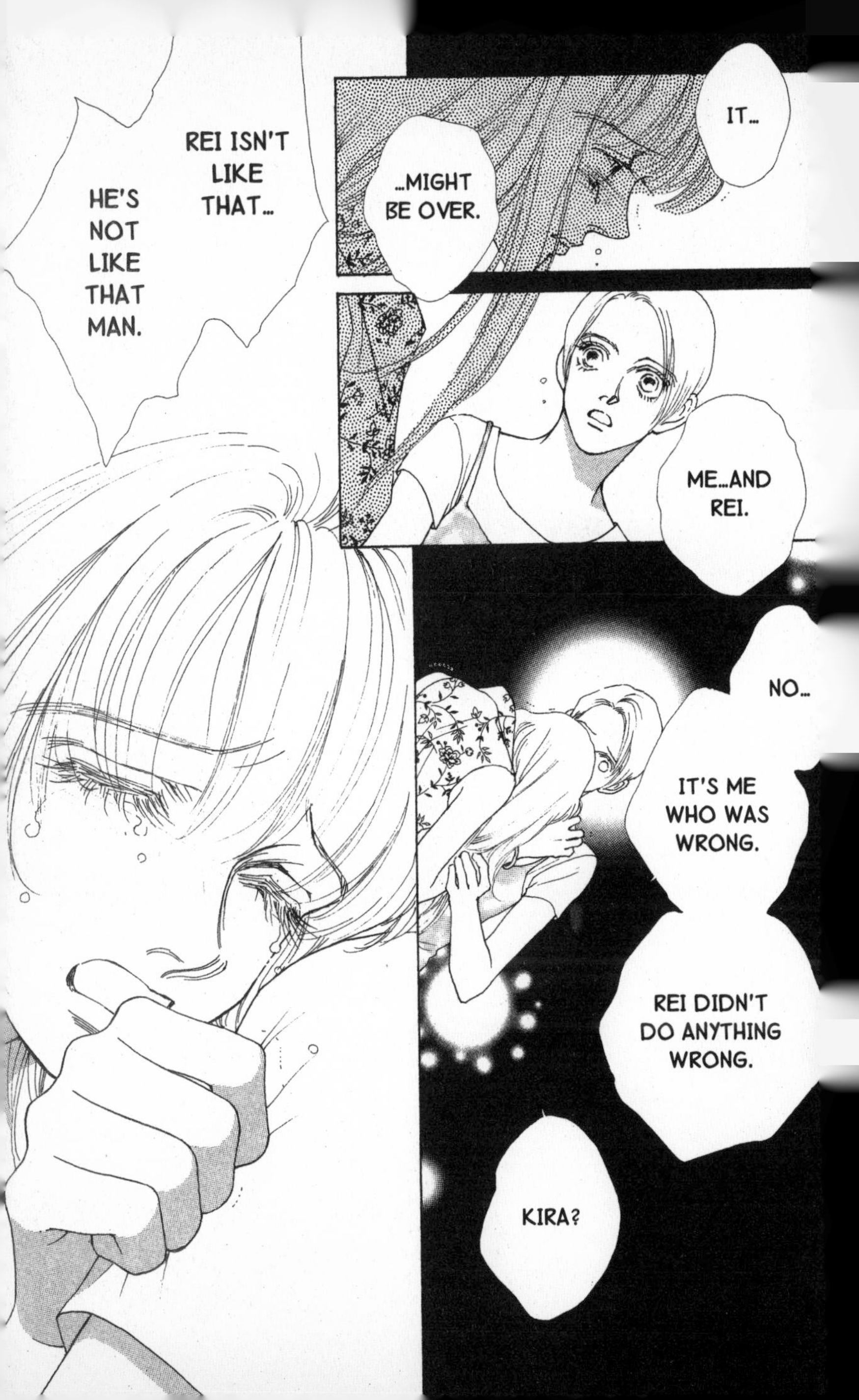
IT...
...MIGHT BE OVER.
ME...AND REI.
NO...
IT'S ME WHO WAS WRONG.
REI DIDN'T DO ANYTHING WRONG.
KIRA?
REI ISN'T LIKE THAT...
HE'S NOT LIKE THAT MAN.

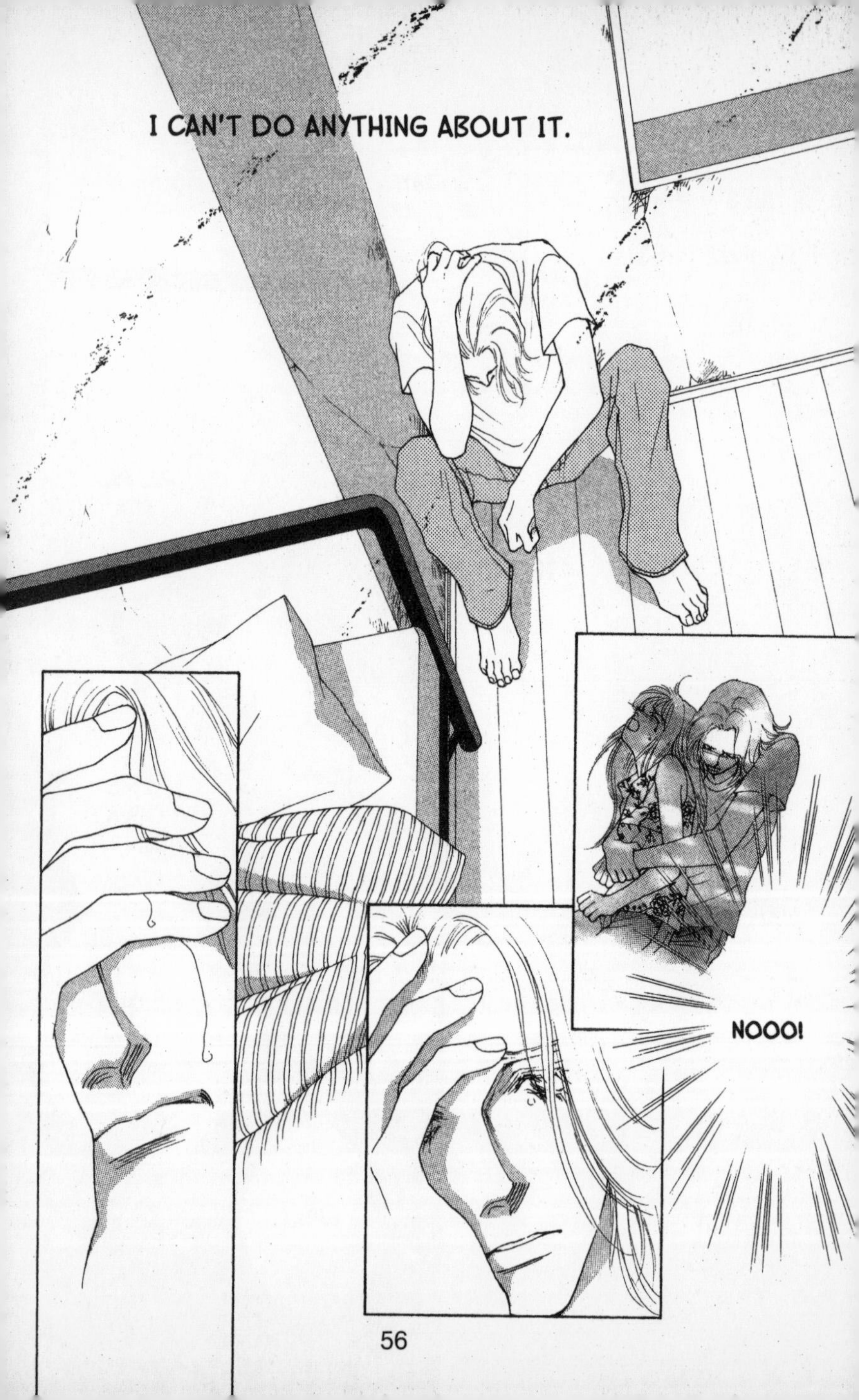
I CAN'T DO ANYTHING ABOUT IT.
NOOO!

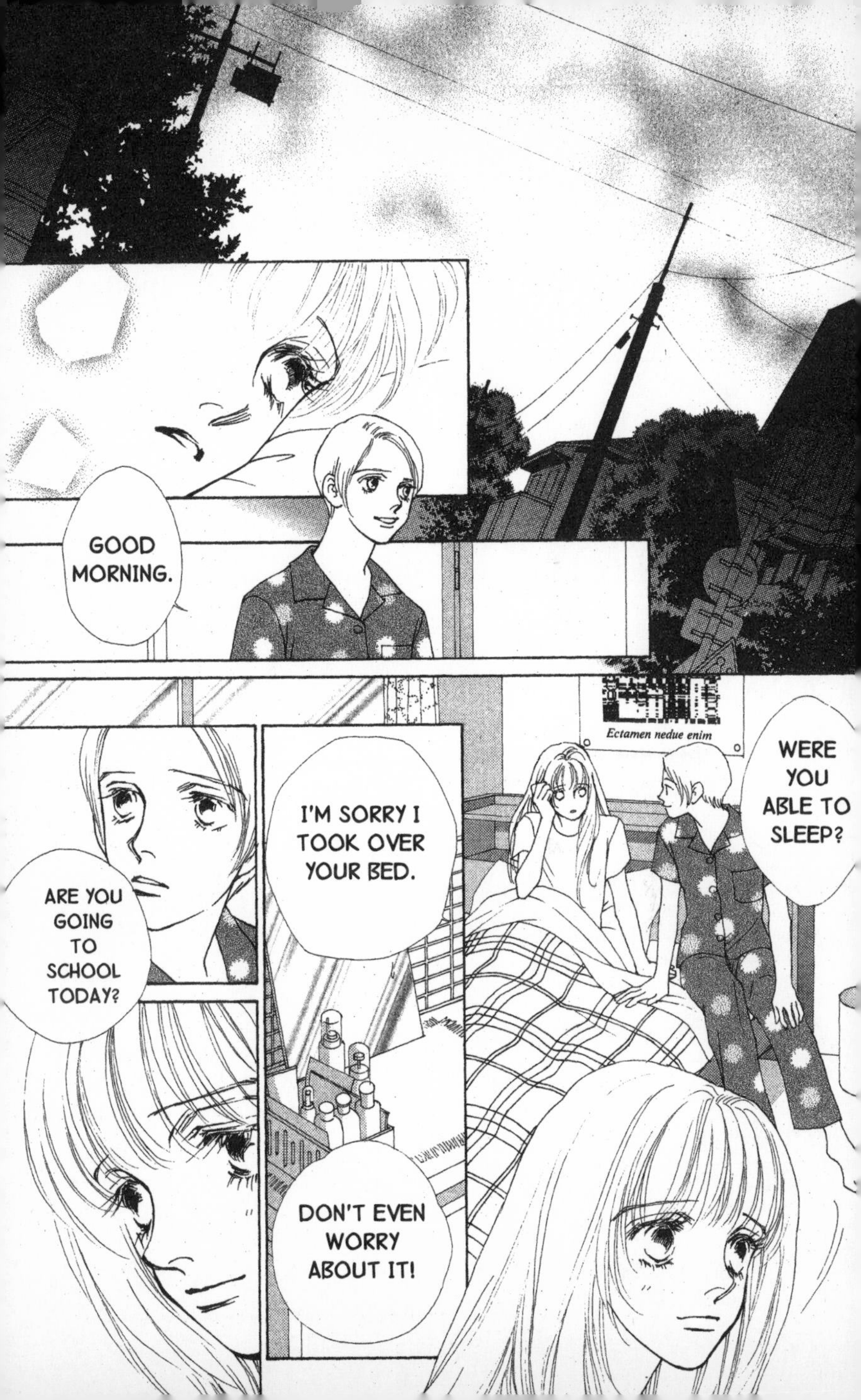
GOOD MORNING.
Ectamen nedue enim
WERE YOU ABLE TO SLEEP?
I'M SORRY I TOOK OVER YOUR BED.
DON'T EVEN WORRY ABOUT IT!
ARE YOU GOING TO SCHOOL TODAY?

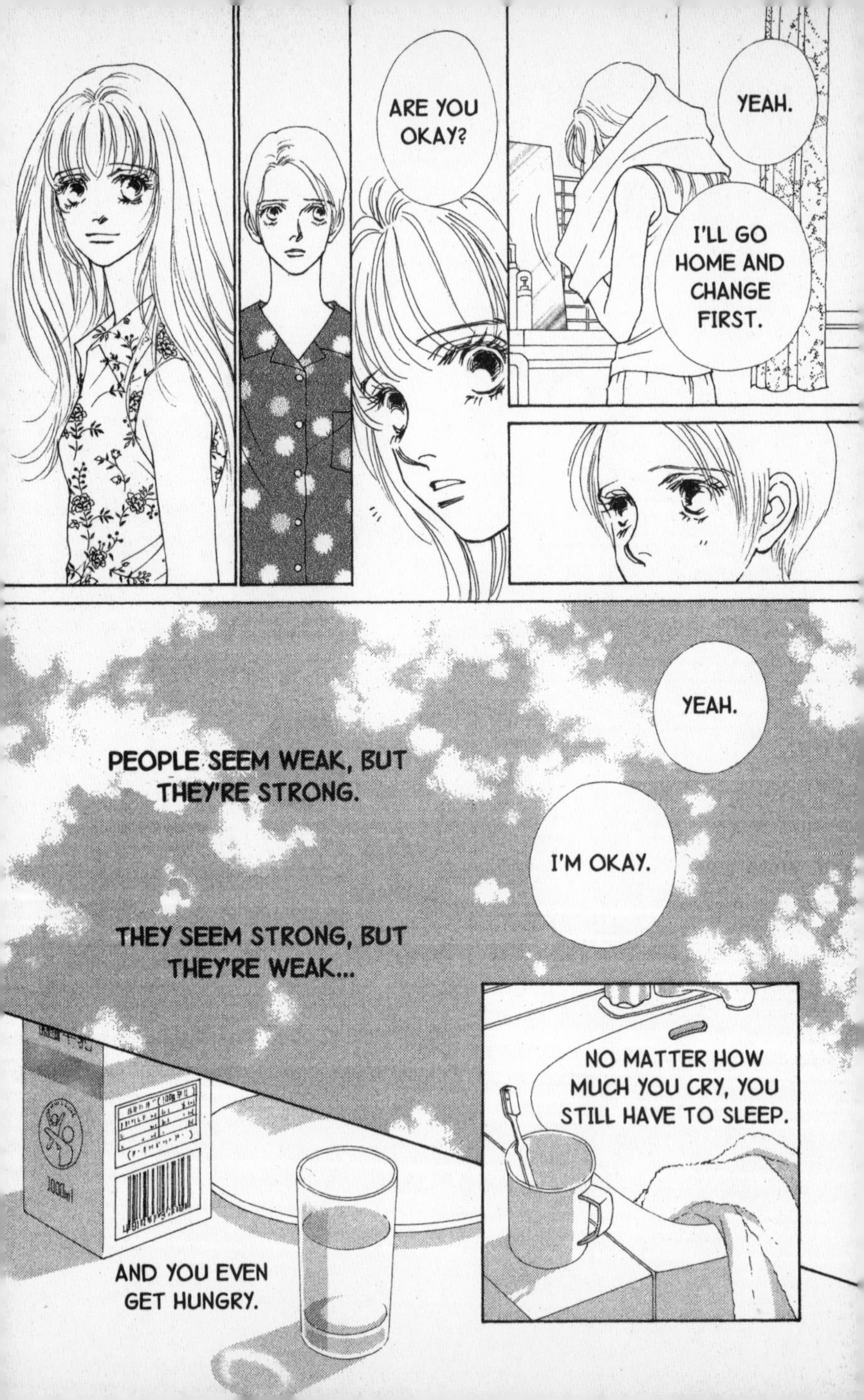
YEAH.
I'LL GO HOME AND CHANGE FIRST.
ARE YOU OKAY?
YEAH.
I'M OKAY.
PEOPLE SEEM WEAK, BUT THEY'RE STRONG.
THEY SEEM STRONG, BUT THEY'RE WEAK...
NO MATTER HOW MUCH YOU CRY, YOU STILL HAVE TO SLEEP.
AND YOU EVEN GET HUNGRY.

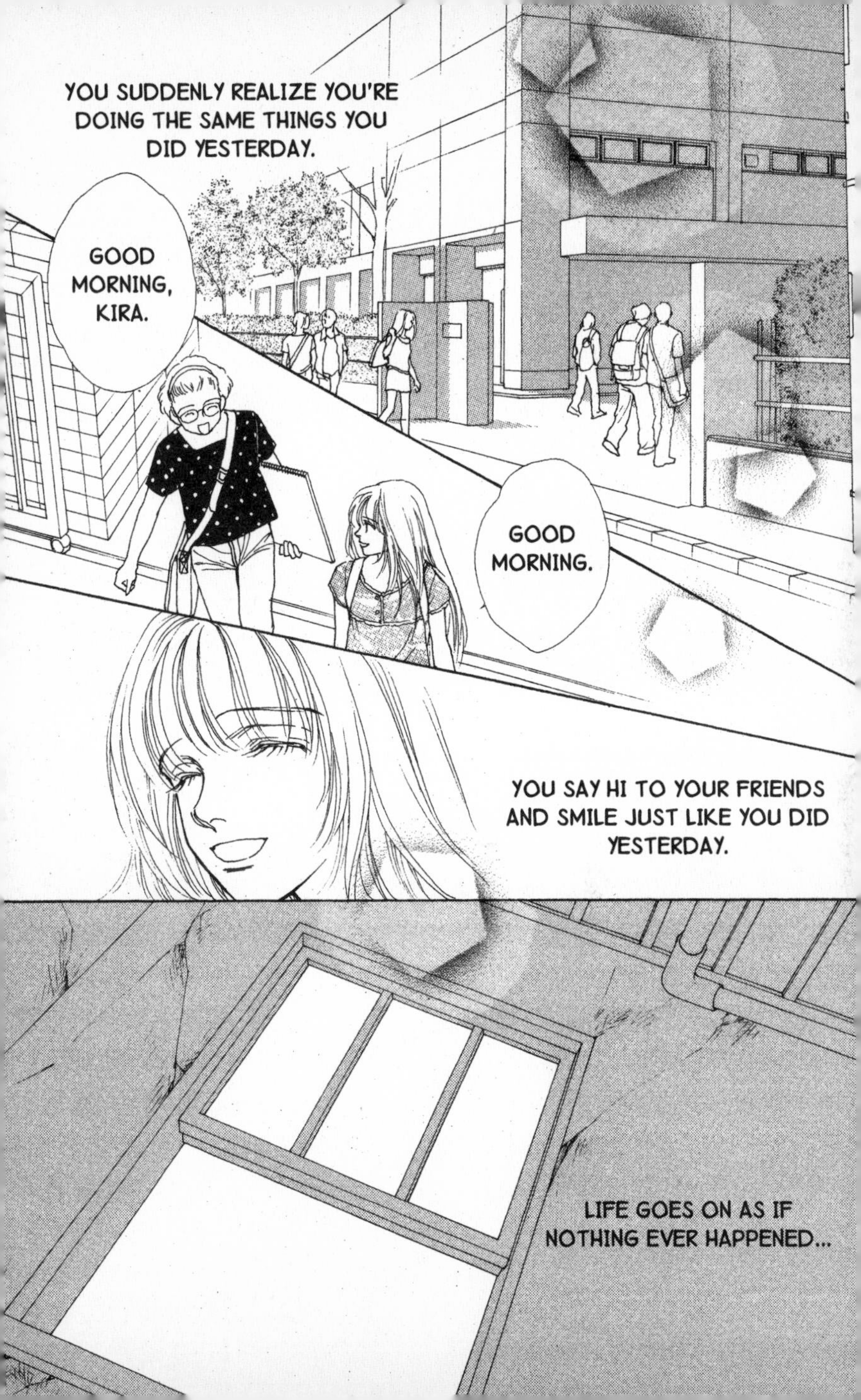
YOU SUDDENLY REALIZE YOU'RE DOING THE SAME THINGS YOU DID YESTERDAY.
GOOD MORNING, KIRA.
GOOD MORNING.
YOU SAY HI TO YOUR FRIENDS AND SMILE JUST LIKE YOU DID YESTERDAY.
LIFE GOES ON AS IF NOTHING EVER HAPPENED...

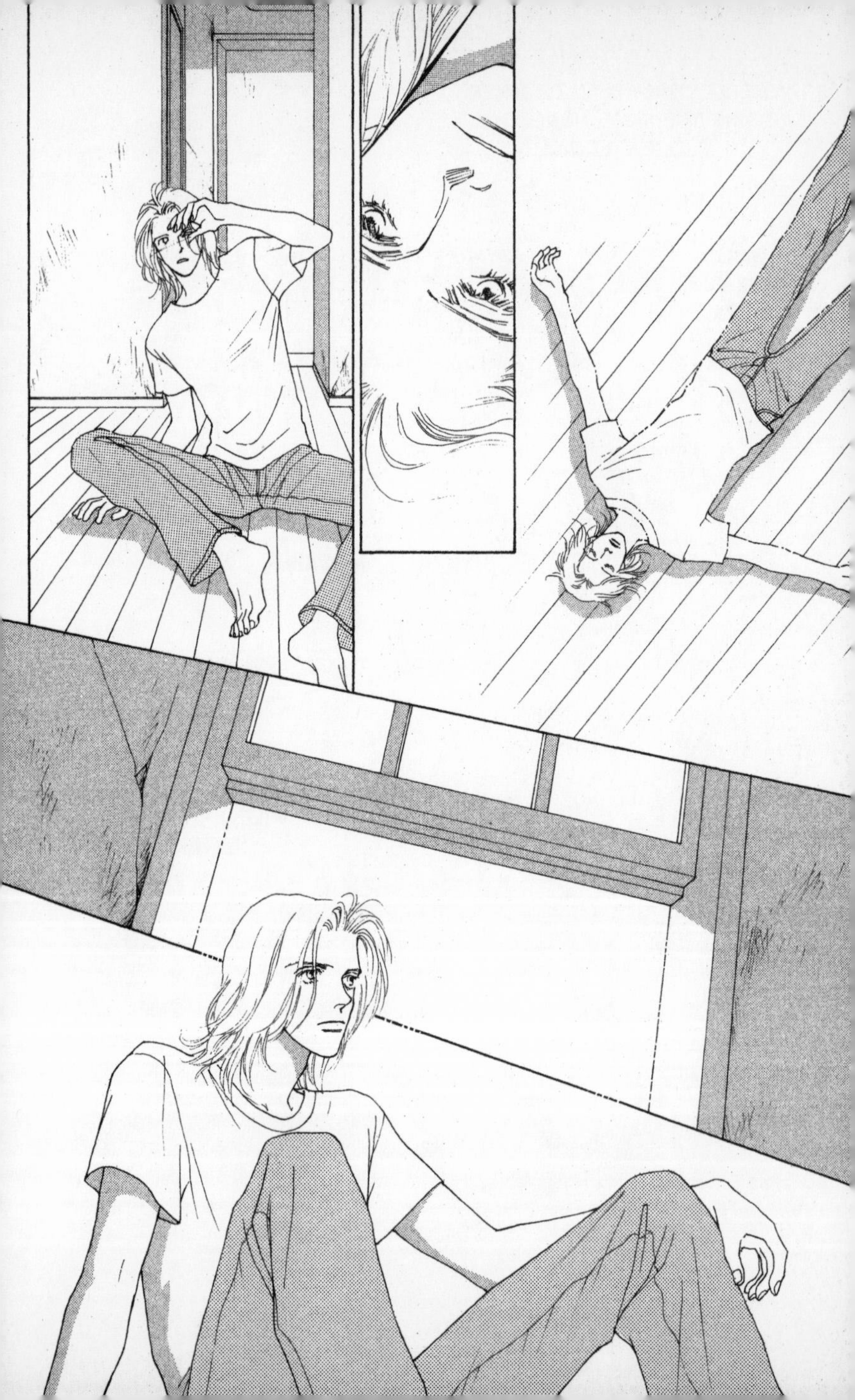

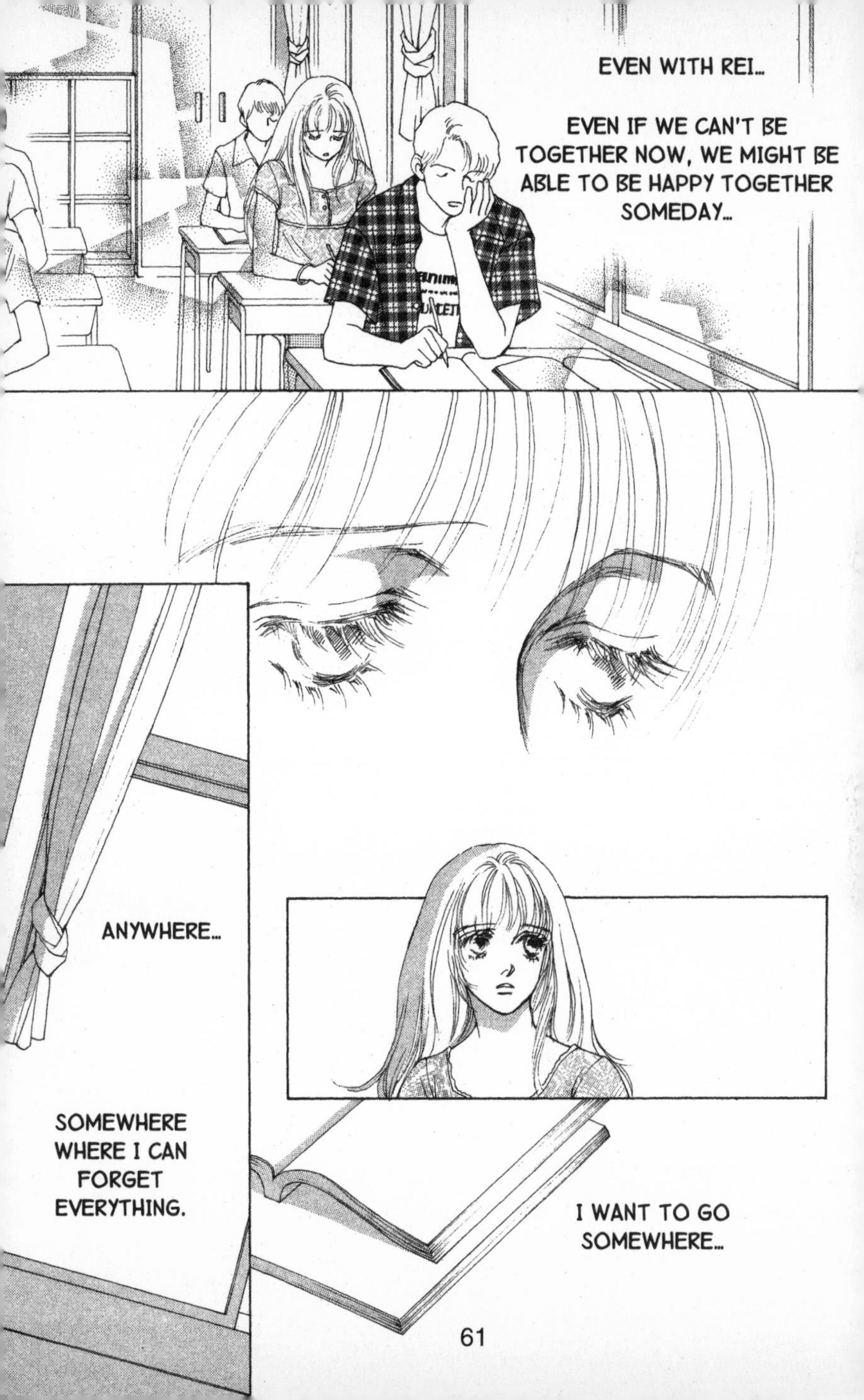
EVEN WITH REI...
EVEN IF WE CAN'T BE TOGETHER NOW, WE MIGHT BE ABLE TO BE HAPPY TOGETHER SOMEDAY...
I WANT TO GO SOMEWHERE...
ANYWHERE...
SOMEWHERE WHERE I CAN FORGET EVERYTHING.

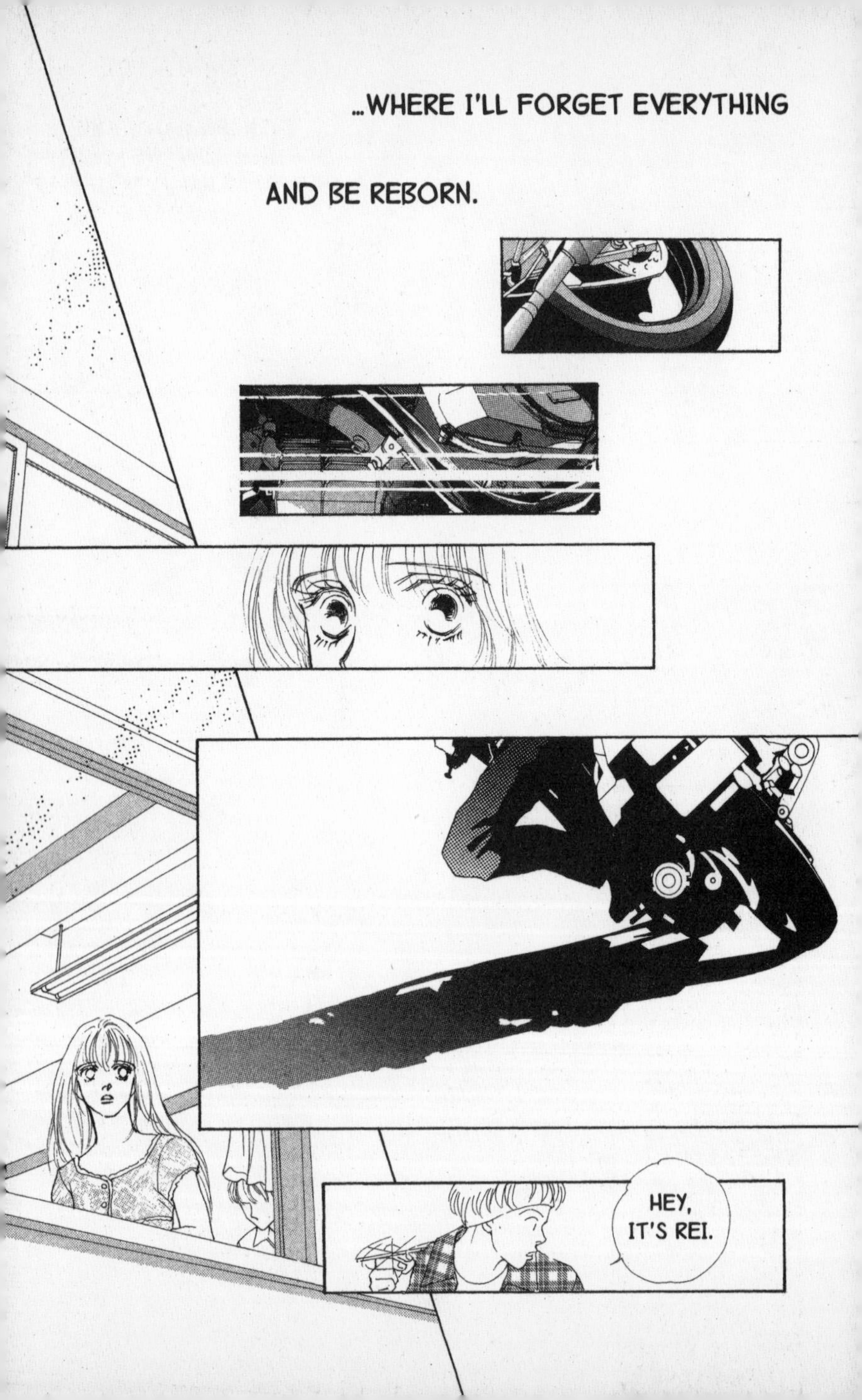
...WHERE I'LL FORGET EVERYTHING
AND BE REBORN.
HEY, IT'S REI.

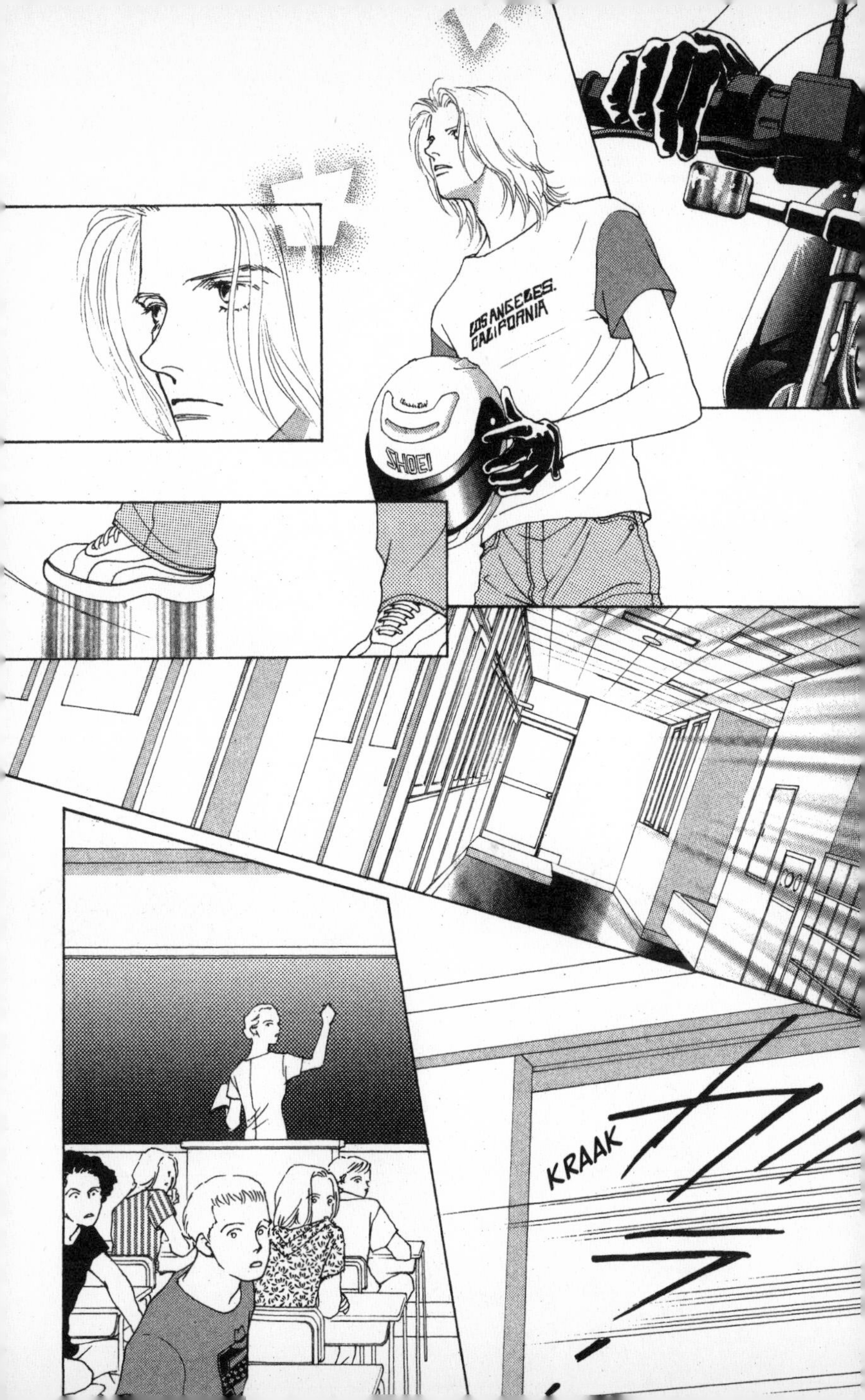
LOS ANGELES.
CALIFORNIA
SHOEI
KRAAK

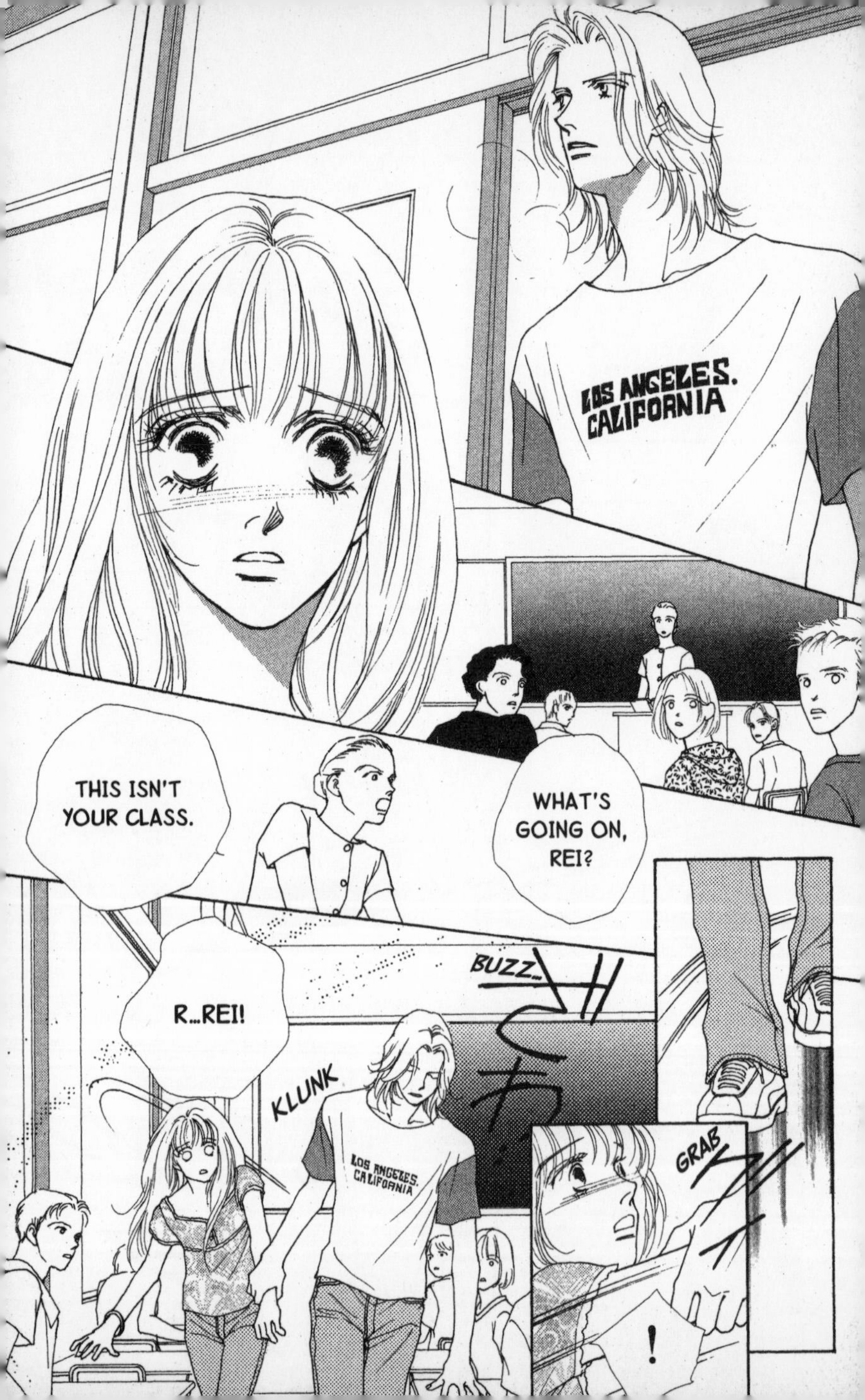
LOS ANGELES. CALIFORNIA
WHAT'S GOING ON, REI?
THIS ISN'T YOUR CLASS.
GRAB
!
BUZZ...
R...REI!
KLUNK
LOS ANGELES. CALIFORNIA

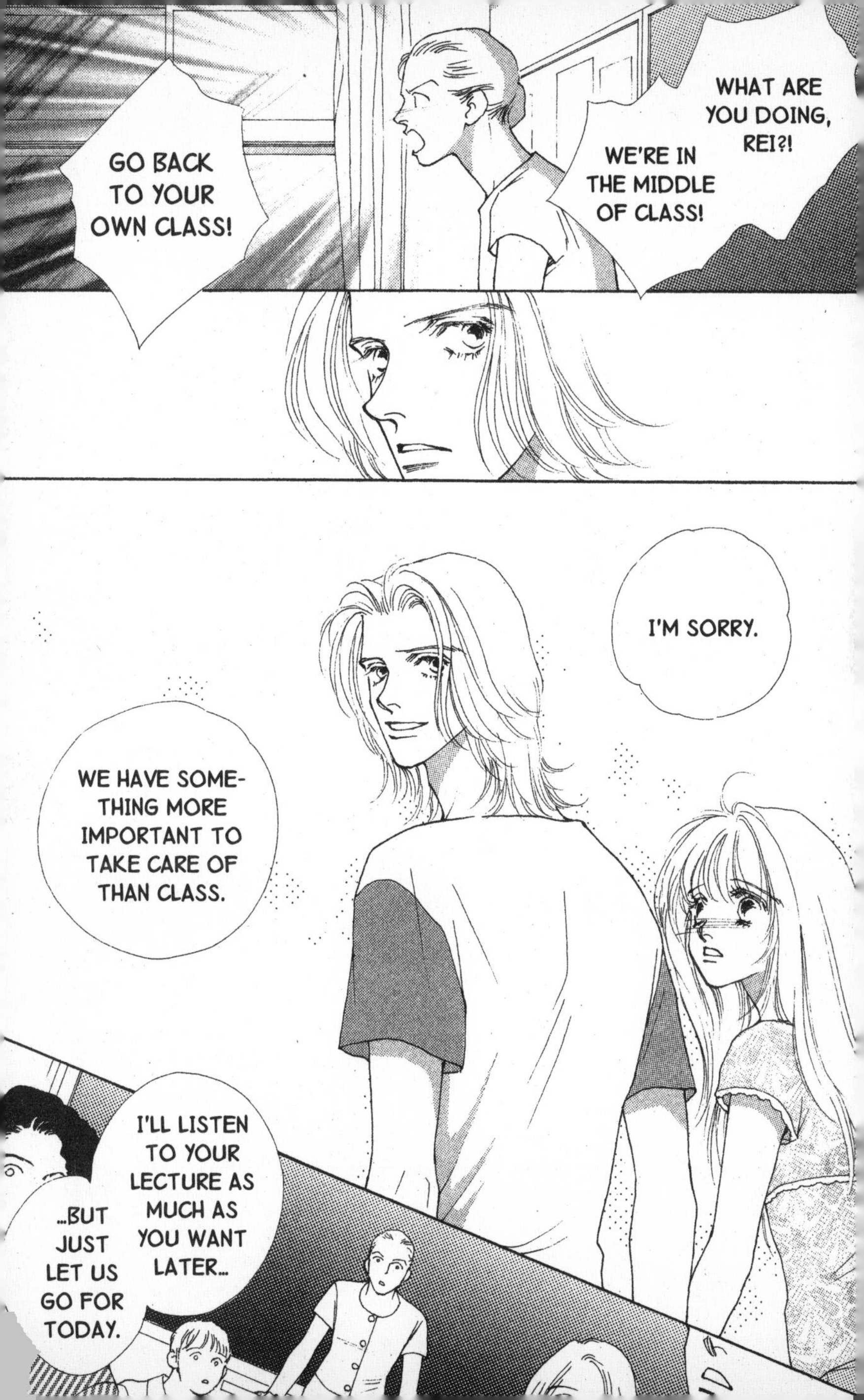
WHAT ARE YOU DOING, REI?!
WE'RE IN THE MIDDLE OF CLASS!
GO BACK TO YOUR OWN CLASS!
I'M SORRY.
WE HAVE SOME-THING MORE IMPORTANT TO TAKE CARE OF THAN CLASS.
I'LL LISTEN TO YOUR LECTURE AS MUCH AS YOU WANT LATER...
...BUT JUST LET US GO FOR TODAY.

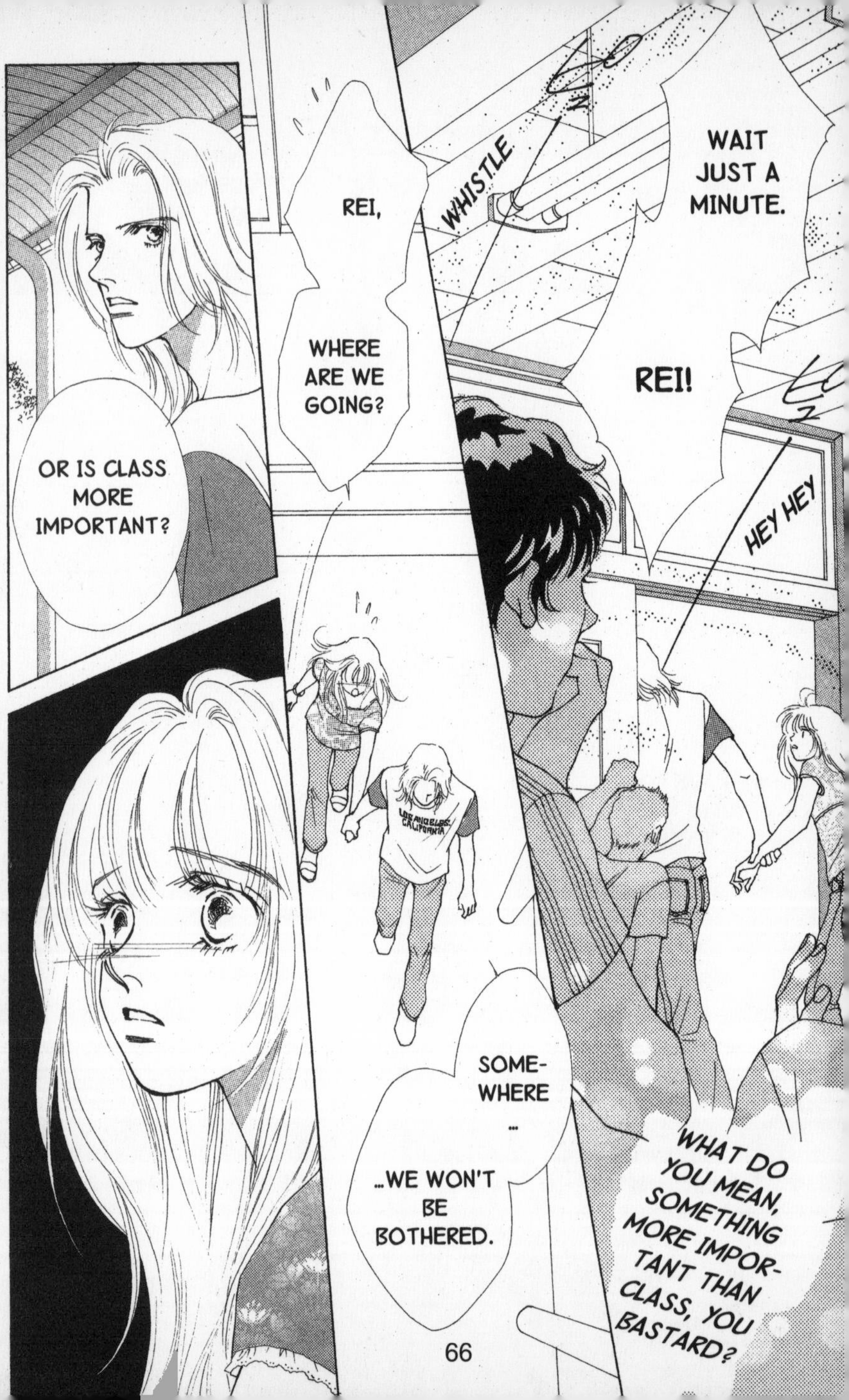

WAIT JUST A MINUTE.
REI!
HEY HEY
WHISTLE
WHAT DO YOU MEAN, SOMETHING MORE IMPORTANT THAN CLASS, YOU BASTARD?
REI,
WHERE ARE WE GOING?
SOMEWHERE...
...WE WON'T BE BOTHERED.
OR IS CLASS MORE IMPORTANT?

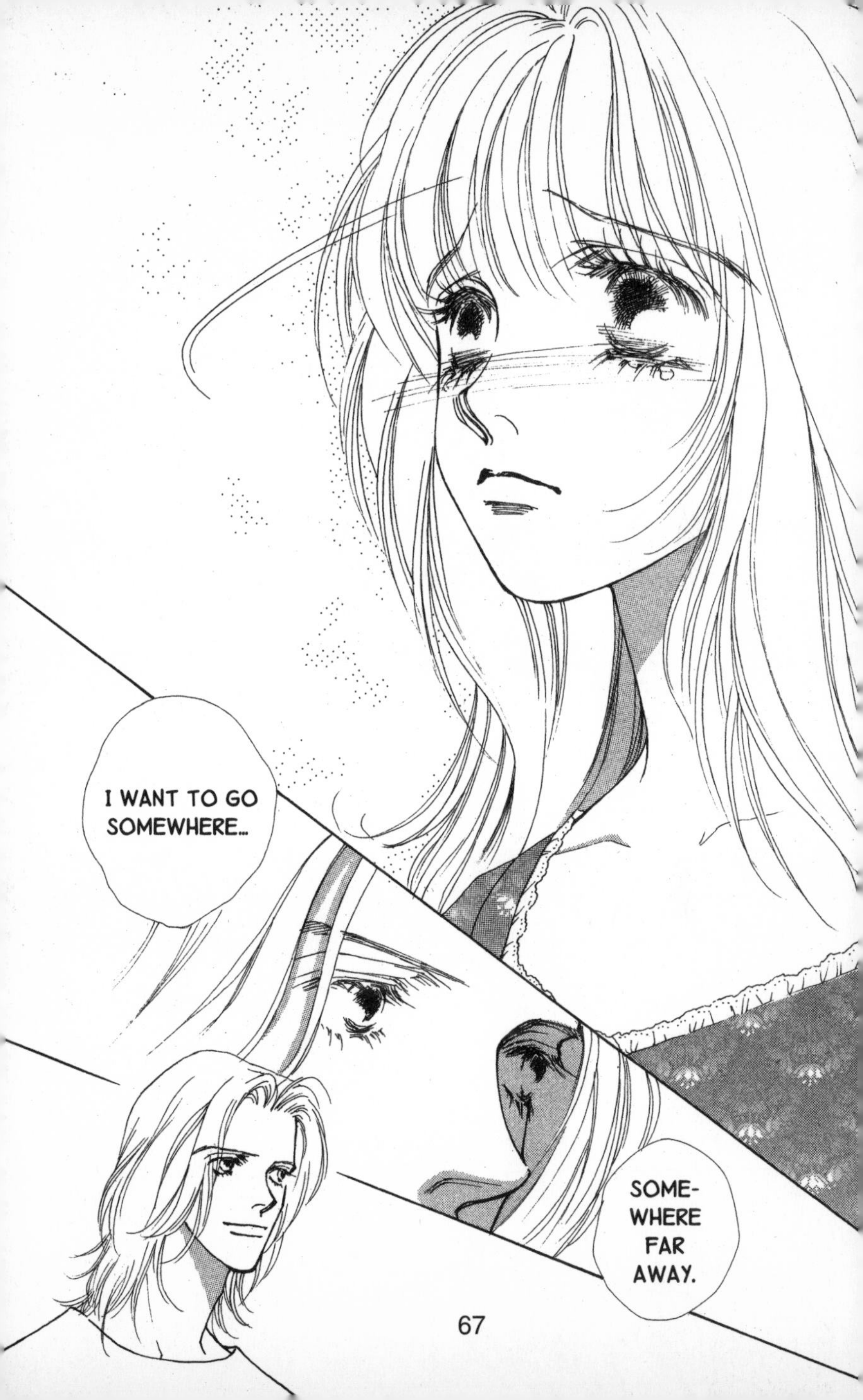
I WANT TO GO SOMEWHERE...
SOME-WHERE FAR AWAY.

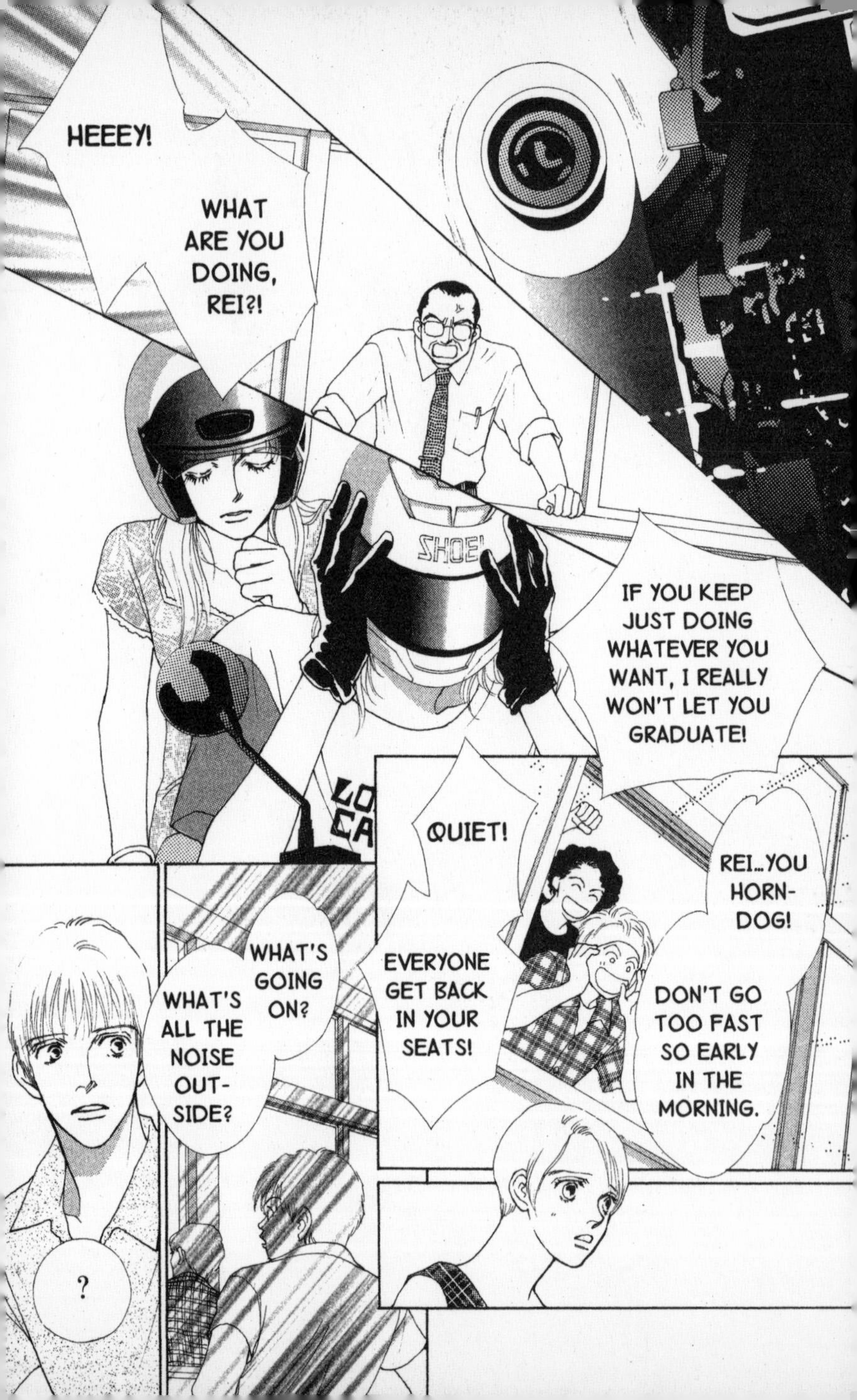
HEEEY!
WHAT ARE YOU DOING, REI?!
IF YOU KEEP JUST DOING WHATEVER YOU WANT, I REALLY WON'T LET YOU GRADUATE!
REI...YOU HORN-DOG!
DON'T GO TOO FAST SO EARLY IN THE MORNING.
QUIET!
EVERYONE GET BACK IN YOUR SEATS!
WHAT'S GOING ON?
WHAT'S ALL THE NOISE OUTSIDE?
?

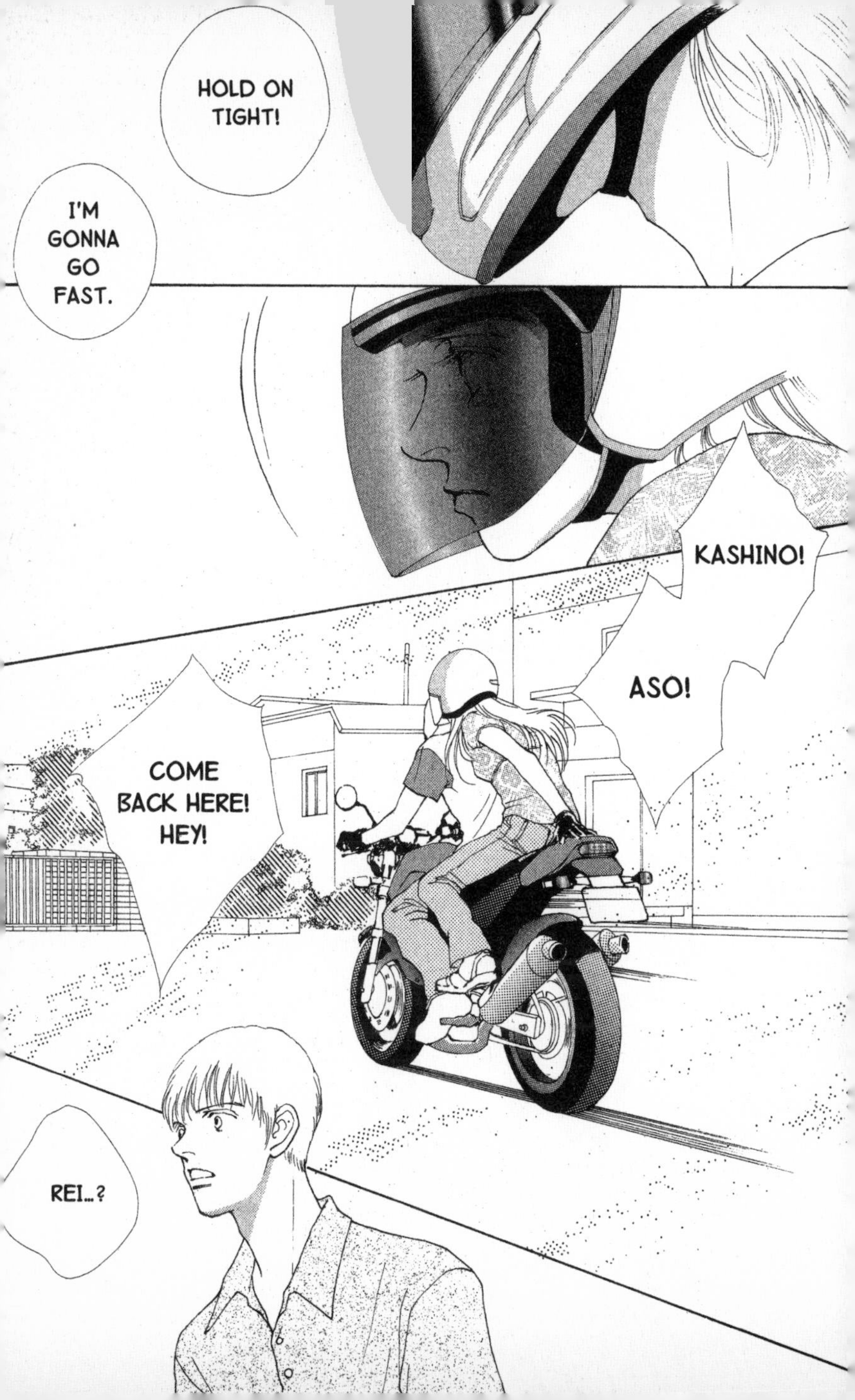
HOLD ON TIGHT!
I'M GONNA GO FAST.
KASHINO!
ASO!
COME BACK HERE! HEY!
REI...?

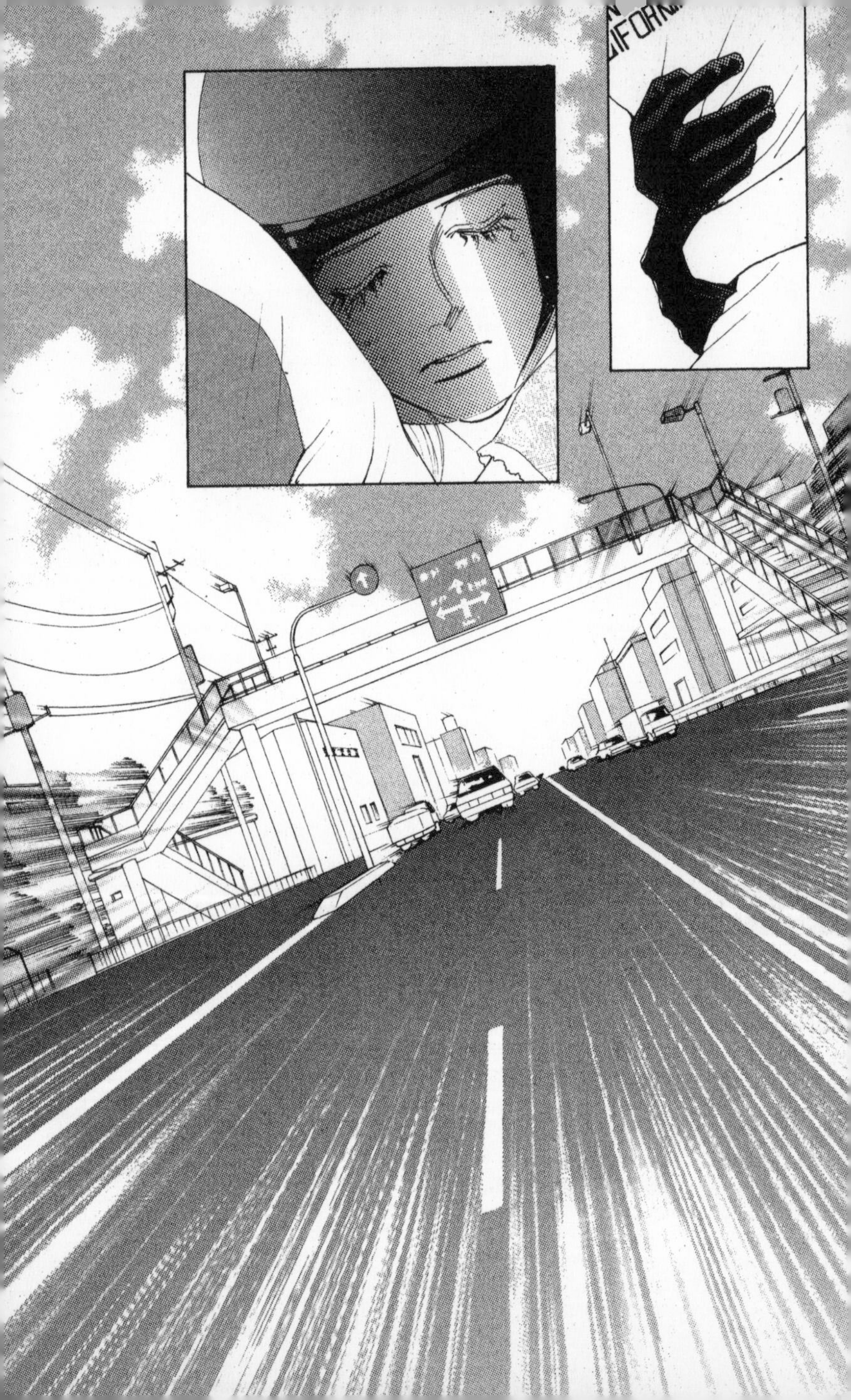

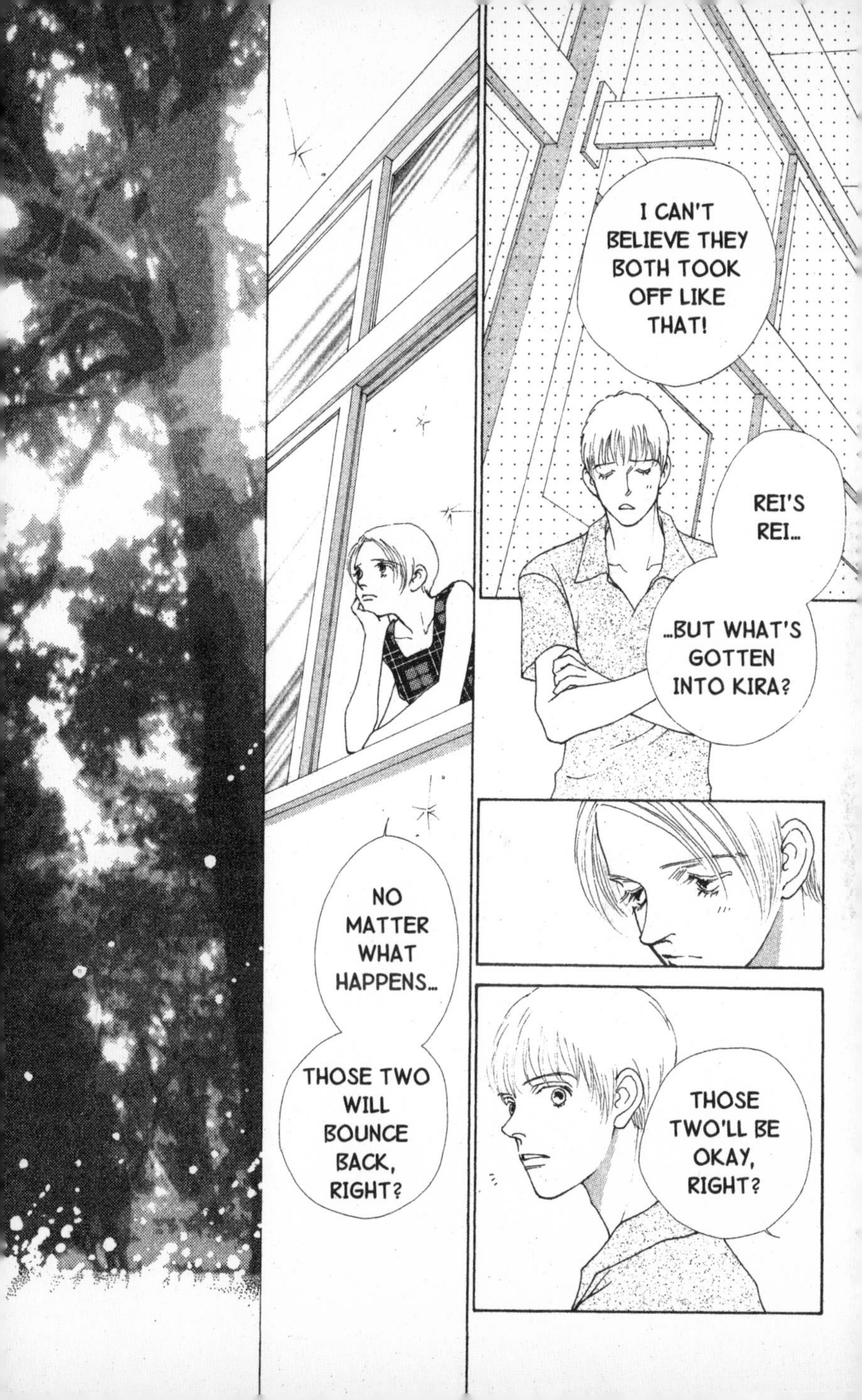
I CAN'T BELIEVE THEY BOTH TOOK OFF LIKE THAT!
REI'S REI...
...BUT WHAT'S GOTTEN INTO KIRA?
THOSE TWO'LL BE OKAY, RIGHT?
NO MATTER WHAT HAPPENS...
THOSE TWO WILL BOUNCE BACK, RIGHT?

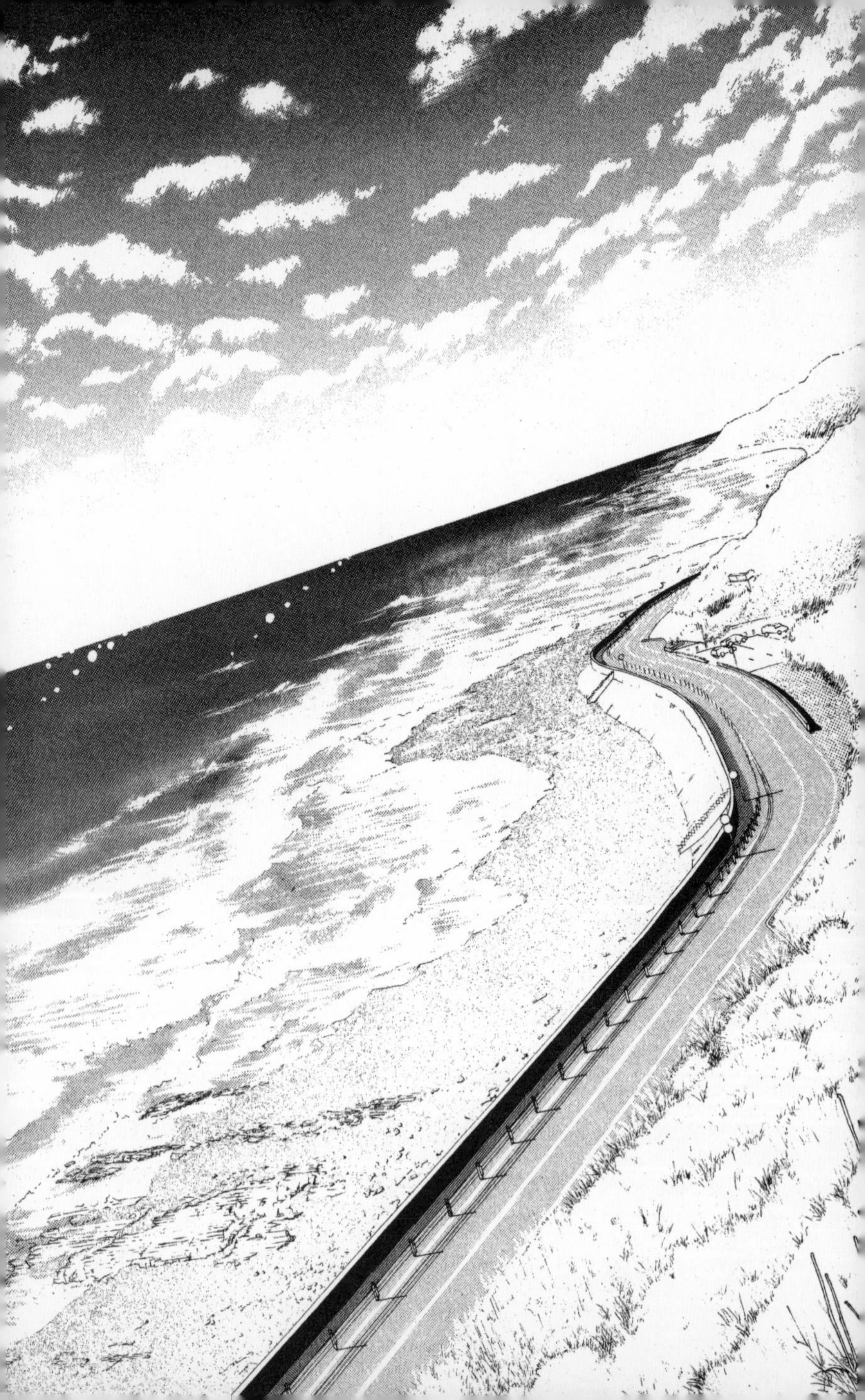

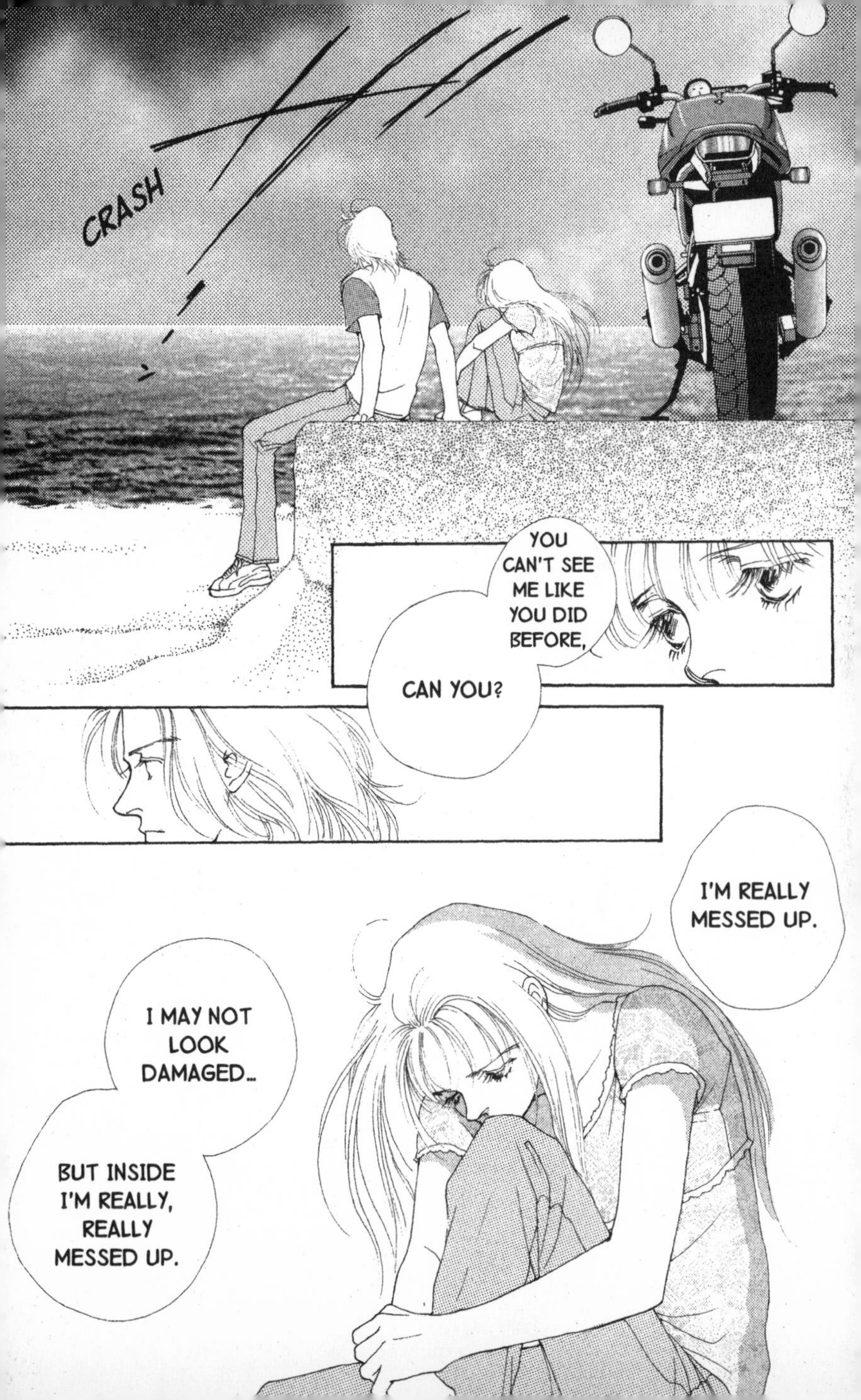
CRASH
YOU CAN'T SEE ME LIKE YOU DID BEFORE,
CAN YOU?
I'M REALLY MESSED UP.
I MAY NOT LOOK DAMAGED...
BUT INSIDE I'M REALLY, REALLY MESSED UP.

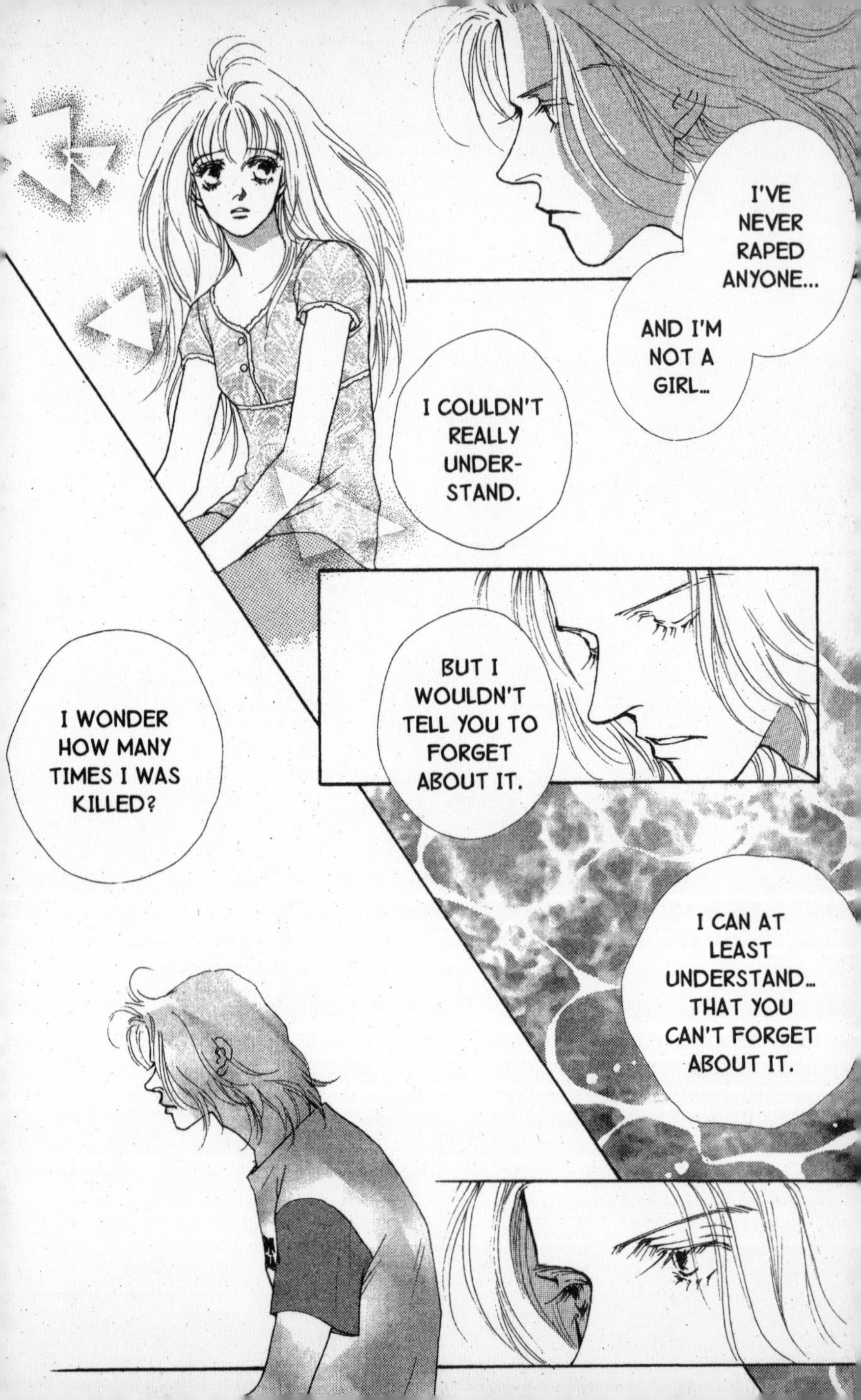
I'VE NEVER RAPED ANYONE...
AND I'M NOT A GIRL...
I COULDN'T REALLY UNDER-STAND.
BUT I WOULDN'T TELL YOU TO FORGET ABOUT IT.
I CAN AT LEAST UNDERSTAND... THAT YOU CAN'T FORGET ABOUT IT.
I WONDER HOW MANY TIMES I WAS KILLED?

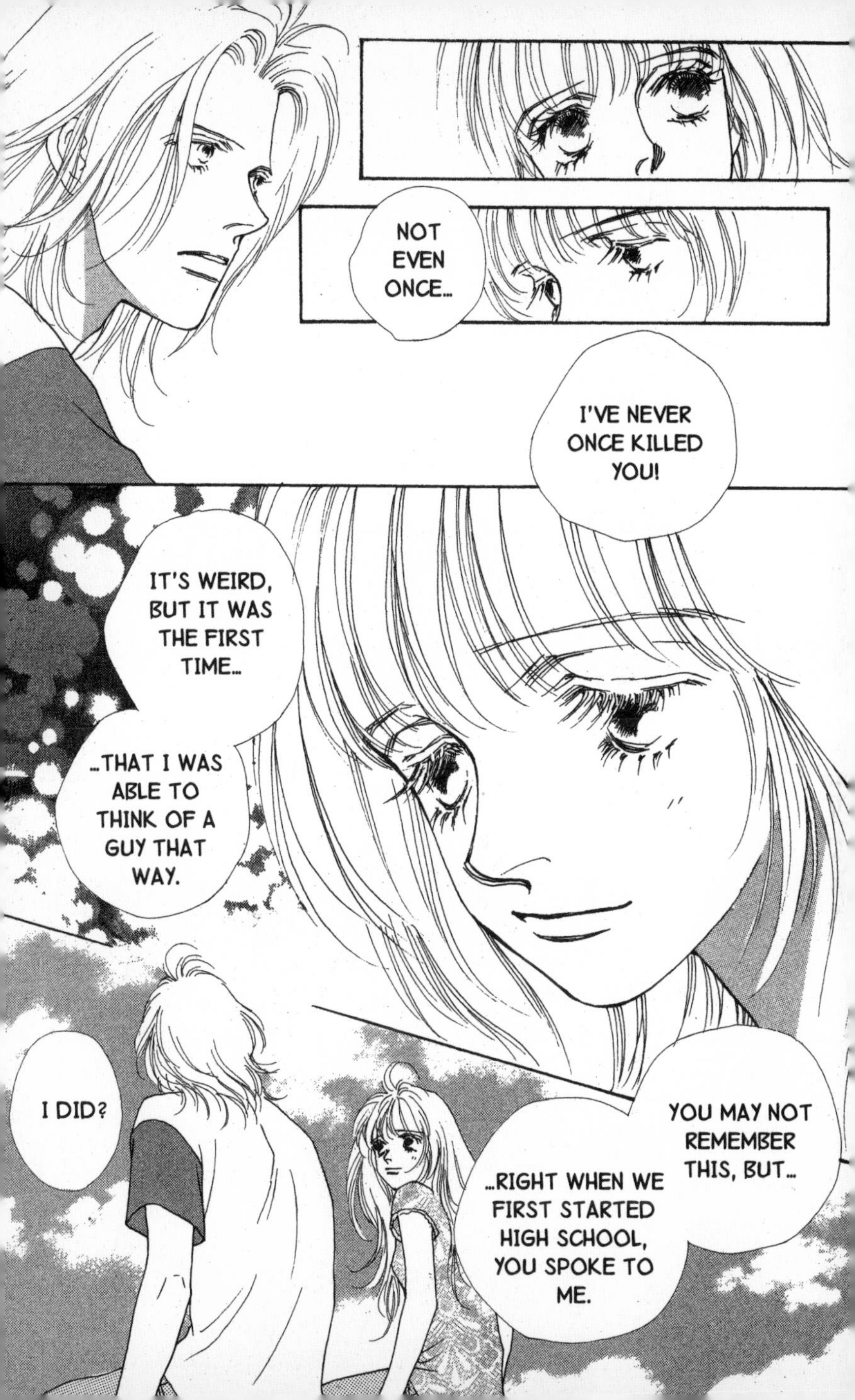
NOT EVEN ONCE...
I'VE NEVER ONCE KILLED YOU!
IT'S WEIRD, BUT IT WAS THE FIRST TIME...
...THAT I WAS ABLE TO THINK OF A GUY THAT WAY.
YOU MAY NOT REMEMBER THIS, BUT...
...RIGHT WHEN WE FIRST STARTED HIGH SCHOOL, YOU SPOKE TO ME.
I DID?

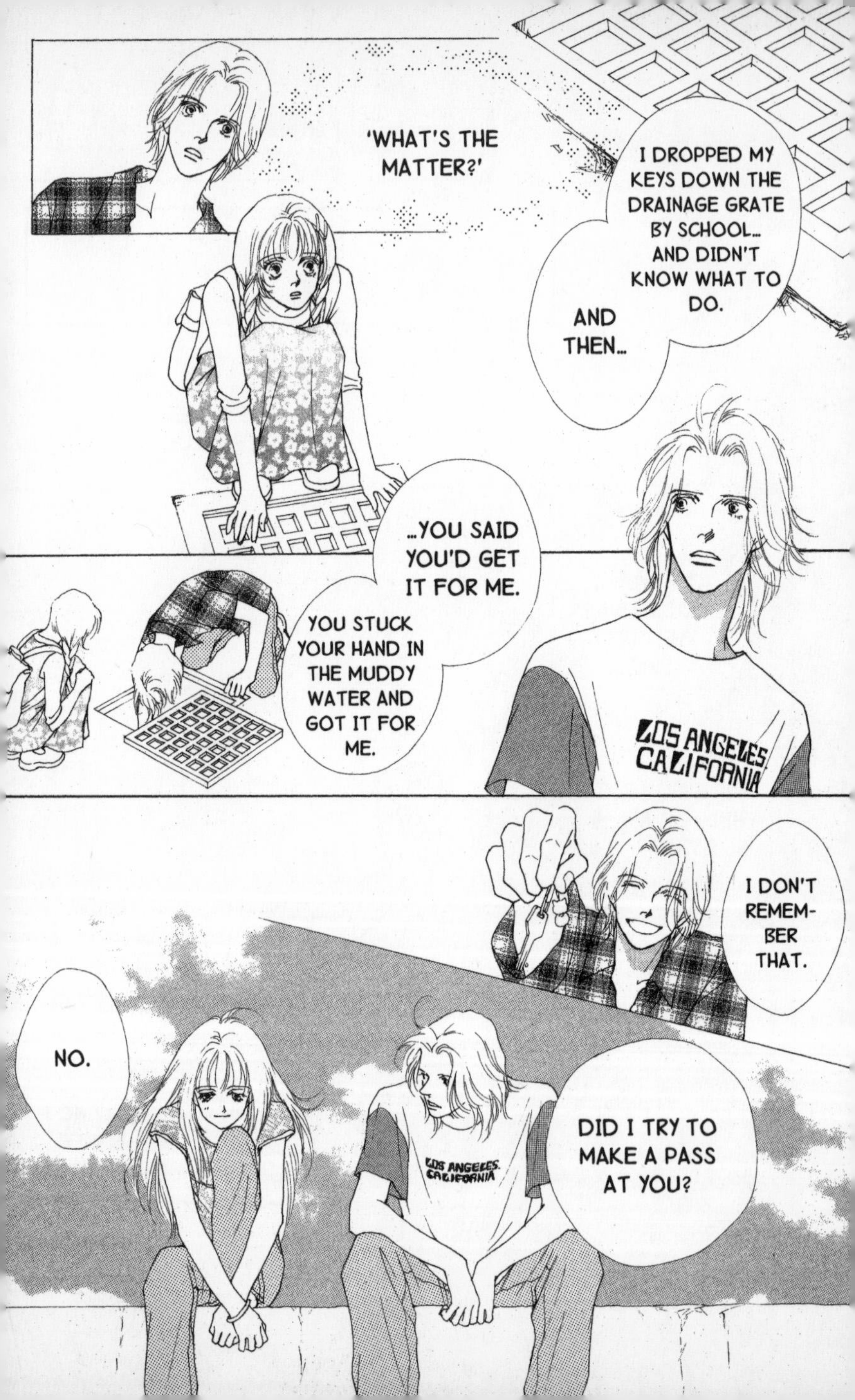
I DROPPED MY KEYS DOWN THE DRAINAGE GRATE BY SCHOOL... AND DIDN'T KNOW WHAT TO DO.
AND THEN...
'WHAT'S THE MATTER?'
...YOU SAID YOU'D GET IT FOR ME.
YOU STUCK YOUR HAND IN THE MUDDY WATER AND GOT IT FOR ME.
LOS ANGELES. CALIFORNIA
I DON'T REMEM-BER THAT.
DID I TRY TO MAKE A PASS AT YOU?
NO.
LOS ANGELES. CALIFORNIA

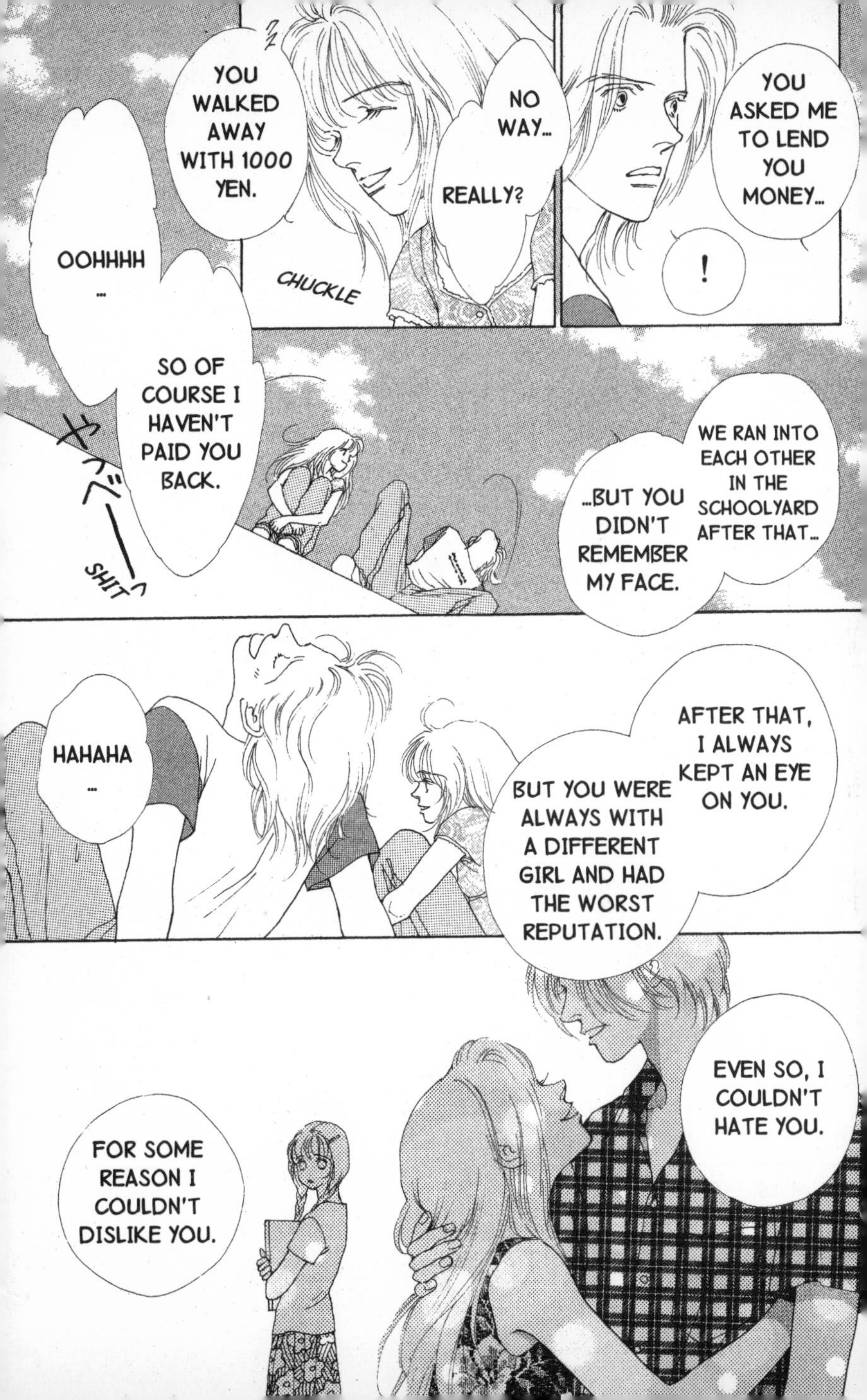
YOU ASKED ME TO LEND YOU MONEY...
!
NO WAY...
REALLY?
YOU WALKED AWAY WITH 1000 YEN.
CHUCKLE
OOHHHH ...
WE RAN INTO EACH OTHER IN THE SCHOOLYARD AFTER THAT...
...BUT YOU DIDN'T REMEMBER MY FACE.
SO OF COURSE I HAVEN'T PAID YOU BACK.
ヤベー
SHIT
AFTER THAT, I ALWAYS KEPT AN EYE ON YOU.
BUT YOU WERE ALWAYS WITH A DIFFERENT GIRL AND HAD THE WORST REPUTATION.
HAHAHA ...
EVEN SO, I COULDN'T HATE YOU.
FOR SOME REASON I COULDN'T DISLIKE YOU.

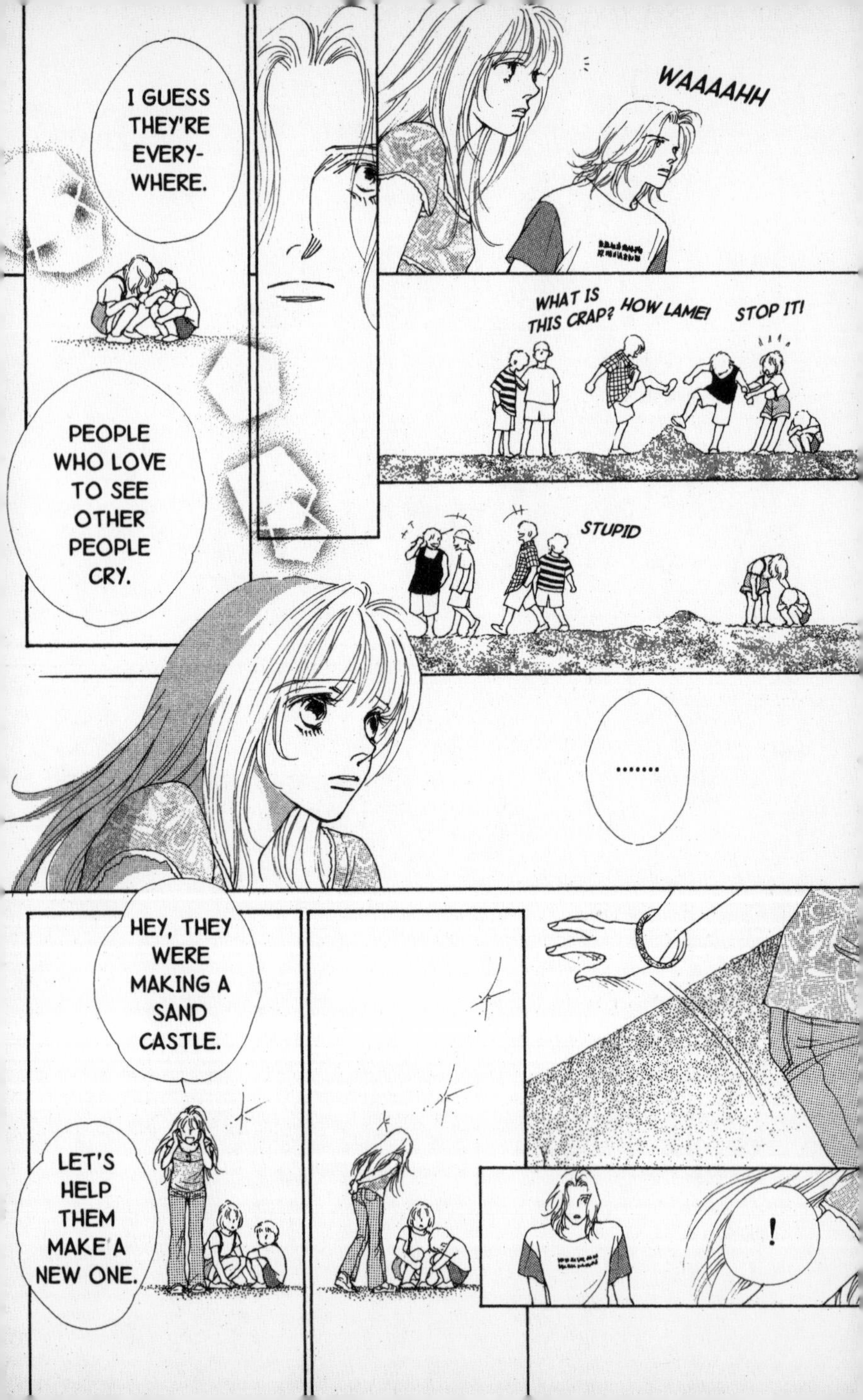
WAAAAHH
STOP IT!
HOW LAME!
WHAT IS THIS CRAP?
STUPID
I GUESS THEY'RE EVERY-WHERE.
PEOPLE WHO LOVE TO SEE OTHER PEOPLE CRY.
....
!
HEY, THEY WERE MAKING A SAND CASTLE.
LET'S HELP THEM MAKE A NEW ONE.

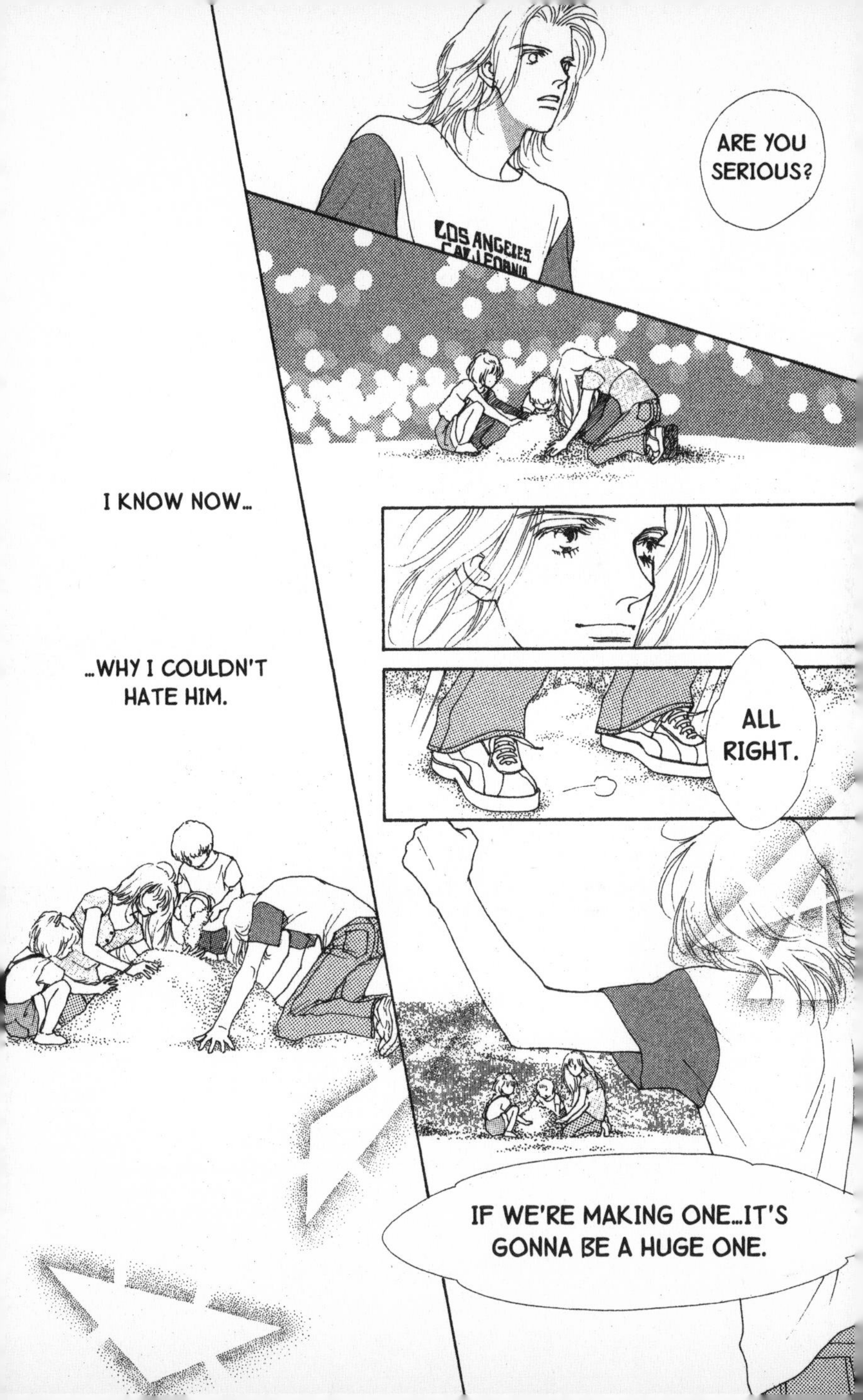
ARE YOU SERIOUS?
LOS ANGELES
ALL RIGHT.
IF WE'RE MAKING ONE...IT'S GONNA BE A HUGE ONE.
I KNOW NOW...
...WHY I COULDN'T HATE HIM.

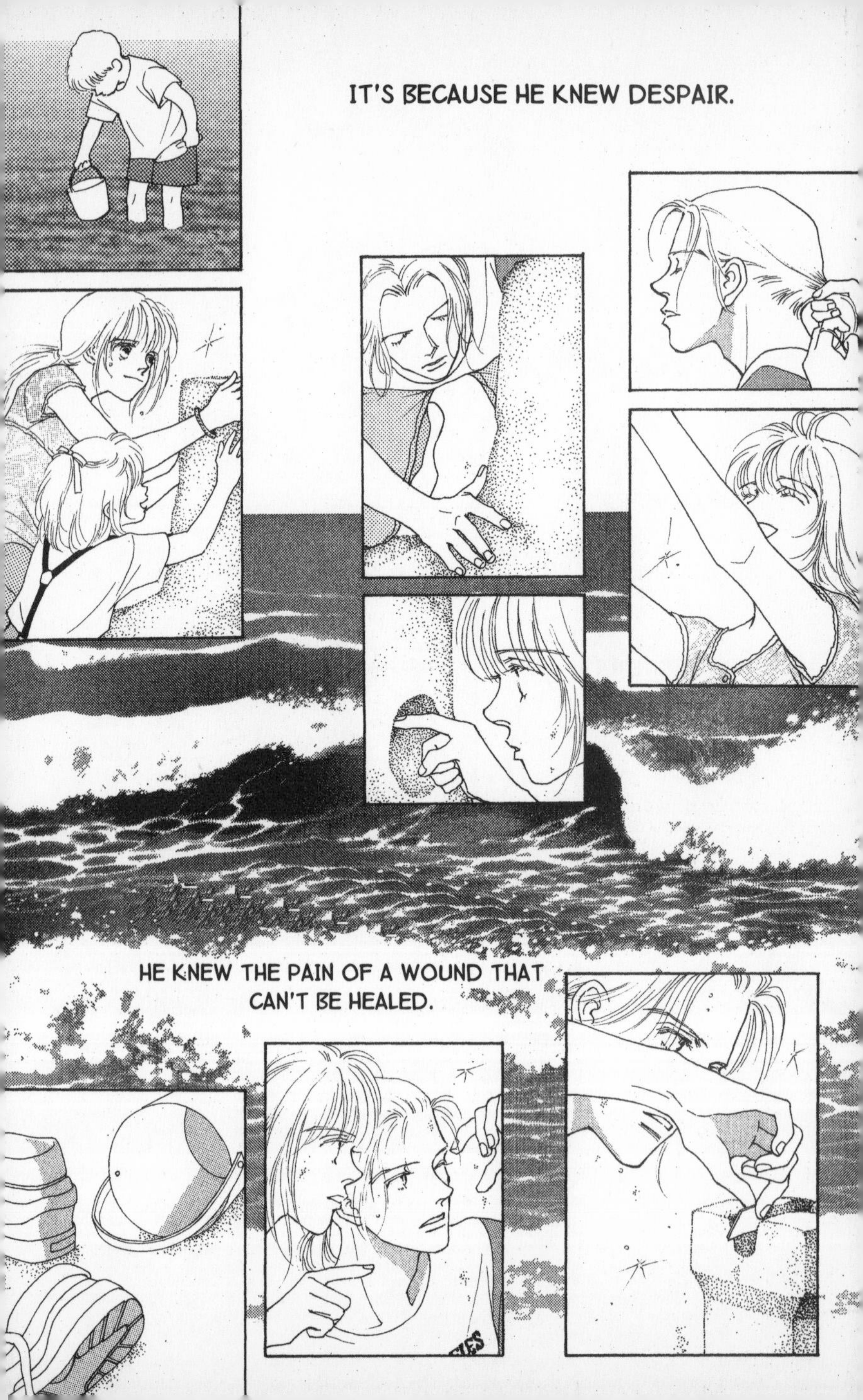
IT'S BECAUSE HE KNEW DESPAIR.
HE KNEW THE PAIN OF A WOUND THAT CAN'T BE HEALED.

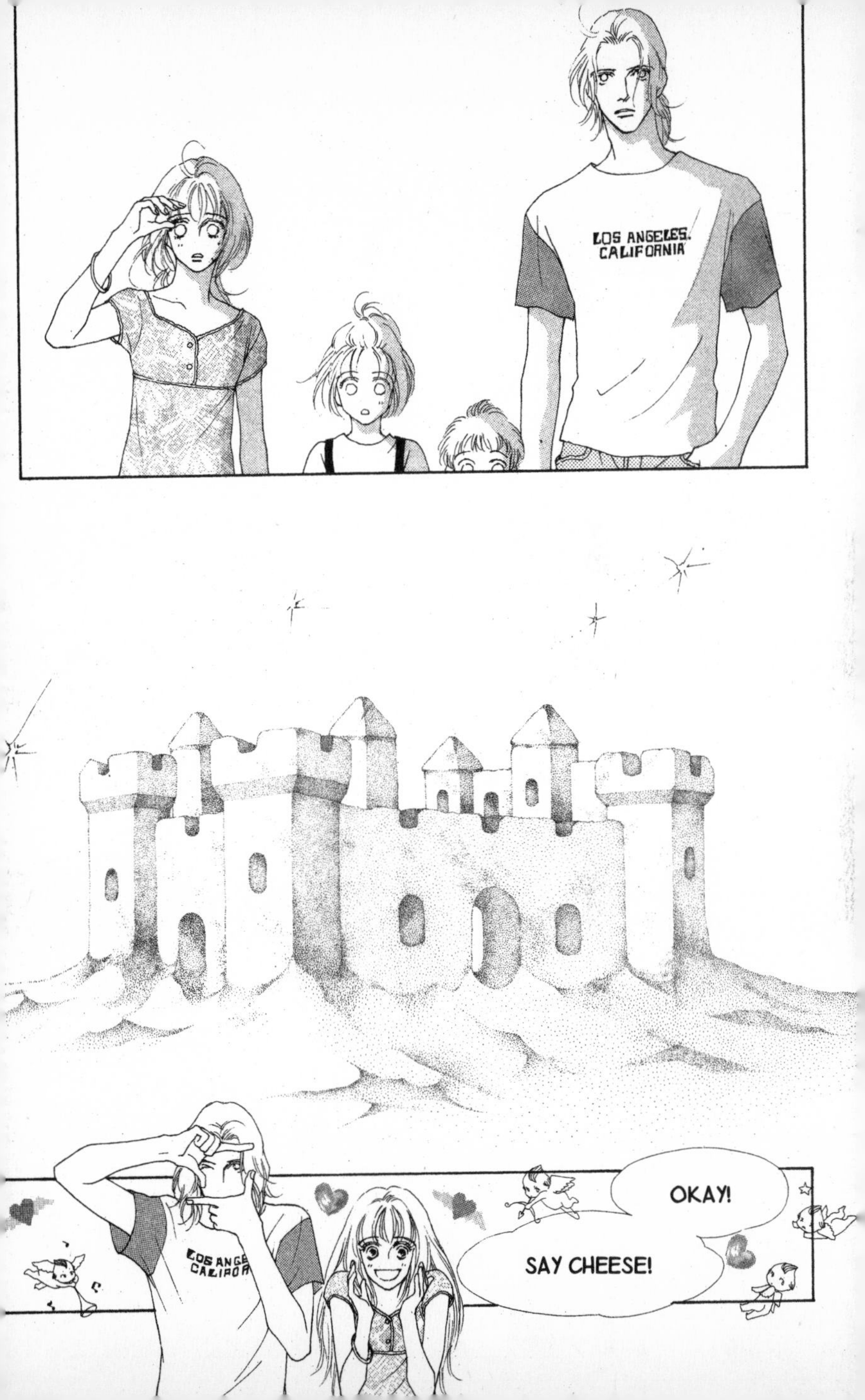
LOS ANGELES.
CALIFORNIA
OKAY!
SAY CHEESE!

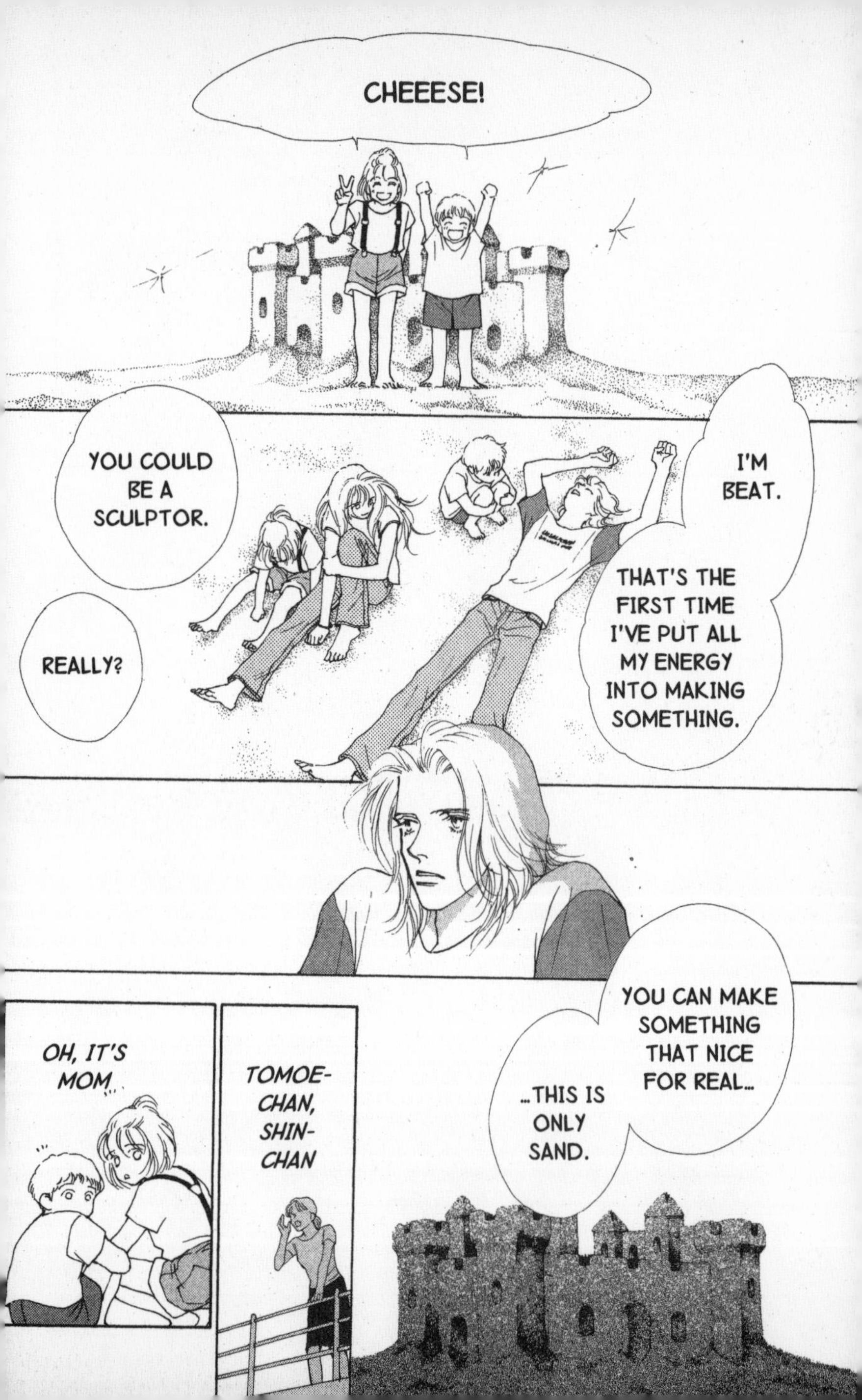
CHEEESE!
I'M BEAT.
THAT'S THE FIRST TIME I'VE PUT ALL MY ENERGY INTO MAKING SOMETHING.
YOU COULD BE A SCULPTOR.
REALLY?
YOU CAN MAKE SOMETHING THAT NICE FOR REAL...
...THIS IS ONLY SAND.
TOMOE-CHAN, SHIN-CHAN
OH, IT'S MOM...

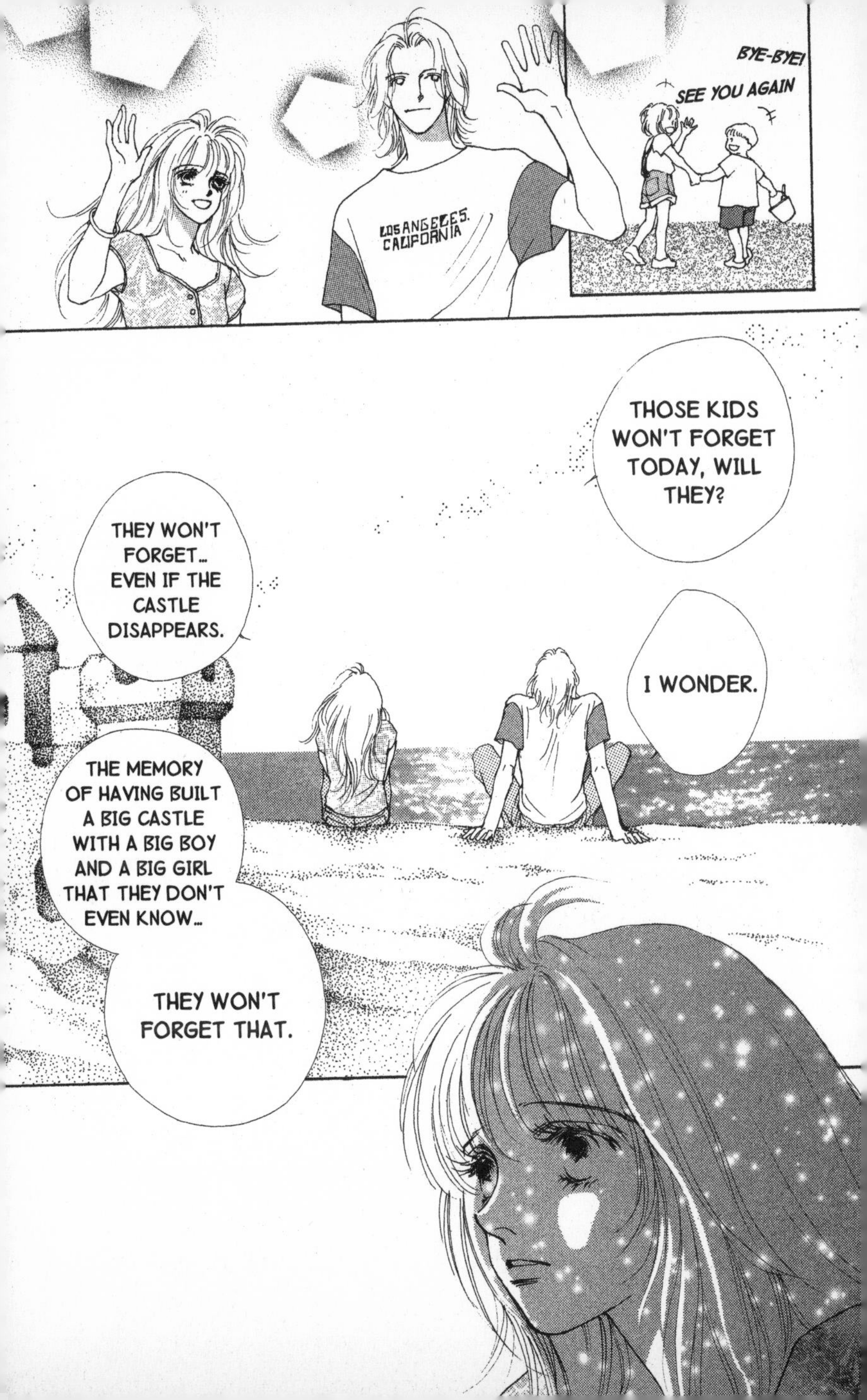

BYE-BYE!
SEE YOU AGAIN
LOS ANGELES. CALIFORNIA
THOSE KIDS WON'T FORGET TODAY, WILL THEY?
THEY WON'T FORGET... EVEN IF THE CASTLE DISAPPEARS.
I WONDER.
THE MEMORY OF HAVING BUILT A BIG CASTLE WITH A BIG BOY AND A BIG GIRL THAT THEY DON'T EVEN KNOW...
THEY WON'T FORGET THAT.

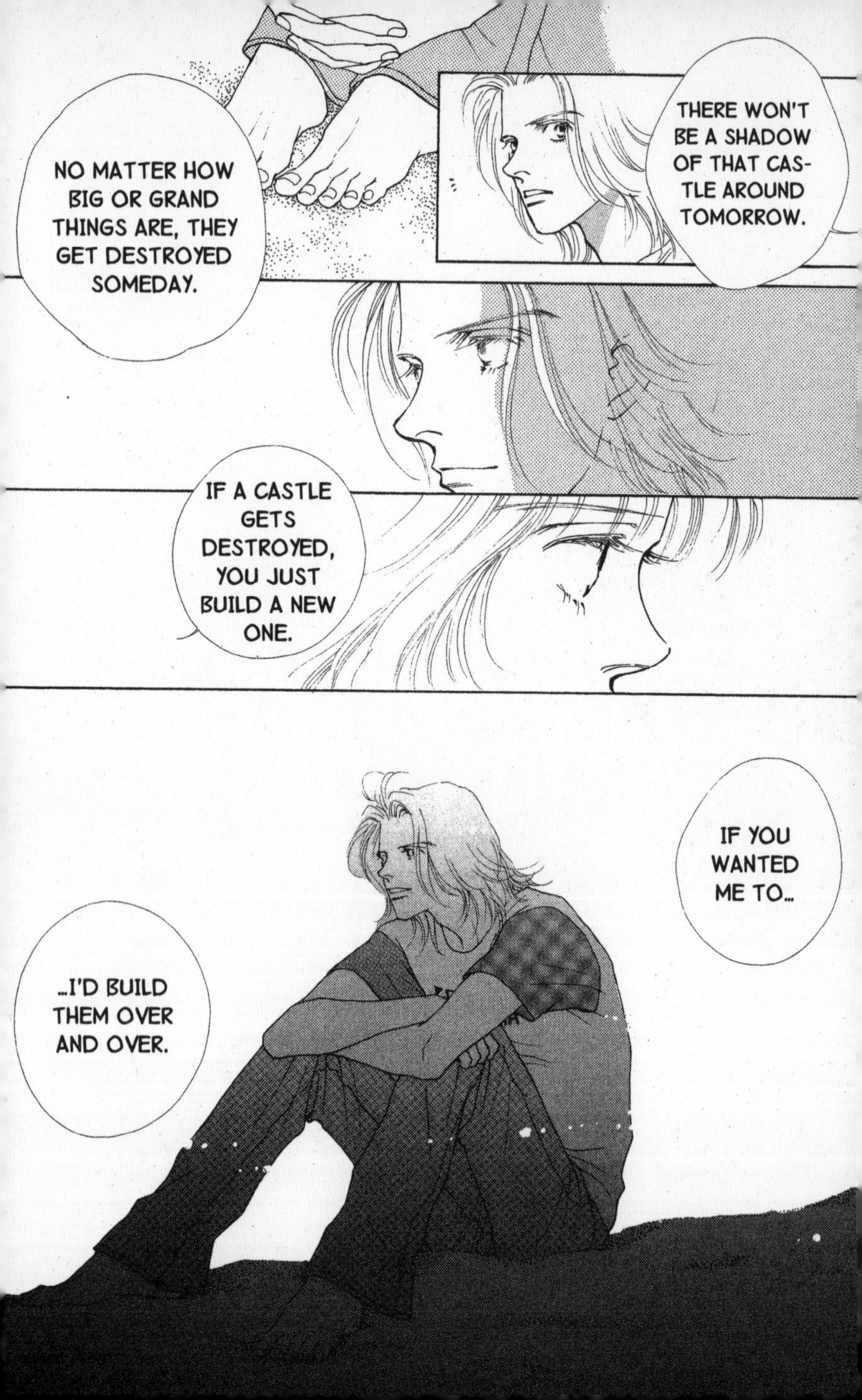
THERE WON'T BE A SHADOW OF THAT CAS-TLE AROUND TOMORROW.
NO MATTER HOW BIG OR GRAND THINGS ARE, THEY GET DESTROYED SOMEDAY.
IF A CASTLE GETS DESTROYED, YOU JUST BUILD A NEW ONE.
IF YOU WANTED ME TO...
...I'D BUILD THEM OVER AND OVER.

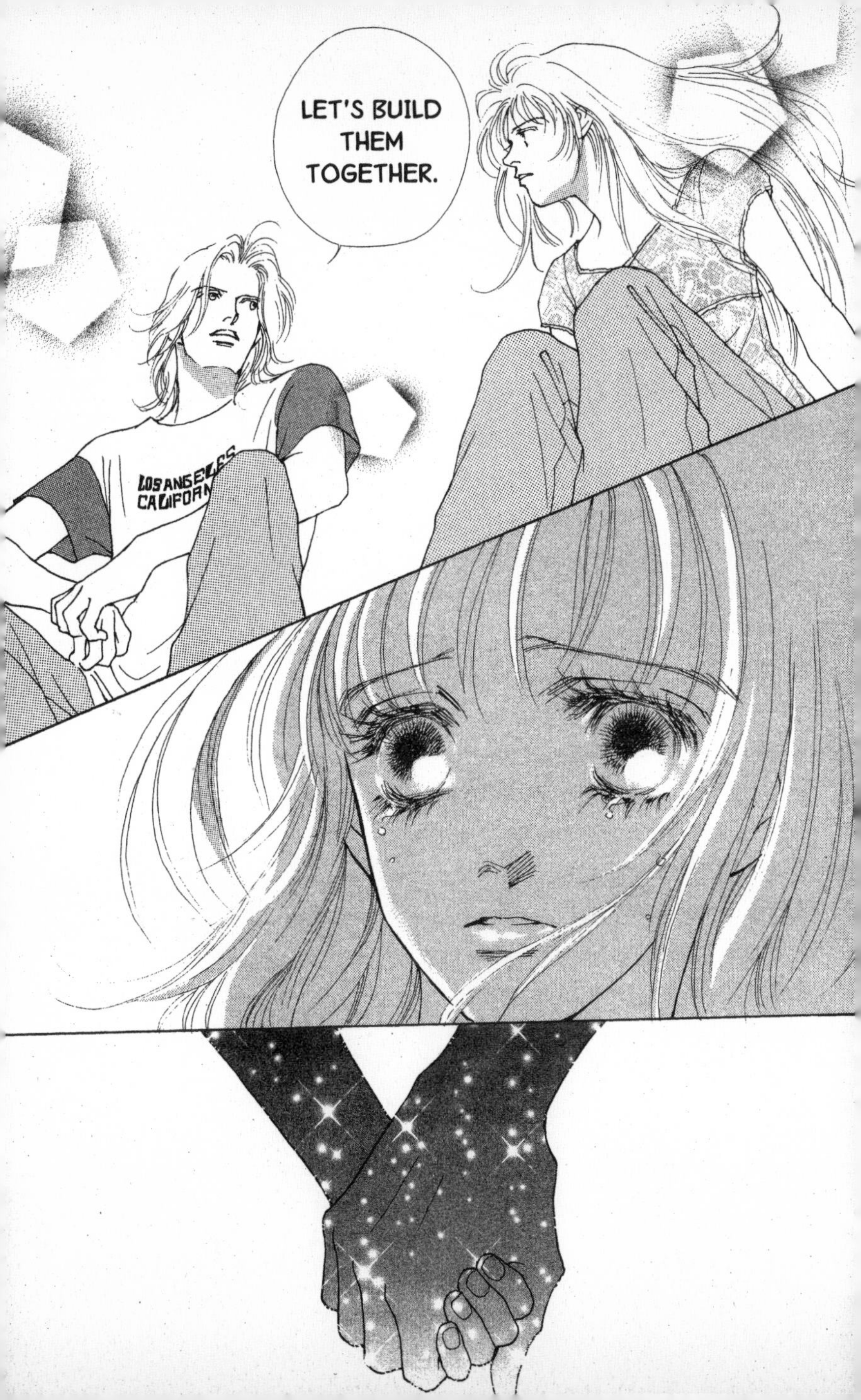
LET'S BUILD THEM TOGETHER.
LOS ANGELES CALIFORN

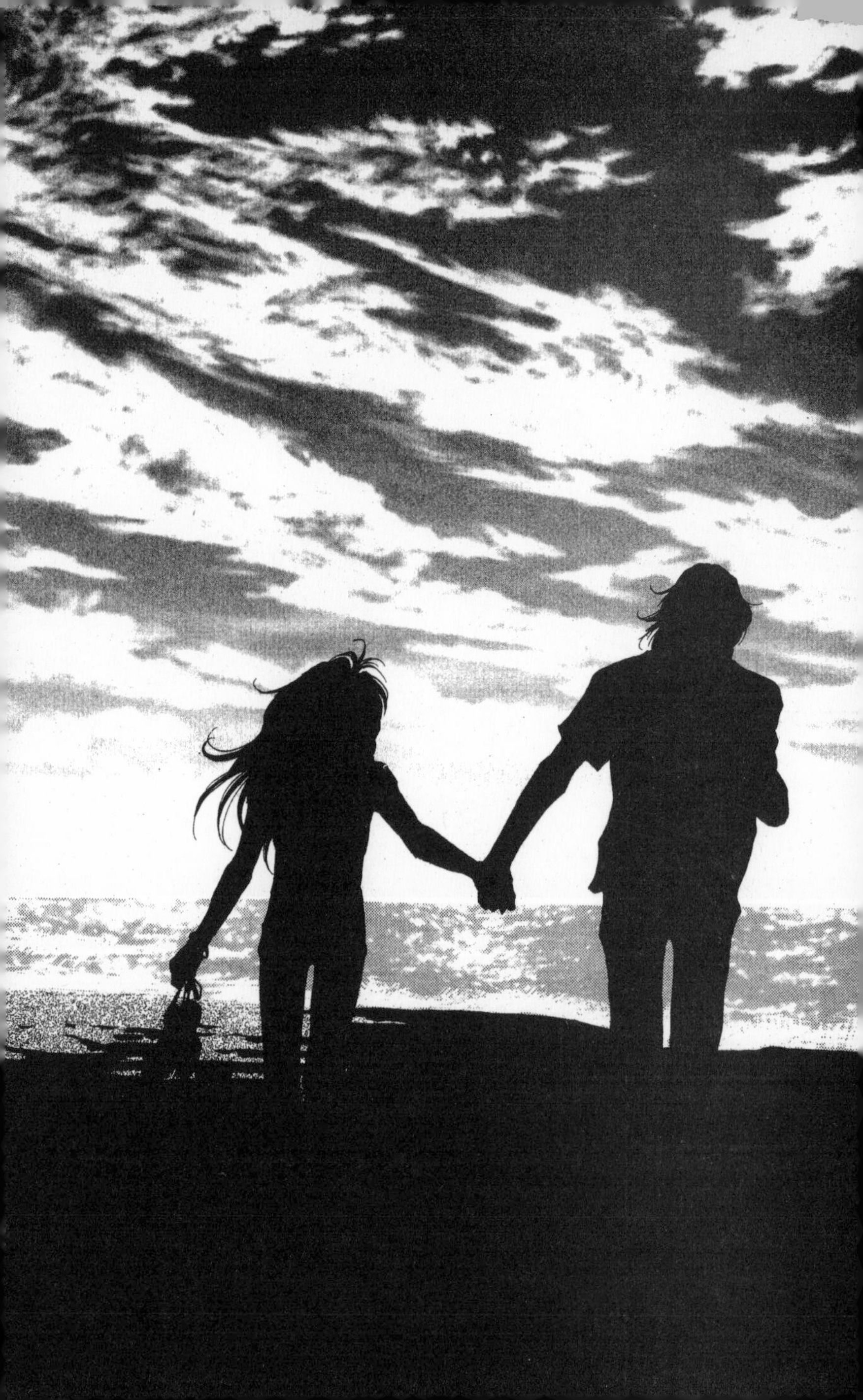

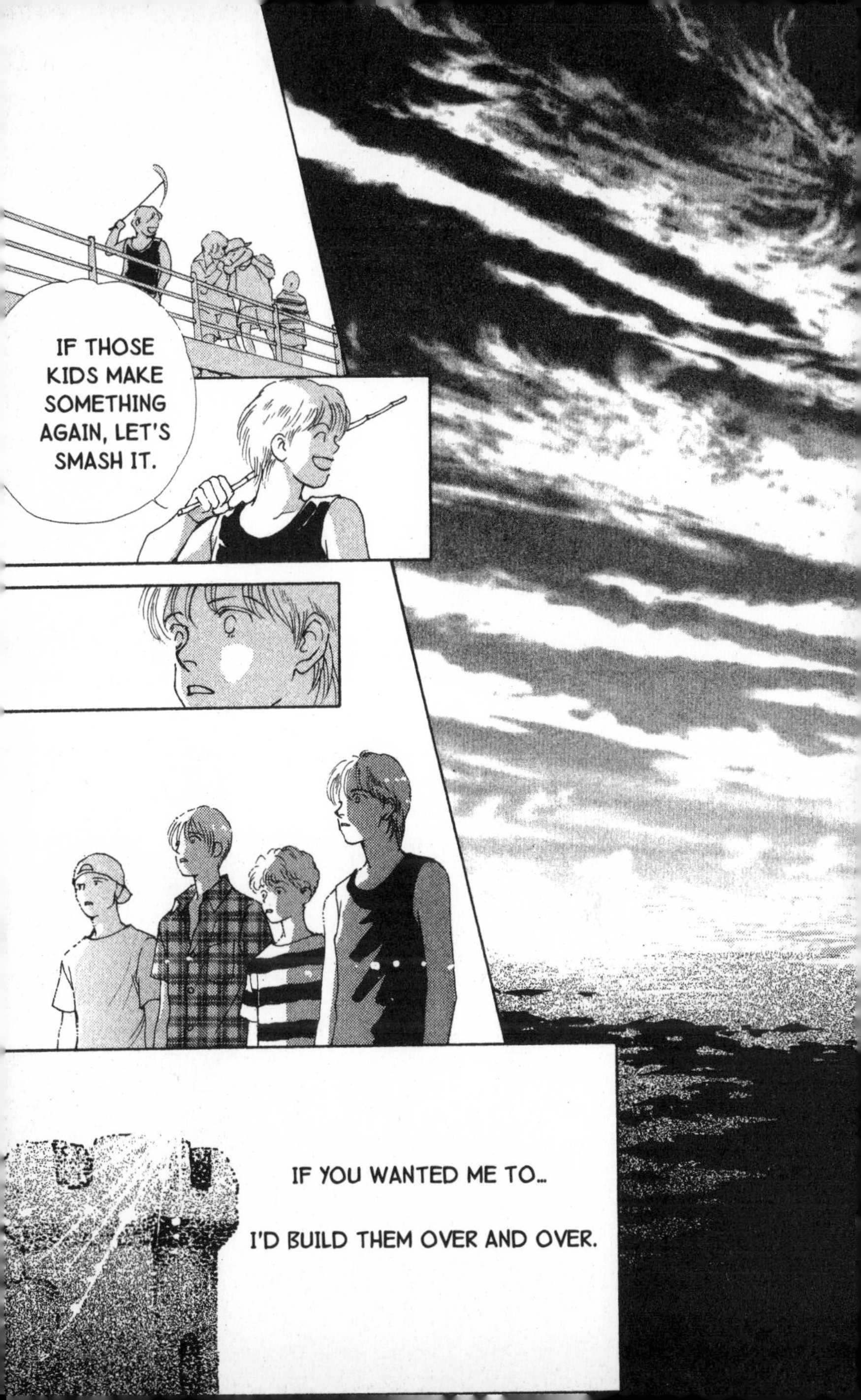
IF THOSE KIDS MAKE SOMETHING AGAIN, LET'S SMASH IT.
IF YOU WANTED ME TO...
I'D BUILD THEM OVER AND OVER.

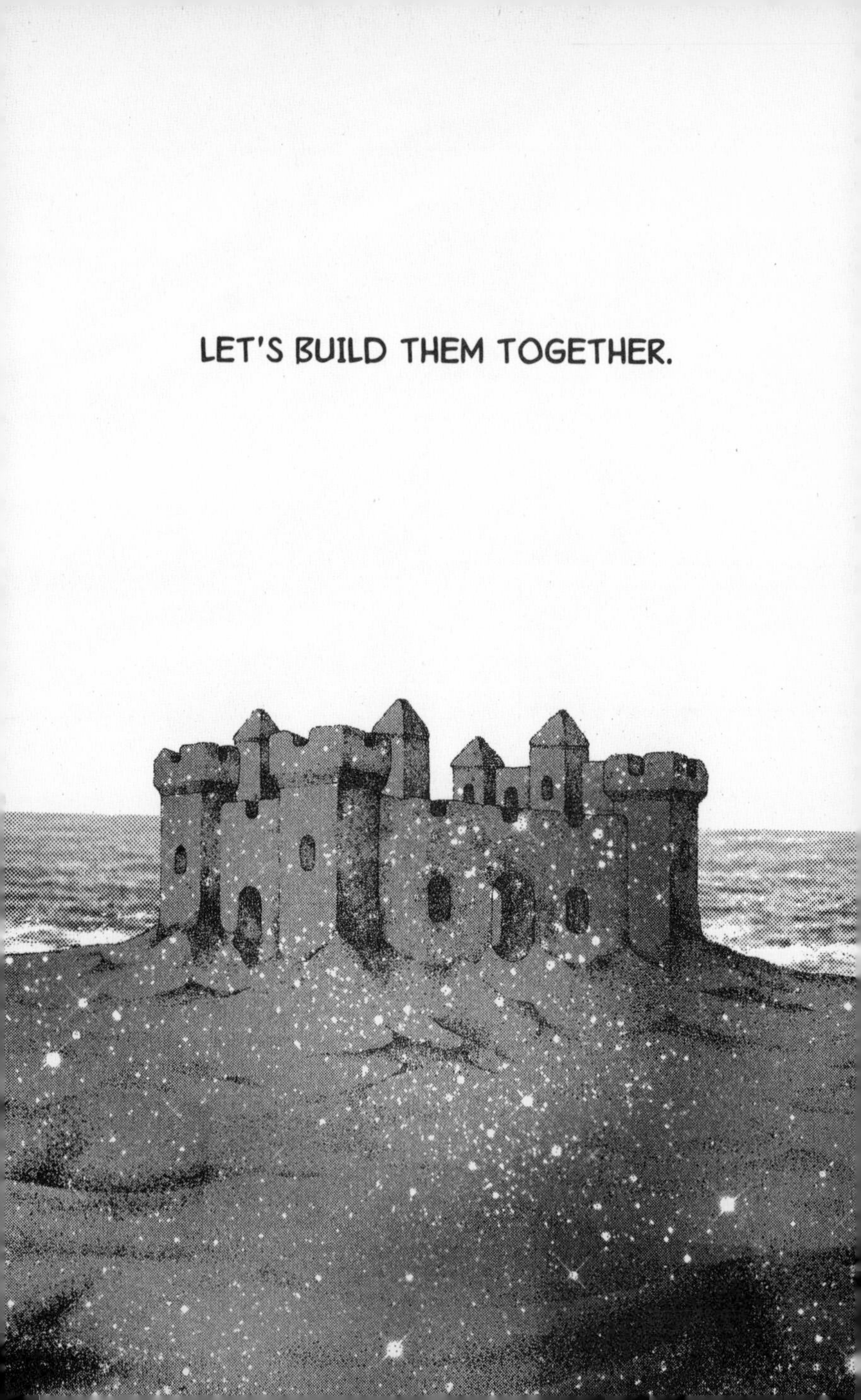
LET'S BUILD THEM TOGETHER.

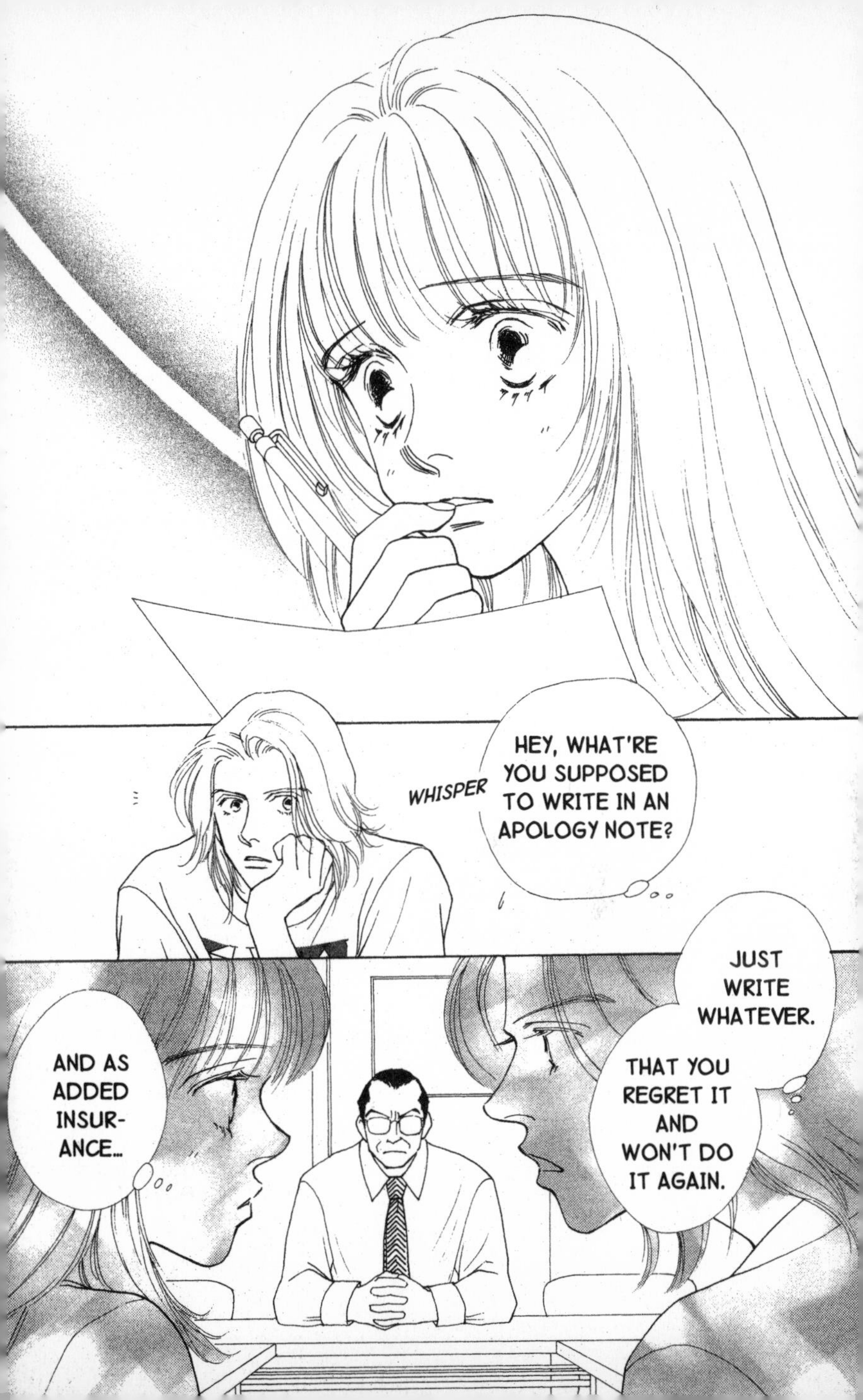
HEY, WHAT'RE YOU SUPPOSED TO WRITE IN AN APOLOGY NOTE?
WHISPER
JUST WRITE WHATEVER.
THAT YOU REGRET IT AND WON'T DO IT AGAIN.
AND AS ADDED INSUR-ANCE...

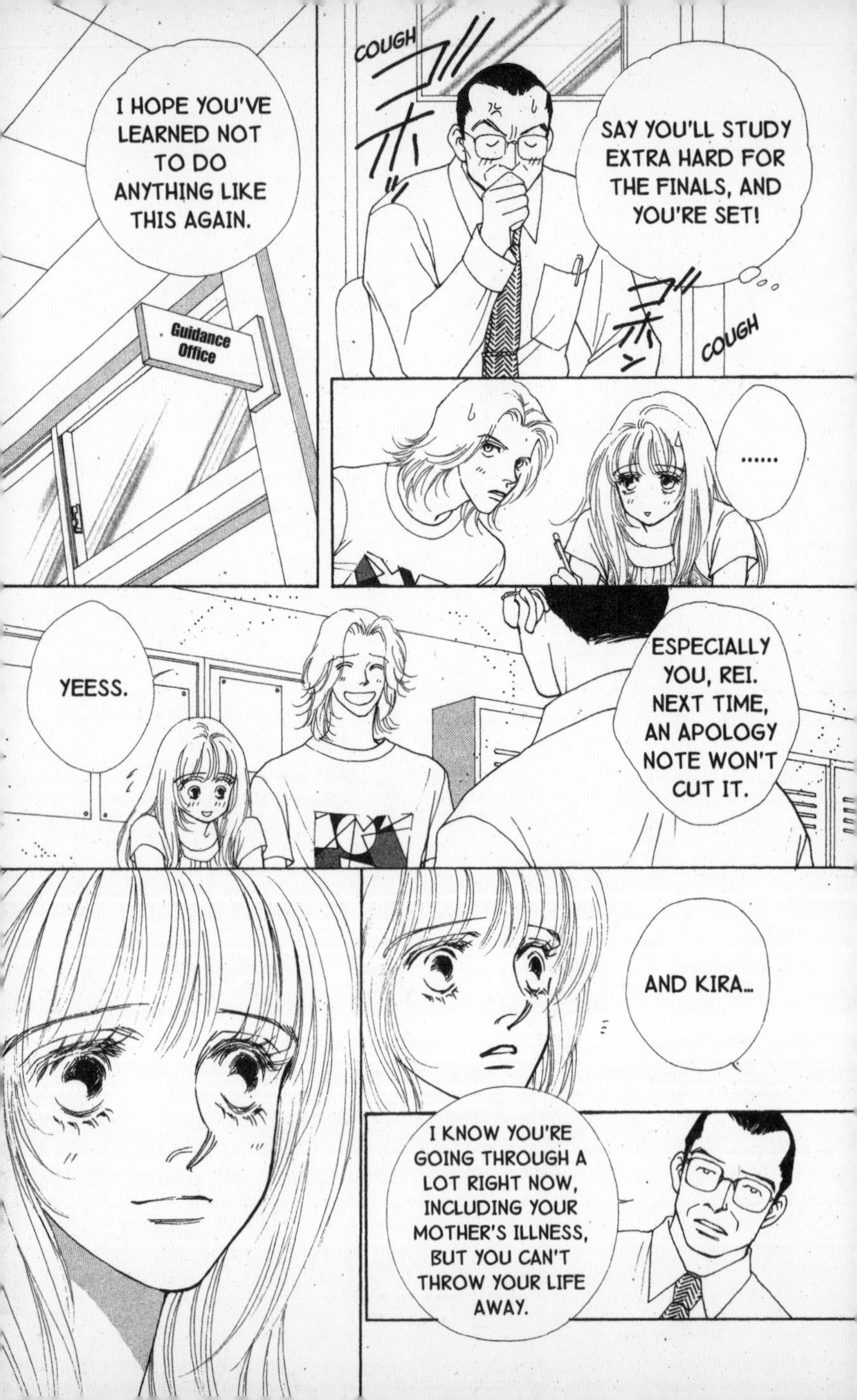
SAY YOU'LL STUDY EXTRA HARD FOR THE FINALS, AND YOU'RE SET!
COUGH
COUGH
......
I HOPE YOU'VE LEARNED NOT TO DO ANYTHING LIKE THIS AGAIN.
Guidance Office
ESPECIALLY YOU, REI. NEXT TIME, AN APOLOGY NOTE WON'T CUT IT.
YEESS.
AND KIRA...
I KNOW YOU'RE GOING THROUGH A LOT RIGHT NOW, INCLUDING YOUR MOTHER'S ILLNESS, BUT YOU CAN'T THROW YOUR LIFE AWAY.

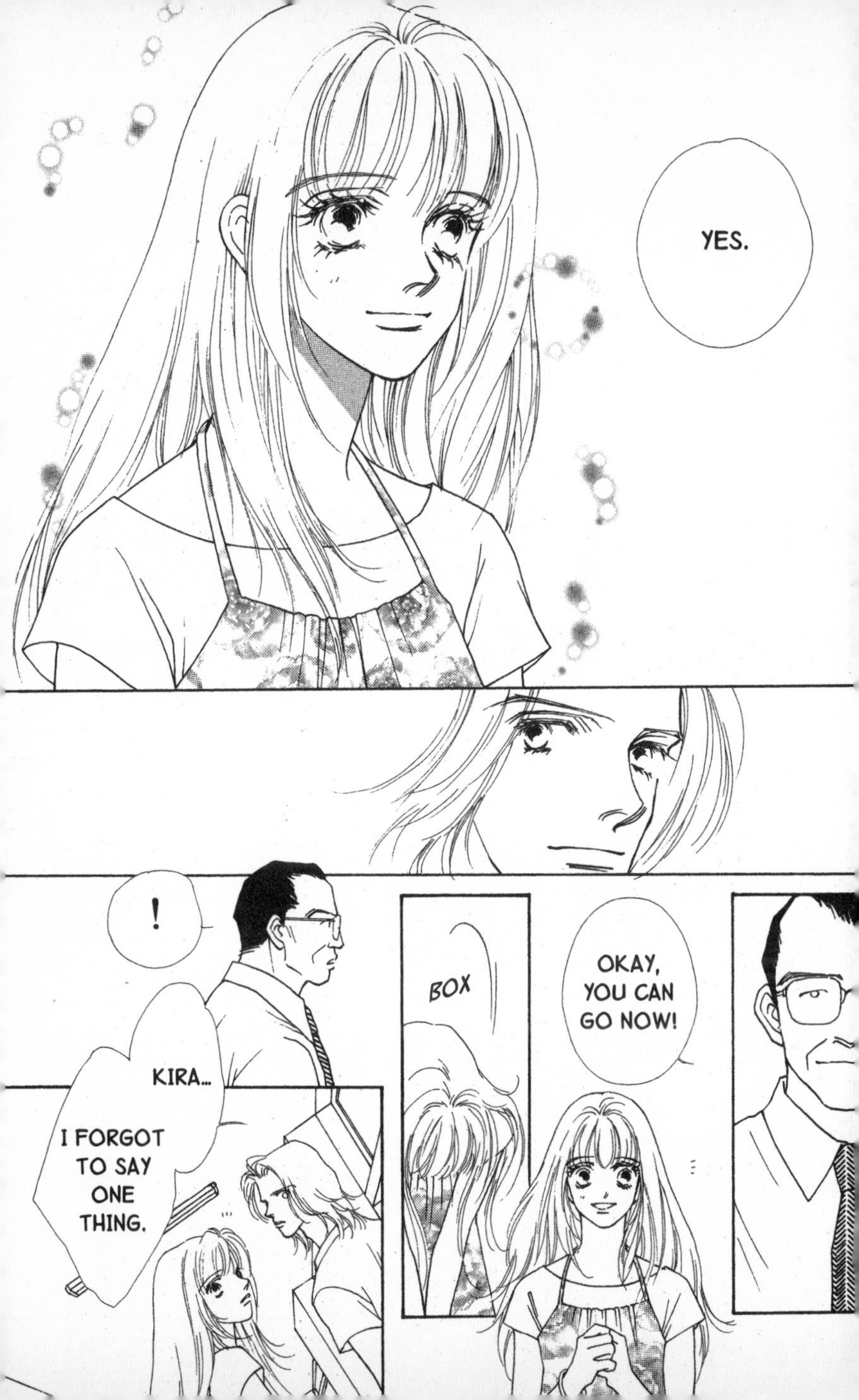
YES.
OKAY, YOU CAN GO NOW!
BOX
!
KIRA...
I FORGOT TO SAY ONE THING.

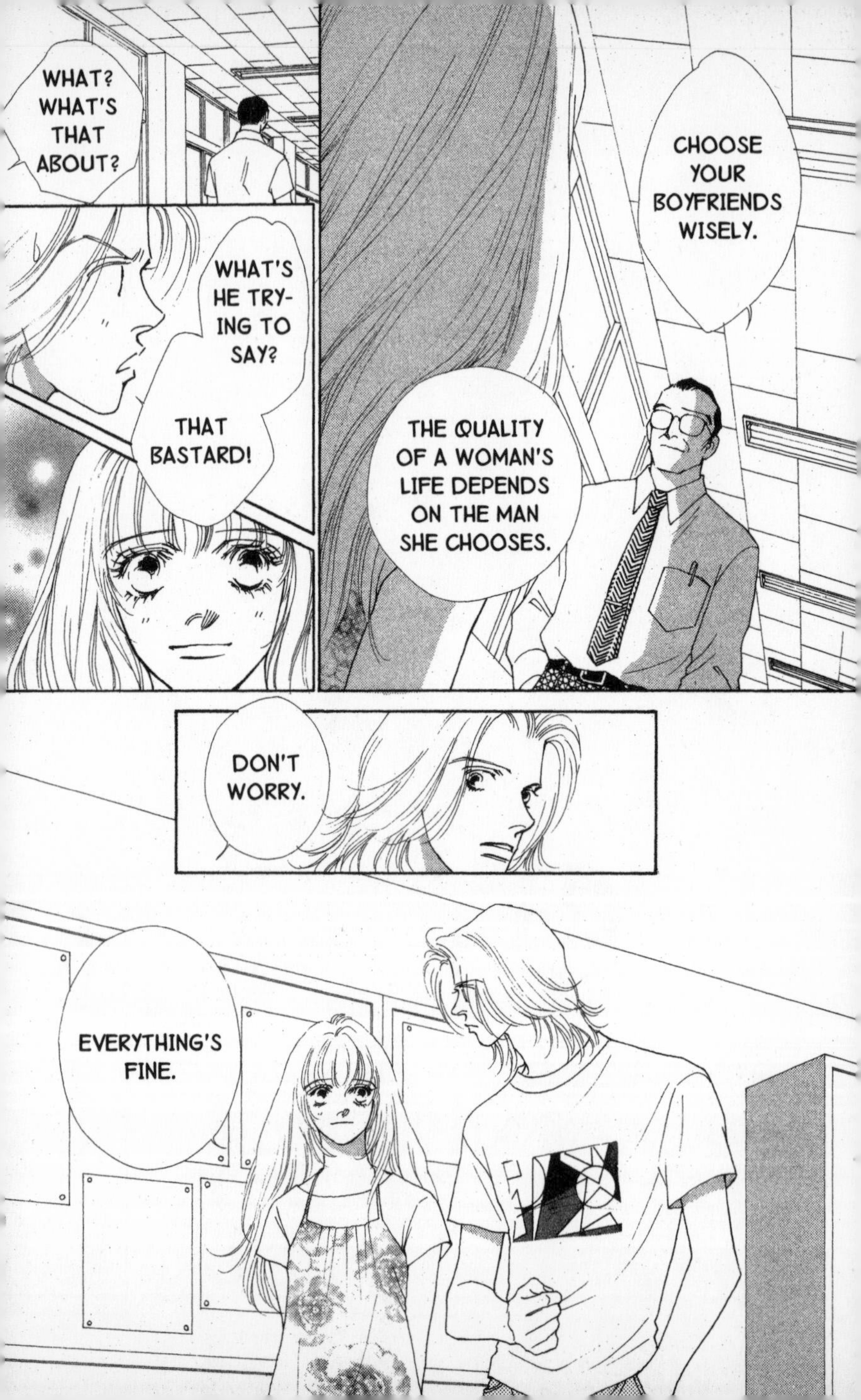
CHOOSE YOUR BOYFRIENDS WISELY.
THE QUALITY OF A WOMAN'S LIFE DEPENDS ON THE MAN SHE CHOOSES.
WHAT? WHAT'S THAT ABOUT?
WHAT'S HE TRY-ING TO SAY?
THAT BASTARD!
DON'T WORRY.
EVERYTHING'S FINE.

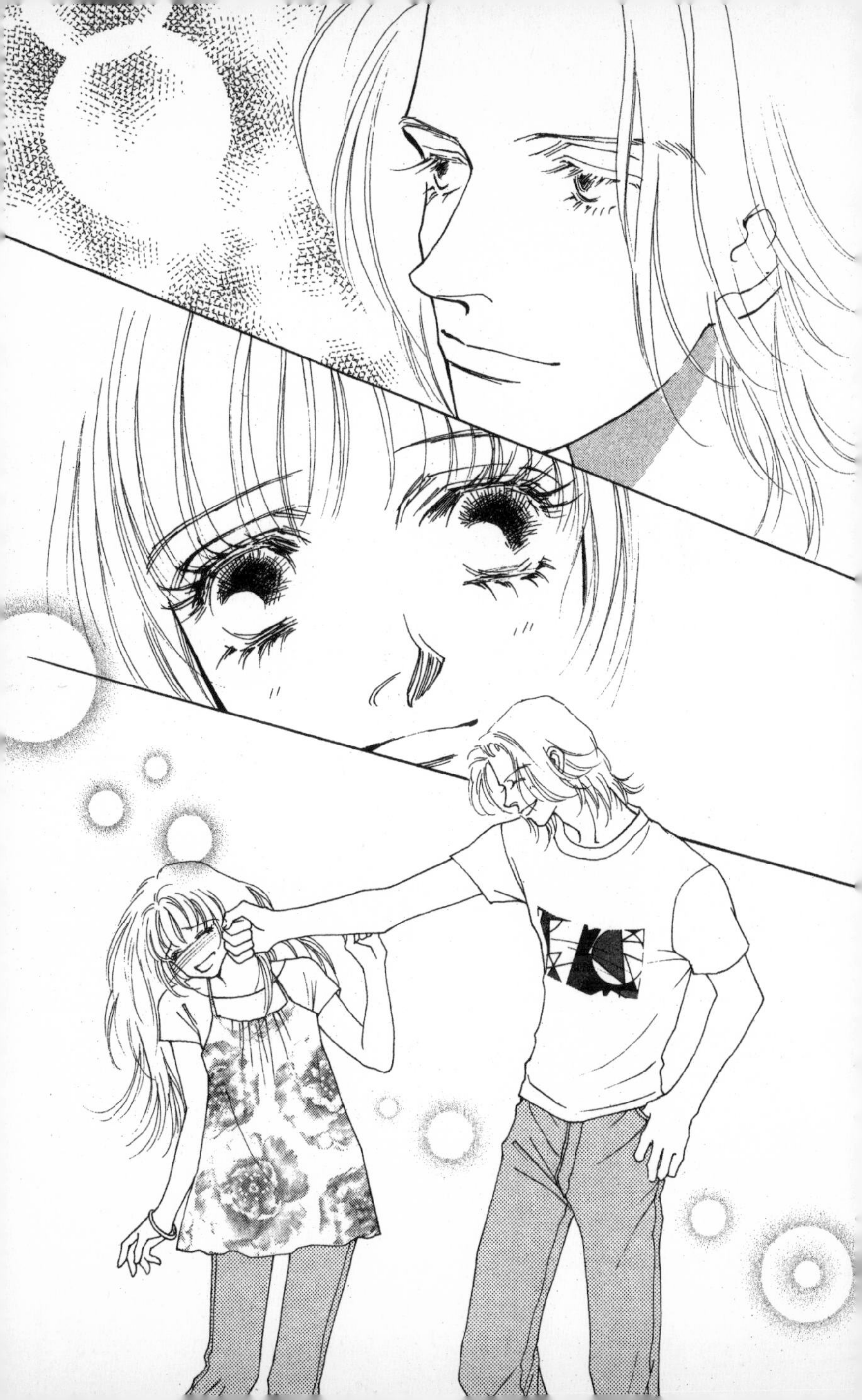

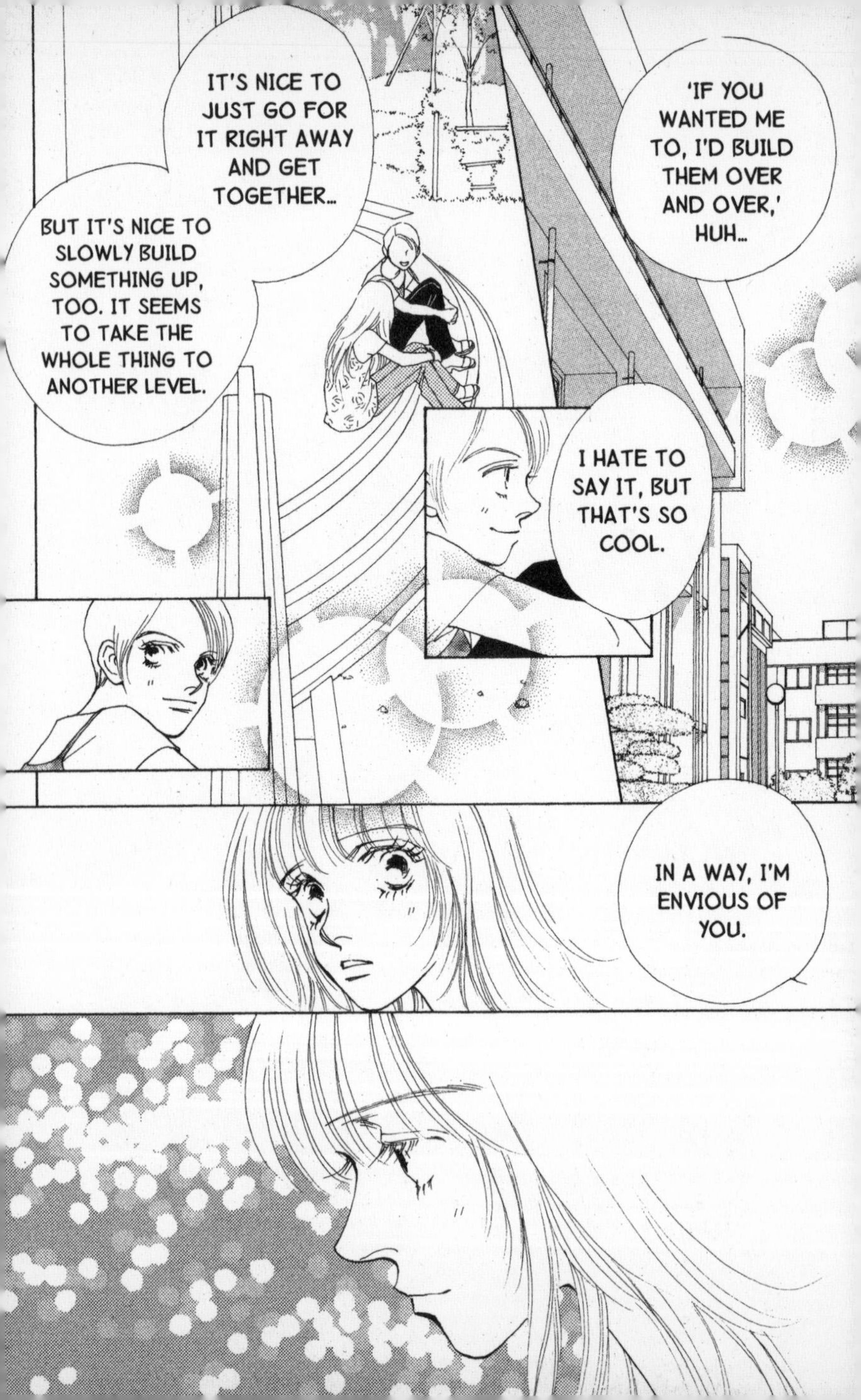
'IF YOU WANTED ME TO, I'D BUILD THEM OVER AND OVER,' HUH...
IT'S NICE TO JUST GO FOR IT RIGHT AWAY AND GET TOGETHER...
BUT IT'S NICE TO SLOWLY BUILD SOMETHING UP, TOO. IT SEEMS TO TAKE THE WHOLE THING TO ANOTHER LEVEL.
I HATE TO SAY IT, BUT THAT'S SO COOL.
IN A WAY, I'M ENVIOUS OF YOU.

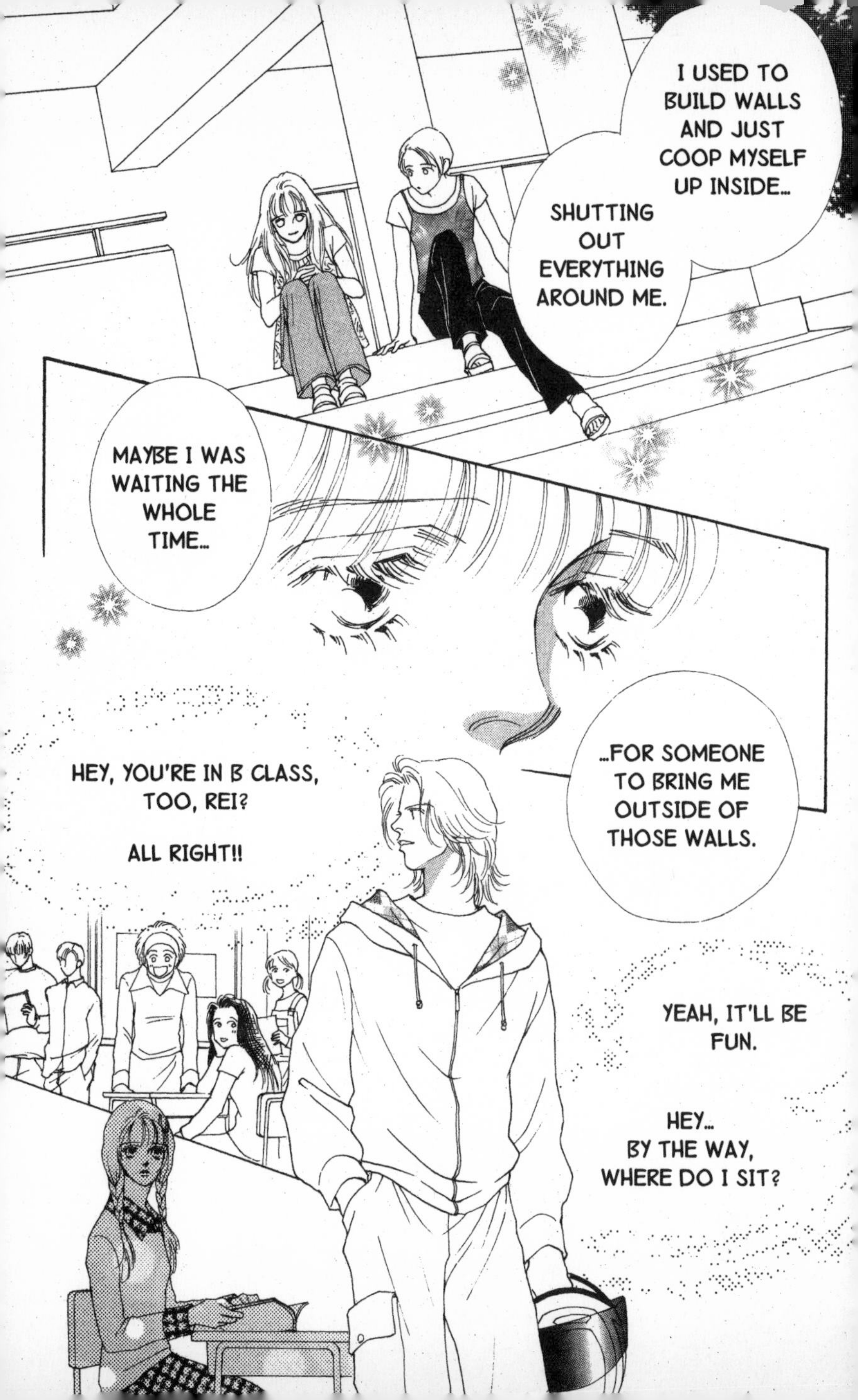
I USED TO BUILD WALLS AND JUST COOP MYSELF UP INSIDE...
SHUTTING OUT EVERYTHING AROUND ME.
MAYBE I WAS WAITING THE WHOLE TIME...
...FOR SOMEONE TO BRING ME OUTSIDE OF THOSE WALLS.
HEY, YOU'RE IN B CLASS, TOO, REI?
ALL RIGHT!!
YEAH, IT'LL BE FUN.
HEY... BY THE WAY, WHERE DO I SIT?

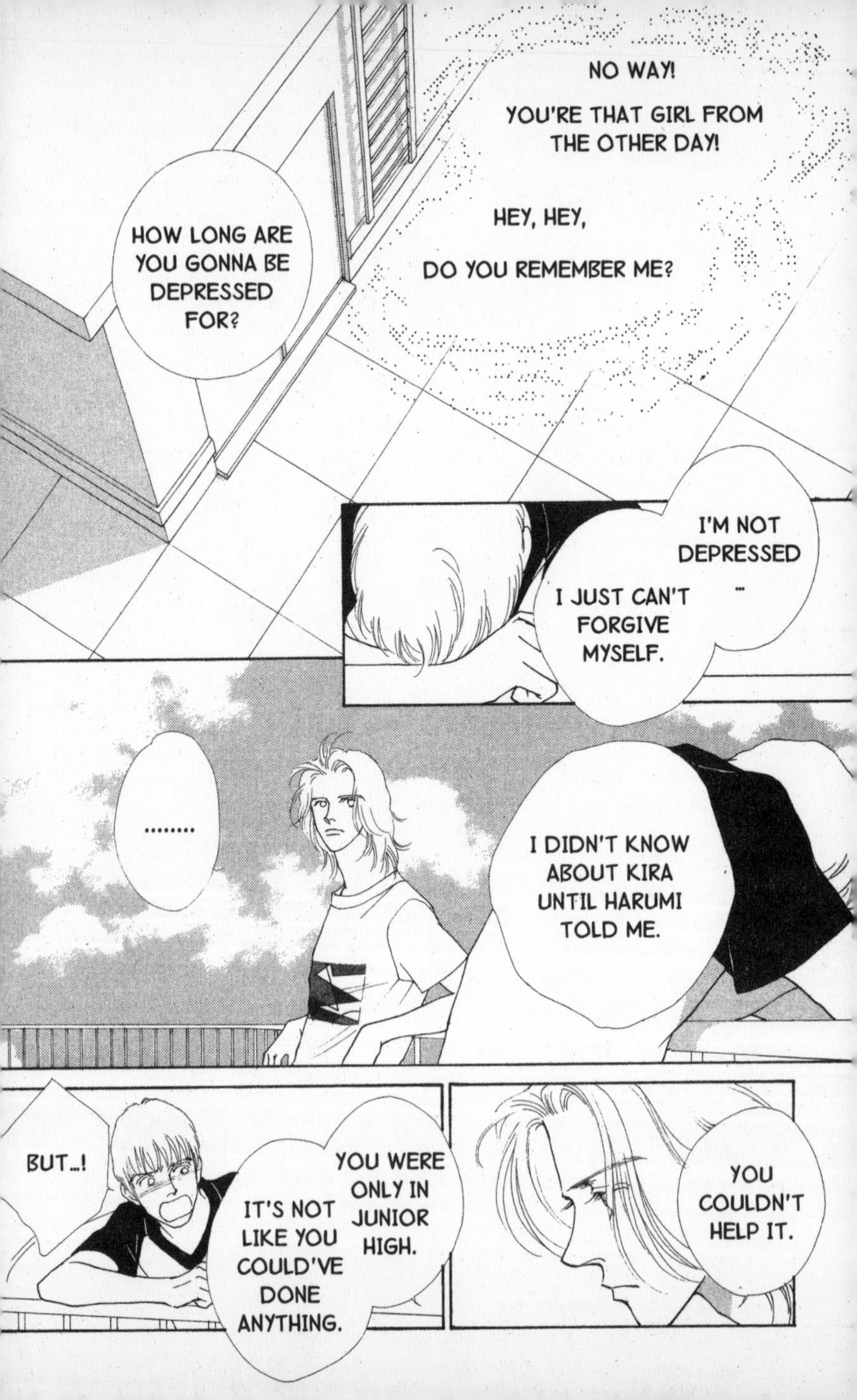
NO WAY!
YOU'RE THAT GIRL FROM THE OTHER DAY!
HEY, HEY,
DO YOU REMEMBER ME?
HOW LONG ARE YOU GONNA BE DEPRESSED FOR?
I'M NOT DEPRESSED ...
I JUST CAN'T FORGIVE MYSELF.
I DIDN'T KNOW ABOUT KIRA UNTIL HARUMI TOLD ME.
....
YOU COULDN'T HELP IT.
YOU WERE ONLY IN JUNIOR HIGH.
IT'S NOT LIKE YOU COULD'VE DONE ANYTHING.
BUT...!

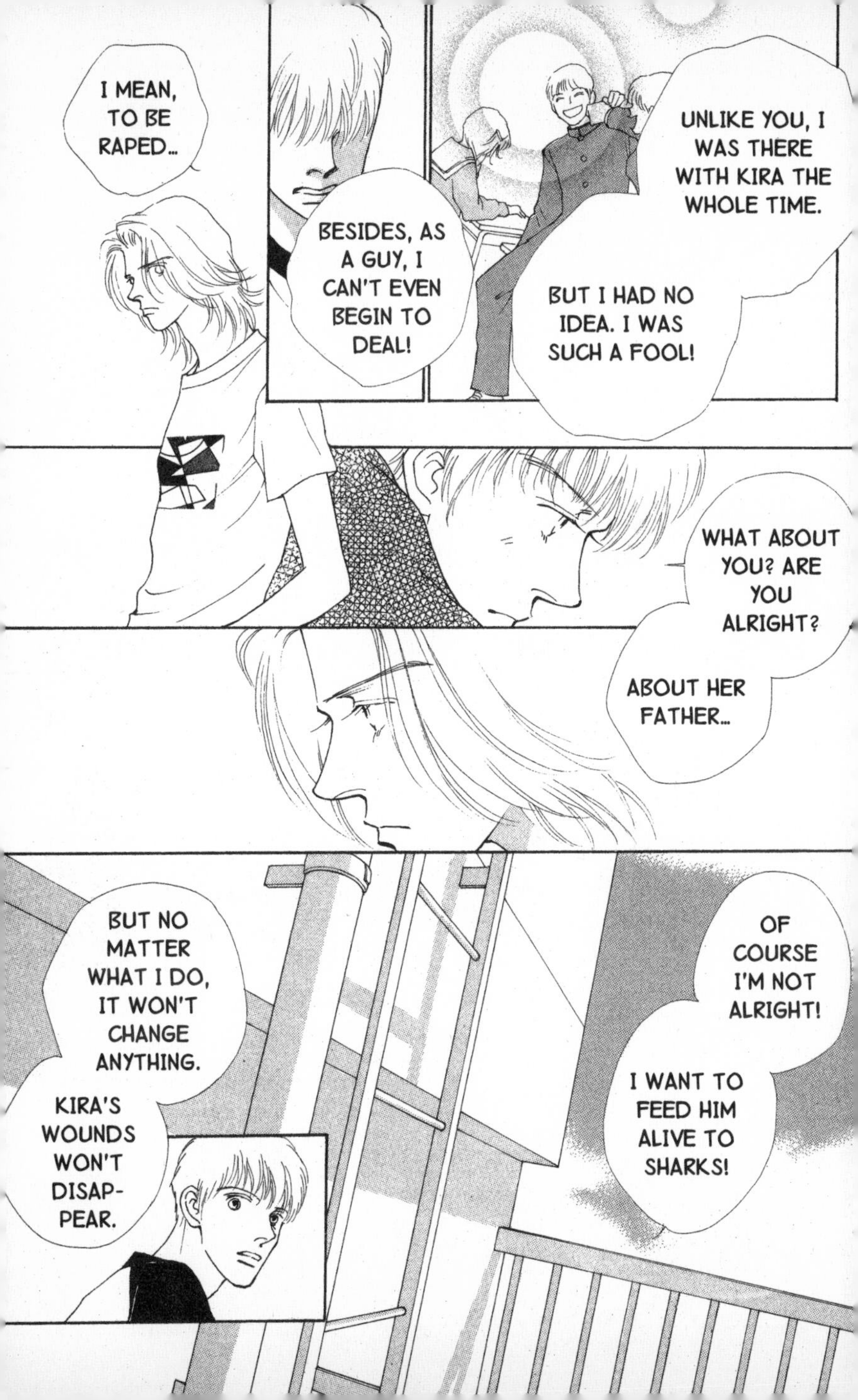
UNLIKE YOU, I WAS THERE WITH KIRA THE WHOLE TIME.
BUT I HAD NO IDEA. I WAS SUCH A FOOL!
BESIDES, AS A GUY, I CAN'T EVEN BEGIN TO DEAL!
I MEAN, TO BE RAPED...
WHAT ABOUT YOU? ARE YOU ALRIGHT?
ABOUT HER FATHER...
OF COURSE I'M NOT ALRIGHT!
I WANT TO FEED HIM ALIVE TO SHARKS!
BUT NO MATTER WHAT I DO, IT WON'T CHANGE ANYTHING.
KIRA'S WOUNDS WON'T DISAP-PEAR.

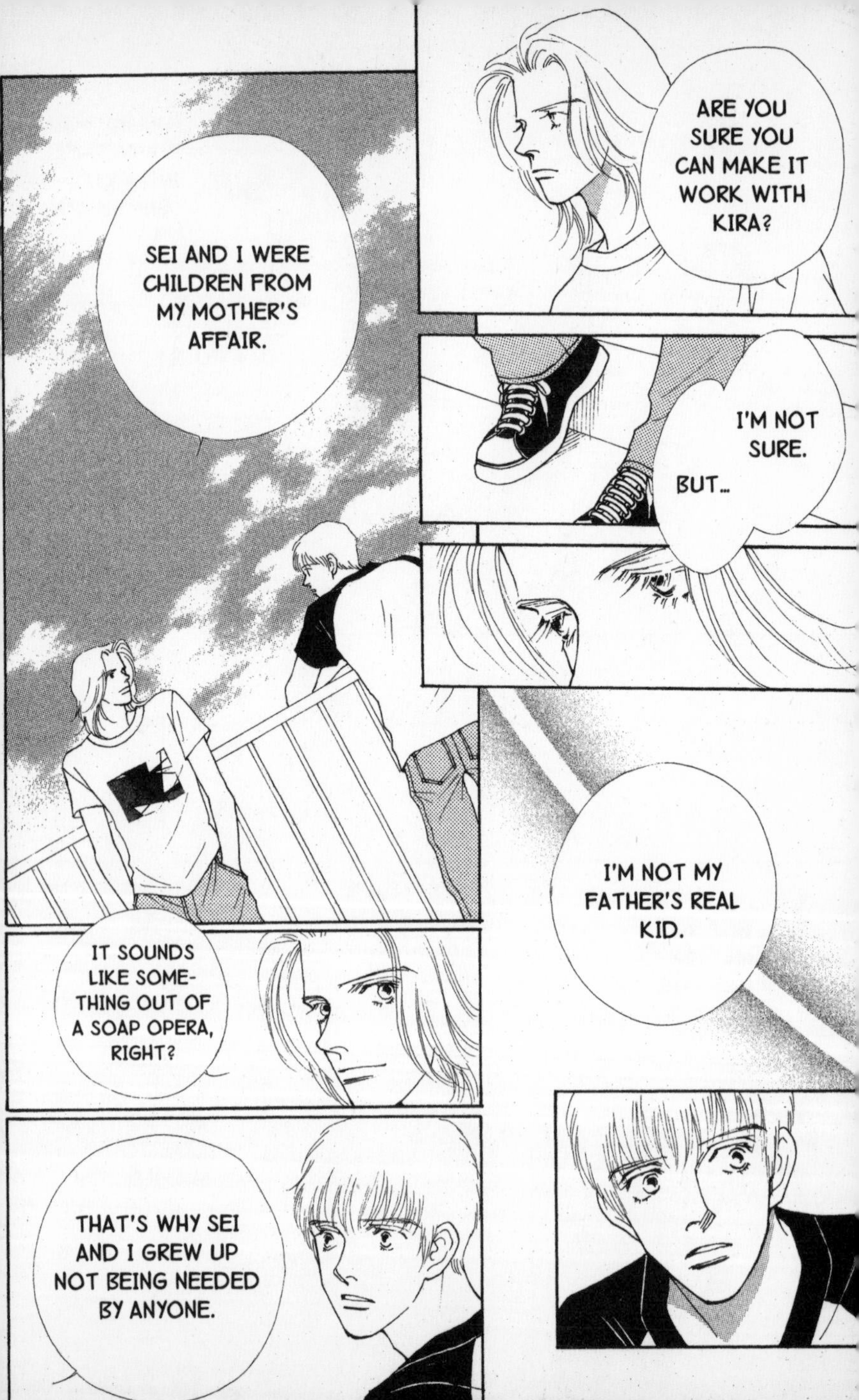
ARE YOU SURE YOU CAN MAKE IT WORK WITH KIRA?
I'M NOT SURE.
BUT...
I'M NOT MY FATHER'S REAL KID.
SEI AND I WERE CHILDREN FROM MY MOTHER'S AFFAIR.
IT SOUNDS LIKE SOME-THING OUT OF A SOAP OPERA, RIGHT?
THAT'S WHY SEI AND I GREW UP NOT BEING NEEDED BY ANYONE.

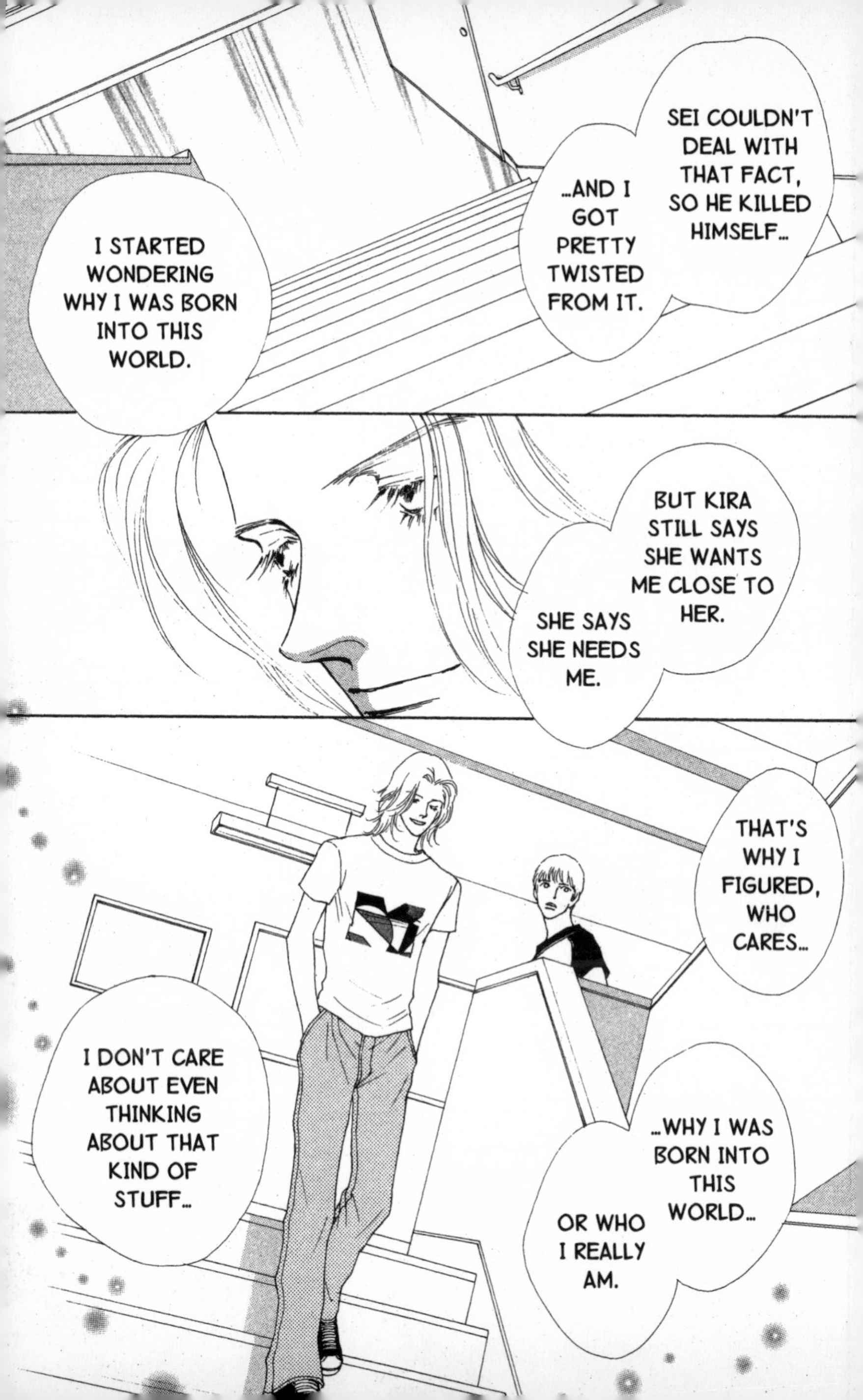
SEI COULDN'T DEAL WITH THAT FACT, SO HE KILLED HIMSELF...
...AND I GOT PRETTY TWISTED FROM IT.
I STARTED WONDERING WHY I WAS BORN INTO THIS WORLD.
BUT KIRA STILL SAYS SHE WANTS ME CLOSE TO HER.
SHE SAYS SHE NEEDS ME.
THAT'S WHY I FIGURED, WHO CARES...
...WHY I WAS BORN INTO THIS WORLD...
OR WHO I REALLY AM.
I DON'T CARE ABOUT EVEN THINKING ABOUT THAT KIND OF STUFF...

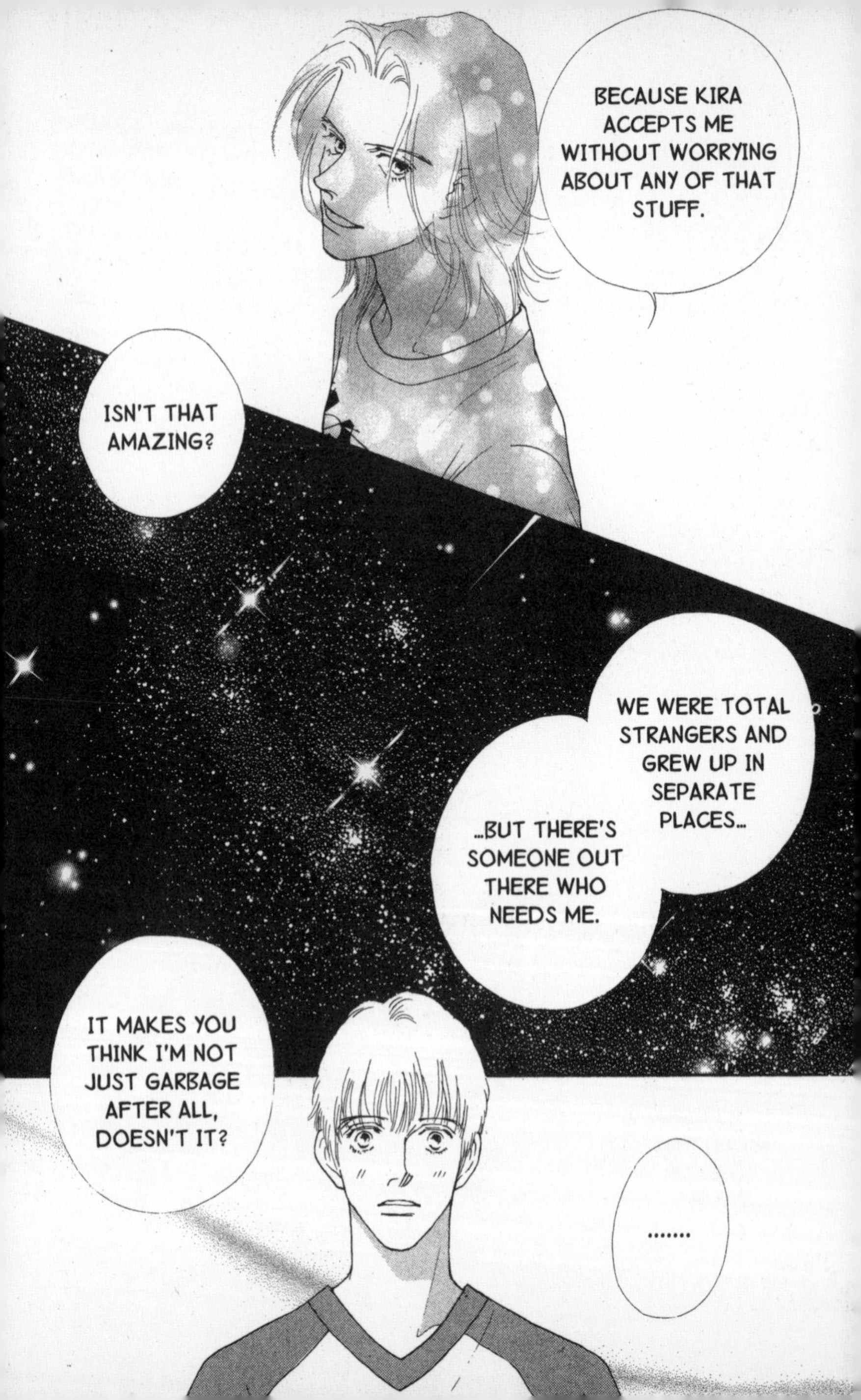
BECAUSE KIRA ACCEPTS ME WITHOUT WORRYING ABOUT ANY OF THAT STUFF.
ISN'T THAT AMAZING?
WE WERE TOTAL STRANGERS AND GREW UP IN SEPARATE PLACES...
...BUT THERE'S SOMEONE OUT THERE WHO NEEDS ME.
IT MAKES YOU THINK I'M NOT JUST GARBAGE AFTER ALL, DOESN'T IT?
....

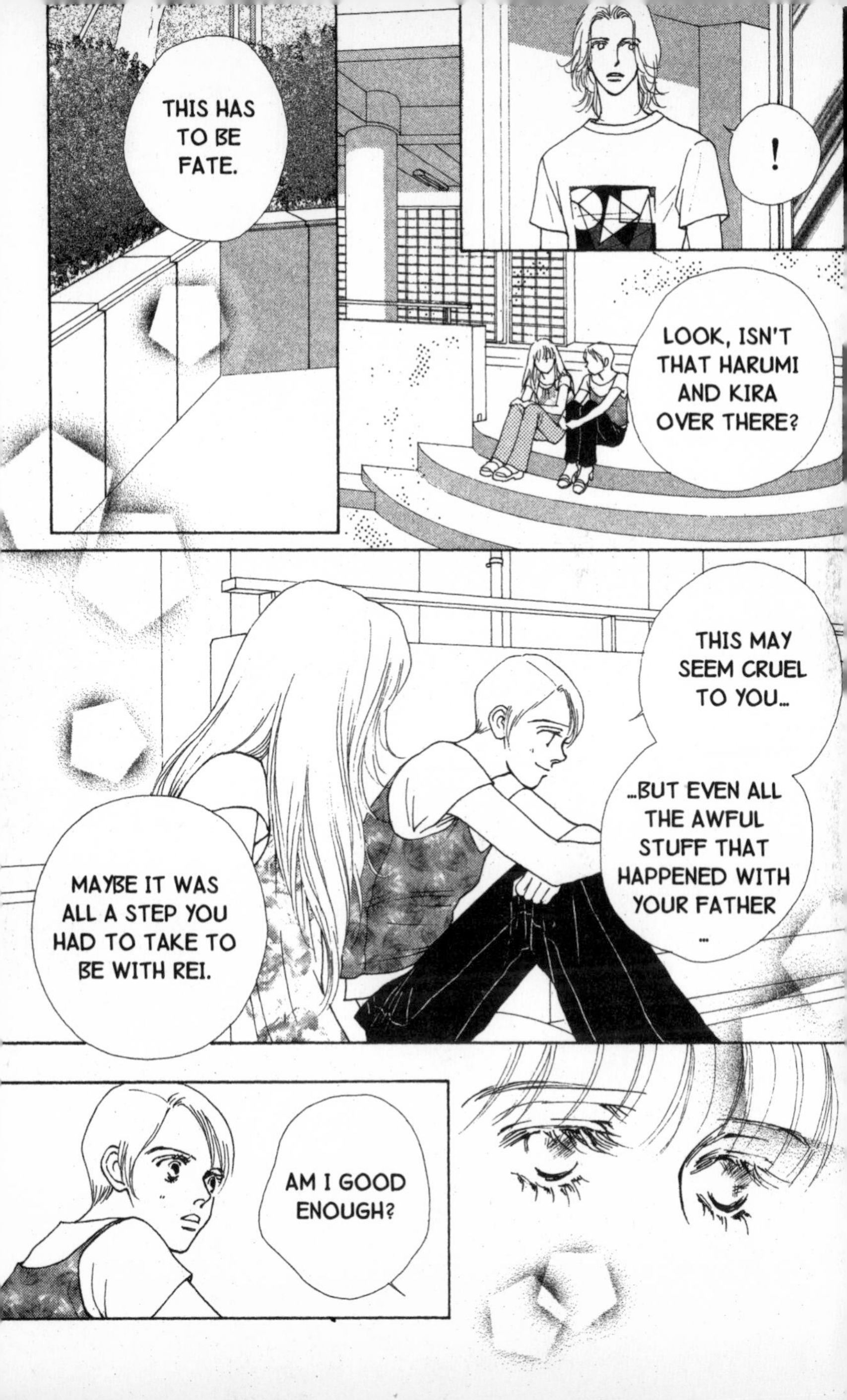
!
LOOK, ISN'T THAT HARUMI AND KIRA OVER THERE?
THIS HAS TO BE FATE.
THIS MAY SEEM CRUEL TO YOU...
...BUT EVEN ALL THE AWFUL STUFF THAT HAPPENED WITH YOUR FATHER ...
MAYBE IT WAS ALL A STEP YOU HAD TO TAKE TO BE WITH REI.
AM I GOOD ENOUGH?

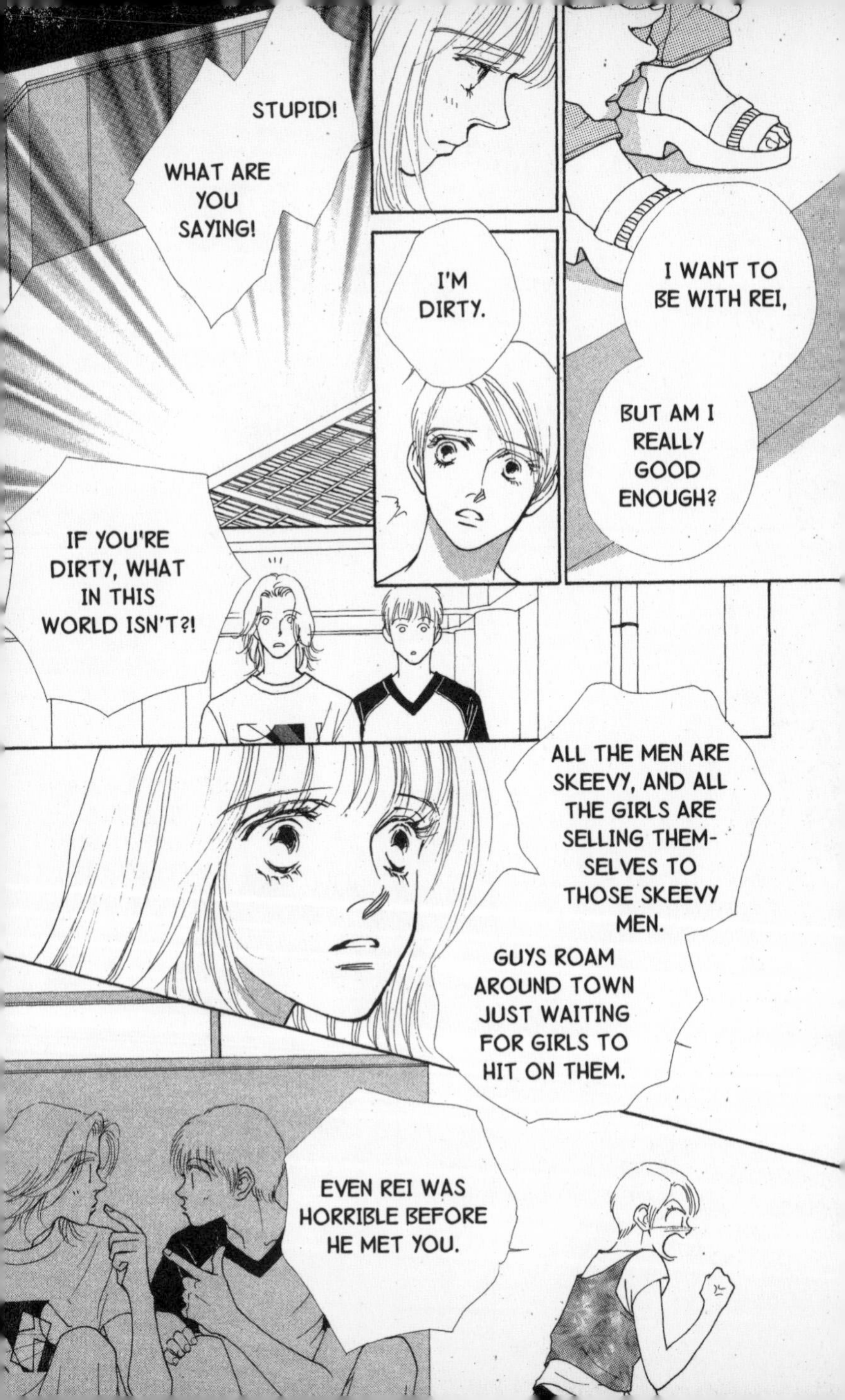
I WANT TO BE WITH REI,
BUT AM I REALLY GOOD ENOUGH?
I'M DIRTY.
STUPID!
WHAT ARE YOU SAYING!
IF YOU'RE DIRTY, WHAT IN THIS WORLD ISN'T?!
ALL THE MEN ARE SKEEVY, AND ALL THE GIRLS ARE SELLING THEM-SELVES TO THOSE SKEEVY MEN.
GUYS ROAM AROUND TOWN JUST WAITING FOR GIRLS TO HIT ON THEM.
EVEN REI WAS HORRIBLE BEFORE HE MET YOU.

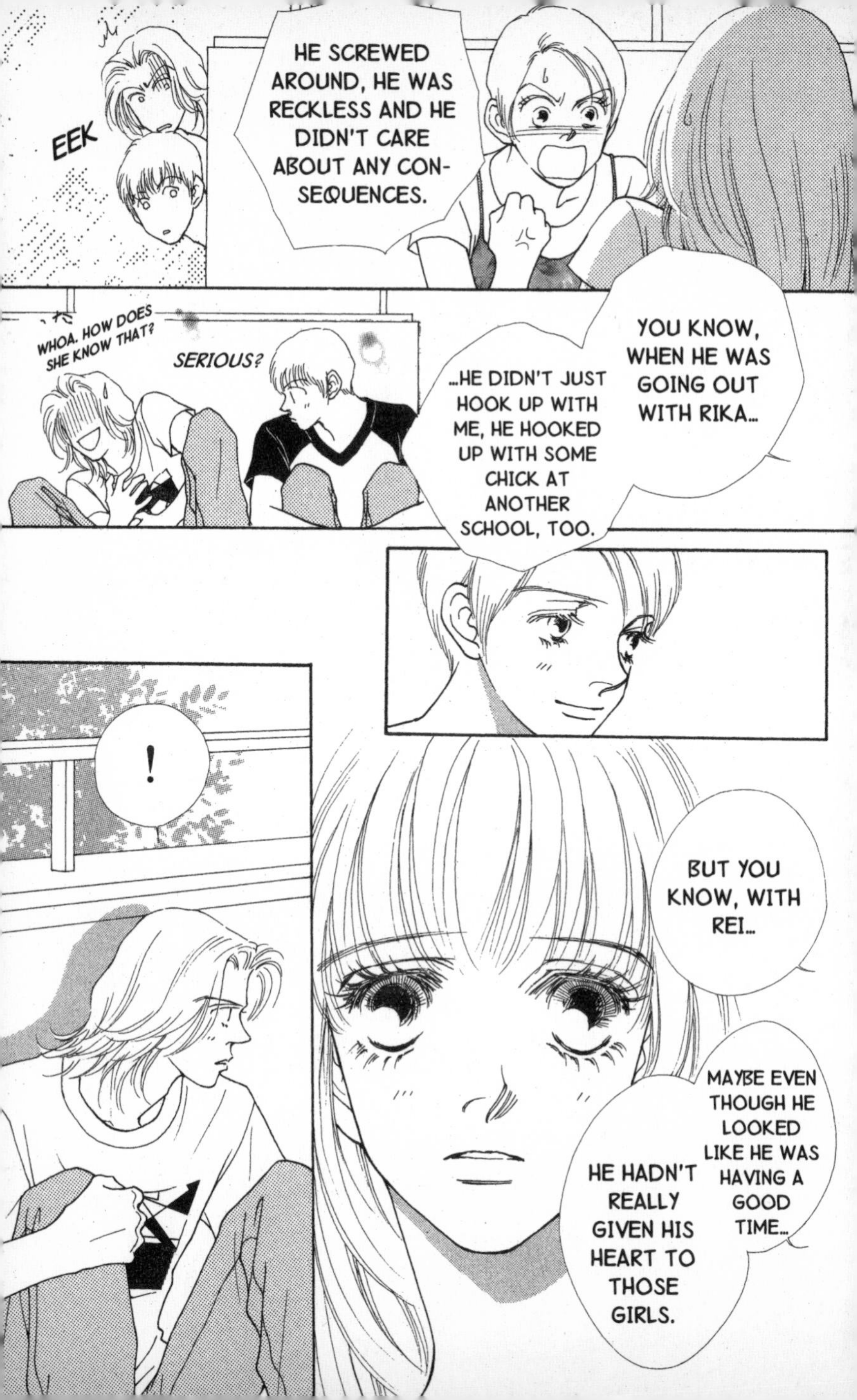
HE SCREWED AROUND, HE WAS RECKLESS AND HE DIDN'T CARE ABOUT ANY CON-SEQUENCES.
EEK
YOU KNOW, WHEN HE WAS GOING OUT WITH RIKA...
...HE DIDN'T JUST HOOK UP WITH ME, HE HOOKED UP WITH SOME CHICK AT ANOTHER SCHOOL, TOO.
SERIOUS?
WHOA. HOW DOES SHE KNOW THAT?
BUT YOU KNOW, WITH REI...
MAYBE EVEN THOUGH HE LOOKED LIKE HE WAS HAVING A GOOD TIME...
HE HADN'T REALLY GIVEN HIS HEART TO THOSE GIRLS.
!

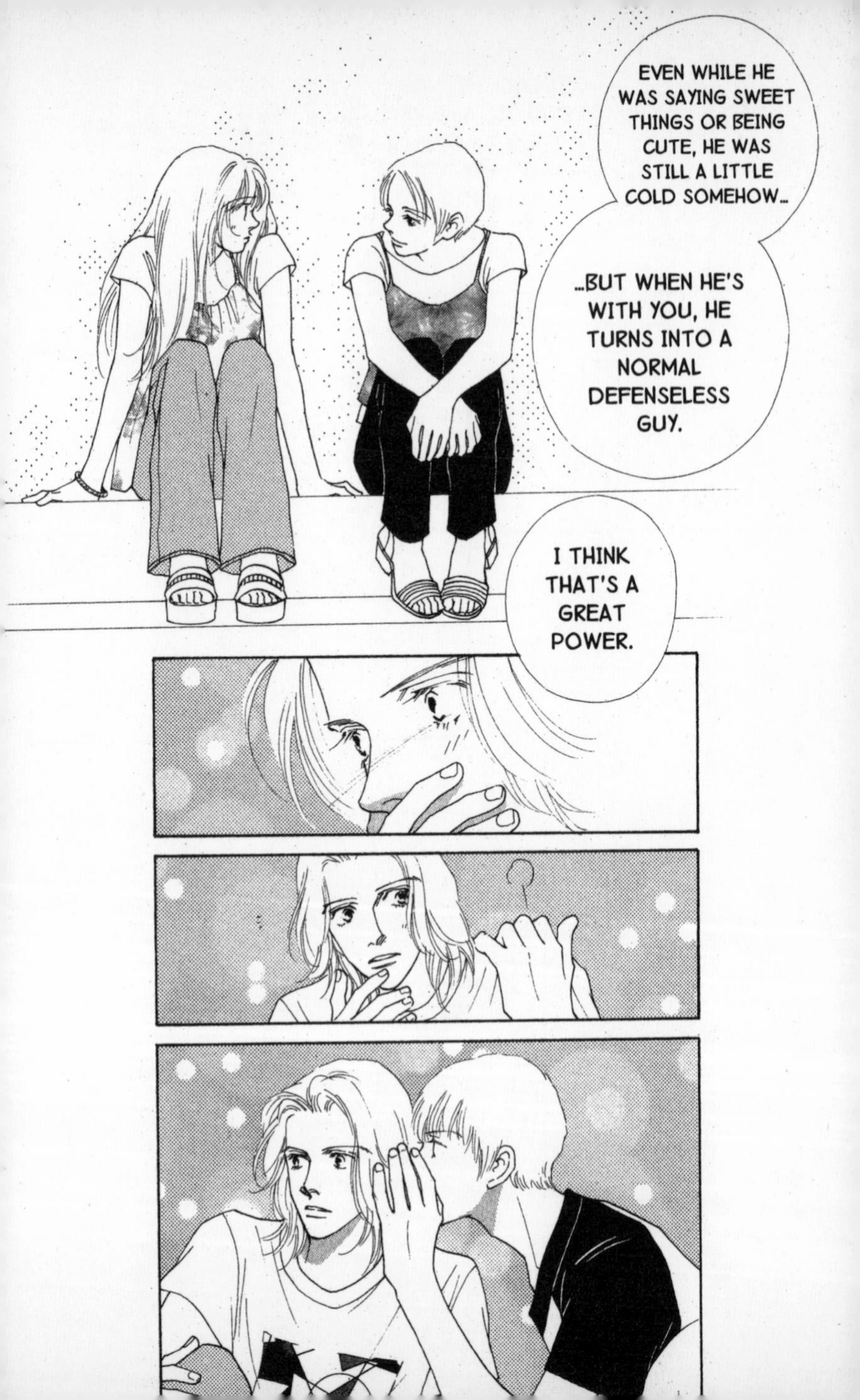
EVEN WHILE HE WAS SAYING SWEET THINGS OR BEING CUTE, HE WAS STILL A LITTLE COLD SOMEHOW...
...BUT WHEN HE'S WITH YOU, HE TURNS INTO A NORMAL DEFENSELESS GUY.
I THINK THAT'S A GREAT POWER.

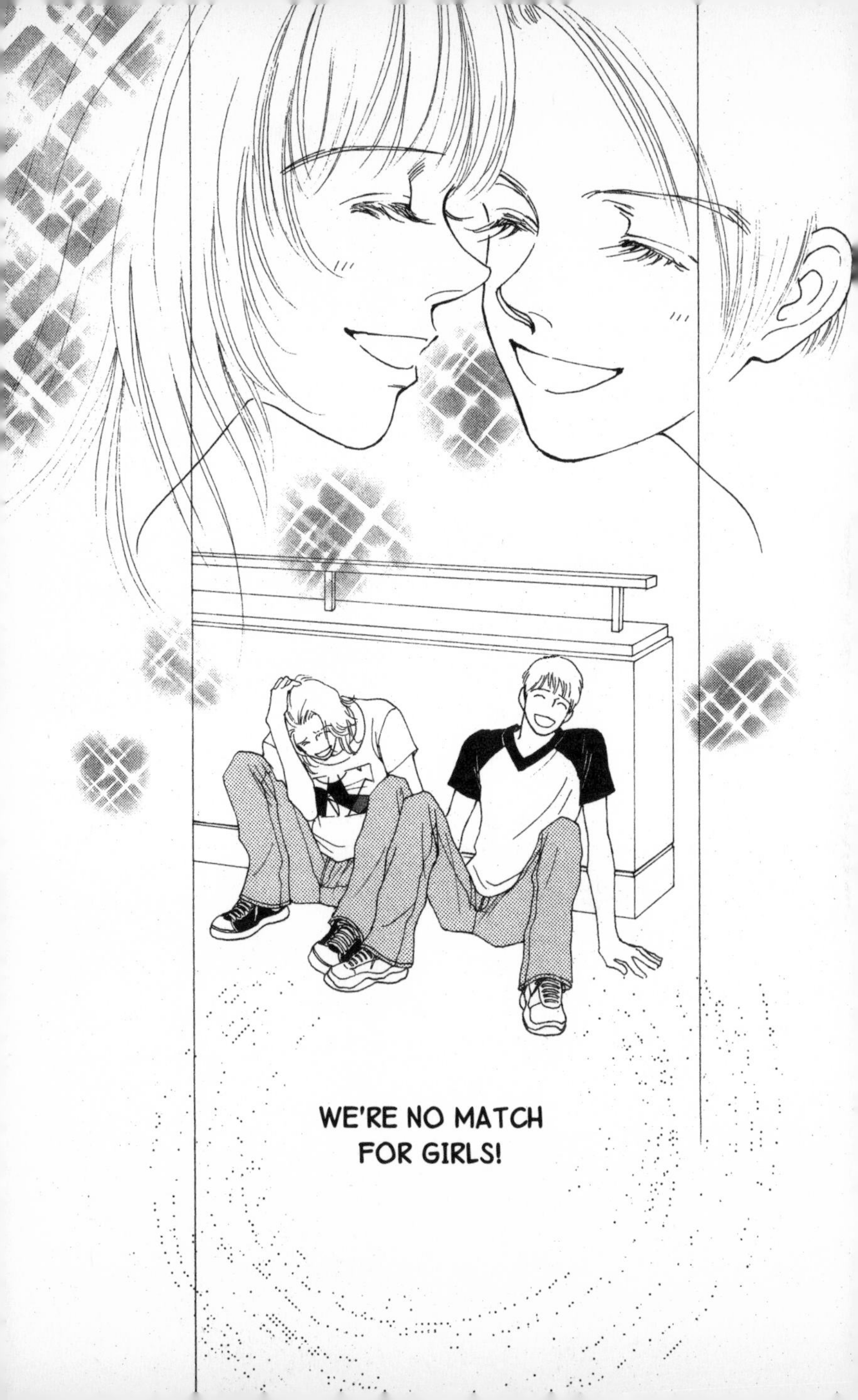
WE'RE NO MATCH
FOR GIRLS!

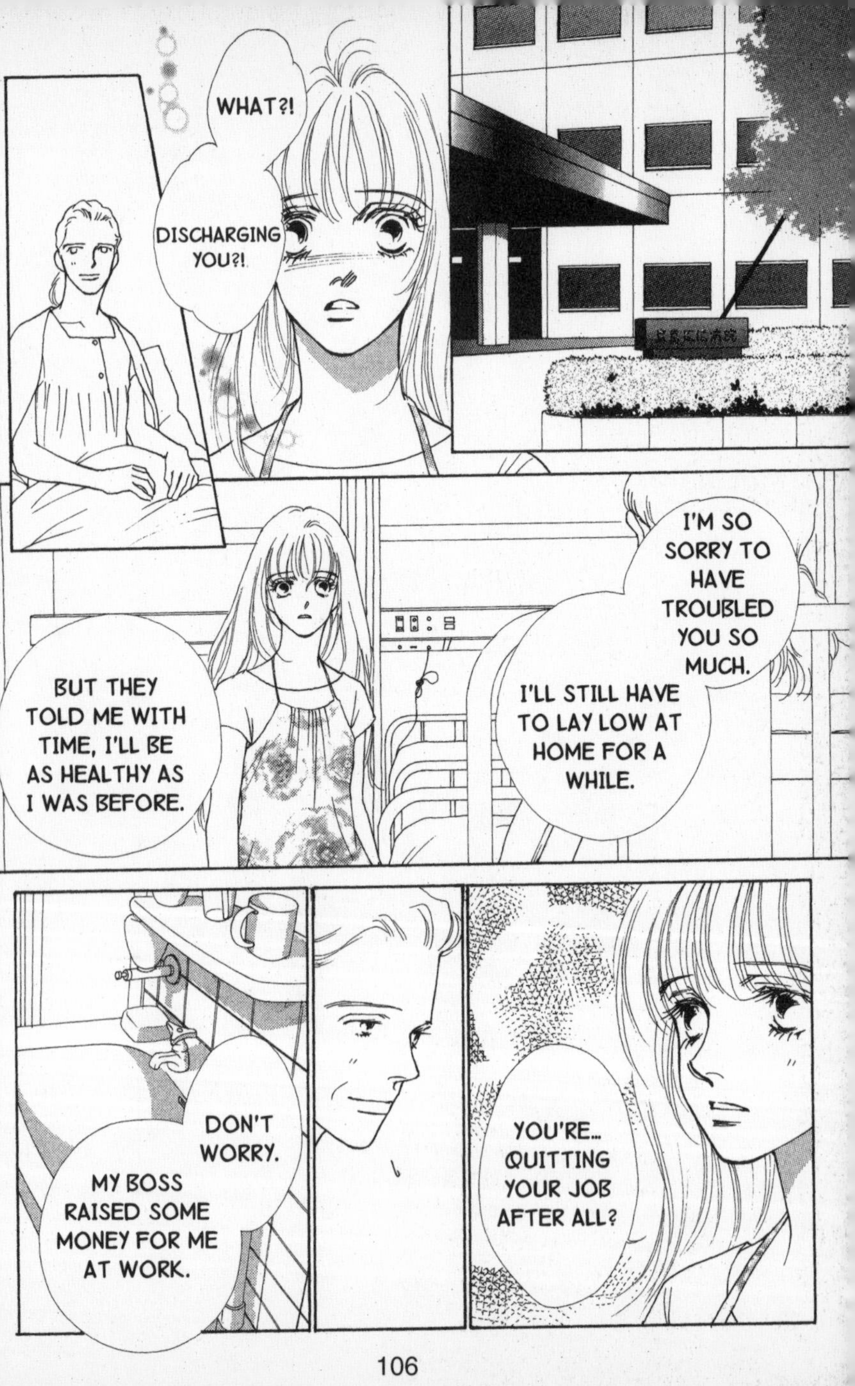
WHAT?!
DISCHARGING YOU?!
I'M SO SORRY TO HAVE TROUBLED YOU SO MUCH.
I'LL STILL HAVE TO LAY LOW AT HOME FOR A WHILE.
BUT THEY TOLD ME WITH TIME, I'LL BE AS HEALTHY AS I WAS BEFORE.
YOU'RE... QUITTING YOUR JOB AFTER ALL?
DON'T WORRY.
MY BOSS RAISED SOME MONEY FOR ME AT WORK.

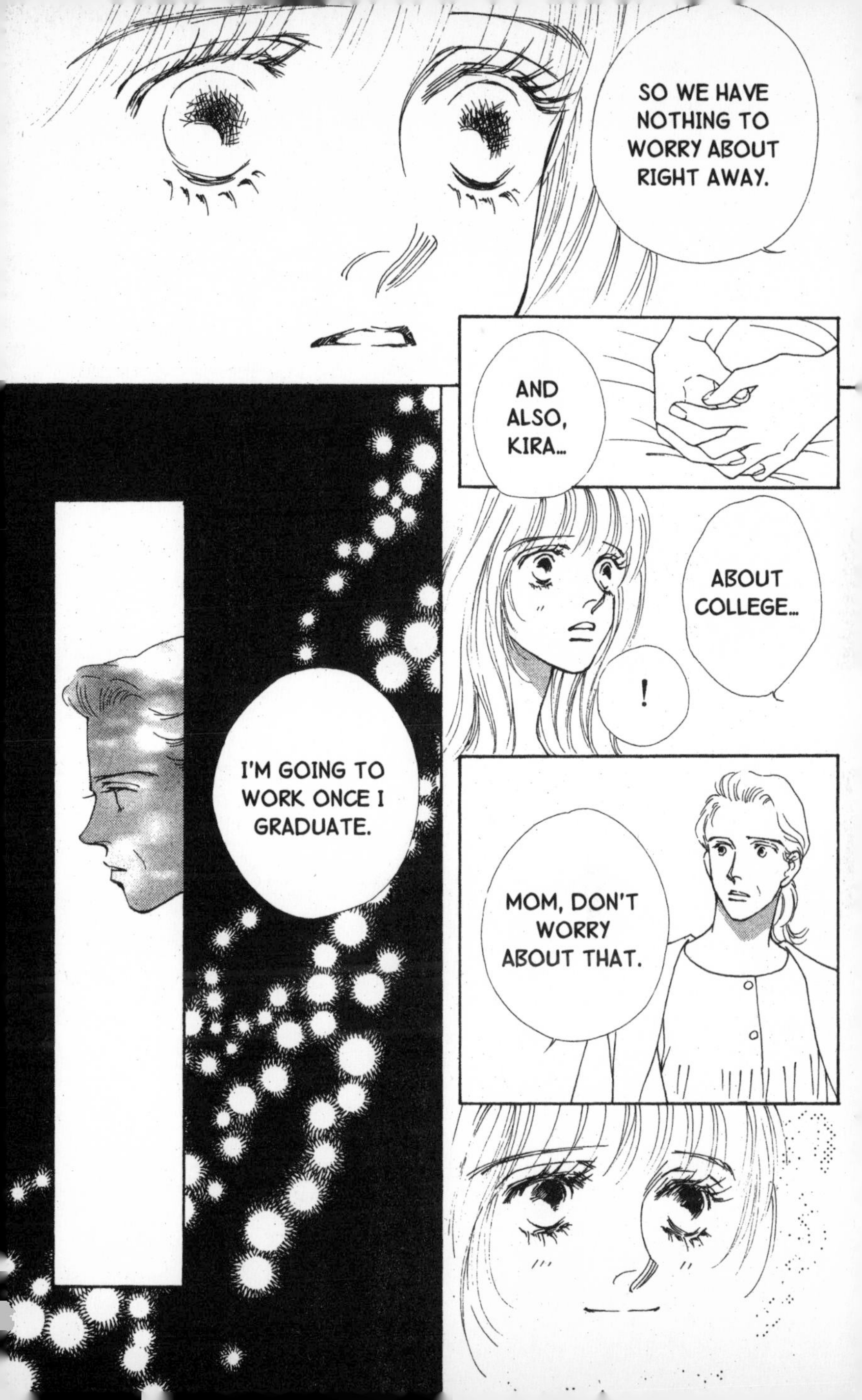

SO WE HAVE NOTHING TO WORRY ABOUT RIGHT AWAY.
AND ALSO, KIRA...
ABOUT COLLEGE...
!
MOM, DON'T WORRY ABOUT THAT.
I'M GOING TO WORK ONCE I GRADUATE.

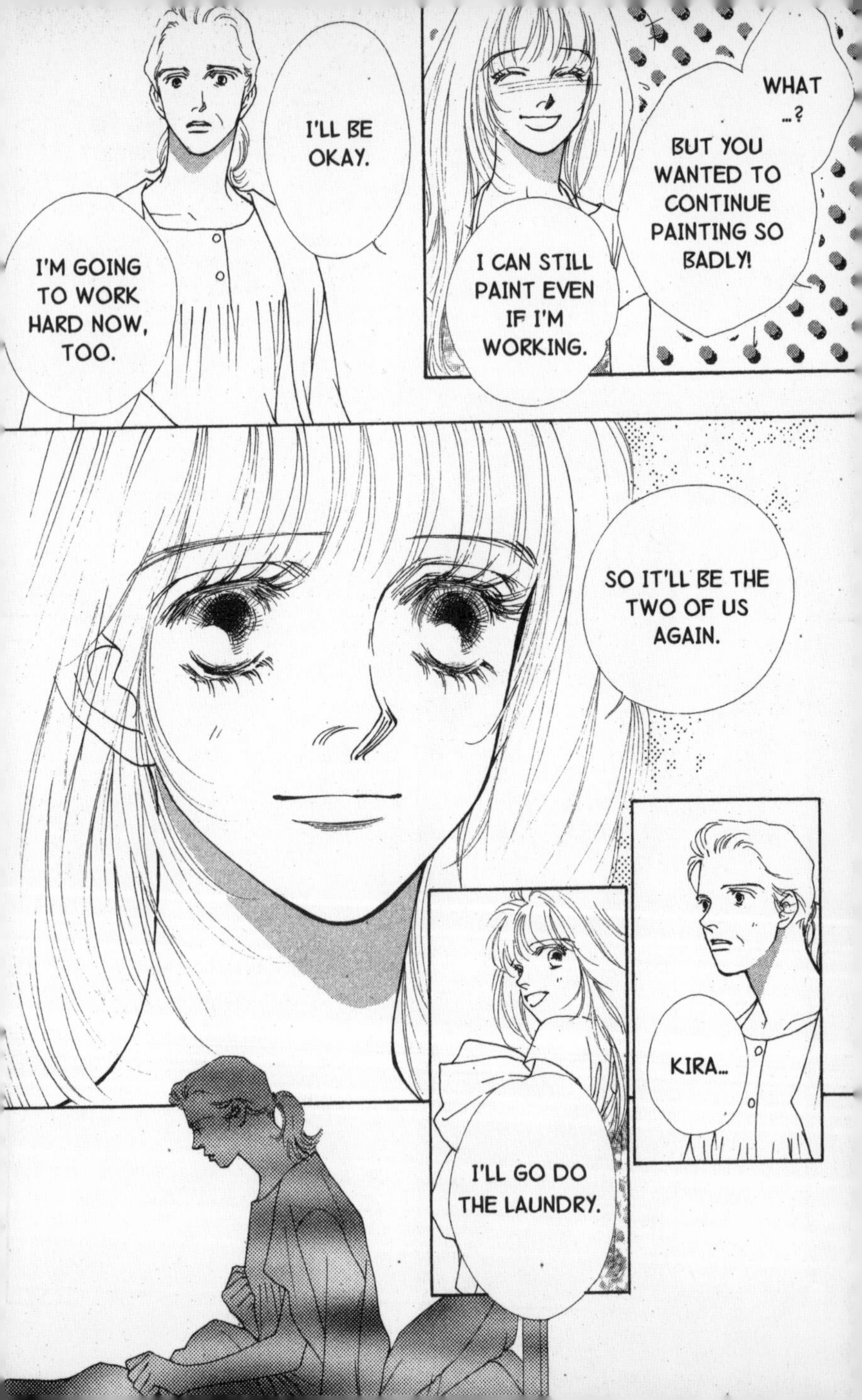
WHAT ...?
BUT YOU WANTED TO CONTINUE PAINTING SO BADLY!
I CAN STILL PAINT EVEN IF I'M WORKING.
I'LL BE OKAY.
I'M GOING TO WORK HARD NOW, TOO.
SO IT'LL BE THE TWO OF US AGAIN.
KIRA...
I'LL GO DO THE LAUNDRY.

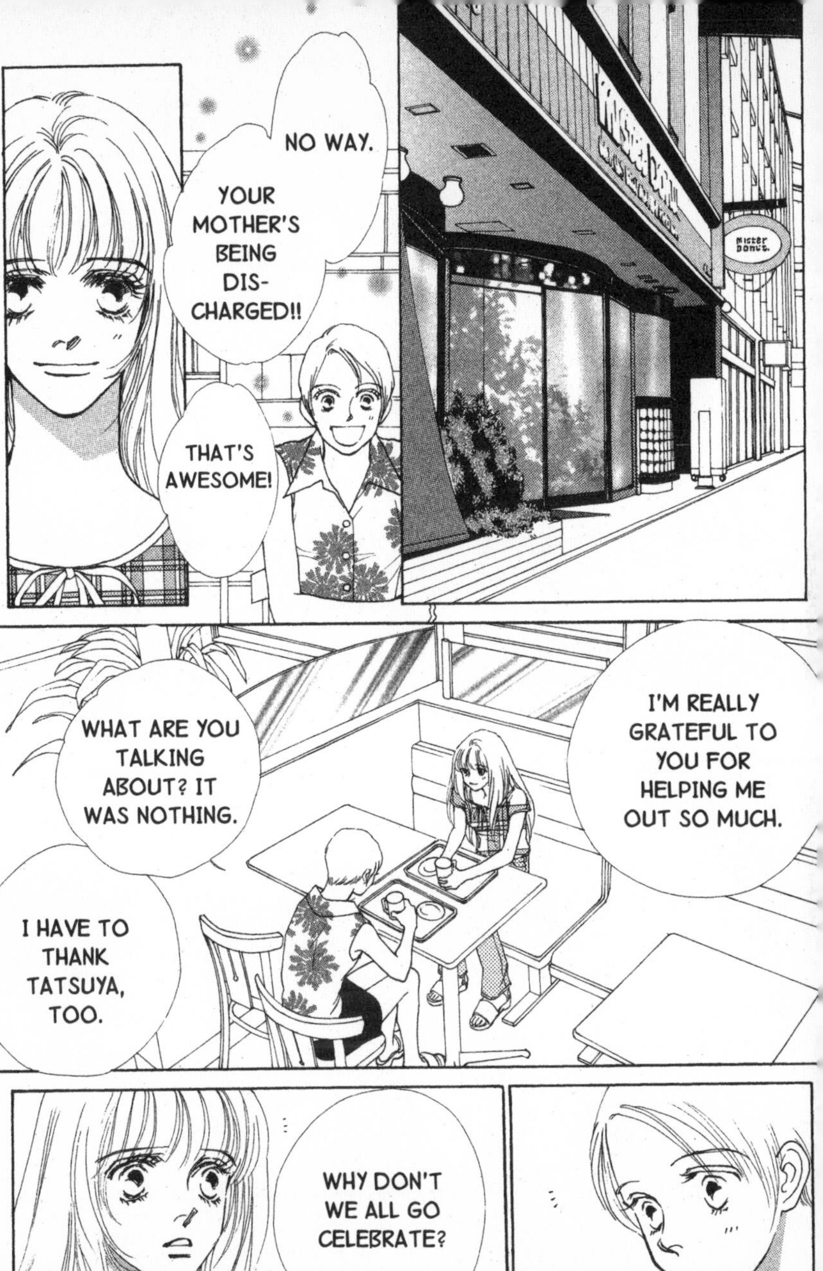
mister Donut.
NO WAY.
YOUR MOTHER'S BEING DIS-CHARGED!!
THAT'S AWESOME!
I'M REALLY GRATEFUL TO YOU FOR HELPING ME OUT SO MUCH.
WHAT ARE YOU TALKING ABOUT? IT WAS NOTHING.
I HAVE TO THANK TATSUYA, TOO.
WHY DON'T WE ALL GO CELEBRATE?

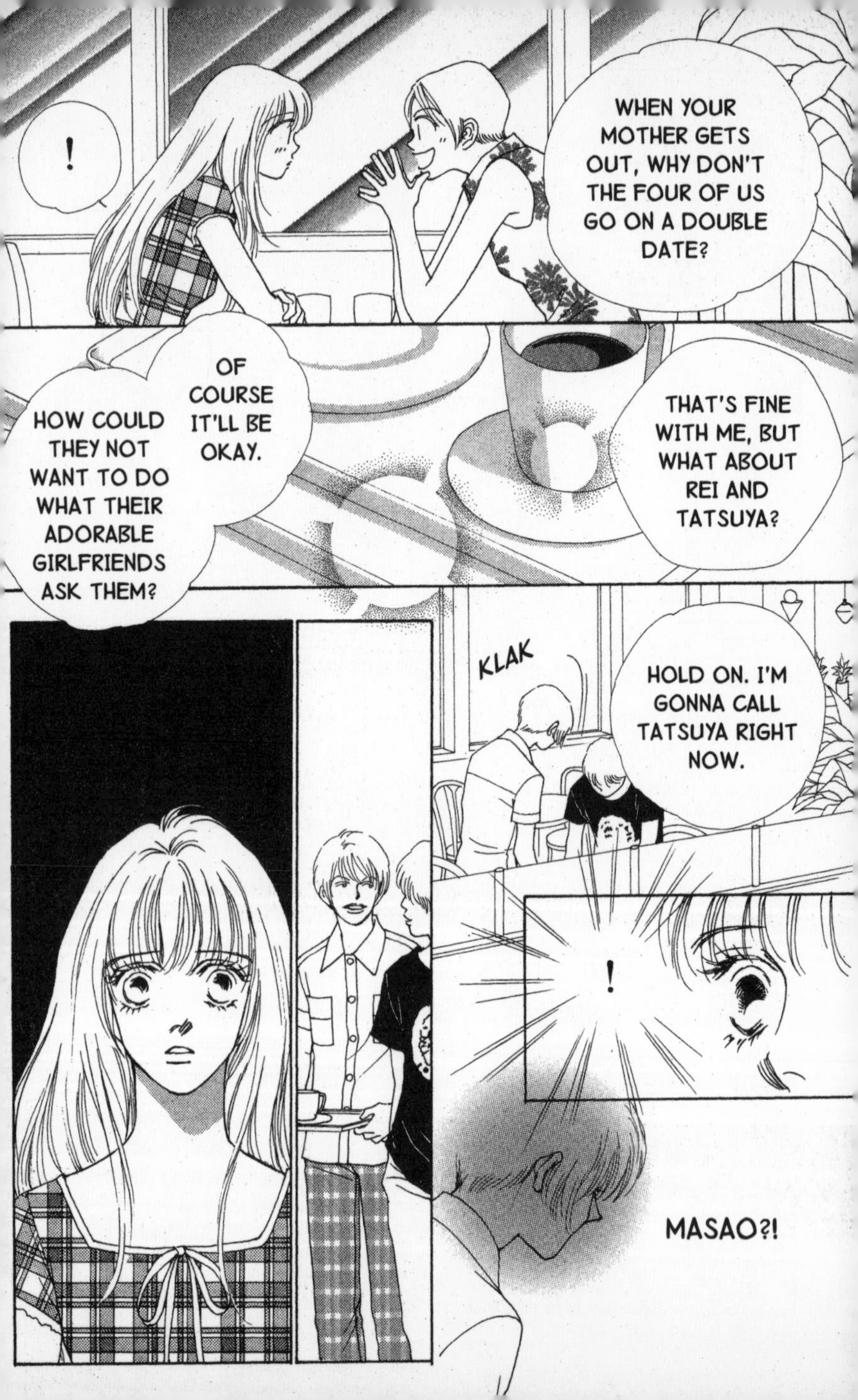
WHEN YOUR MOTHER GETS OUT, WHY DON'T THE FOUR OF US GO ON A DOUBLE DATE?
!
THAT'S FINE WITH ME, BUT WHAT ABOUT REI AND TATSUYA?
OF COURSE IT'LL BE OKAY.
HOW COULD THEY NOT WANT TO DO WHAT THEIR ADORABLE GIRLFRIENDS ASK THEM?
HOLD ON. I'M GONNA CALL TATSUYA RIGHT NOW.
KLAK
!
MASAO?!

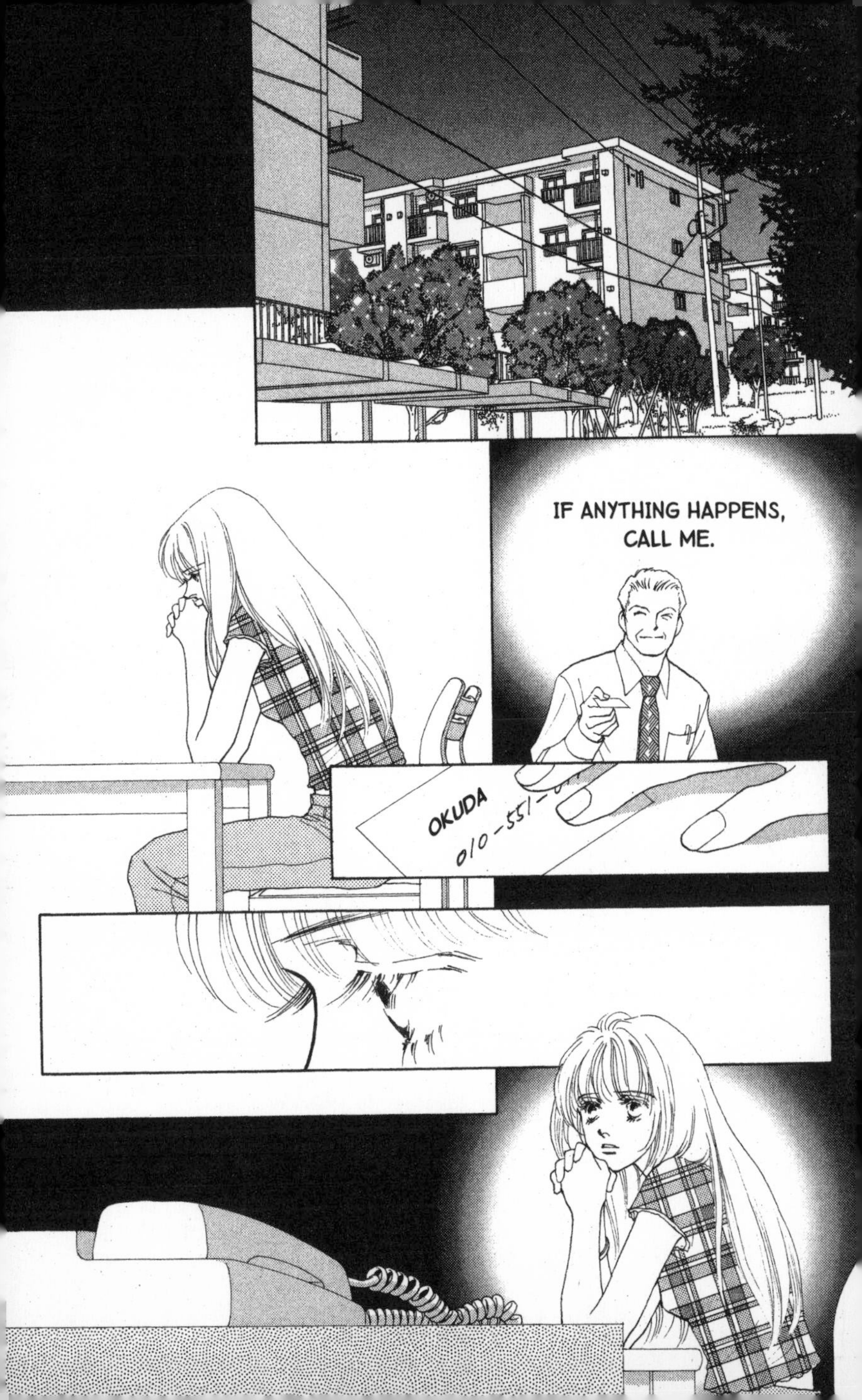
IF ANYTHING HAPPENS, CALL ME.
OKUDA
010-551-0

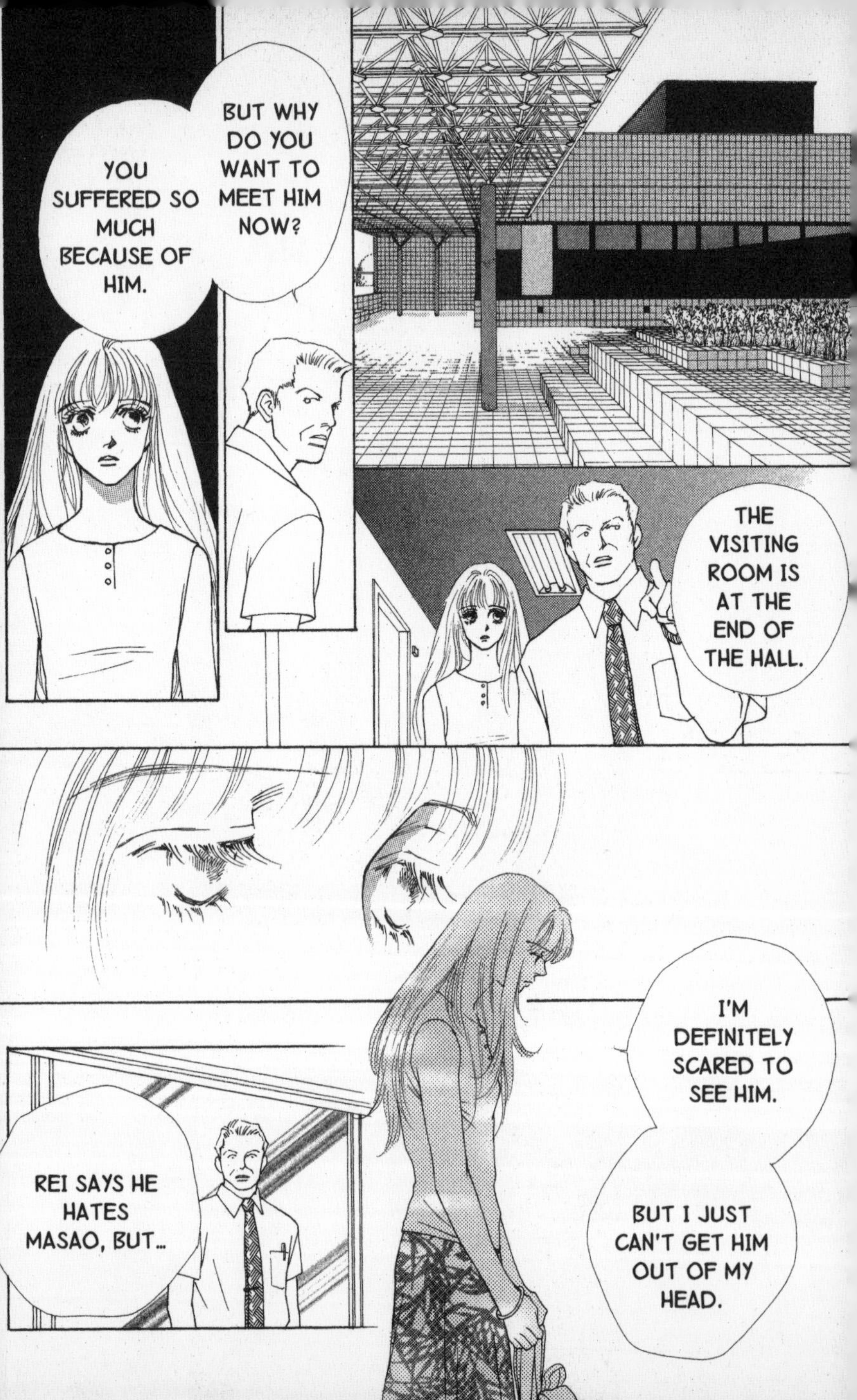
THE VISITING ROOM IS AT THE END OF THE HALL.
BUT WHY DO YOU WANT TO MEET HIM NOW?
YOU SUFFERED SO MUCH BECAUSE OF HIM.
I'M DEFINITELY SCARED TO SEE HIM.
BUT I JUST CAN'T GET HIM OUT OF MY HEAD.
REI SAYS HE HATES MASAO, BUT...

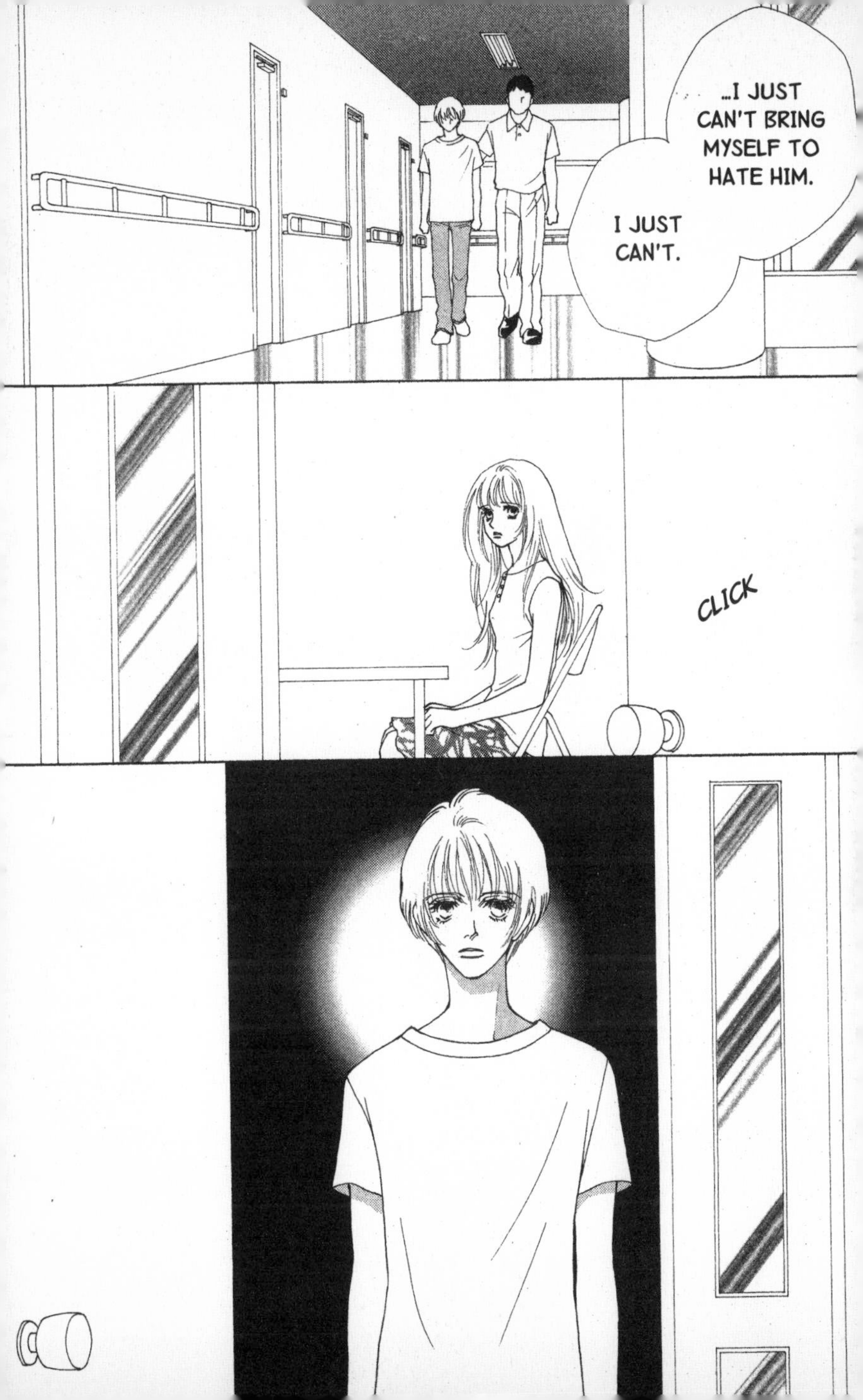
...I JUST CAN'T BRING MYSELF TO HATE HIM.
I JUST CAN'T.
CLICK

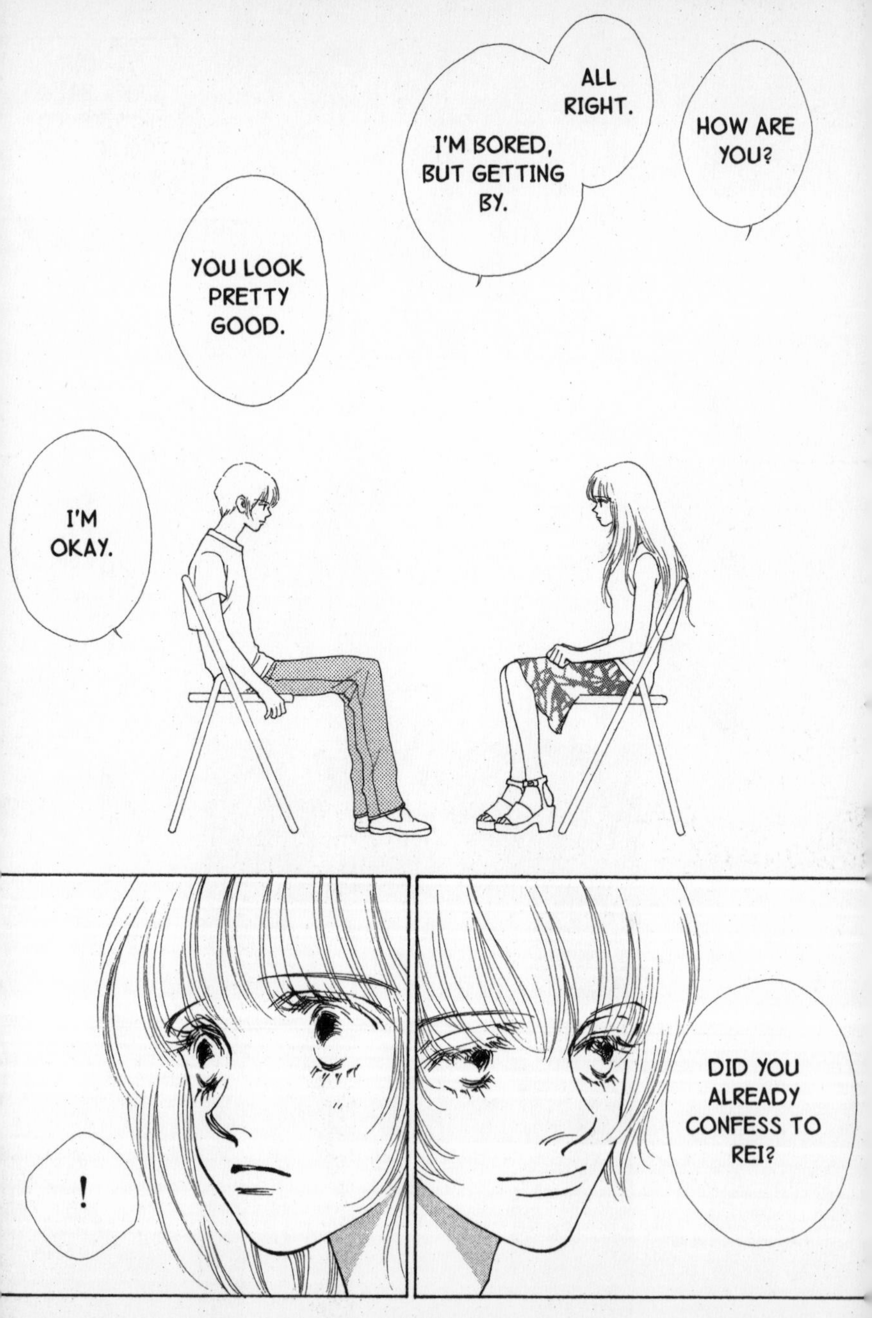
HOW ARE YOU?
ALL RIGHT.
I'M BORED, BUT GETTING BY.
YOU LOOK PRETTY GOOD.
I'M OKAY.
DID YOU ALREADY CONFESS TO REI?
!

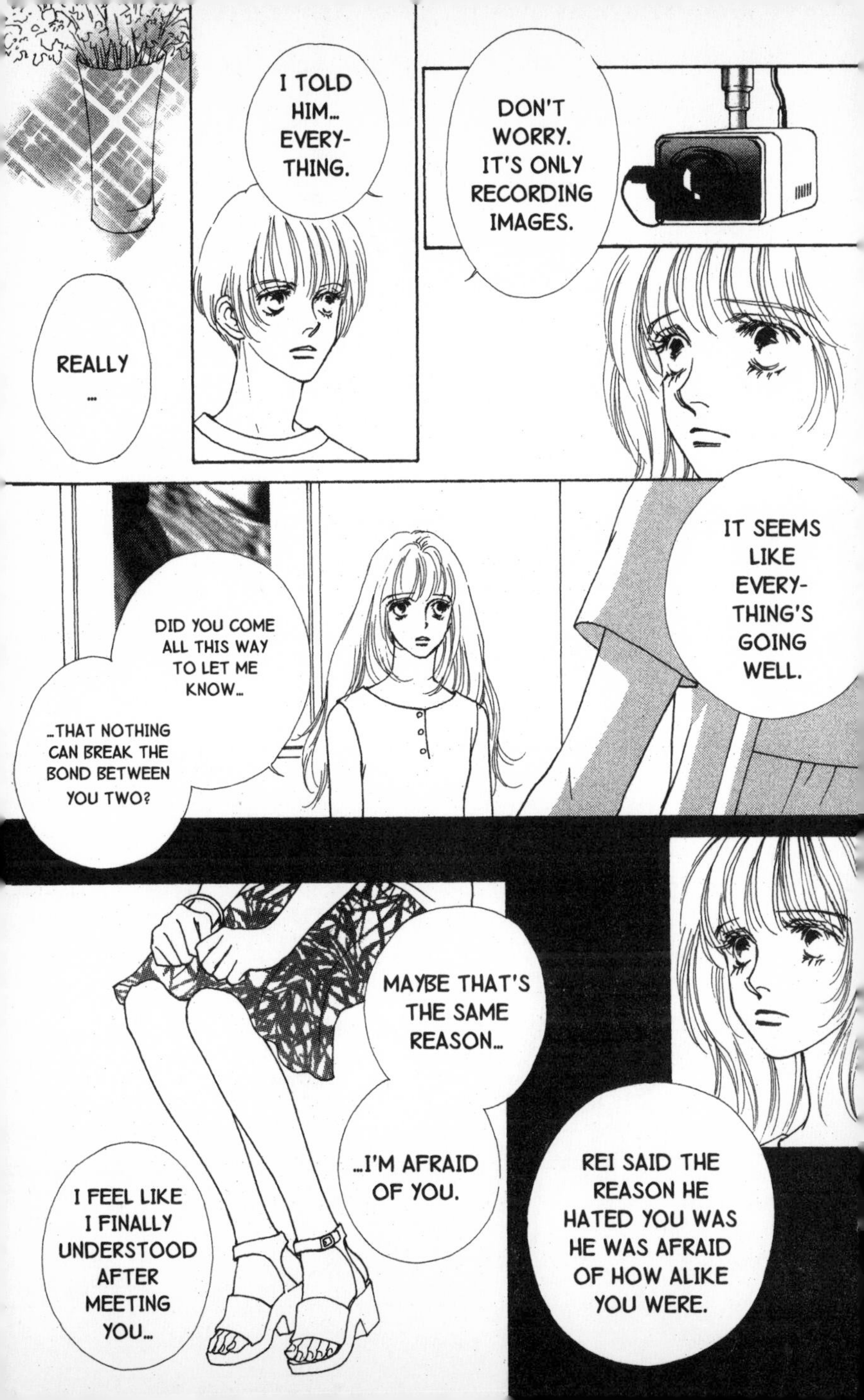
DON'T WORRY. IT'S ONLY RECORDING IMAGES.
I TOLD HIM... EVERY-THING.
REALLY ...
IT SEEMS LIKE EVERY-THING'S GOING WELL.
DID YOU COME ALL THIS WAY TO LET ME KNOW...
...THAT NOTHING CAN BREAK THE BOND BETWEEN YOU TWO?
REI SAID THE REASON HE HATED YOU WAS HE WAS AFRAID OF HOW ALIKE YOU WERE.
MAYBE THAT'S THE SAME REASON...
...I'M AFRAID OF YOU.
I FEEL LIKE I FINALLY UNDERSTOOD AFTER MEETING YOU...

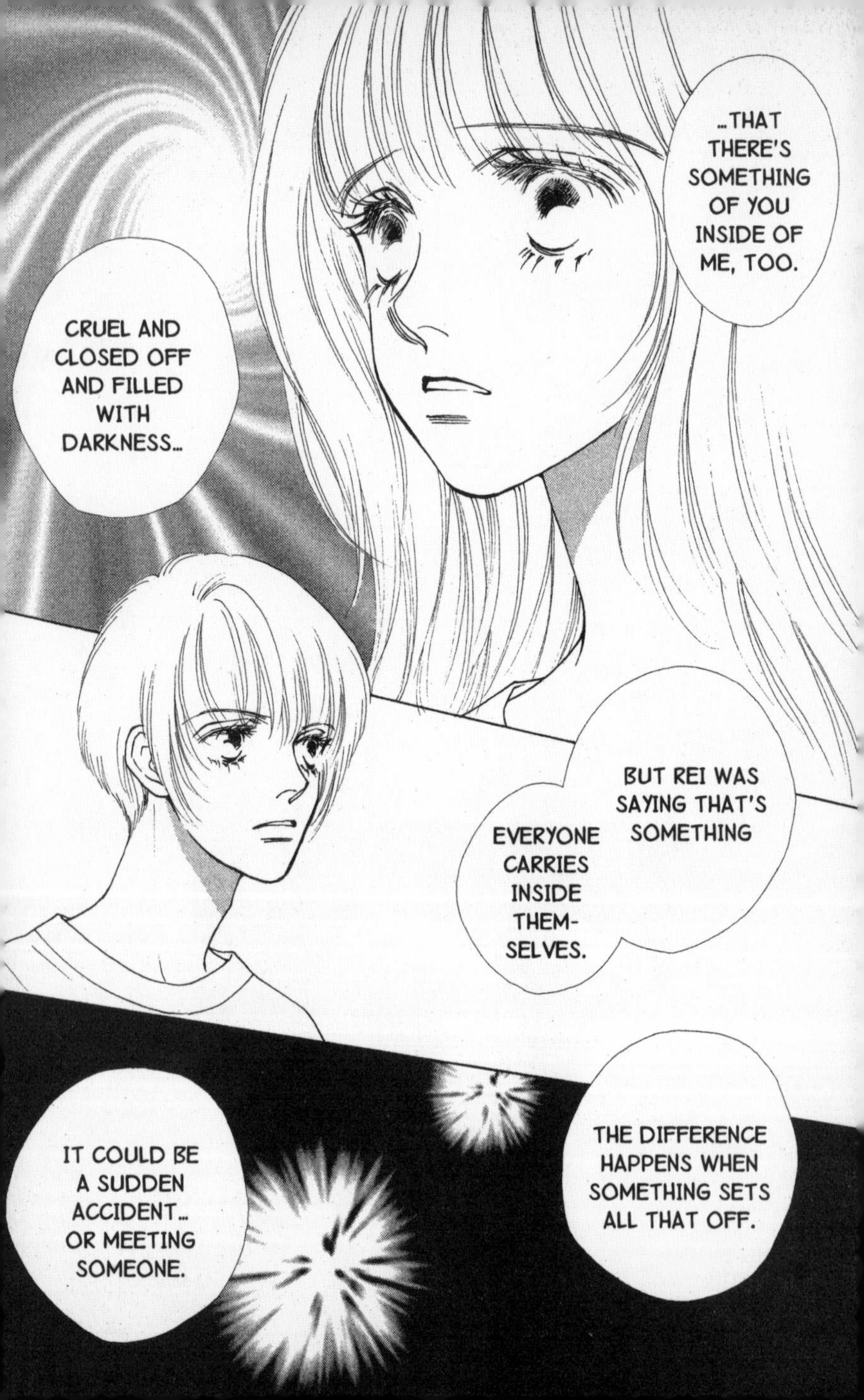
...THAT THERE'S SOMETHING OF YOU INSIDE OF ME, TOO.
CRUEL AND CLOSED OFF AND FILLED WITH DARKNESS...
BUT REI WAS SAYING THAT'S SOMETHING
EVERYONE CARRIES INSIDE THEM-SELVES.
THE DIFFERENCE HAPPENS WHEN SOMETHING SETS ALL THAT OFF.
IT COULD BE A SUDDEN ACCIDENT... OR MEETING SOMEONE.

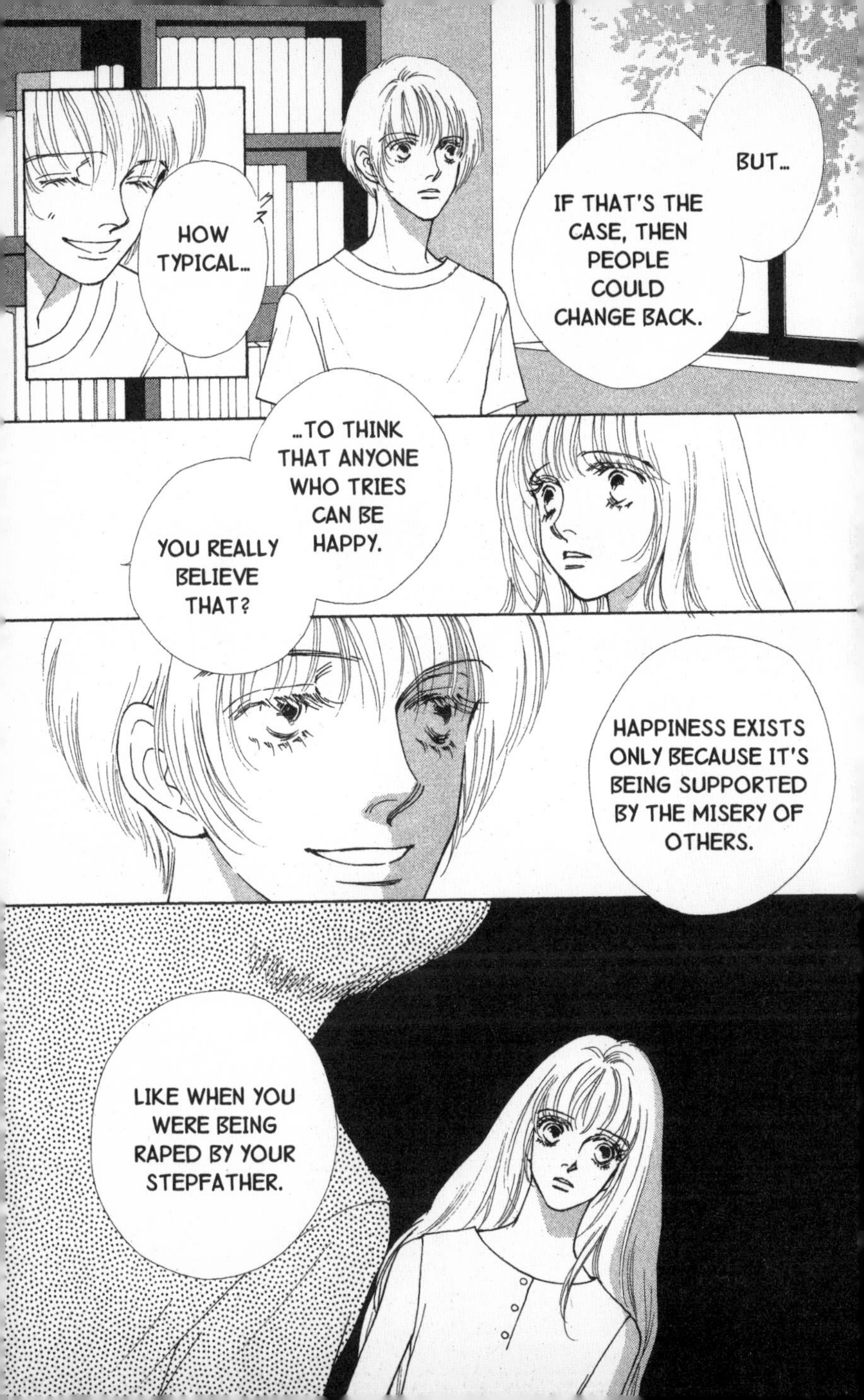
BUT...
IF THAT'S THE CASE, THEN PEOPLE COULD CHANGE BACK.
HOW TYPICAL...
...TO THINK THAT ANYONE WHO TRIES CAN BE HAPPY.
YOU REALLY BELIEVE THAT?
HAPPINESS EXISTS ONLY BECAUSE IT'S BEING SUPPORTED BY THE MISERY OF OTHERS.
LIKE WHEN YOU WERE BEING RAPED BY YOUR STEPFATHER.

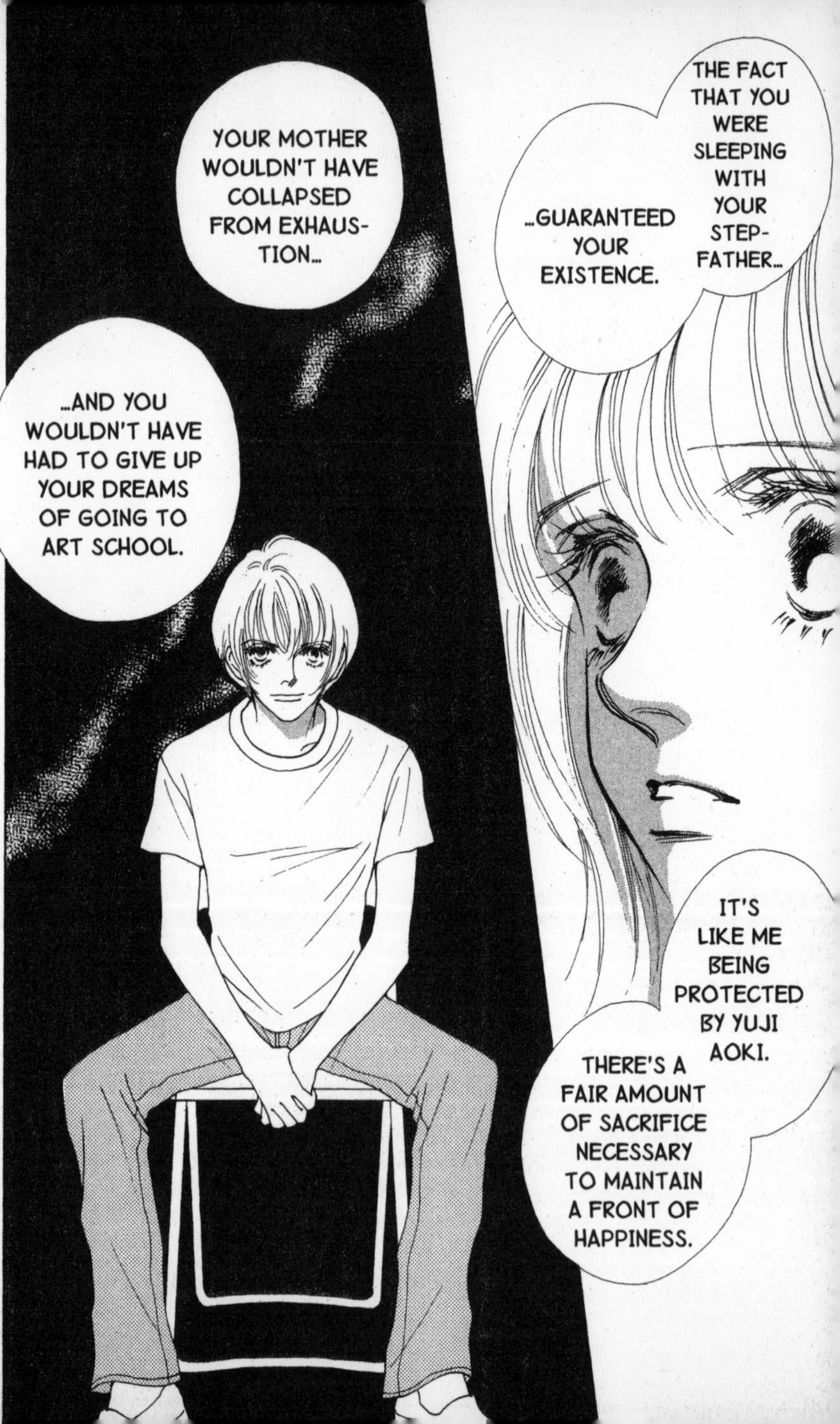
THE FACT THAT YOU WERE SLEEPING WITH YOUR STEP-FATHER...
...GUARANTEED YOUR EXISTENCE.
IT'S LIKE ME BEING PROTECTED BY YUJI AOKI.
THERE'S A FAIR AMOUNT OF SACRIFICE NECESSARY TO MAINTAIN A FRONT OF HAPPINESS.
YOUR MOTHER WOULDN'T HAVE COLLAPSED FROM EXHAUS-TION...
...AND YOU WOULDN'T HAVE HAD TO GIVE UP YOUR DREAMS OF GOING TO ART SCHOOL.

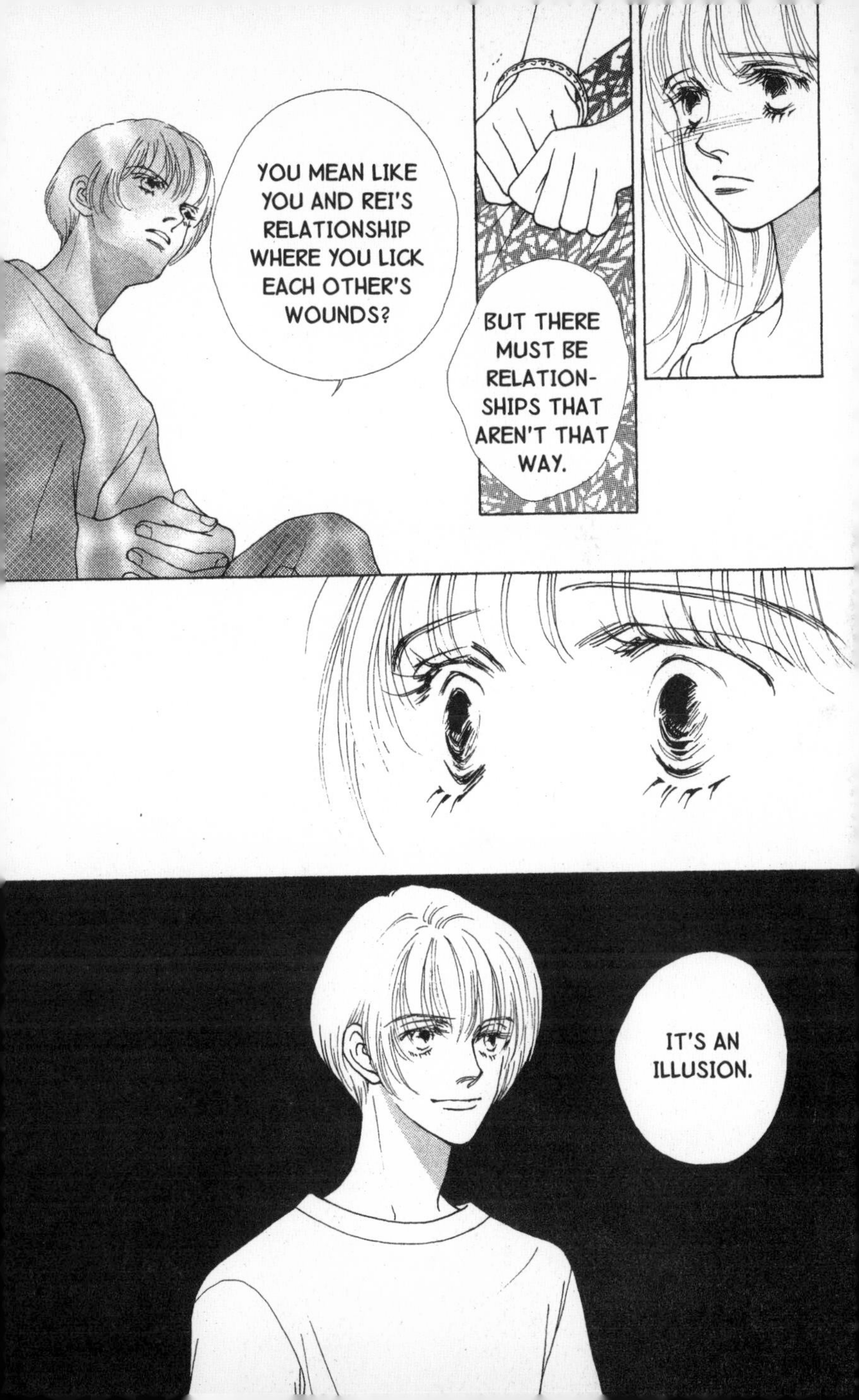
BUT THERE MUST BE RELATIONSHIPS THAT AREN'T THAT WAY.
YOU MEAN LIKE YOU AND REI'S RELATIONSHIP WHERE YOU LICK EACH OTHER'S WOUNDS?
IT'S AN ILLUSION.

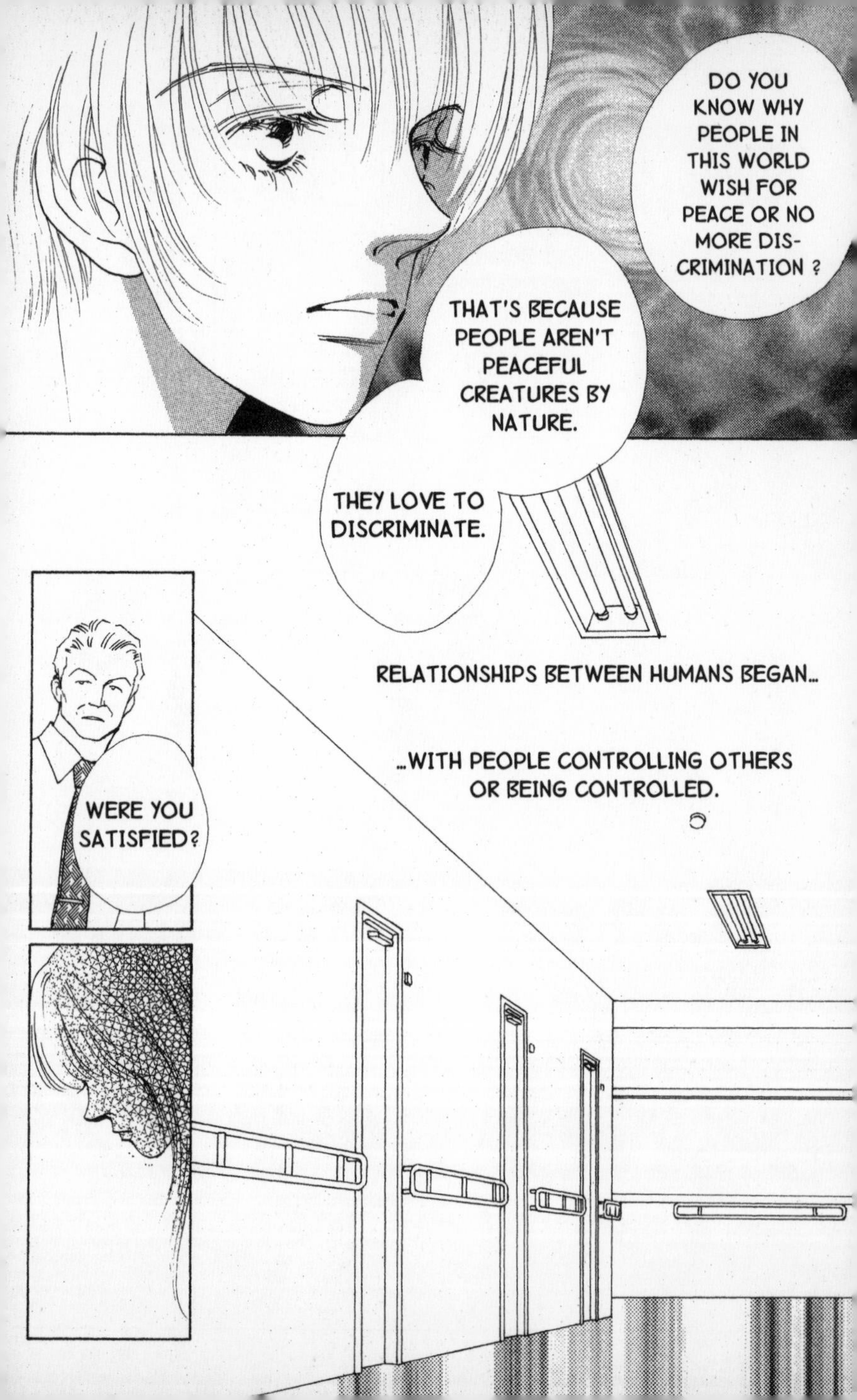
DO YOU KNOW WHY PEOPLE IN THIS WORLD WISH FOR PEACE OR NO MORE DIS-CRIMINATION ?
THAT'S BECAUSE PEOPLE AREN'T PEACEFUL CREATURES BY NATURE.
THEY LOVE TO DISCRIMINATE.
RELATIONSHIPS BETWEEN HUMANS BEGAN...
...WITH PEOPLE CONTROLLING OTHERS OR BEING CONTROLLED.
WERE YOU SATISFIED?

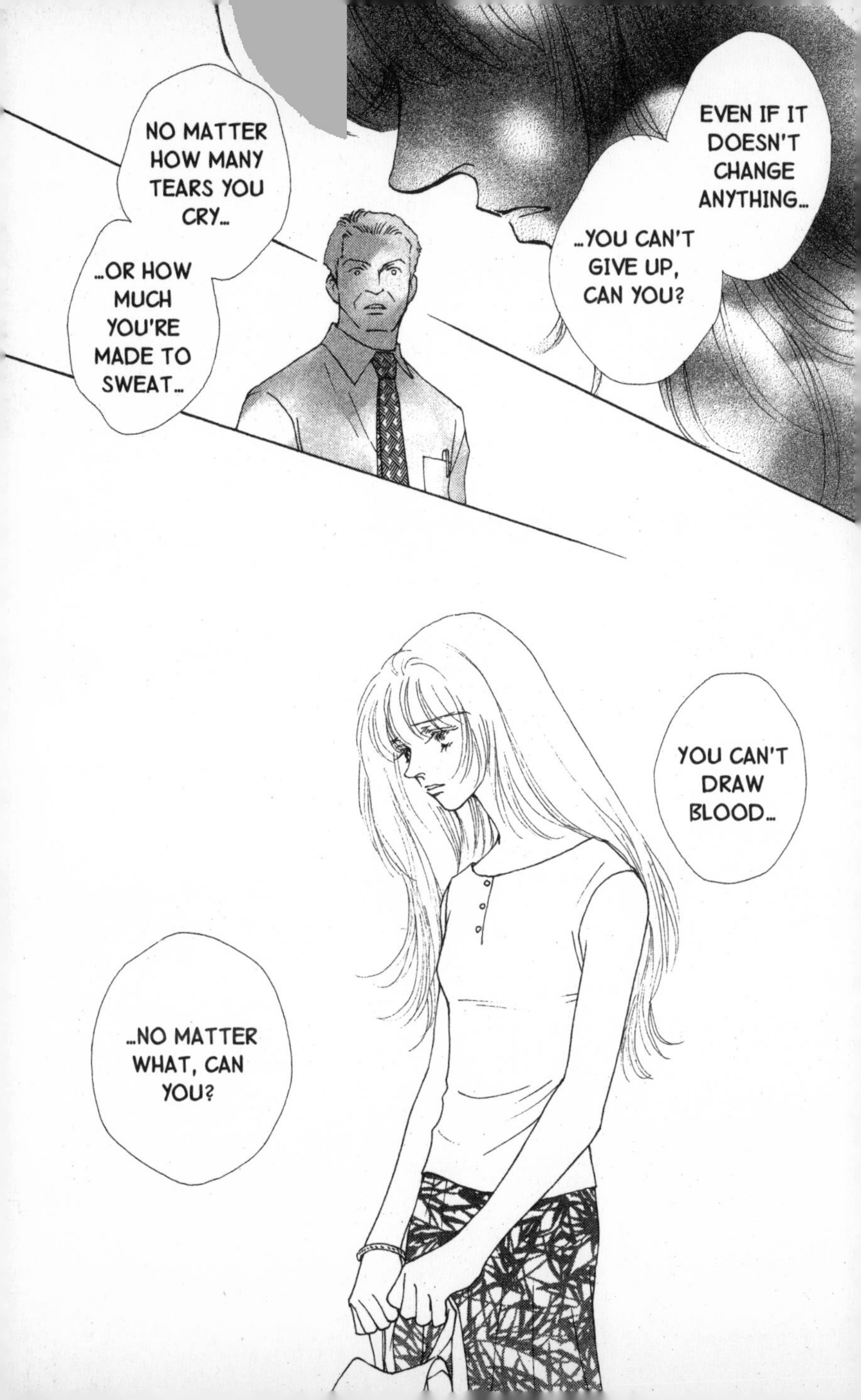
EVEN IF IT DOESN'T CHANGE ANYTHING...
...YOU CAN'T GIVE UP, CAN YOU?
NO MATTER HOW MANY TEARS YOU CRY...
...OR HOW MUCH YOU'RE MADE TO SWEAT...
YOU CAN'T DRAW BLOOD...
...NO MATTER WHAT, CAN YOU?

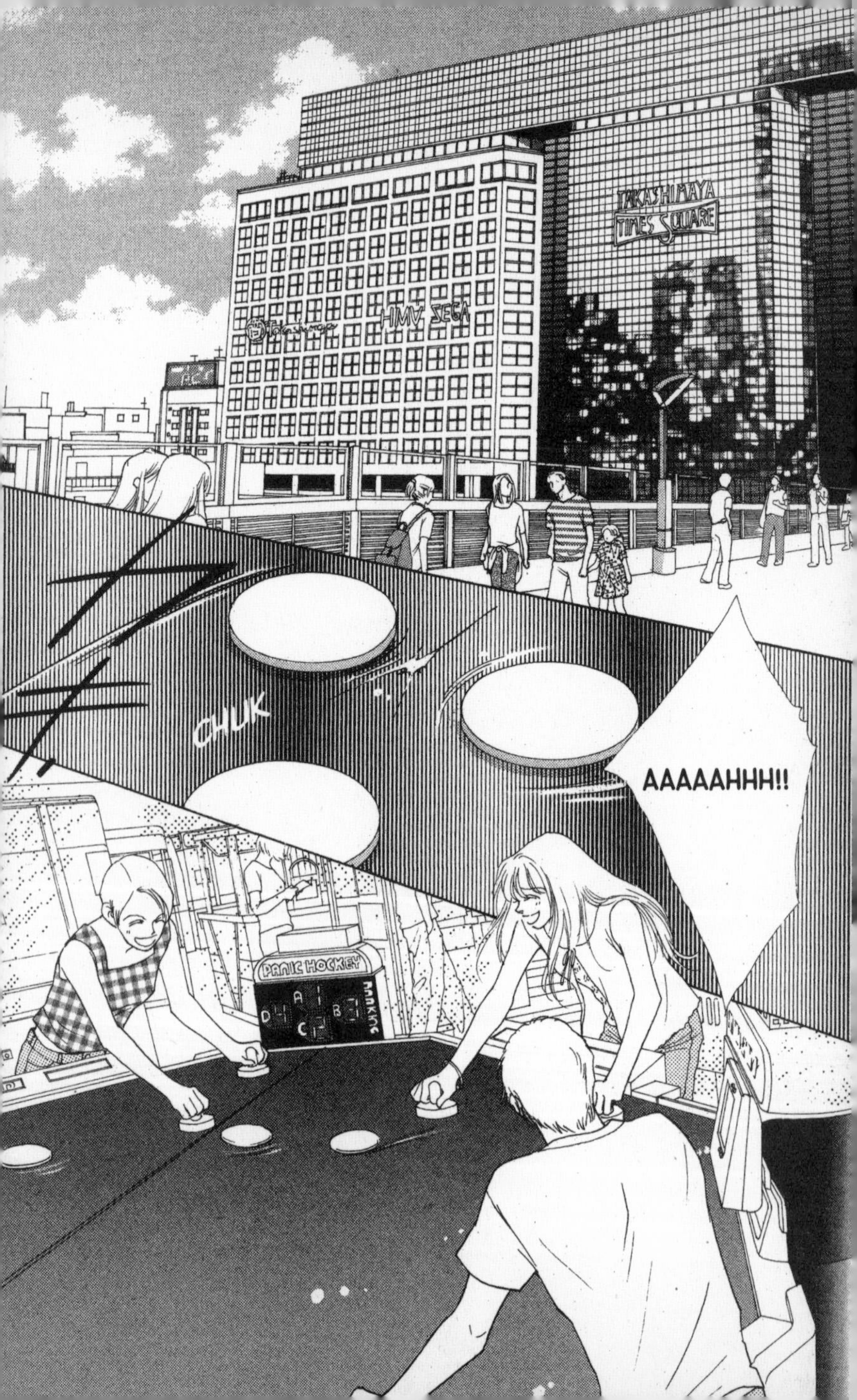
TAKASHIMAYA
TIMES SQUARE
HMV SEGA
AAAAAHHH!!
CHUK
PANIC HOCKEY

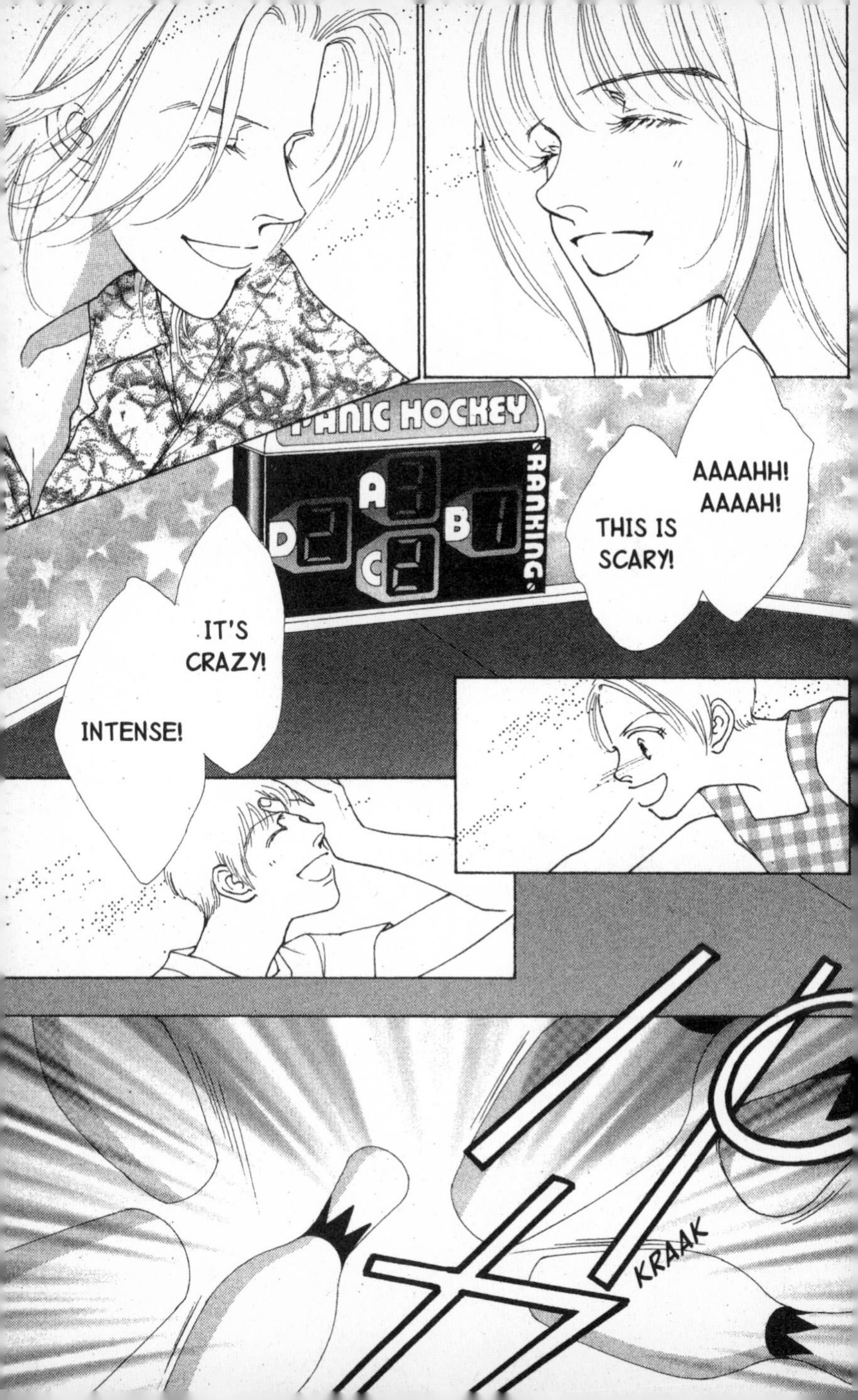
PANIC HOCKEY
RANKING
A
B
C
D
AAAAHH! AAAAH! THIS IS SCARY!
IT'S CRAZY! INTENSE!
KRAAK

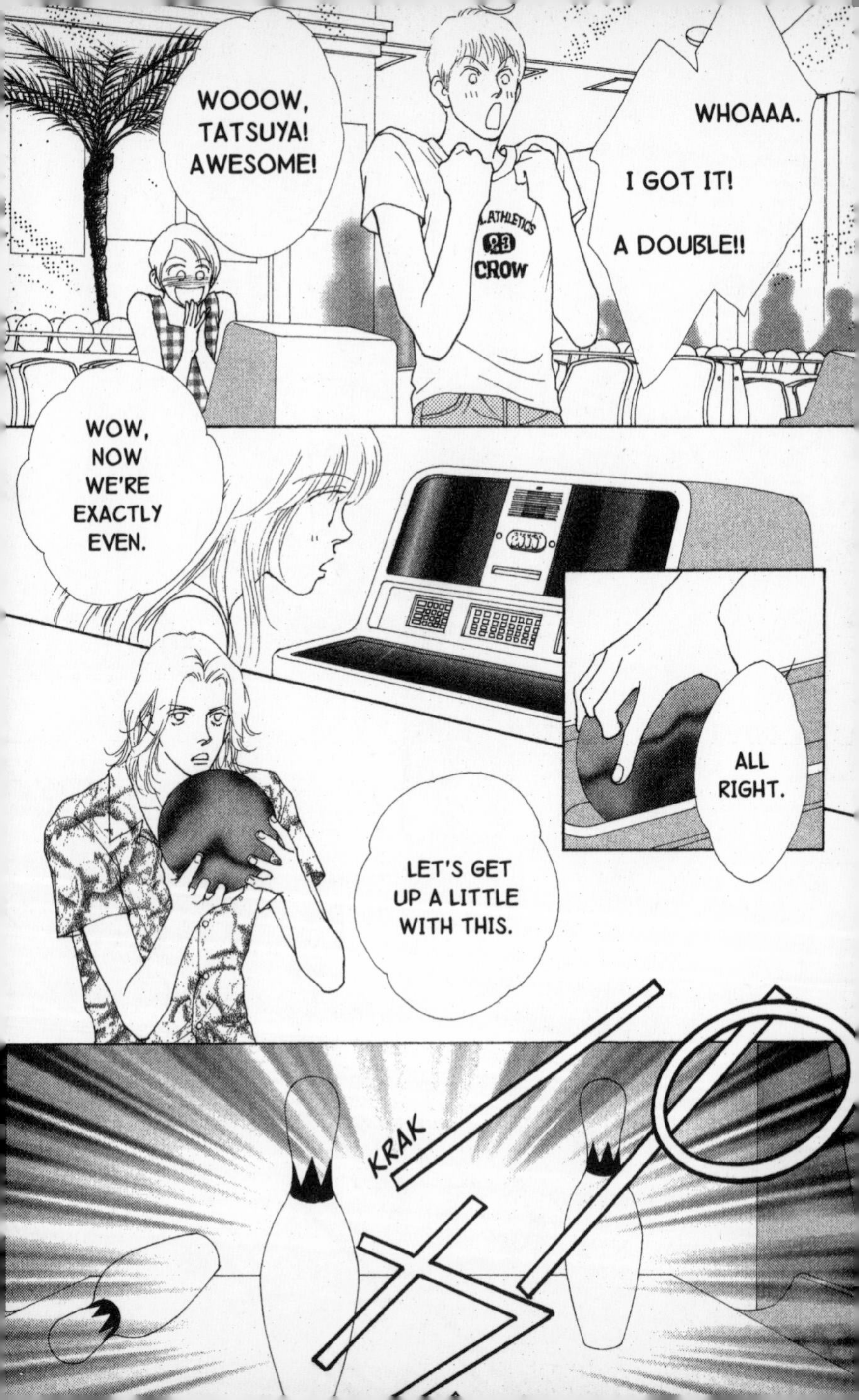
WHOAAA.
I GOT IT!
A DOUBLE!!
WOOOW, TATSUYA! AWESOME!
WOW, NOW WE'RE EXACTLY EVEN.
ALL RIGHT.
LET'S GET UP A LITTLE WITH THIS.
KRAK

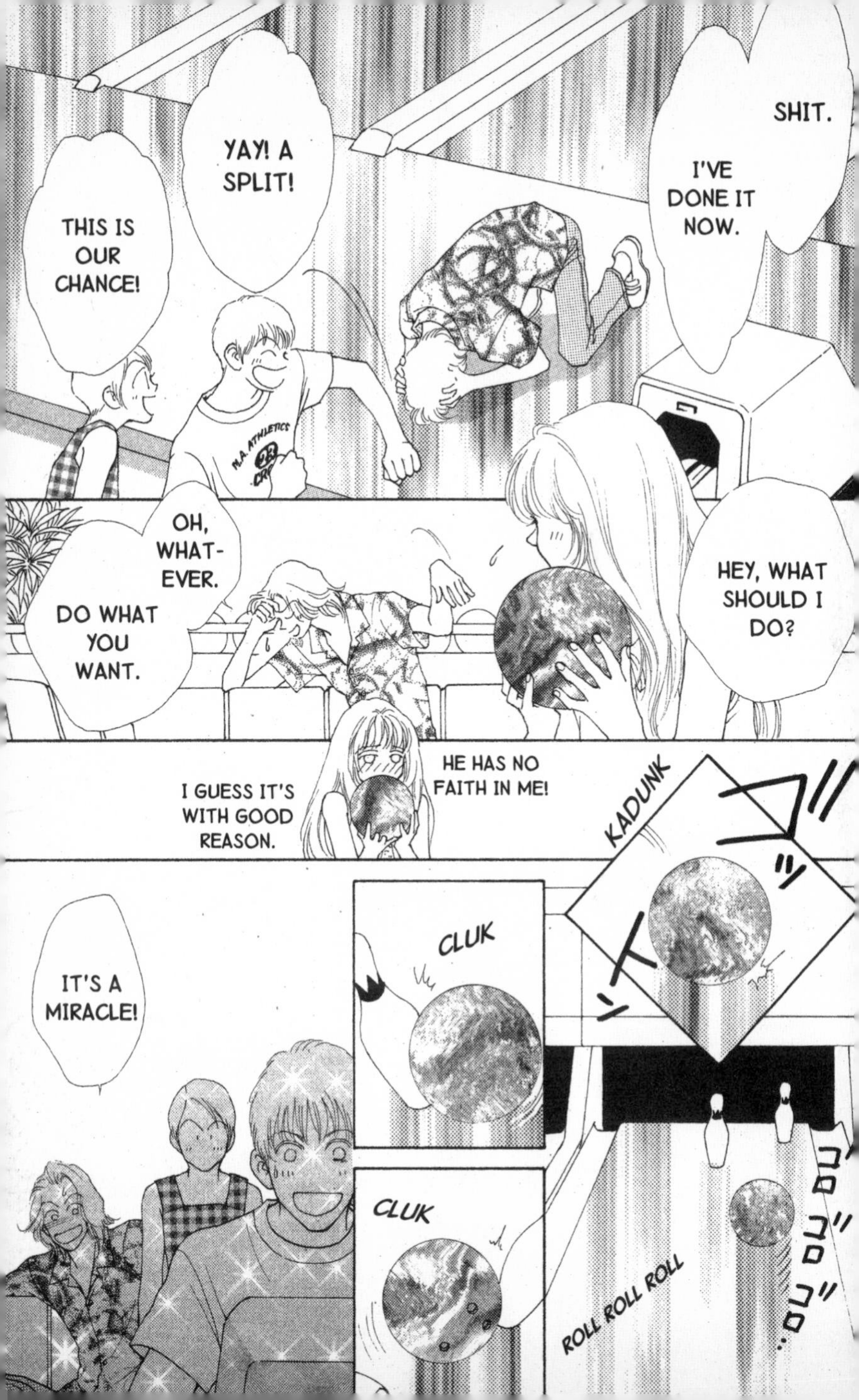
SHIT.
I'VE DONE IT NOW.
YAY! A SPLIT!
THIS IS OUR CHANCE!
HEY, WHAT SHOULD I DO?
OH, WHAT-EVER.
DO WHAT YOU WANT.
HE HAS NO FAITH IN ME!
I GUESS IT'S WITH GOOD REASON.
KADUNK
CLUK
CLUK
ROLL ROLL ROLL
IT'S A MIRACLE!

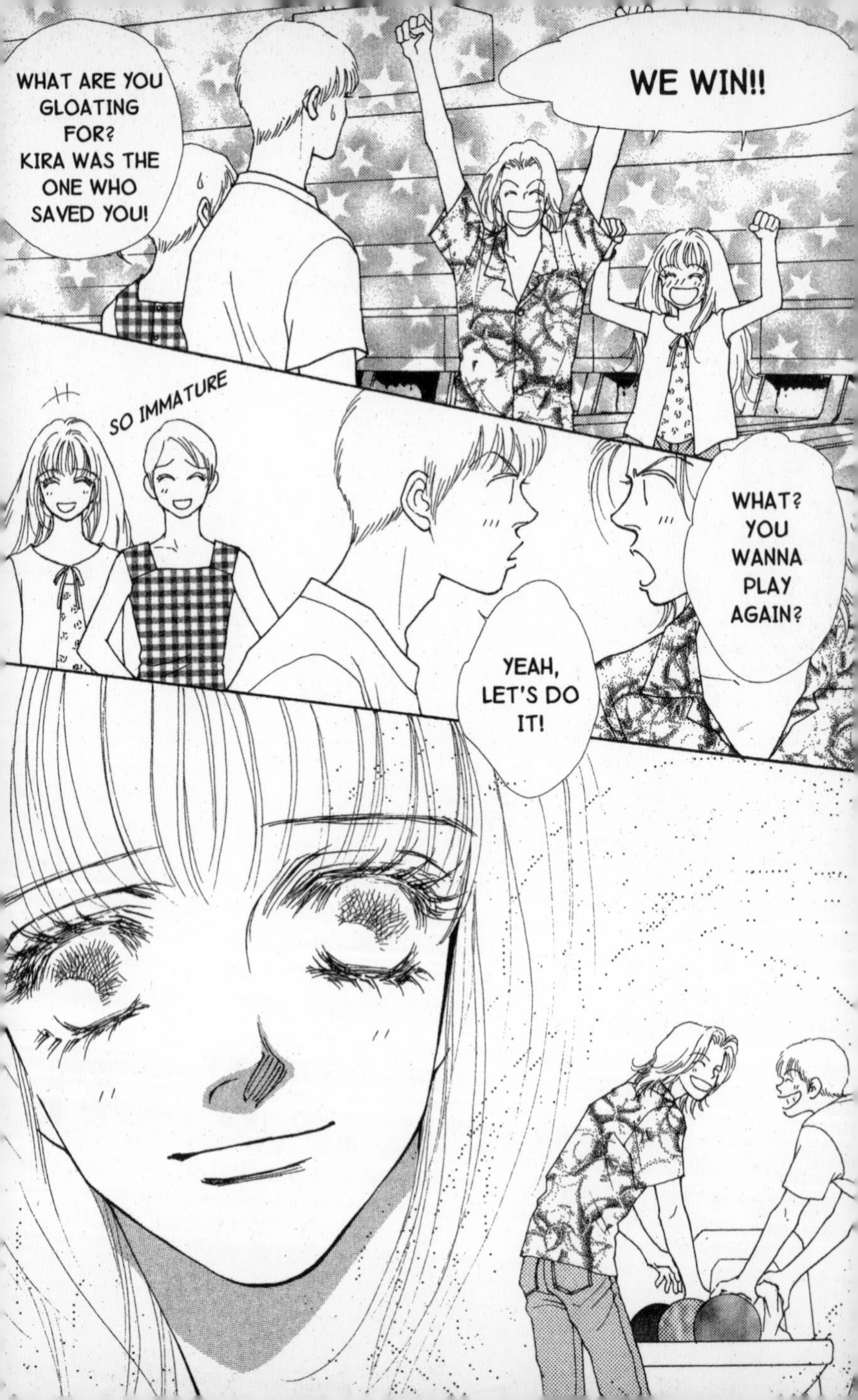
WE WIN!!
WHAT ARE YOU GLOATING FOR? KIRA WAS THE ONE WHO SAVED YOU!
WHAT? YOU WANNA PLAY AGAIN?
YEAH, LET'S DO IT!
SO IMMATURE

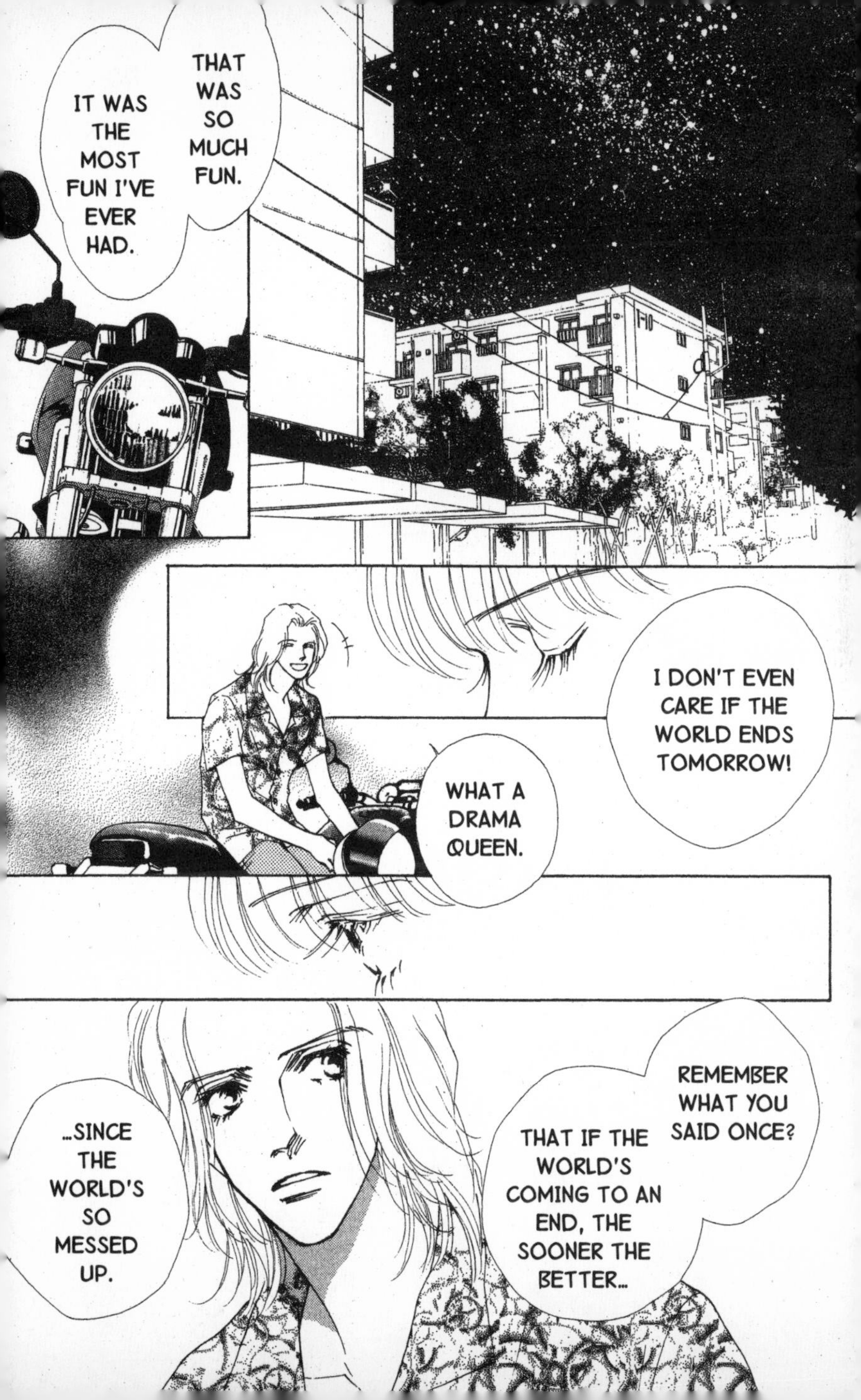
THAT WAS SO MUCH FUN.
IT WAS THE MOST FUN I'VE EVER HAD.
I DON'T EVEN CARE IF THE WORLD ENDS TOMORROW!
WHAT A DRAMA QUEEN.
REMEMBER WHAT YOU SAID ONCE?
THAT IF THE WORLD'S COMING TO AN END, THE SOONER THE BETTER...
...SINCE THE WORLD'S SO MESSED UP.

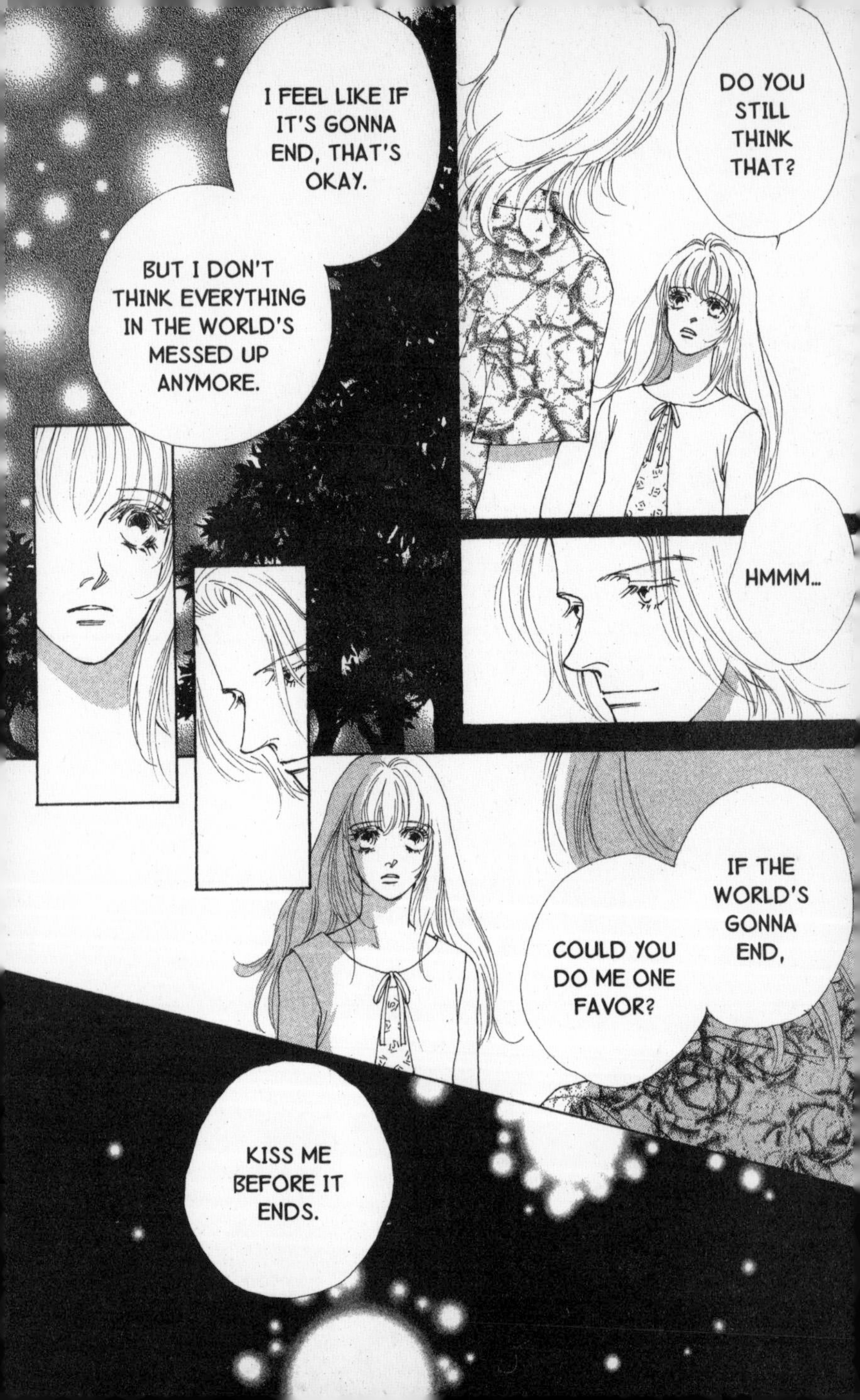
DO YOU STILL THINK THAT?
HMMM...
I FEEL LIKE IF IT'S GONNA END, THAT'S OKAY.
BUT I DON'T THINK EVERYTHING IN THE WORLD'S MESSED UP ANYMORE.
IF THE WORLD'S GONNA END,
COULD YOU DO ME ONE FAVOR?
KISS ME BEFORE IT ENDS.

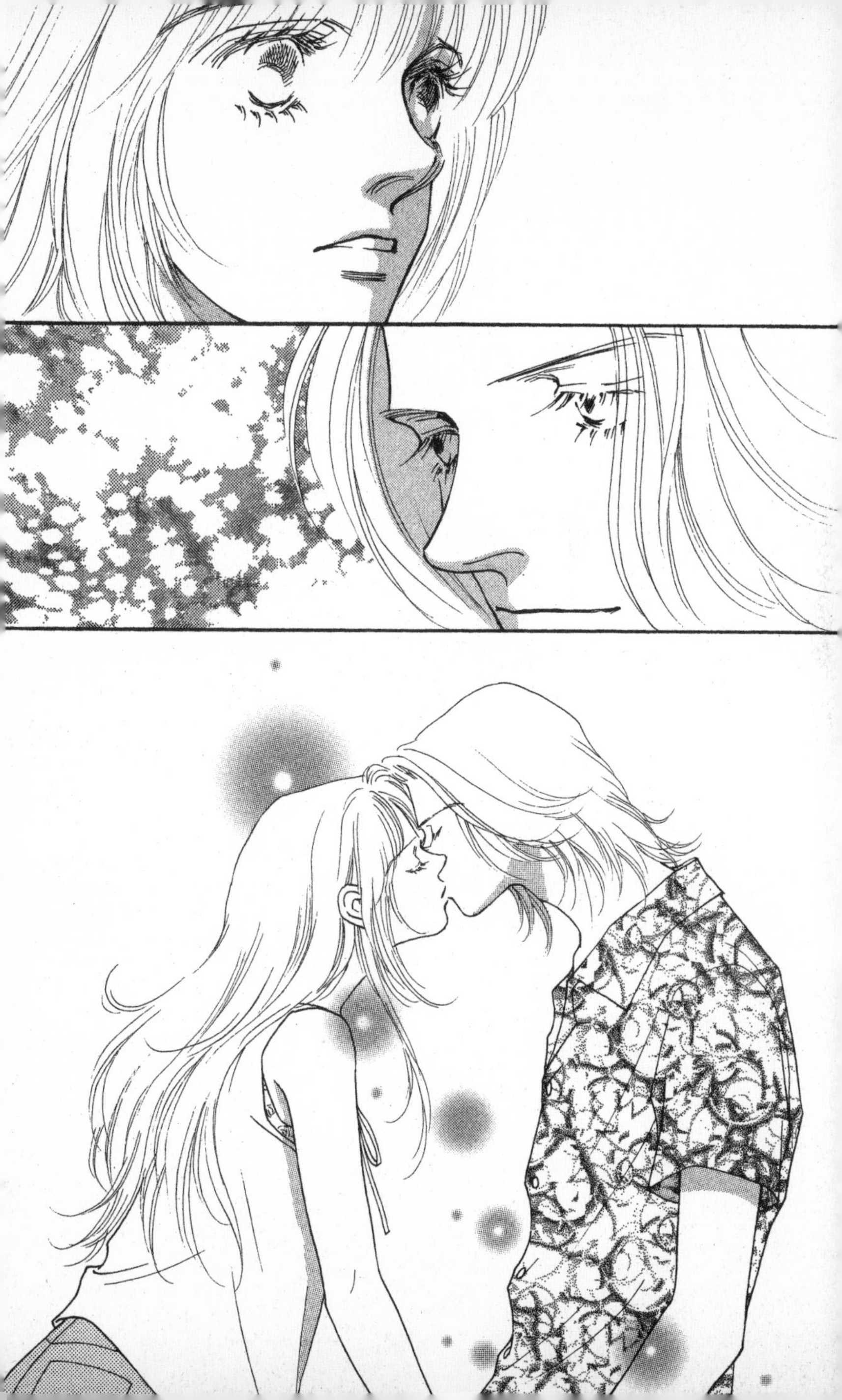

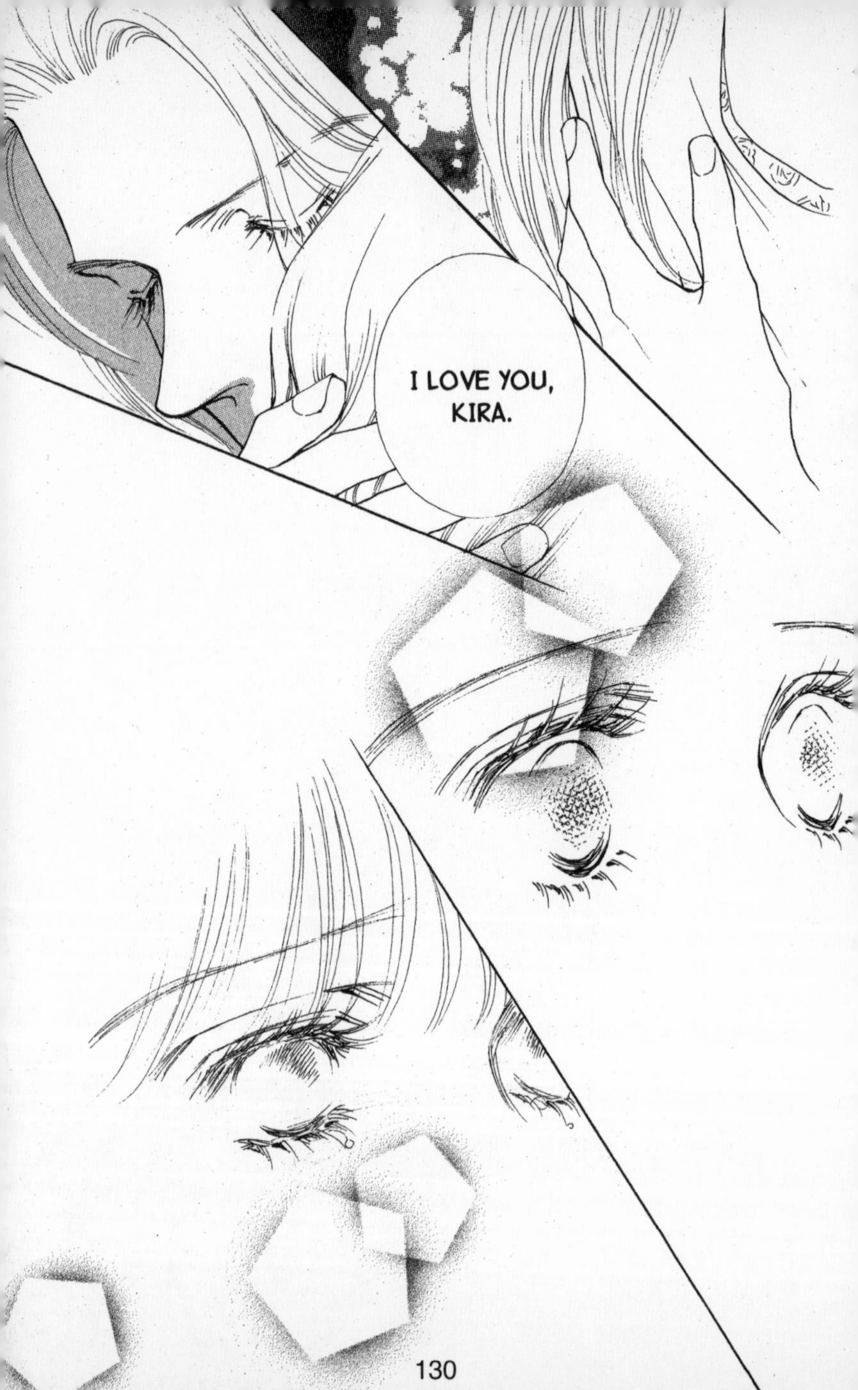
I LOVE YOU, KIRA.

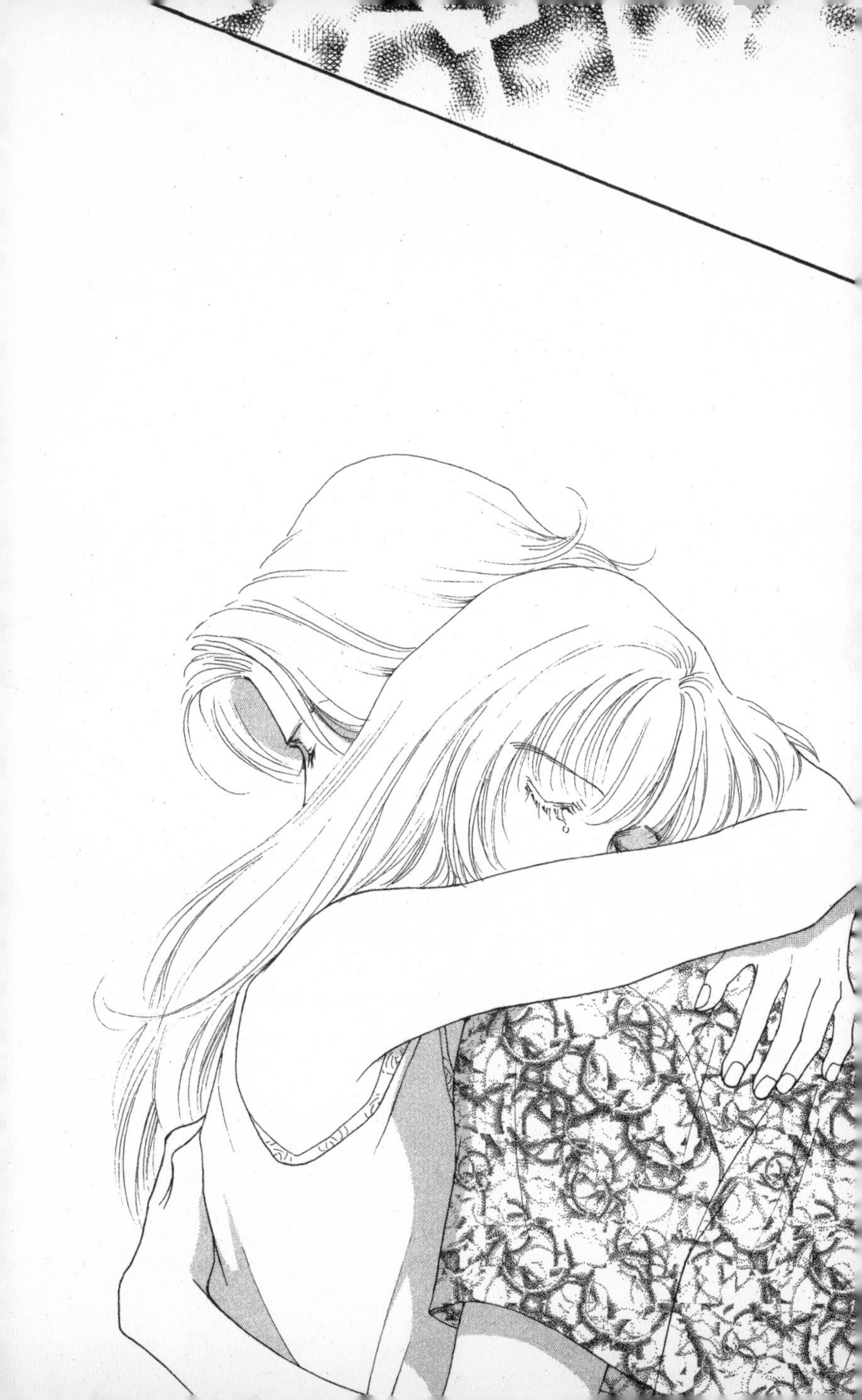

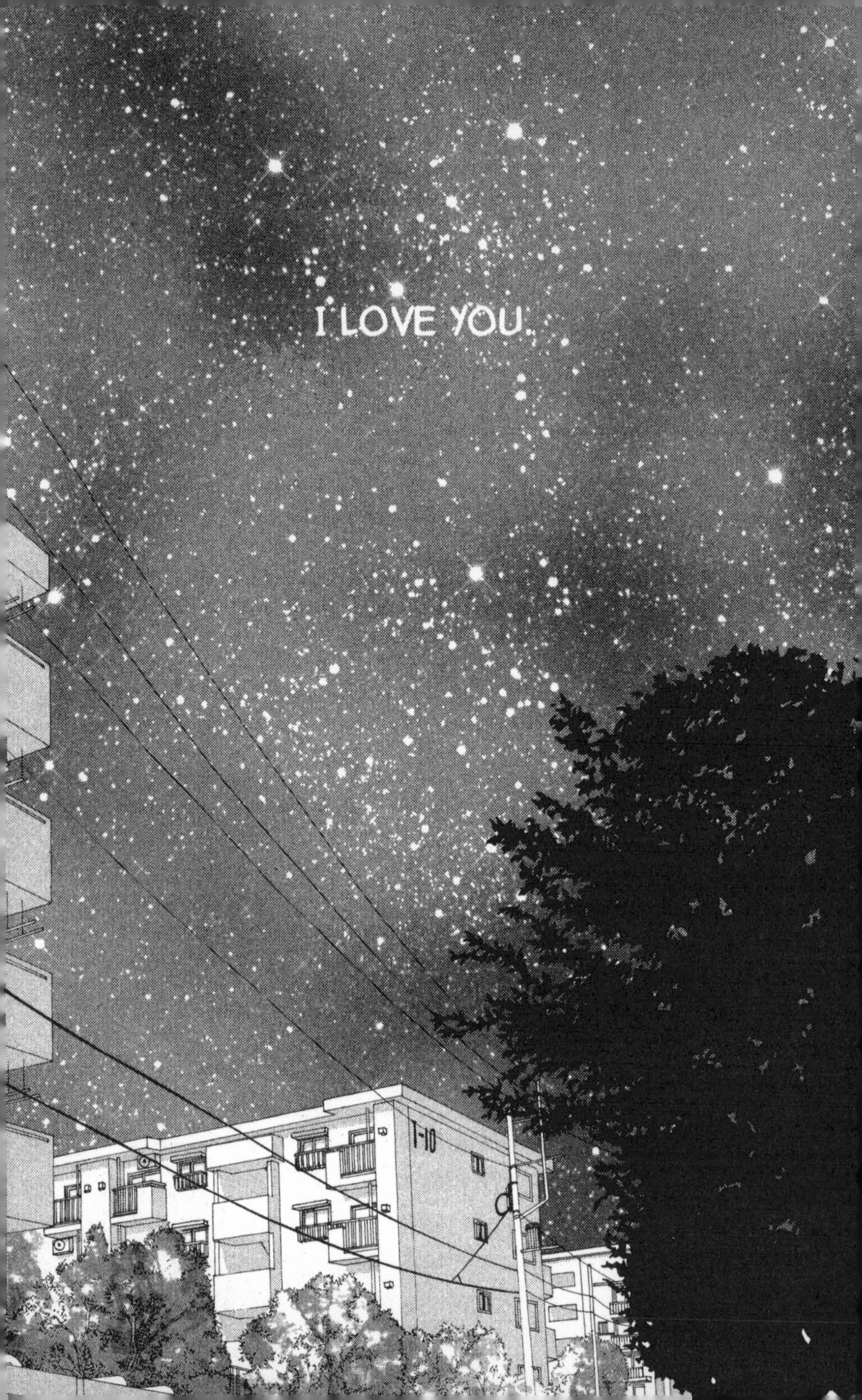
I LOVE YOU.
1-10

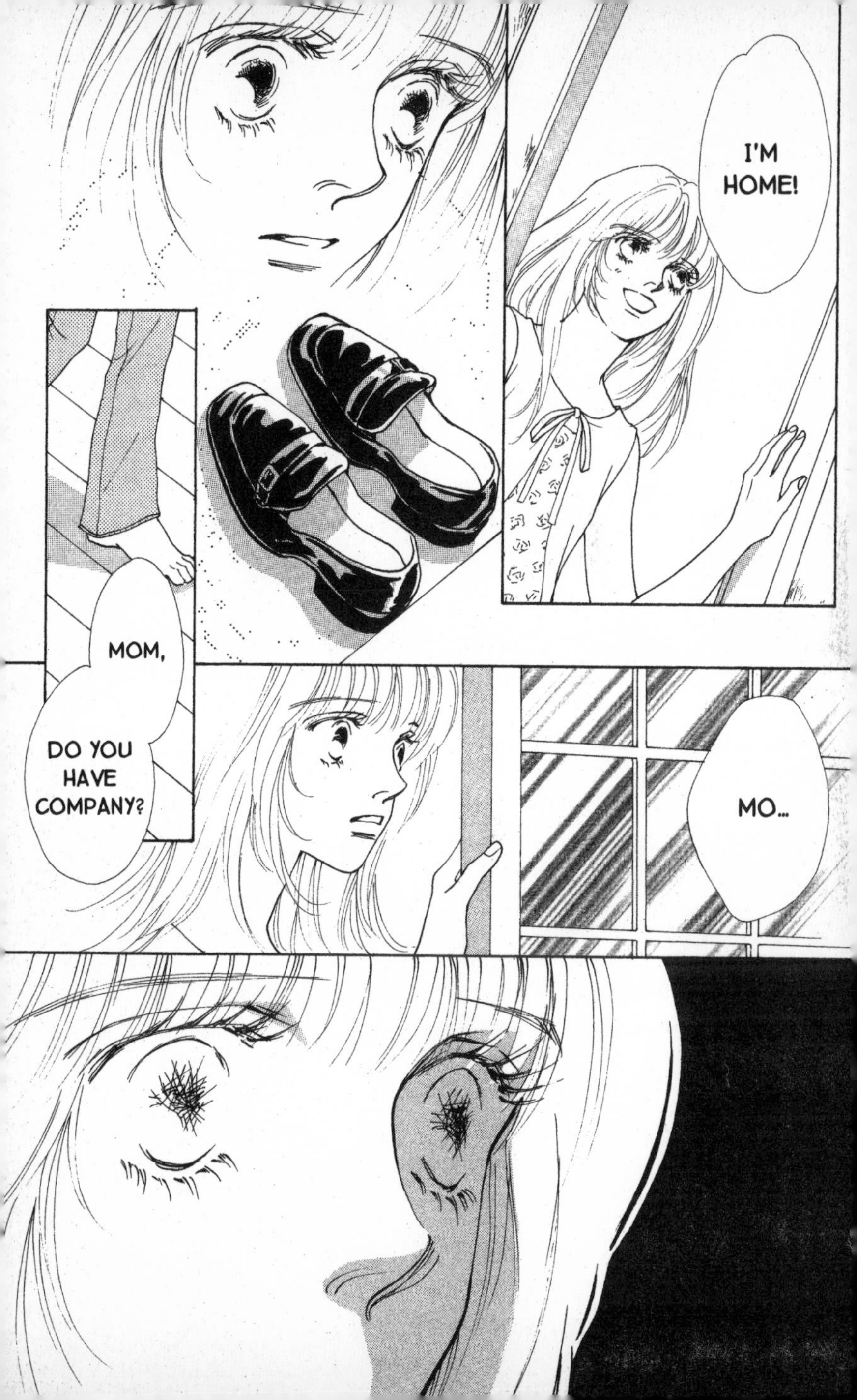
I'M HOME!
MOM, DO YOU HAVE COMPANY?
MO...

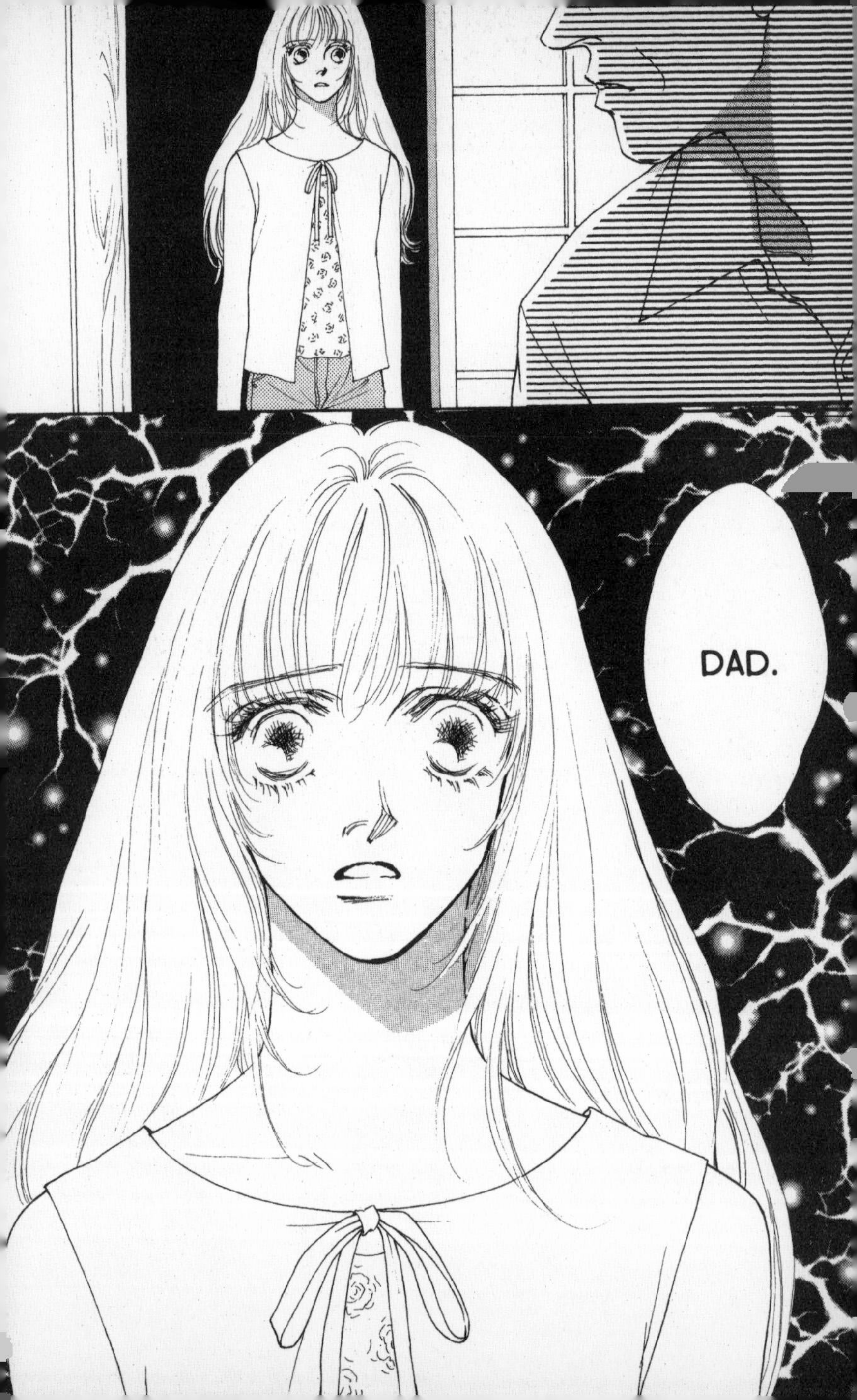
DAD.

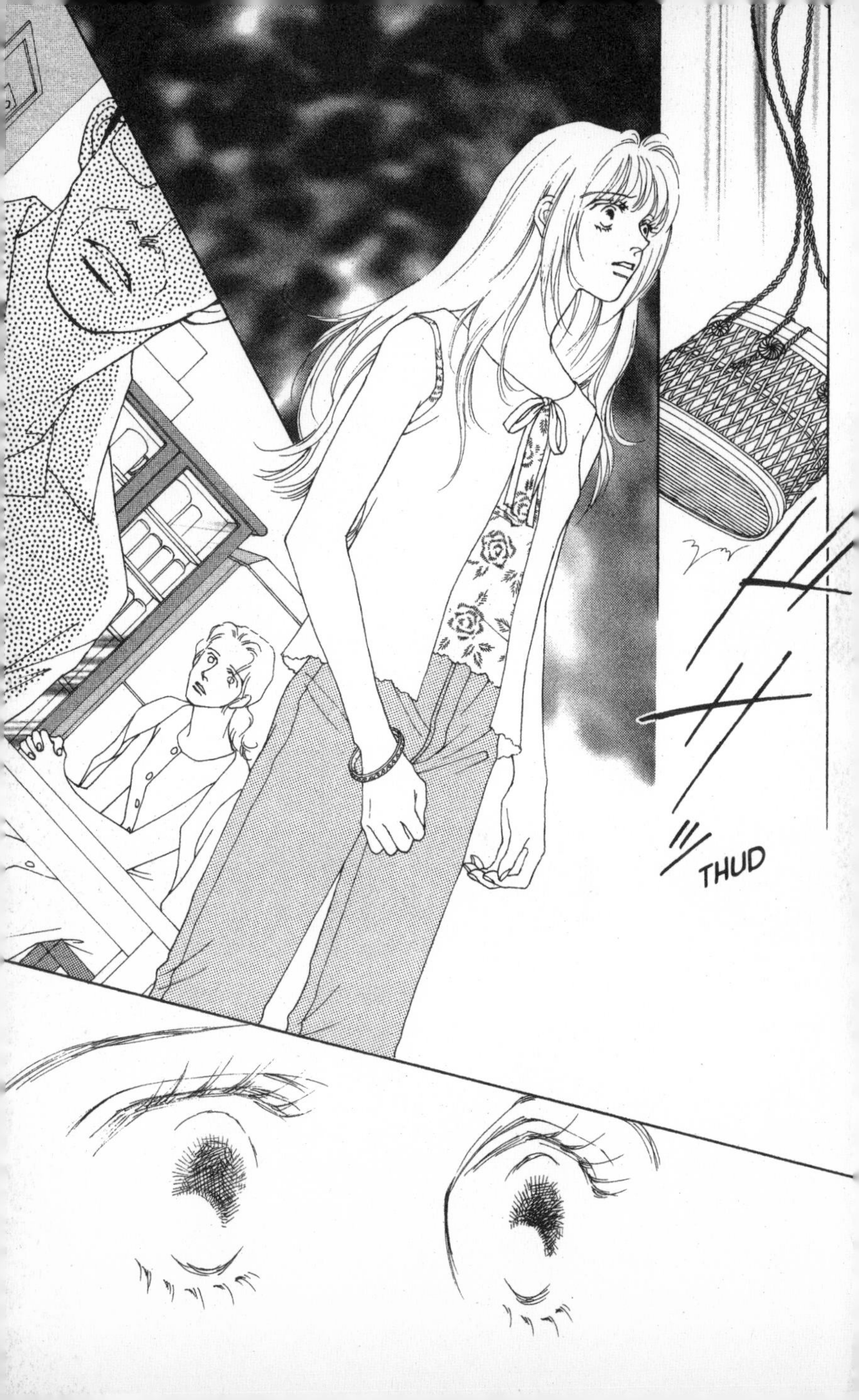
THUD

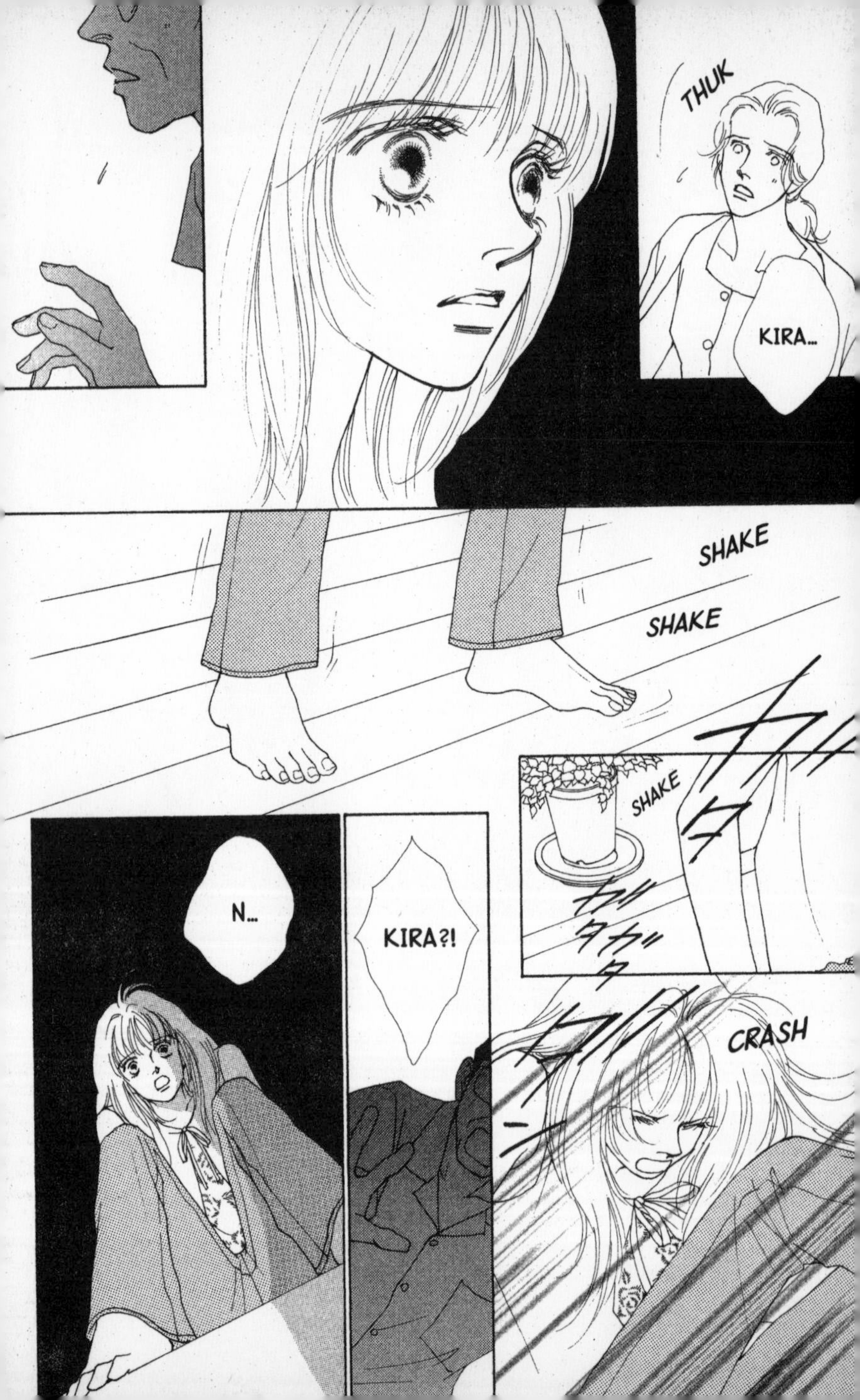
THUK
KIRA...
SHAKE
SHAKE
SHAKE
CRASH
KIRA?!
N...

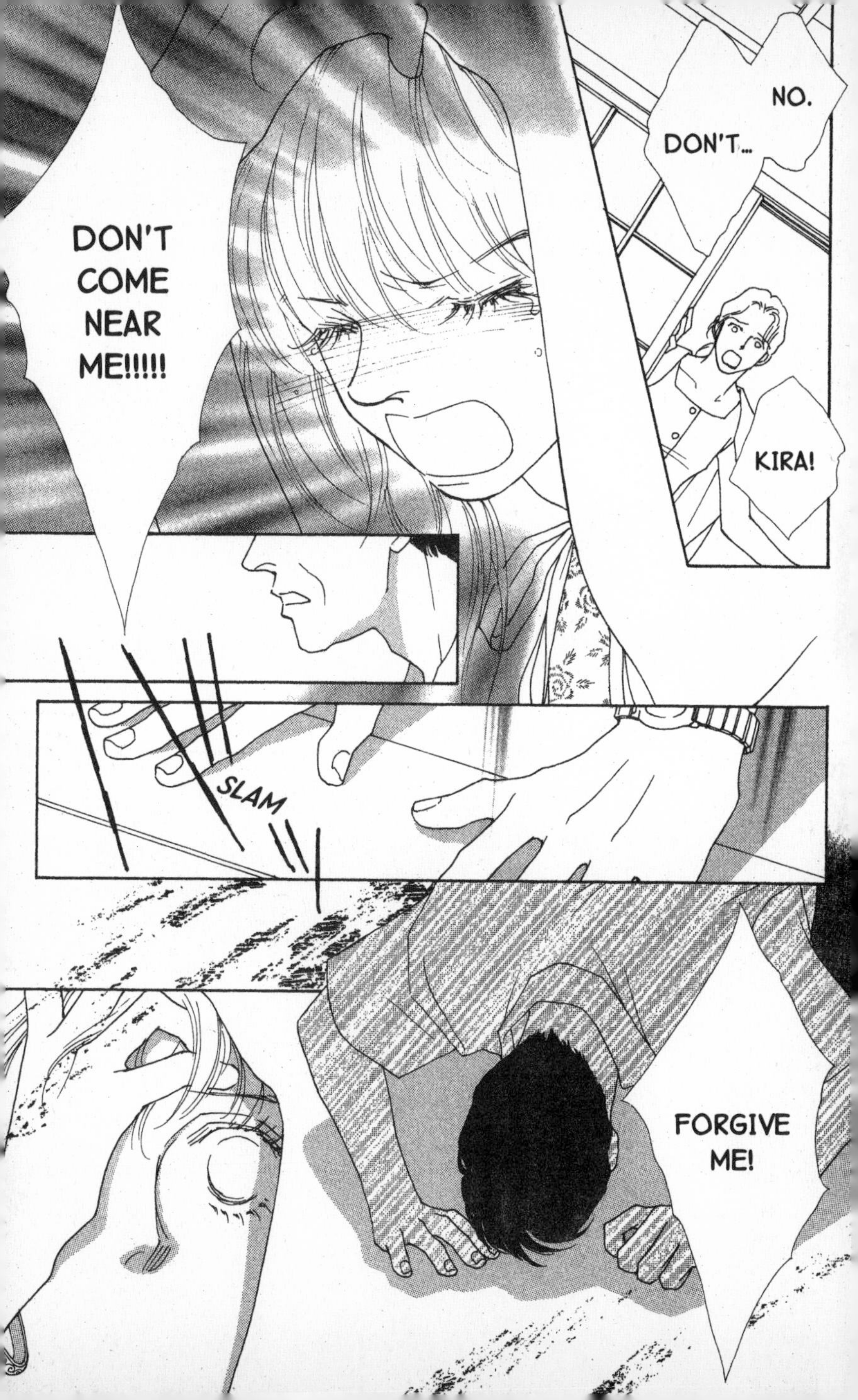
NO.
DON'T...
KIRA!
DON'T COME NEAR ME!!!!!
SLAM
FORGIVE ME!

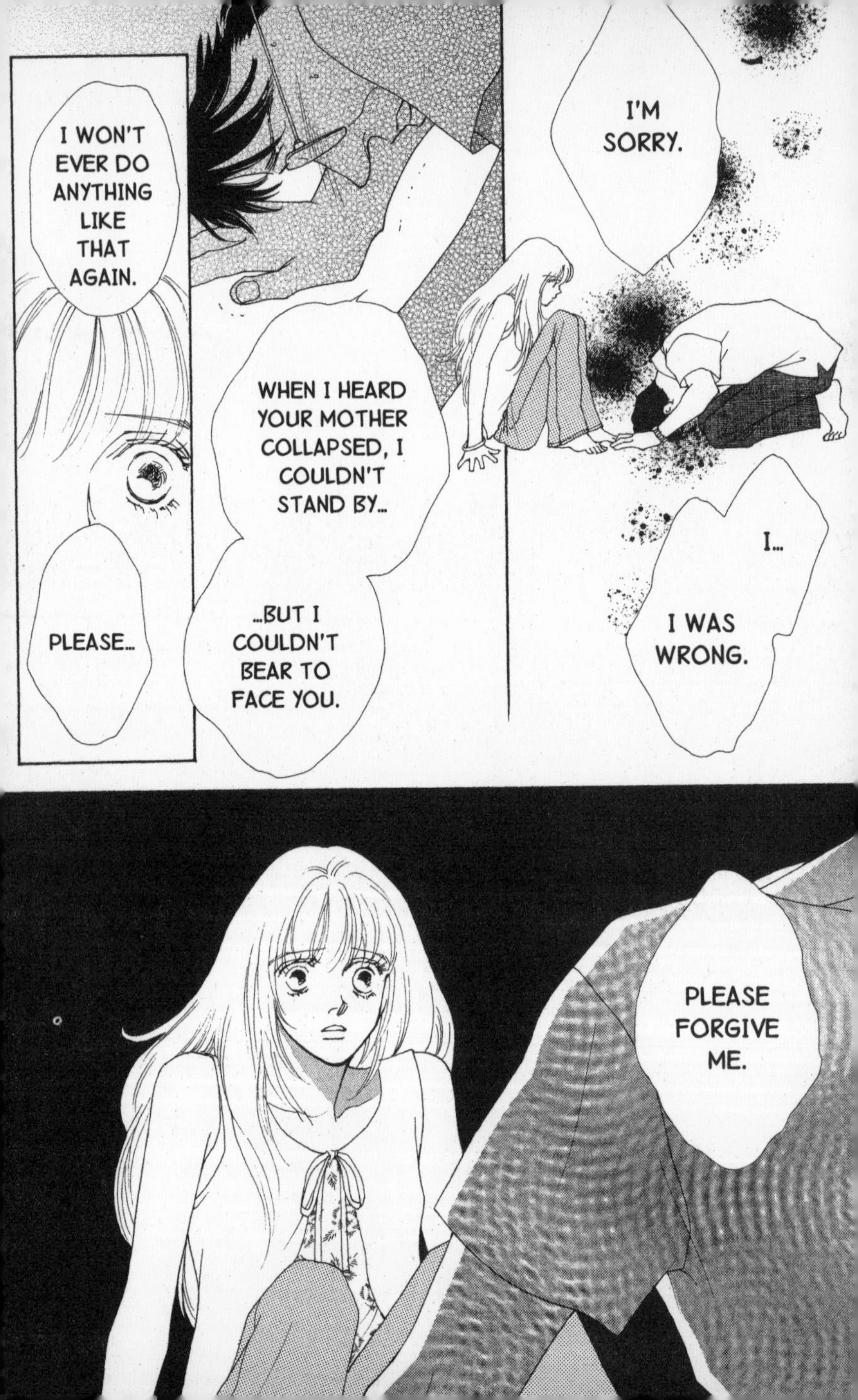
I'M SORRY.
I...
I WAS WRONG.
WHEN I HEARD YOUR MOTHER COLLAPSED, I COULDN'T STAND BY...
...BUT I COULDN'T BEAR TO FACE YOU.
I WON'T EVER DO ANYTHING LIKE THAT AGAIN.
PLEASE...
PLEASE FORGIVE ME.

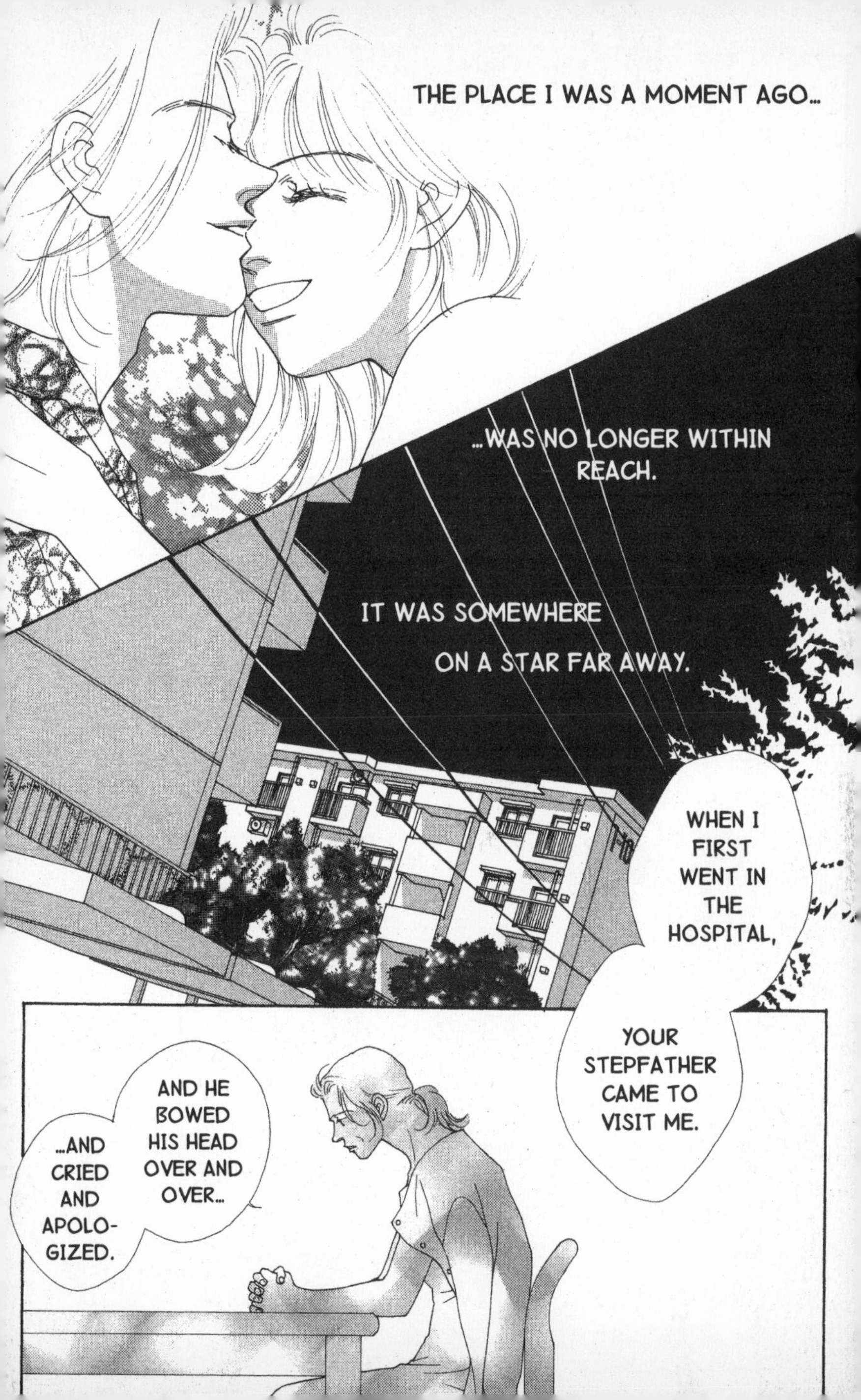
THE PLACE I WAS A MOMENT AGO...
...WAS NO LONGER WITHIN REACH.
IT WAS SOMEWHERE ON A STAR FAR AWAY.
WHEN I FIRST WENT IN THE HOSPITAL,
YOUR STEPFATHER CAME TO VISIT ME.
AND HE BOWED HIS HEAD OVER AND OVER...
...AND CRIED AND APOLOGIZED.

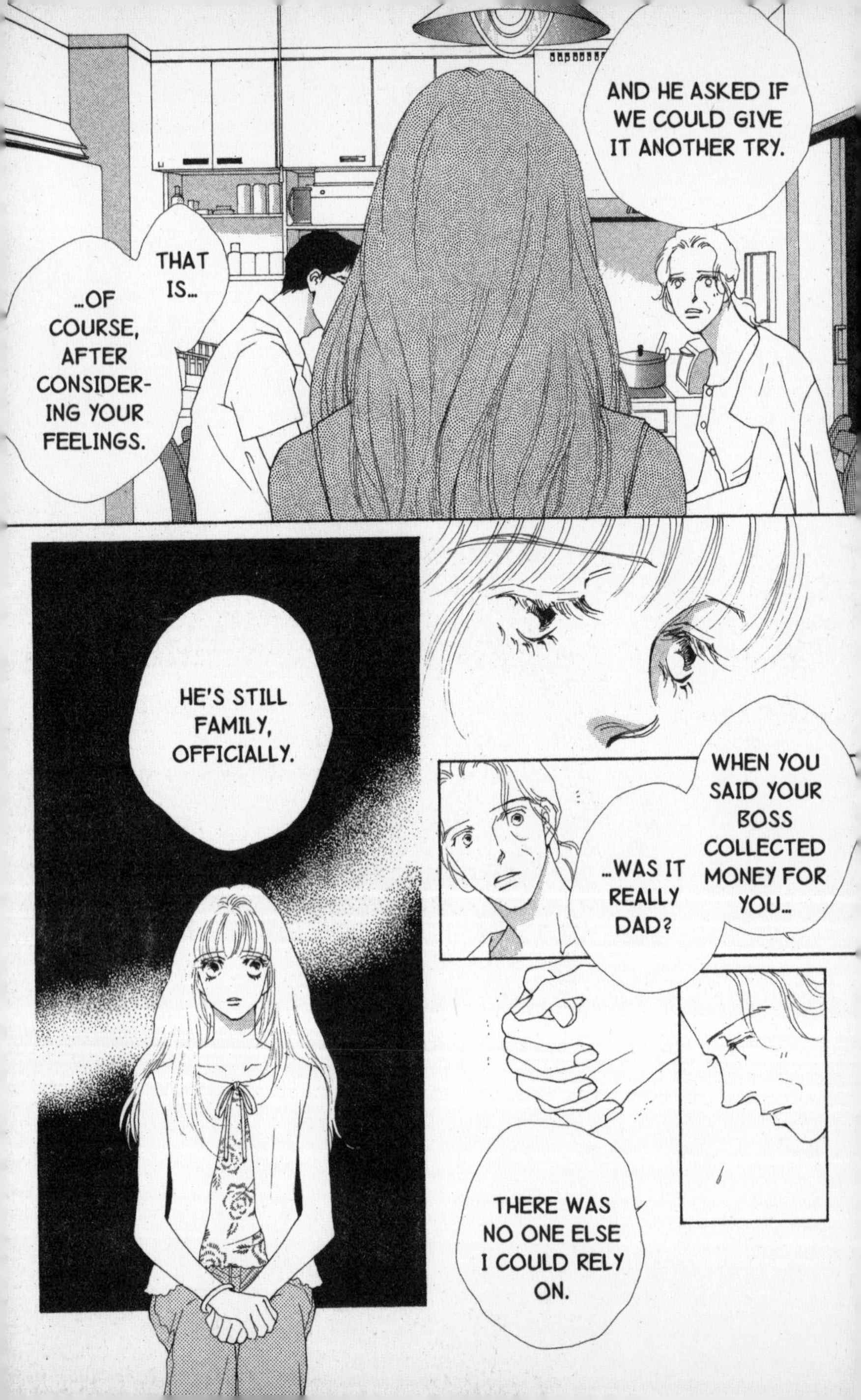
AND HE ASKED IF WE COULD GIVE IT ANOTHER TRY.
THAT IS...
...OF COURSE, AFTER CONSIDER-ING YOUR FEELINGS.
WHEN YOU SAID YOUR BOSS COLLECTED MONEY FOR YOU...
...WAS IT REALLY DAD?
THERE WAS NO ONE ELSE I COULD RELY ON.
HE'S STILL FAMILY, OFFICIALLY.

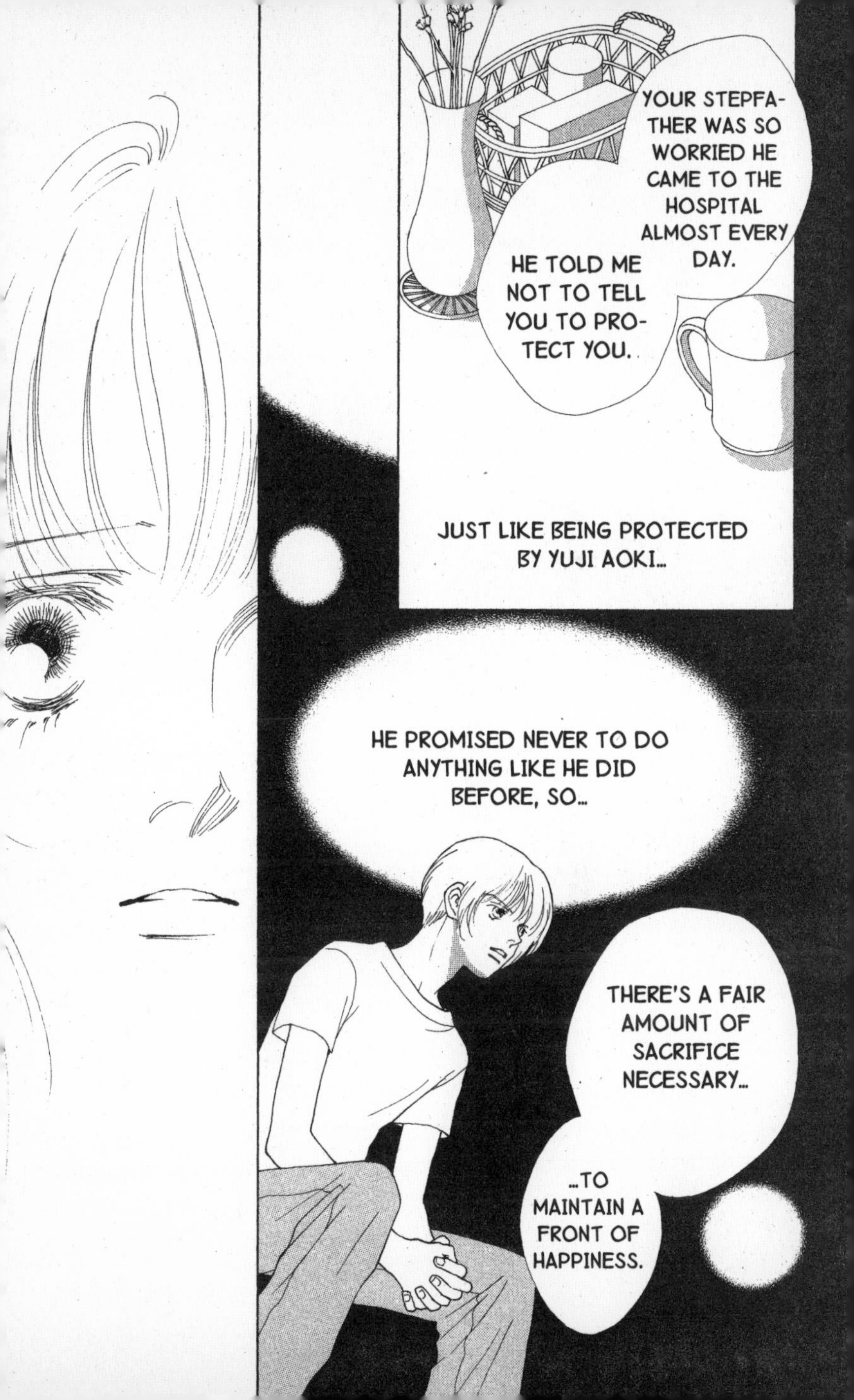
YOUR STEPFA-THER WAS SO WORRIED HE CAME TO THE HOSPITAL ALMOST EVERY DAY.
HE TOLD ME NOT TO TELL YOU TO PRO-TECT YOU.
JUST LIKE BEING PROTECTED BY YUJI AOKI...
HE PROMISED NEVER TO DO ANYTHING LIKE HE DID BEFORE, SO...
THERE'S A FAIR AMOUNT OF SACRIFICE NECESSARY...
...TO MAINTAIN A FRONT OF HAPPINESS.

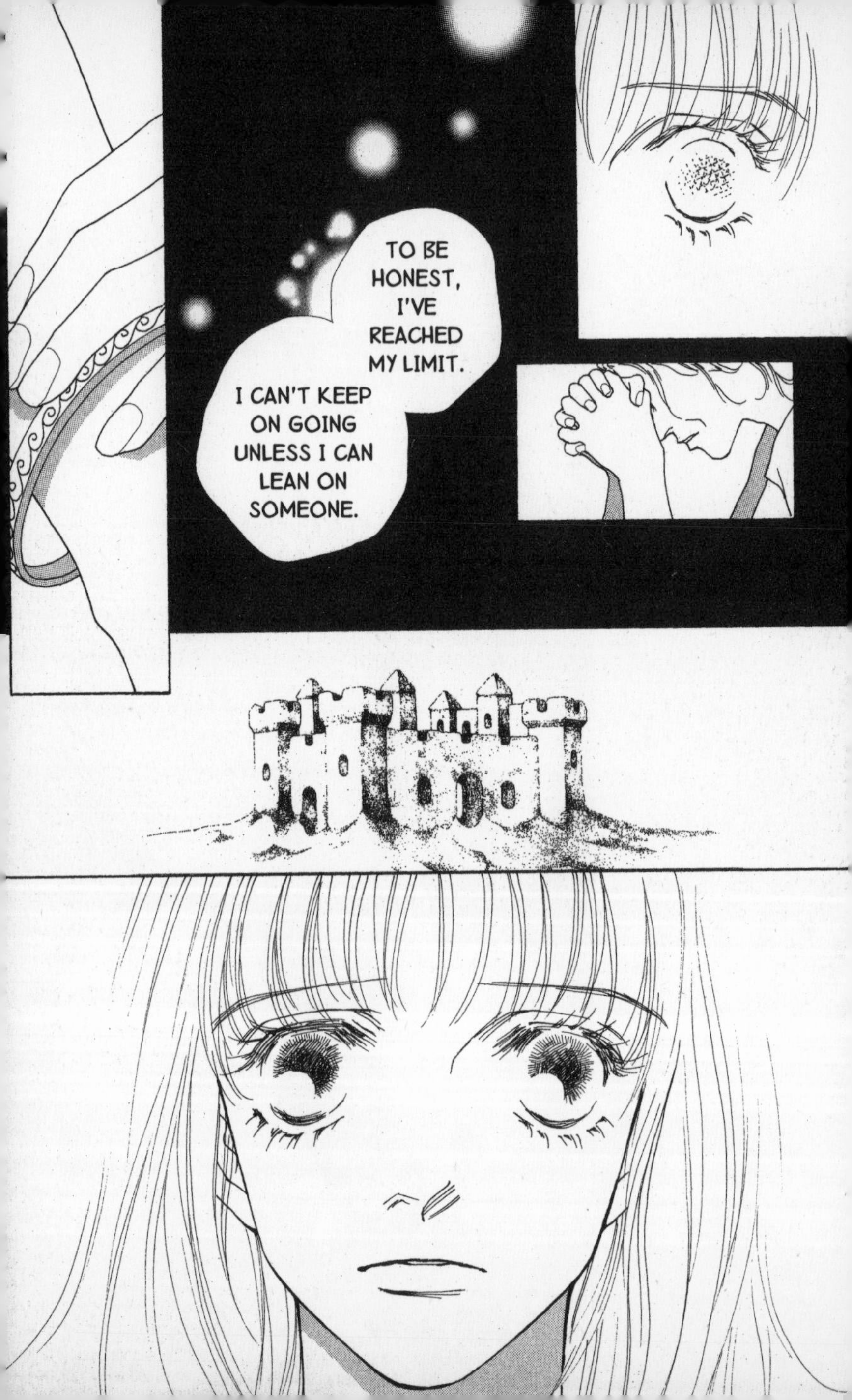
TO BE HONEST, I'VE REACHED MY LIMIT.
I CAN'T KEEP ON GOING UNLESS I CAN LEAN ON SOMEONE.

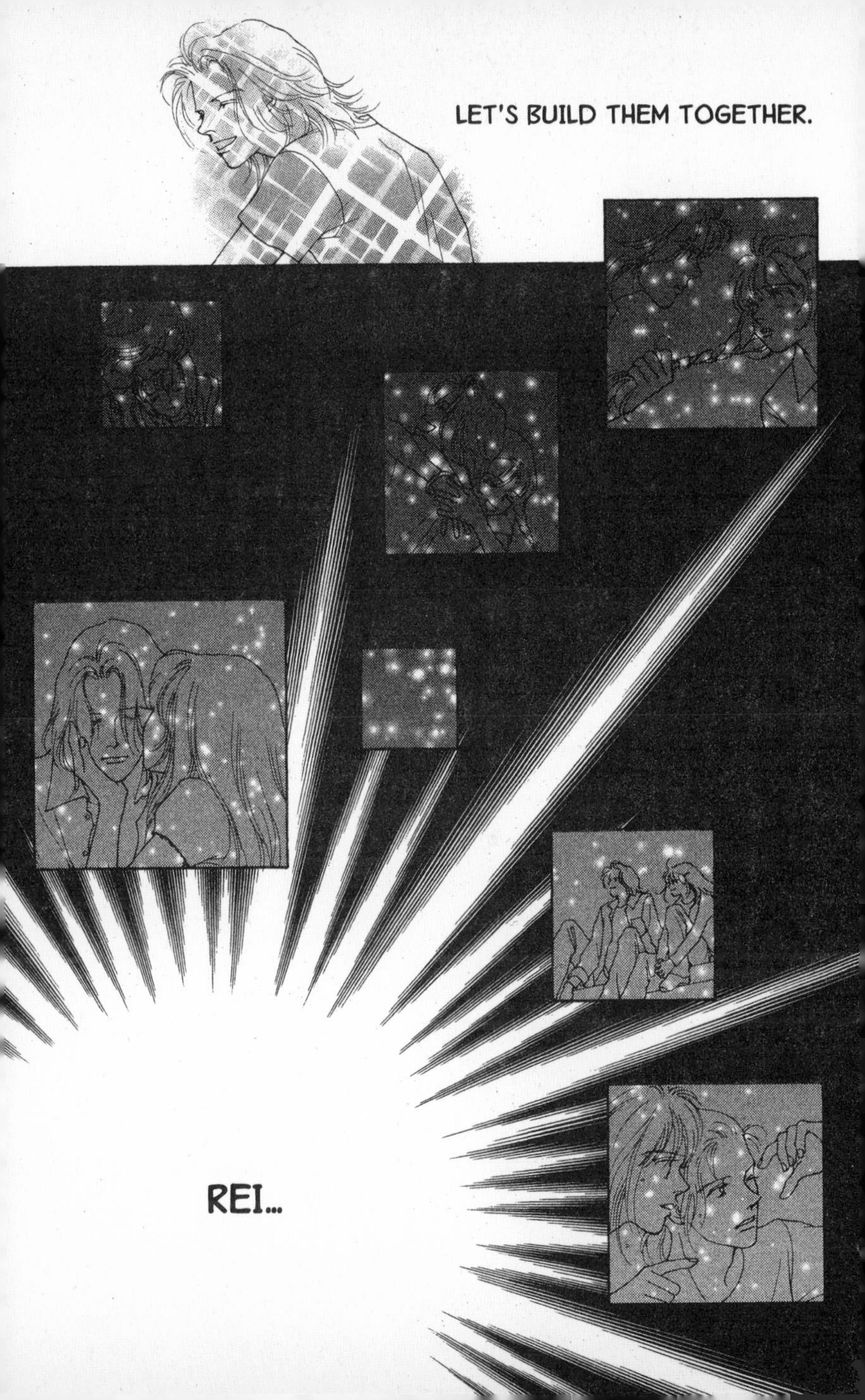
LET'S BUILD THEM TOGETHER.
REI...

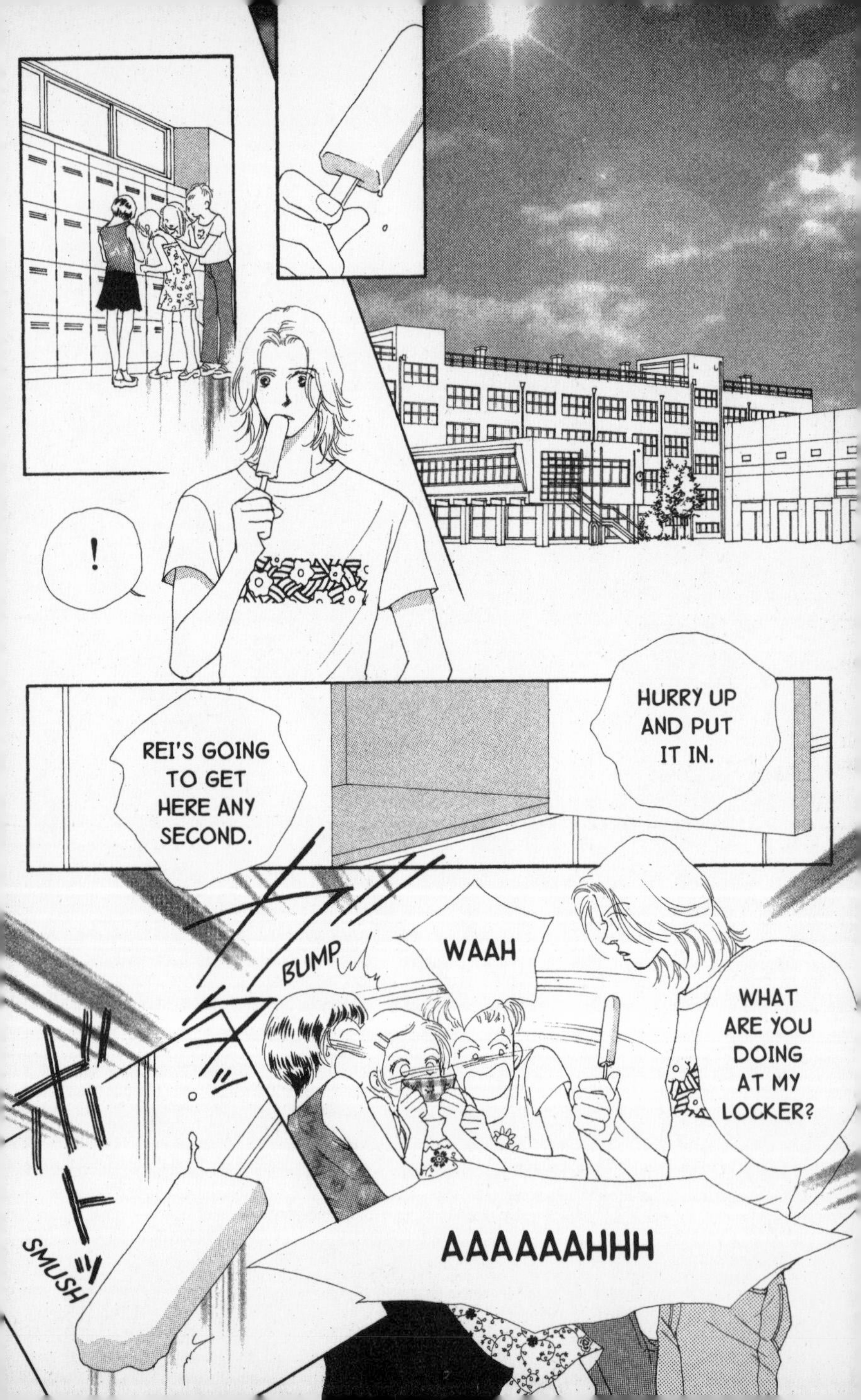
!
HURRY UP AND PUT IT IN.
REI'S GOING TO GET HERE ANY SECOND.
WHAT ARE YOU DOING AT MY LOCKER?
WAAH
BUMP
AAAAAAHHH
SMUSH

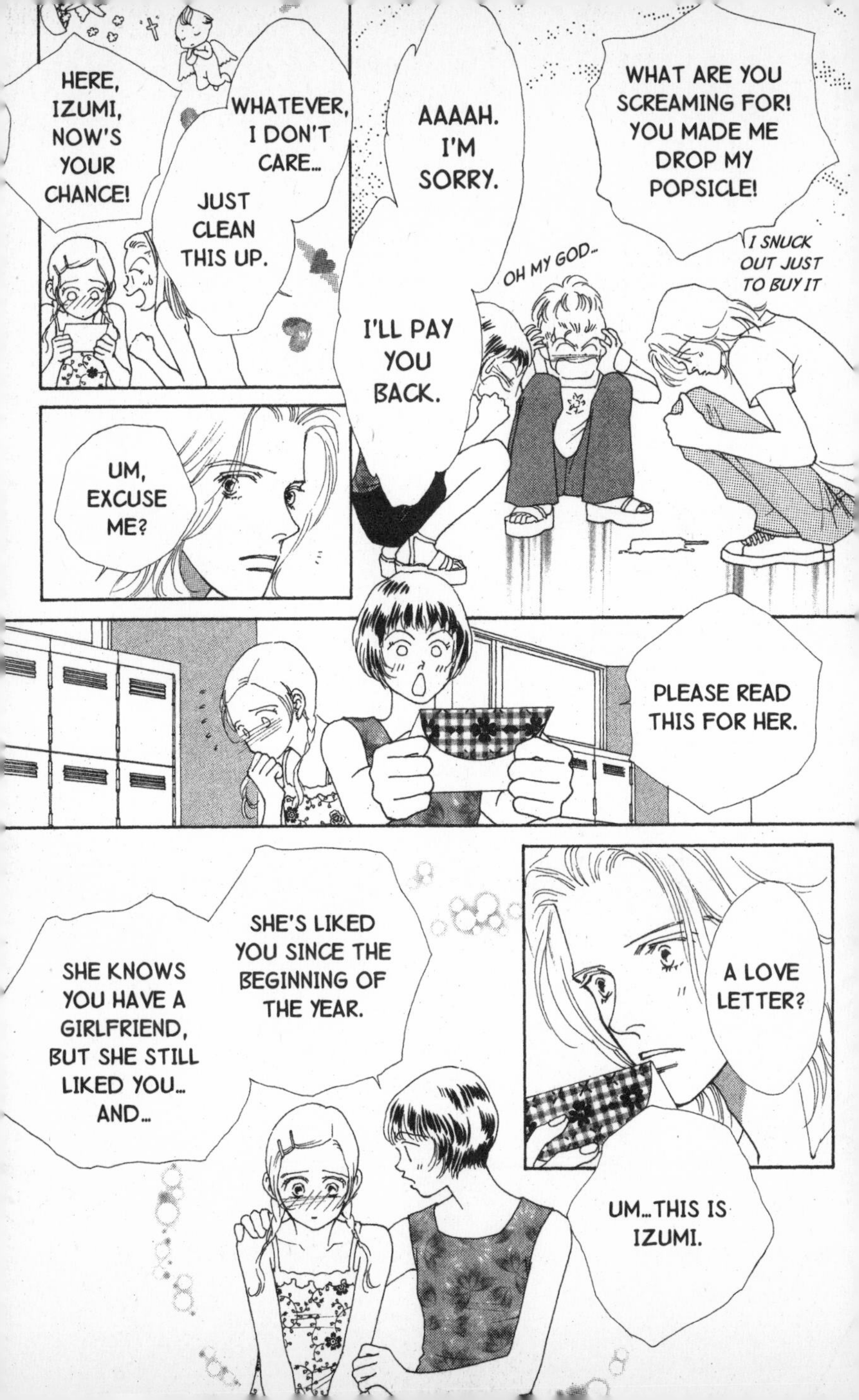
WHAT ARE YOU SCREAMING FOR! YOU MADE ME DROP MY POPSICLE!
I SNUCK OUT JUST TO BUY IT
AAAAH. I'M SORRY.
OH MY GOD...
I'LL PAY YOU BACK.
WHATEVER, I DON'T CARE...
JUST CLEAN THIS UP.
HERE, IZUMI, NOW'S YOUR CHANCE!
UM, EXCUSE ME?
PLEASE READ THIS FOR HER.
A LOVE LETTER?
UM...THIS IS IZUMI.
SHE'S LIKED YOU SINCE THE BEGINNING OF THE YEAR.
SHE KNOWS YOU HAVE A GIRLFRIEND, BUT SHE STILL LIKED YOU... AND...

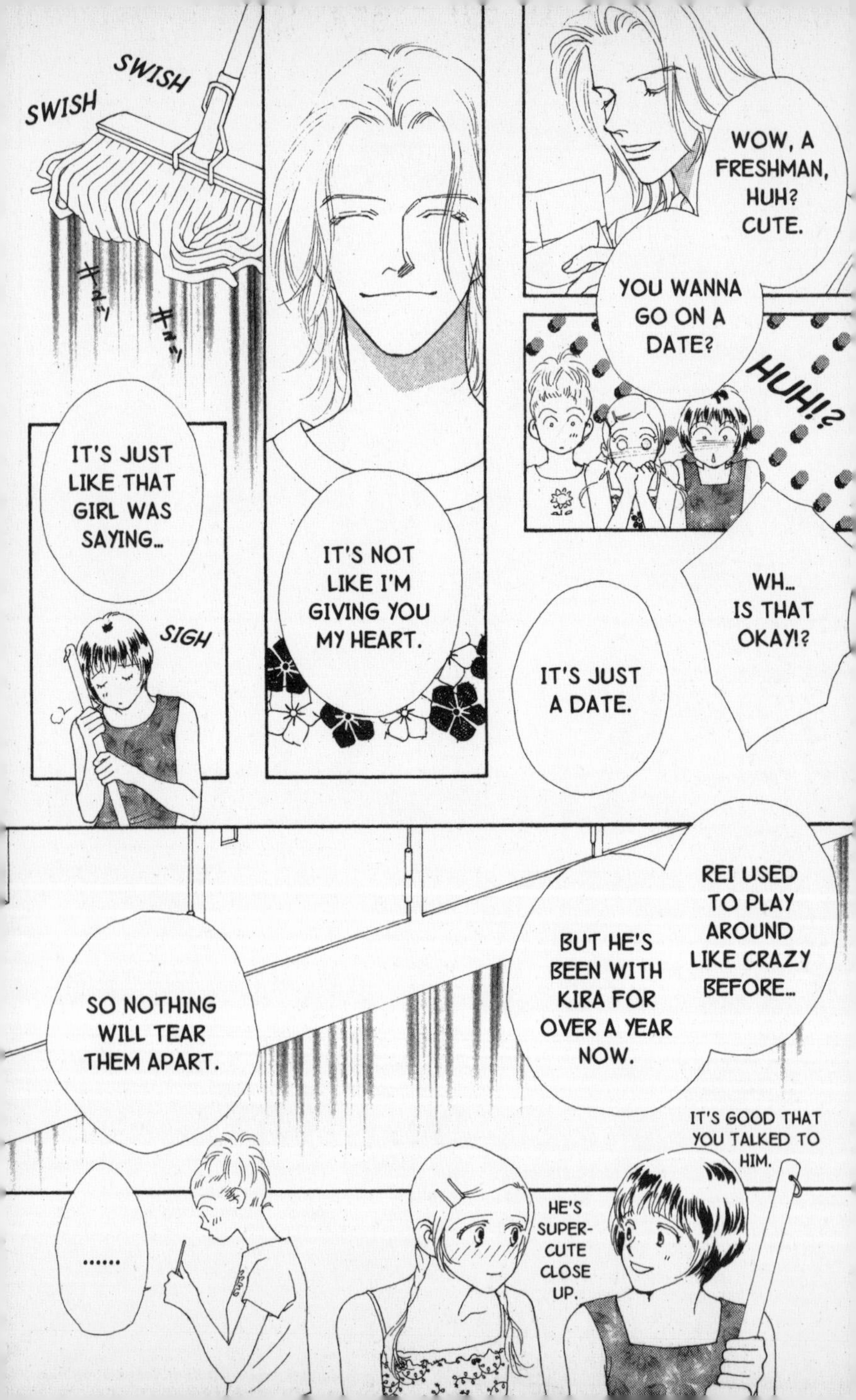
WOW, A FRESHMAN, HUH? CUTE.
YOU WANNA GO ON A DATE?
HUH!?
WH... IS THAT OKAY!?
IT'S JUST A DATE.
IT'S NOT LIKE I'M GIVING YOU MY HEART.
SWISH
SWISH
IT'S JUST LIKE THAT GIRL WAS SAYING...
SIGH
REI USED TO PLAY AROUND LIKE CRAZY BEFORE...
BUT HE'S BEEN WITH KIRA FOR OVER A YEAR NOW.
SO NOTHING WILL TEAR THEM APART.
IT'S GOOD THAT YOU TALKED TO HIM.
HE'S SUPER-CUTE CLOSE UP.
......

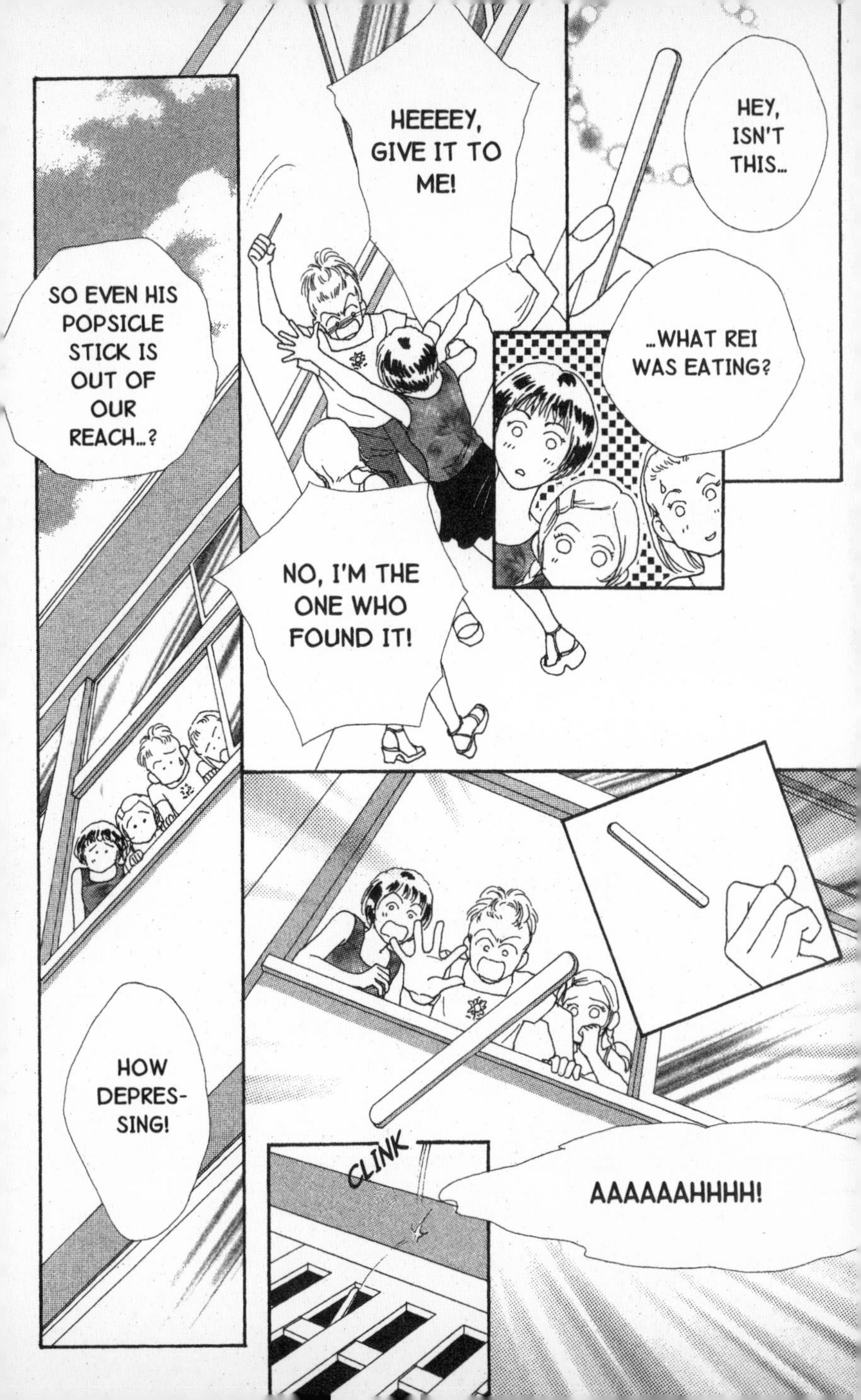
HEY, ISN'T THIS...
...WHAT REI WAS EATING?
HEEEEY, GIVE IT TO ME!
NO, I'M THE ONE WHO FOUND IT!
AAAAAAHHHH!
CLINK
SO EVEN HIS POPSICLE STICK IS OUT OF OUR REACH...?
HOW DEPRES-SING!

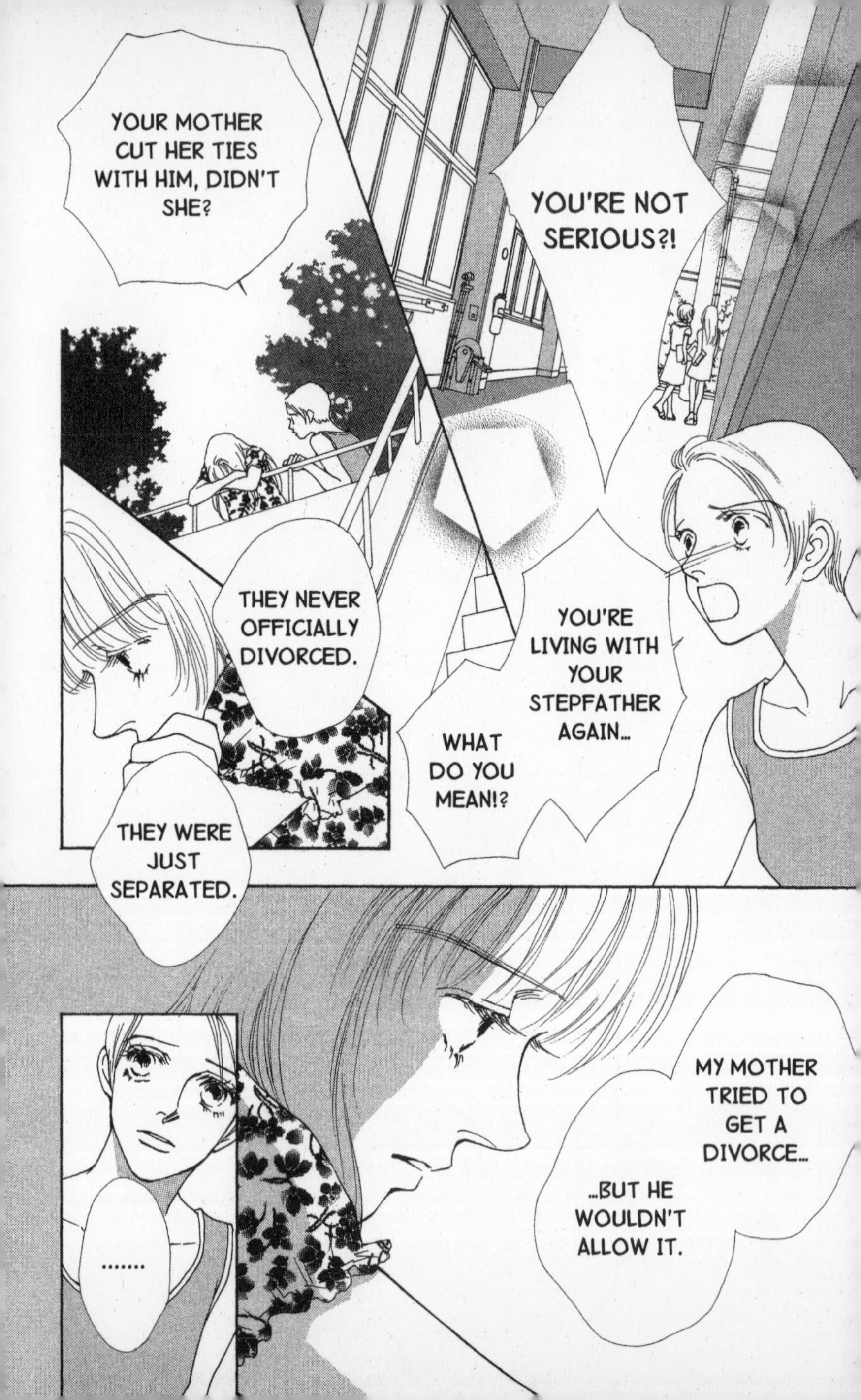
YOU'RE NOT SERIOUS?!
YOUR MOTHER CUT HER TIES WITH HIM, DIDN'T SHE?
YOU'RE LIVING WITH YOUR STEPFATHER AGAIN...
WHAT DO YOU MEAN!?
THEY NEVER OFFICIALLY DIVORCED.
THEY WERE JUST SEPARATED.
MY MOTHER TRIED TO GET A DIVORCE...
...BUT HE WOULDN'T ALLOW IT.
....

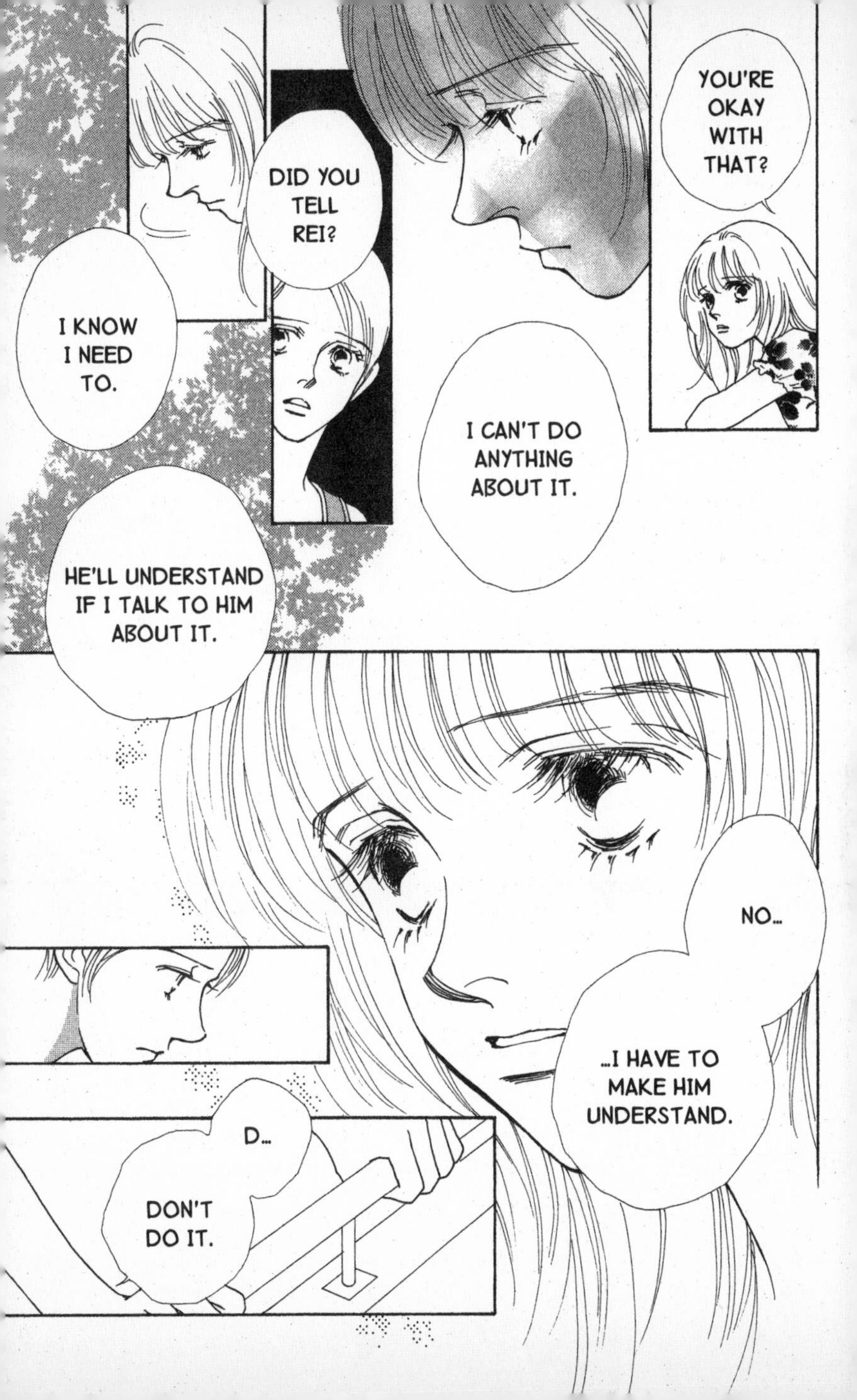
YOU'RE OKAY WITH THAT?
I CAN'T DO ANYTHING ABOUT IT.
DID YOU TELL REI?
I KNOW I NEED TO.
HE'LL UNDERSTAND IF I TALK TO HIM ABOUT IT.
NO...
...I HAVE TO MAKE HIM UNDERSTAND.
D...
DON'T DO IT.

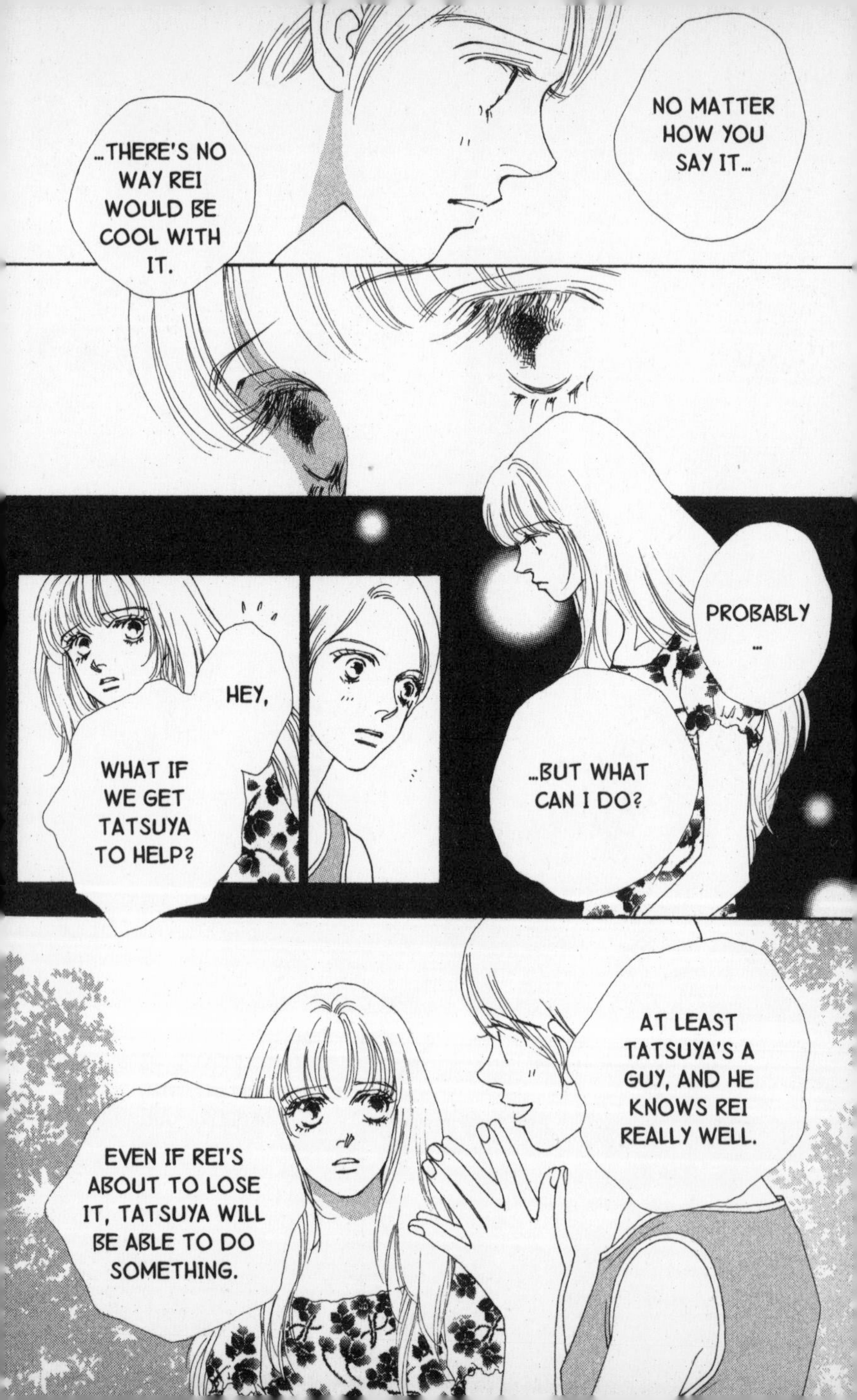
NO MATTER HOW YOU SAY IT...
...THERE'S NO WAY REI WOULD BE COOL WITH IT.
PROBABLY ...
...BUT WHAT CAN I DO?
HEY,
WHAT IF WE GET TATSUYA TO HELP?
AT LEAST TATSUYA'S A GUY, AND HE KNOWS REI REALLY WELL.
EVEN IF REI'S ABOUT TO LOSE IT, TATSUYA WILL BE ABLE TO DO SOMETHING.

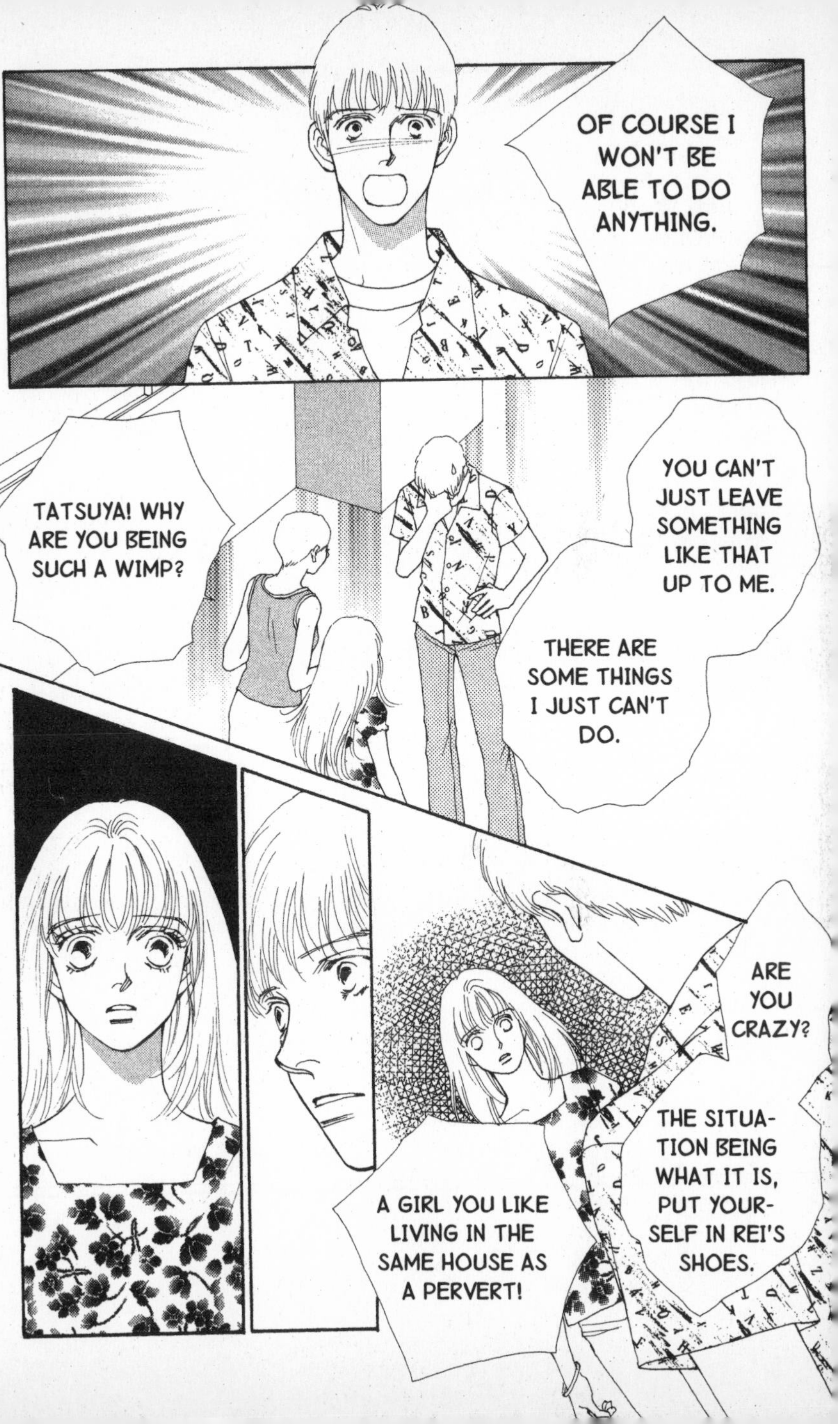
OF COURSE I WON'T BE ABLE TO DO ANYTHING.
YOU CAN'T JUST LEAVE SOMETHING LIKE THAT UP TO ME.
THERE ARE SOME THINGS I JUST CAN'T DO.
TATSUYA! WHY ARE YOU BEING SUCH A WIMP?
ARE YOU CRAZY?
THE SITUA-TION BEING WHAT IT IS, PUT YOUR-SELF IN REI'S SHOES.
A GIRL YOU LIKE LIVING IN THE SAME HOUSE AS A PERVERT!

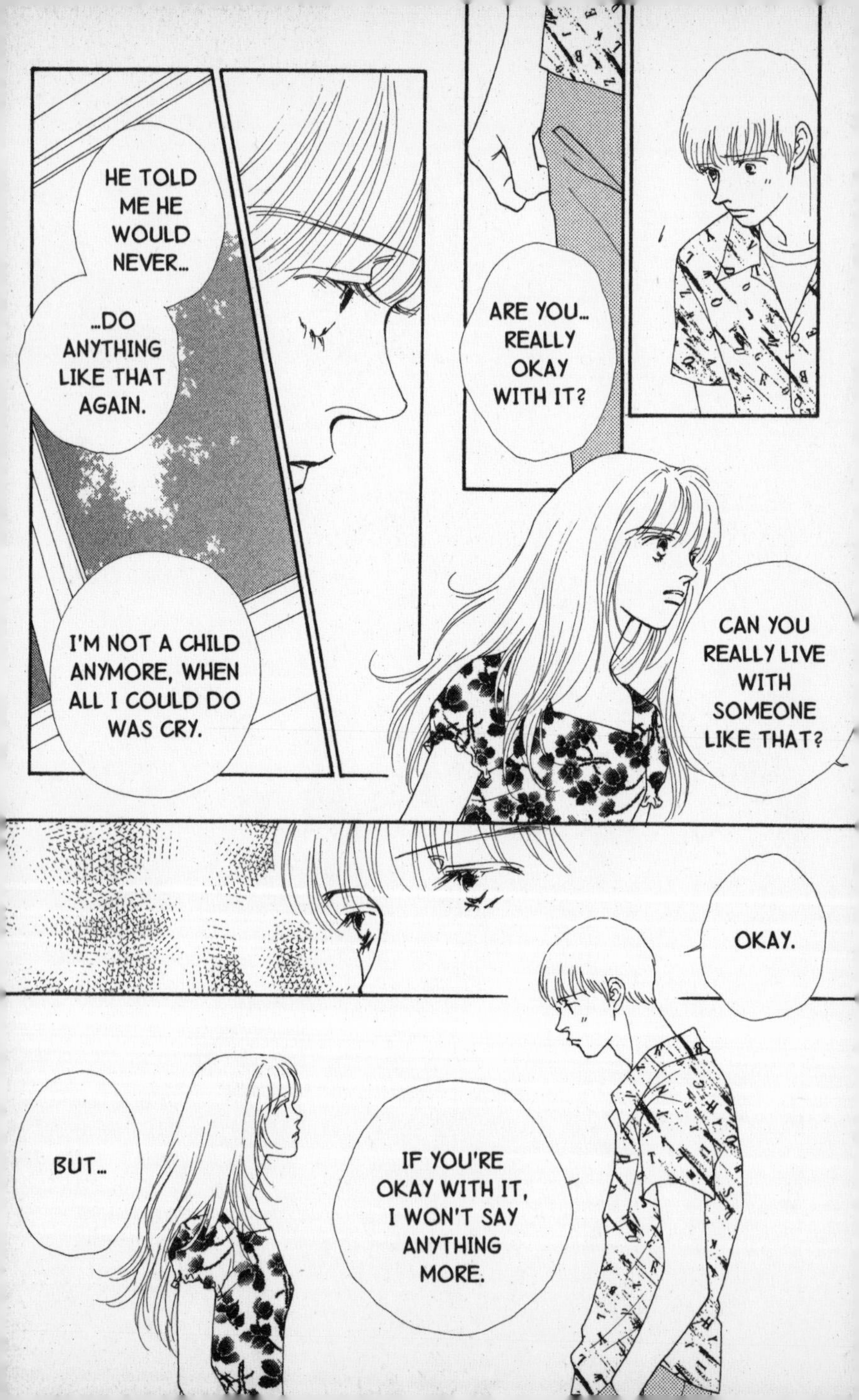
ARE YOU... REALLY OKAY WITH IT?
CAN YOU REALLY LIVE WITH SOMEONE LIKE THAT?
HE TOLD ME HE WOULD NEVER...
...DO ANYTHING LIKE THAT AGAIN.
I'M NOT A CHILD ANYMORE, WHEN ALL I COULD DO WAS CRY.
OKAY.
IF YOU'RE OKAY WITH IT, I WON'T SAY ANYTHING MORE.
BUT...

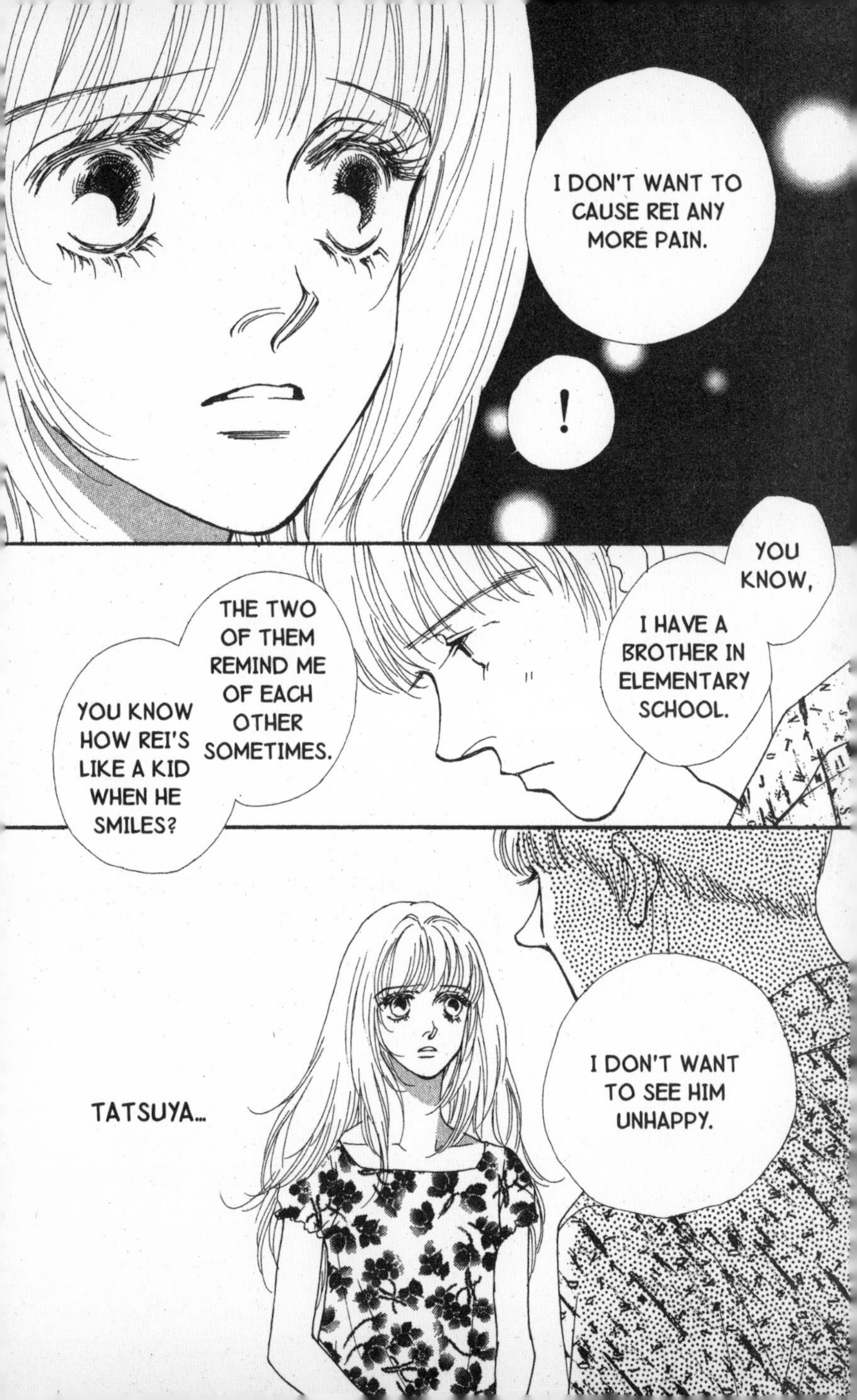
I DON'T WANT TO CAUSE REI ANY MORE PAIN.
!
YOU KNOW,
I HAVE A BROTHER IN ELEMENTARY SCHOOL.
THE TWO OF THEM REMIND ME OF EACH OTHER SOMETIMES.
YOU KNOW HOW REI'S LIKE A KID WHEN HE SMILES?
I DON'T WANT TO SEE HIM UNHAPPY.
TATSUYA...

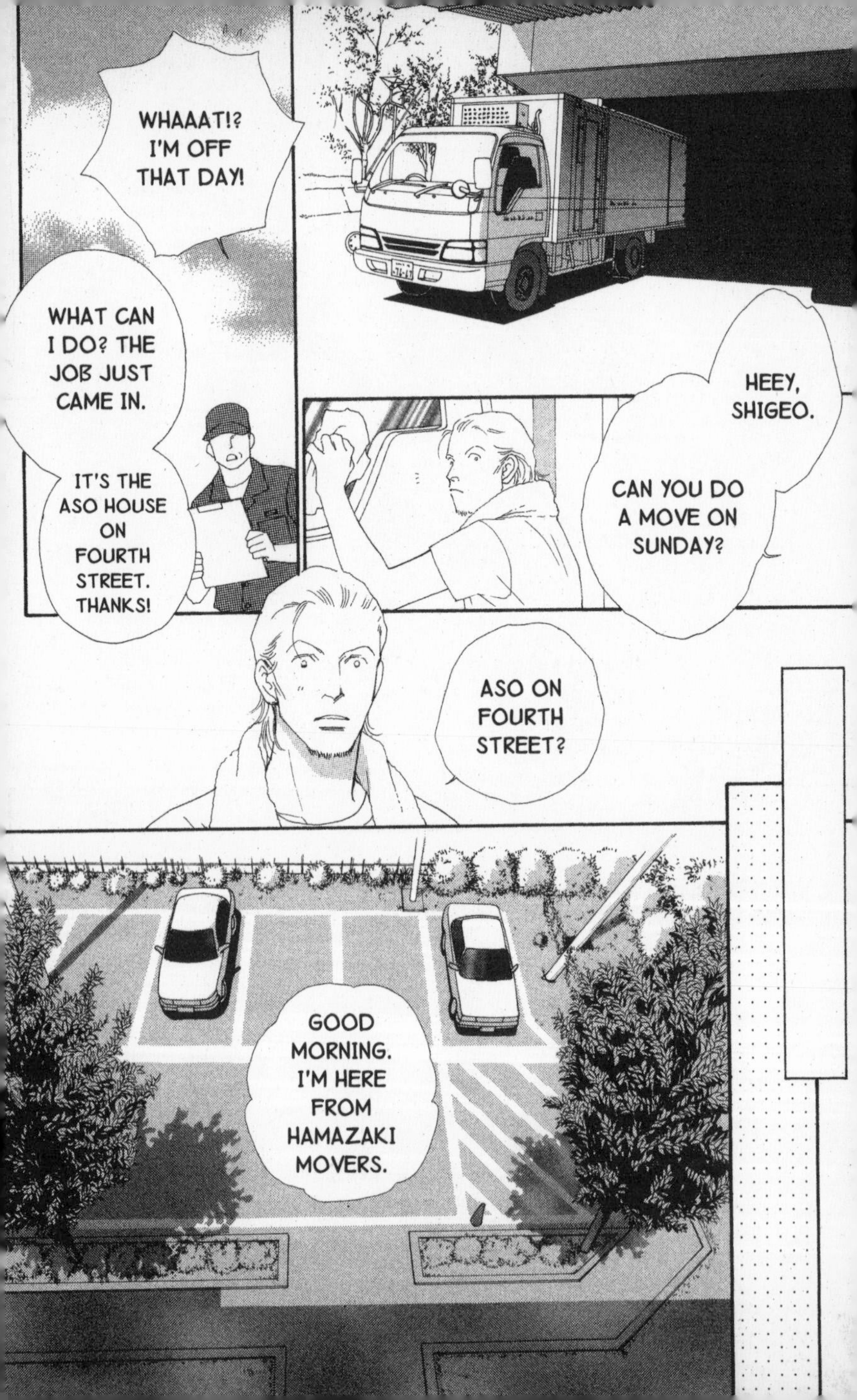
HEEY, SHIGEO.
CAN YOU DO A MOVE ON SUNDAY?
WHAAAT!? I'M OFF THAT DAY!
WHAT CAN I DO? THE JOB JUST CAME IN.
IT'S THE ASO HOUSE ON FOURTH STREET. THANKS!
ASO ON FOURTH STREET?
GOOD MORNING. I'M HERE FROM HAMAZAKI MOVERS.

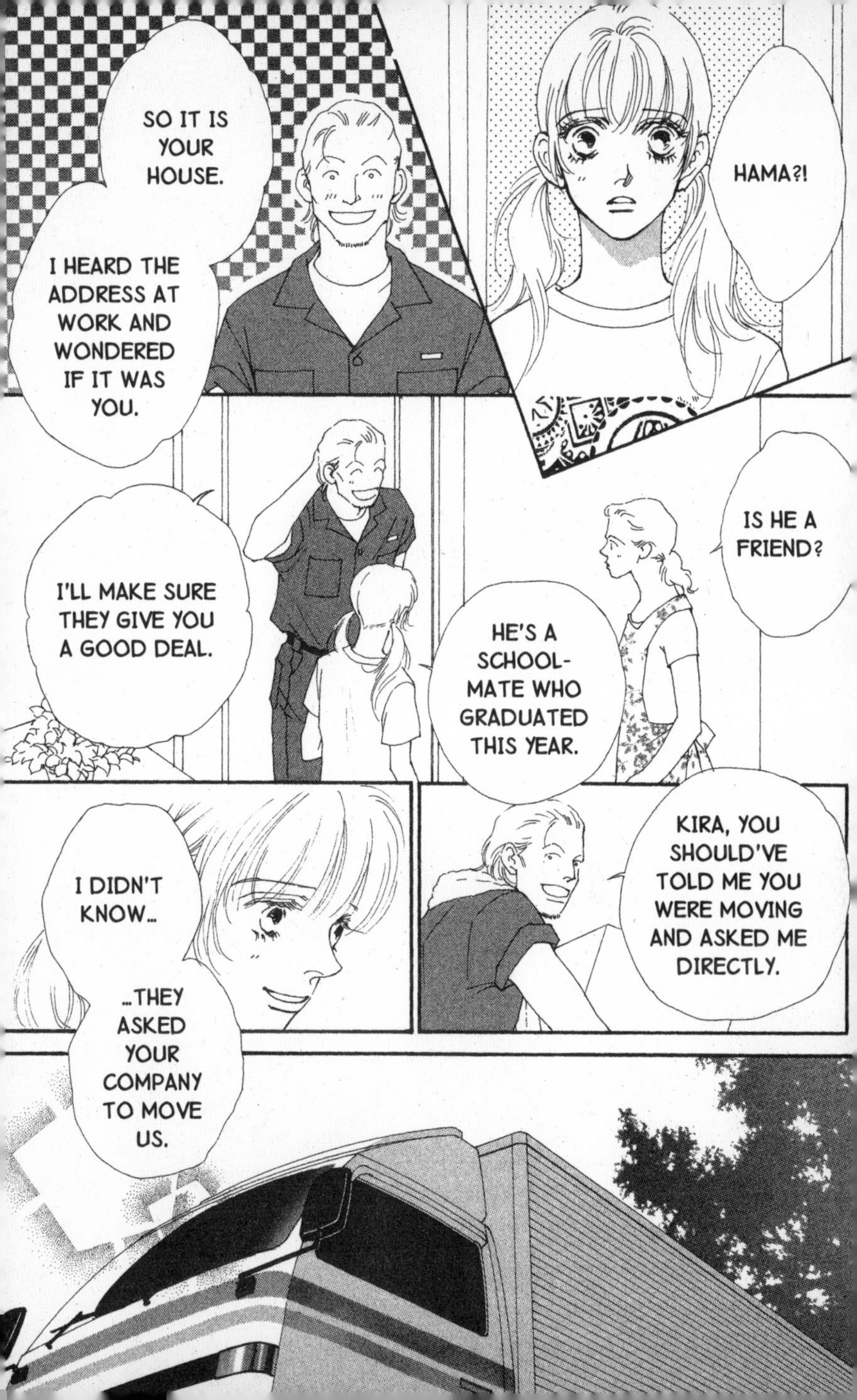
HAMA?!
SO IT IS YOUR HOUSE.
I HEARD THE ADDRESS AT WORK AND WONDERED IF IT WAS YOU.
IS HE A FRIEND?
HE'S A SCHOOL-MATE WHO GRADUATED THIS YEAR.
I'LL MAKE SURE THEY GIVE YOU A GOOD DEAL.
KIRA, YOU SHOULD'VE TOLD ME YOU WERE MOVING AND ASKED ME DIRECTLY.
I DIDN'T KNOW...
...THEY ASKED YOUR COMPANY TO MOVE US.

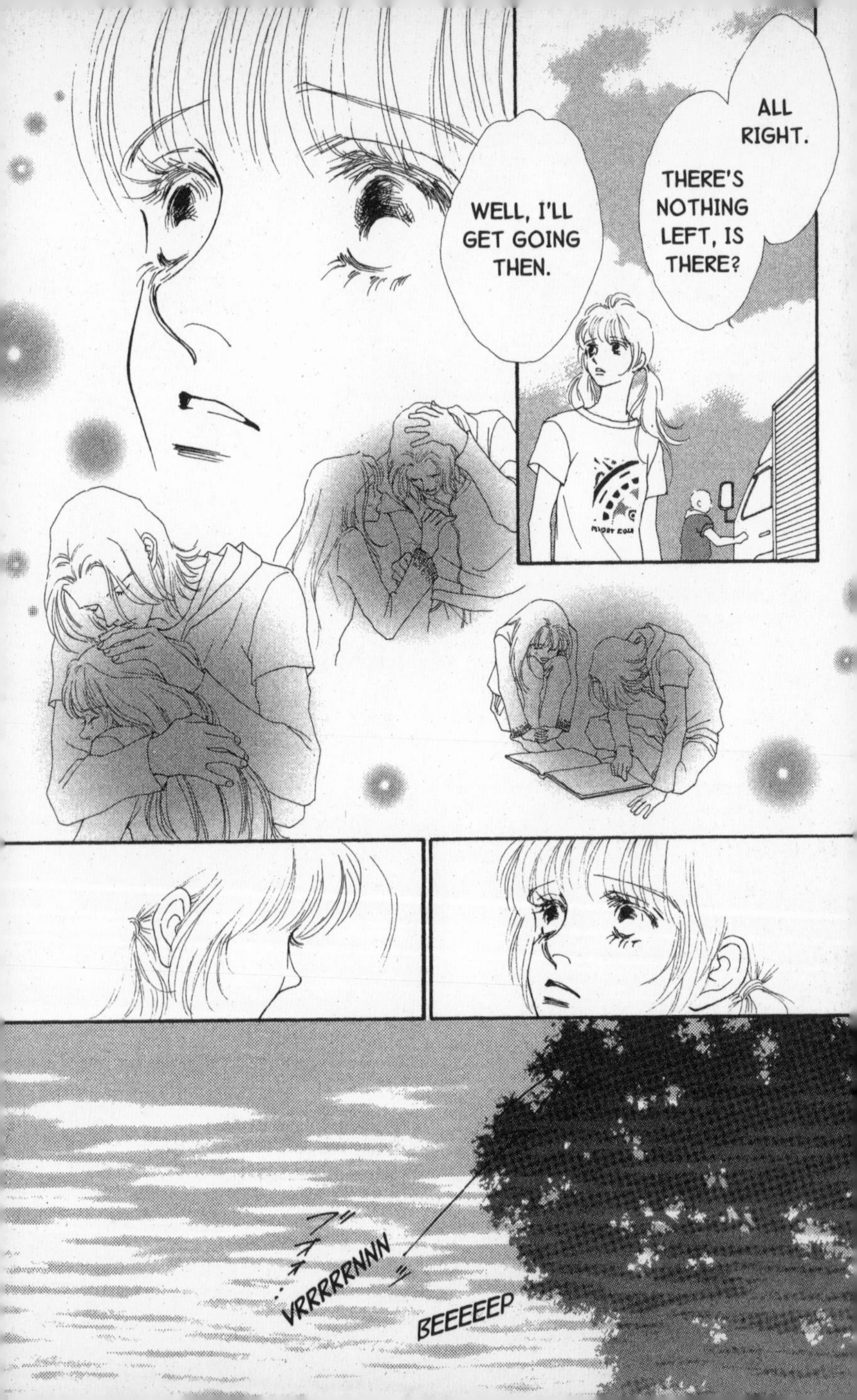
ALL RIGHT.
THERE'S NOTHING LEFT, IS THERE?
WELL, I'LL GET GOING THEN.
VRRRRRNNN
BEEEEEEP

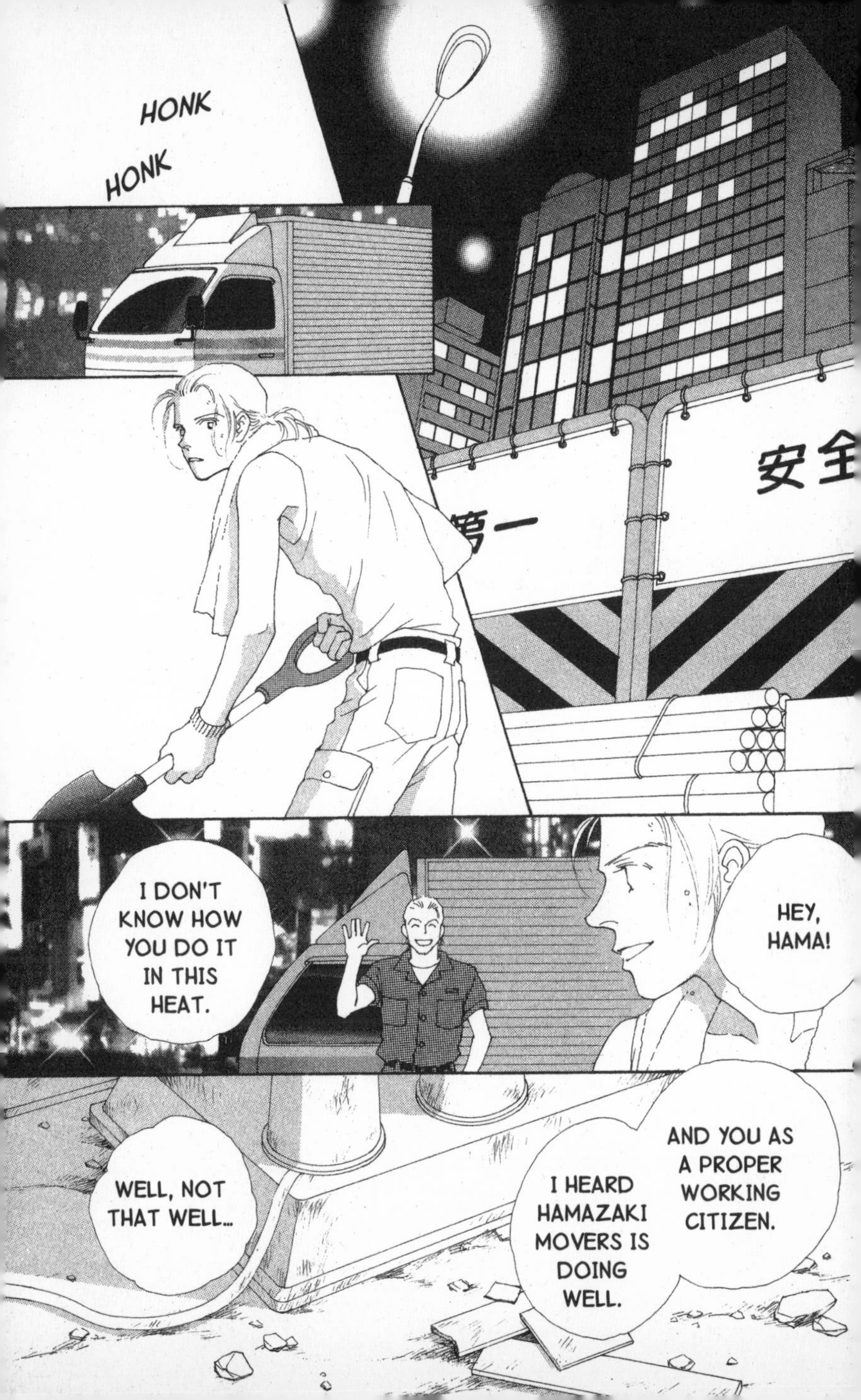
HONK
HONK
安全
第一
HEY, HAMA!
I DON'T KNOW HOW YOU DO IT IN THIS HEAT.
AND YOU AS A PROPER WORKING CITIZEN.
I HEARD HAMAZAKI MOVERS IS DOING WELL.
WELL, NOT THAT WELL...

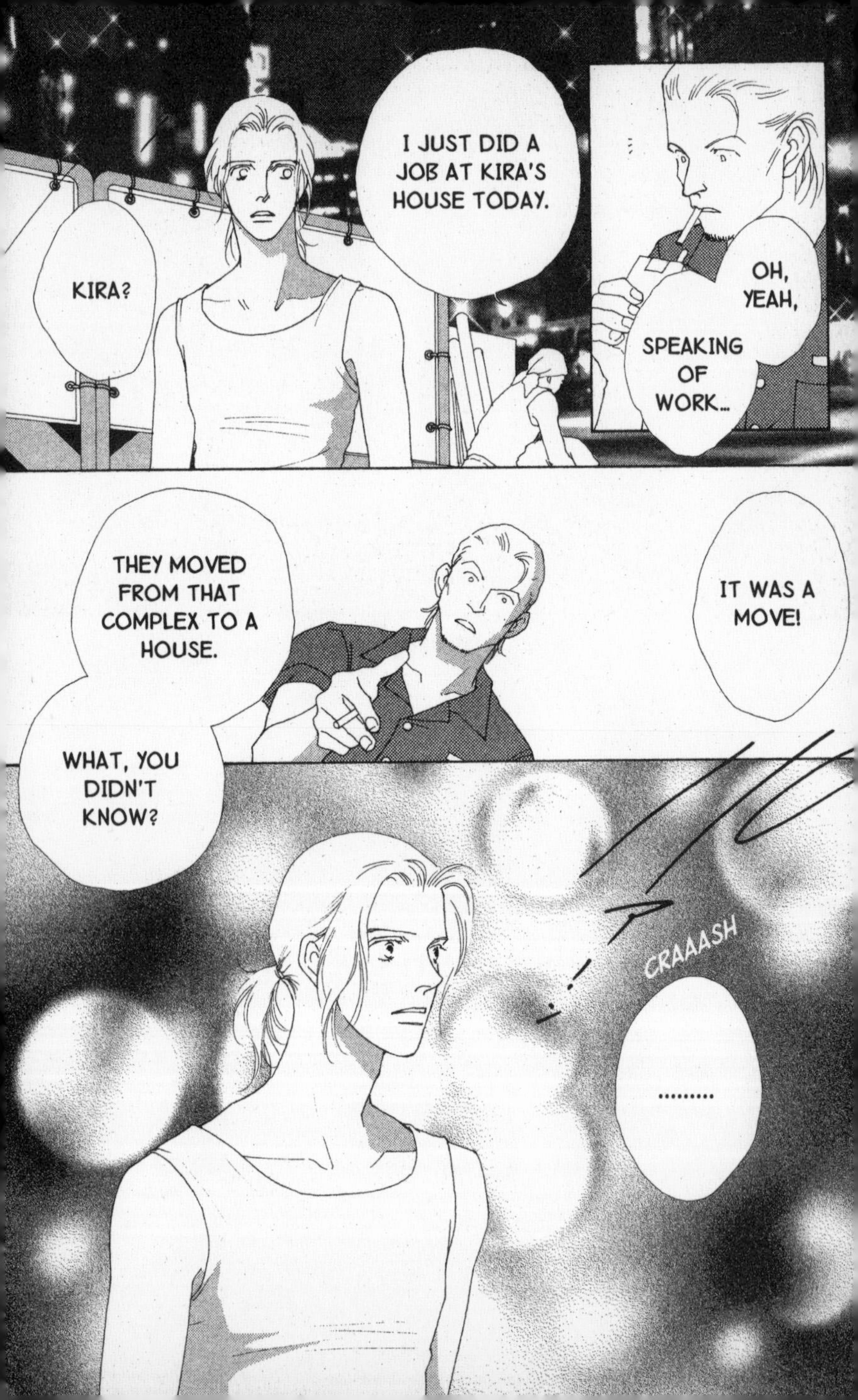
OH, YEAH,
SPEAKING OF WORK...
I JUST DID A JOB AT KIRA'S HOUSE TODAY.
KIRA?
IT WAS A MOVE!
THEY MOVED FROM THAT COMPLEX TO A HOUSE.
WHAT, YOU DIDN'T KNOW?
CRAAASH
....

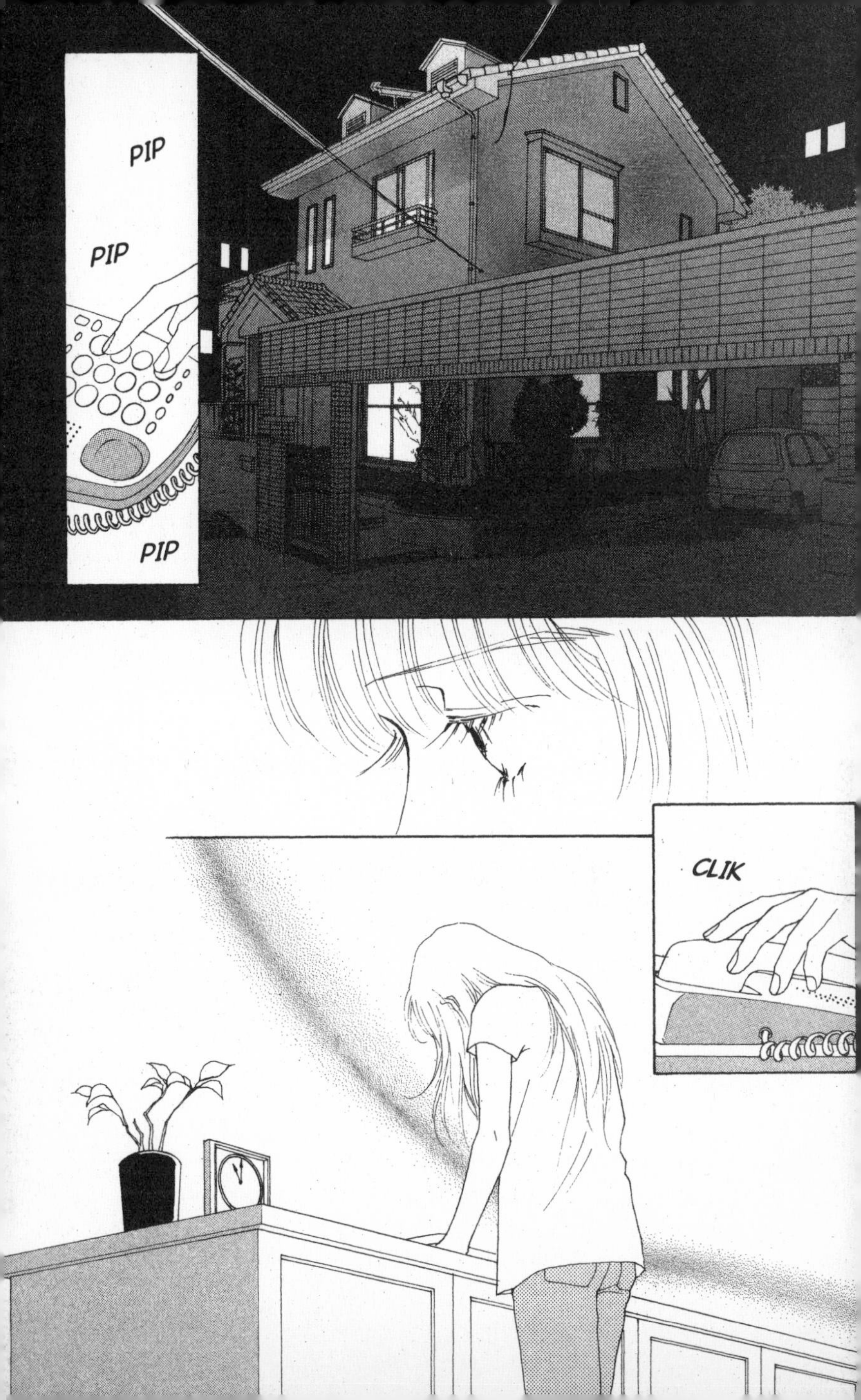
PIP
PIP
PIP
CLIK

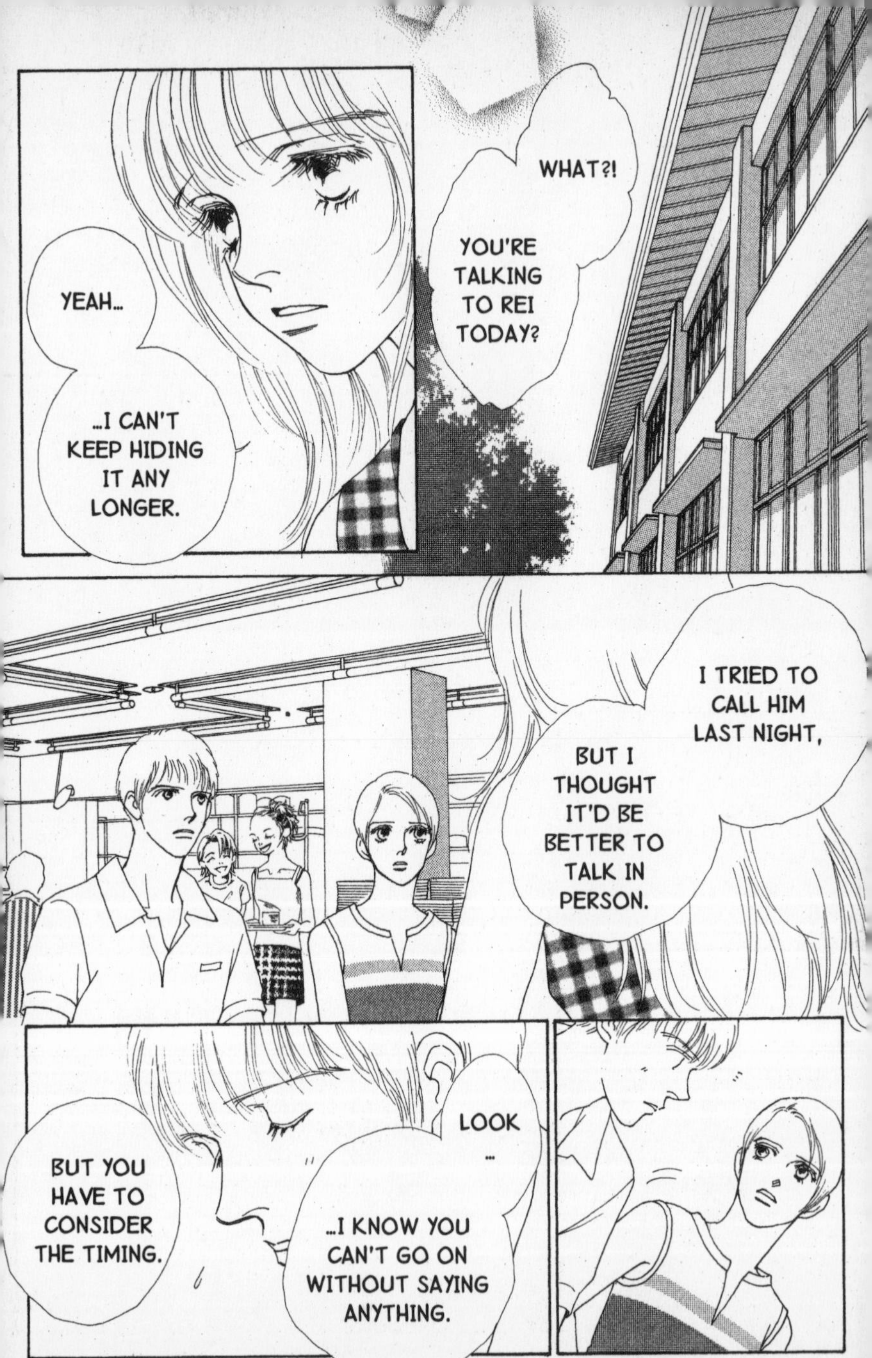
WHAT?!
YOU'RE TALKING TO REI TODAY?
YEAH...
...I CAN'T KEEP HIDING IT ANY LONGER.
I TRIED TO CALL HIM LAST NIGHT,
BUT I THOUGHT IT'D BE BETTER TO TALK IN PERSON.
LOOK...
...I KNOW YOU CAN'T GO ON WITHOUT SAYING ANYTHING.
BUT YOU HAVE TO CONSIDER THE TIMING.

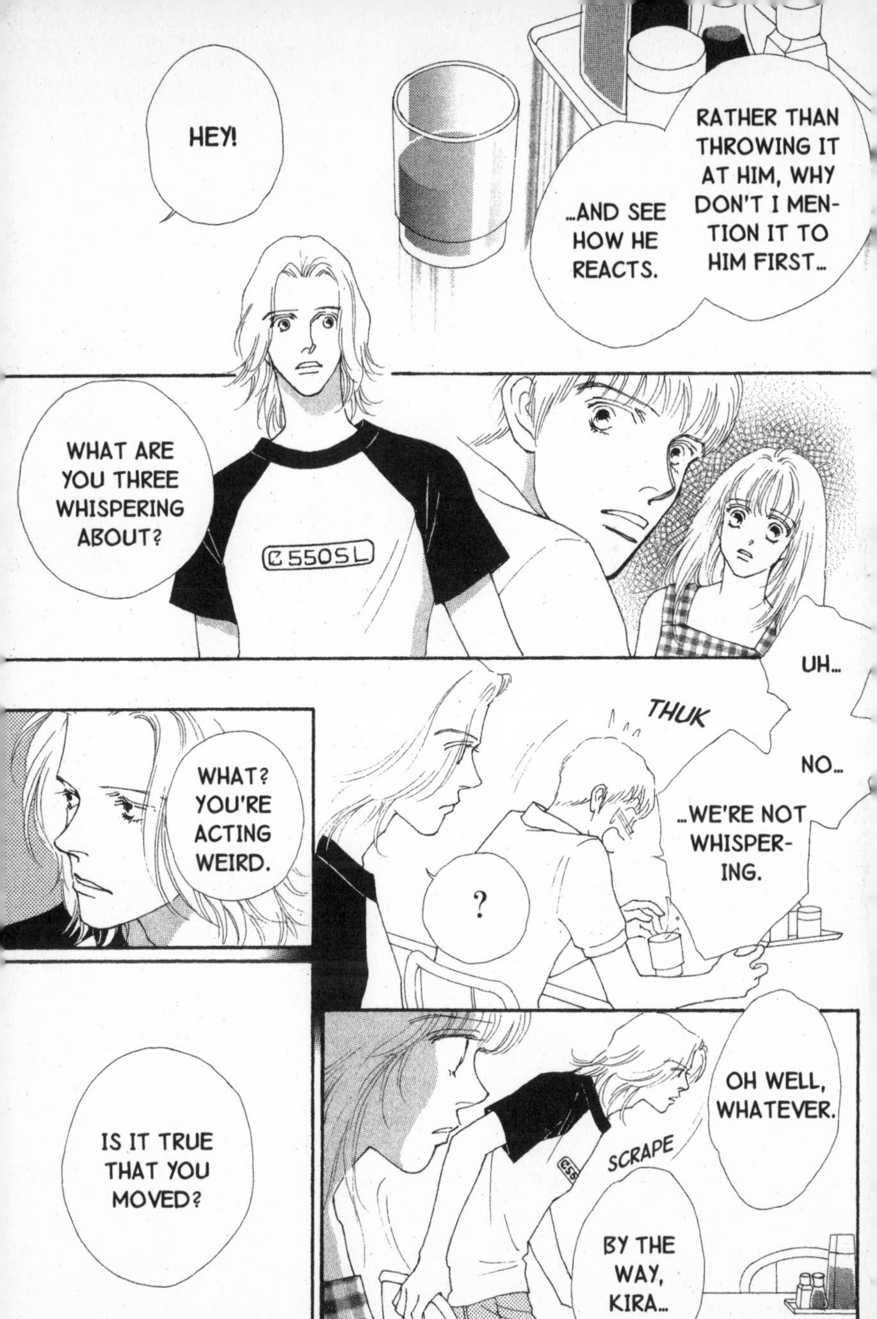
RATHER THAN THROWING IT AT HIM, WHY DON'T I MEN-TION IT TO HIM FIRST...
...AND SEE HOW HE REACTS.
HEY!
WHAT ARE YOU THREE WHISPERING ABOUT?
C550SL
UH...
THUK
NO...
...WE'RE NOT WHISPER-ING.
?
WHAT? YOU'RE ACTING WEIRD.
OH WELL, WHATEVER.
SCRAPE
BY THE WAY, KIRA...
IS IT TRUE THAT YOU MOVED?

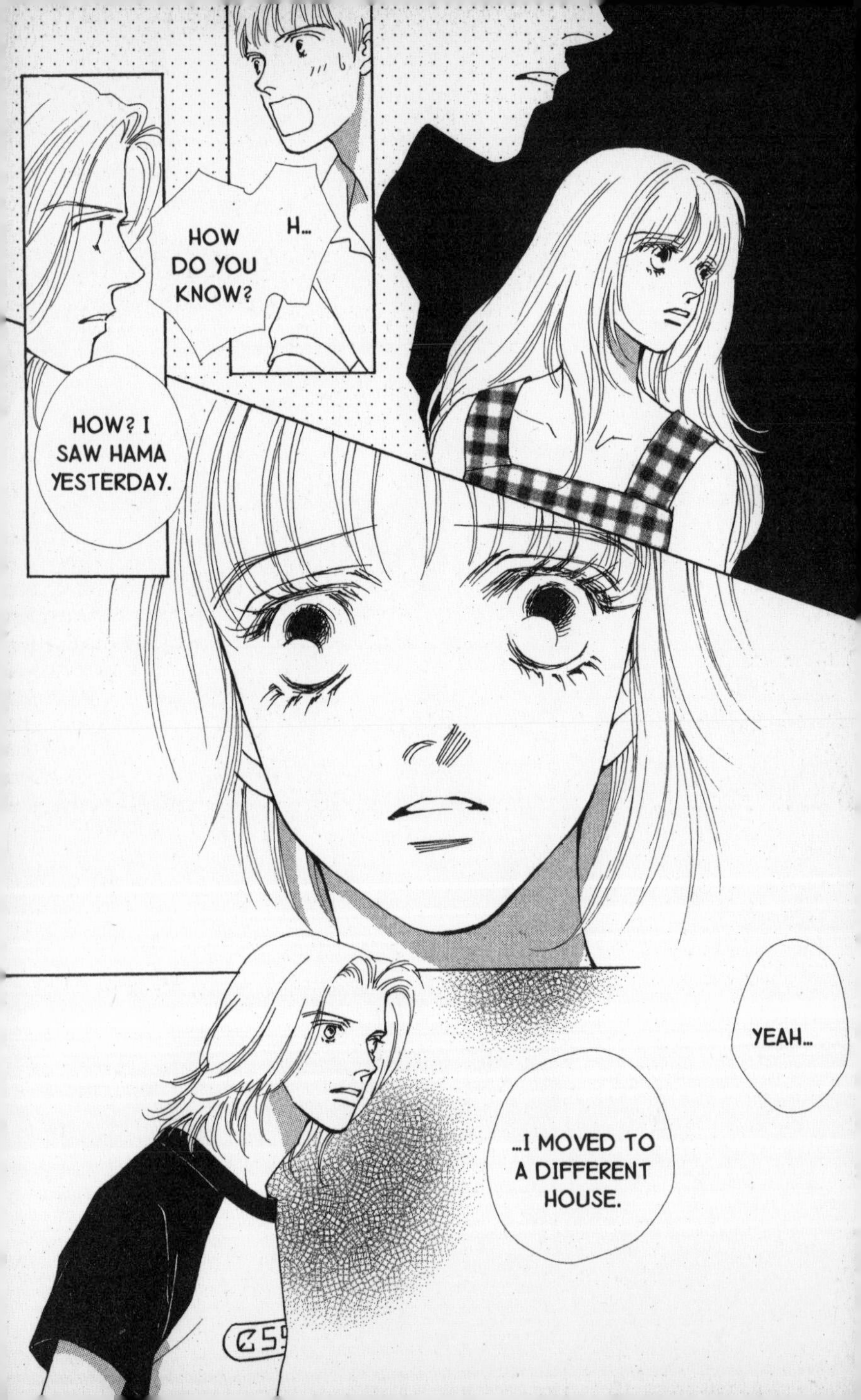
H... HOW DO YOU KNOW?
HOW? I SAW HAMA YESTERDAY.
YEAH...
...I MOVED TO A DIFFERENT HOUSE.

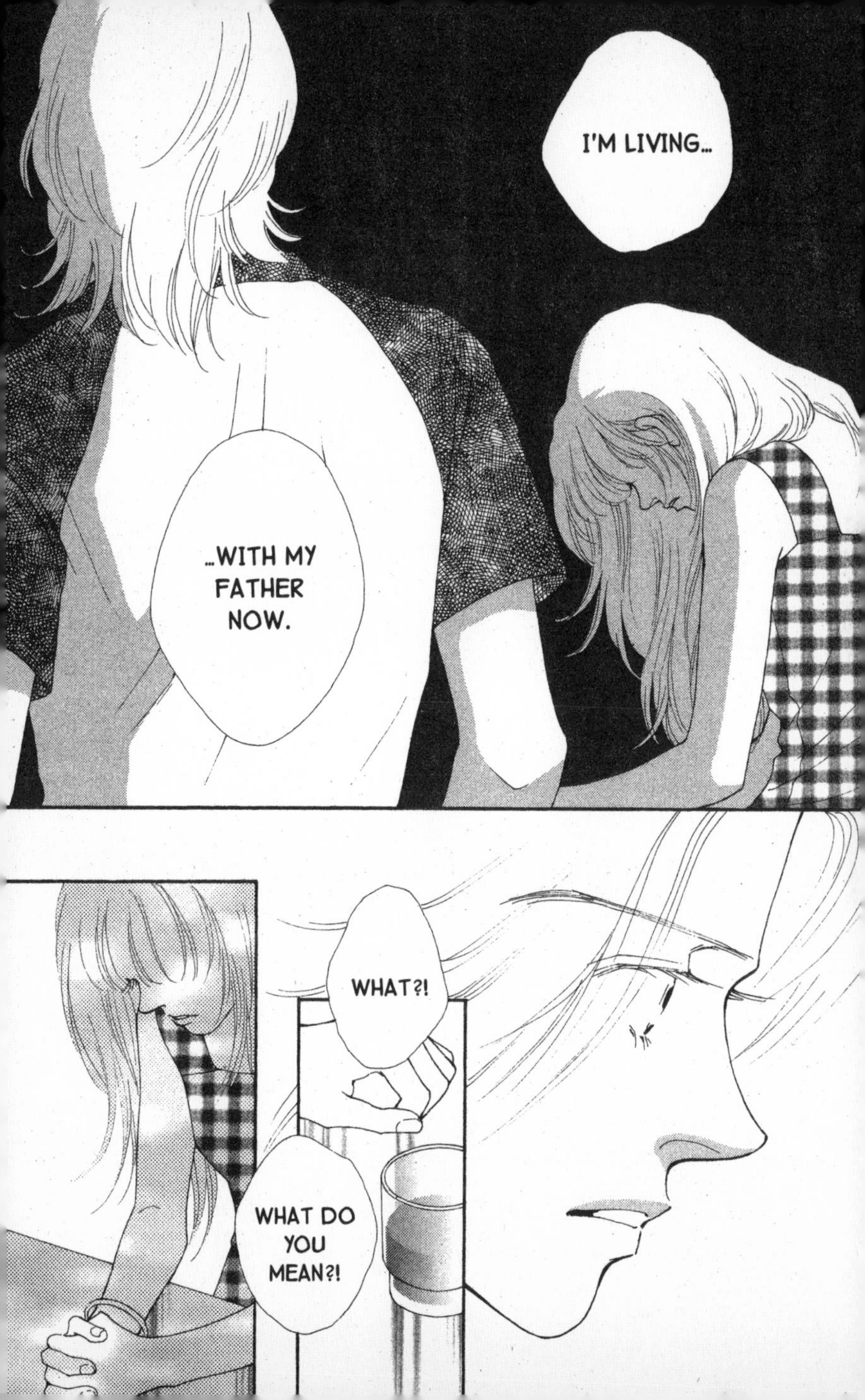
I'M LIVING...
...WITH MY FATHER NOW.
WHAT?!
WHAT DO YOU MEAN?!

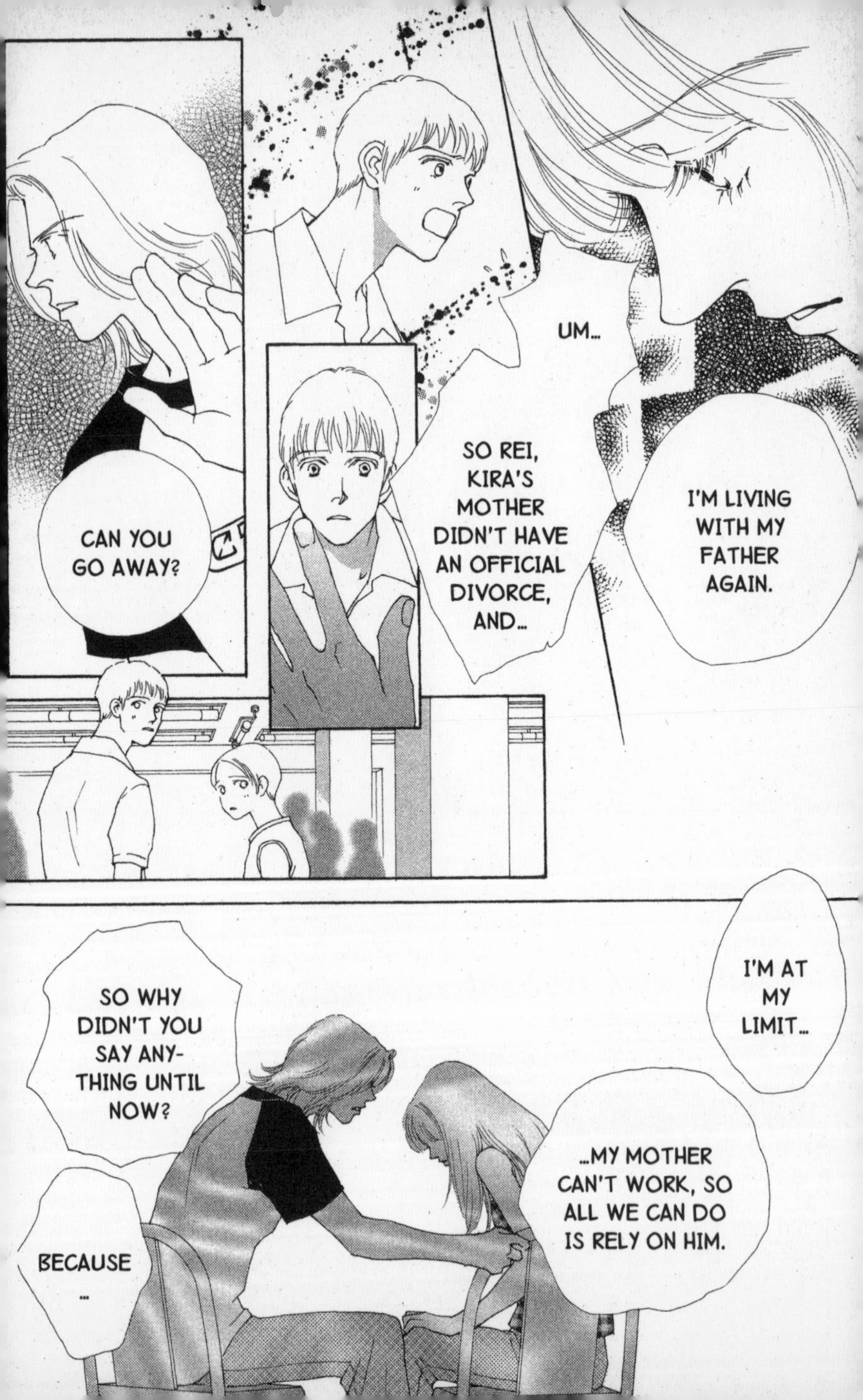
UM...
I'M LIVING WITH MY FATHER AGAIN.
SO REI, KIRA'S MOTHER DIDN'T HAVE AN OFFICIAL DIVORCE, AND...
CAN YOU GO AWAY?
I'M AT MY LIMIT...
...MY MOTHER CAN'T WORK, SO ALL WE CAN DO IS RELY ON HIM.
SO WHY DIDN'T YOU SAY ANY-THING UNTIL NOW?
BECAUSE ...

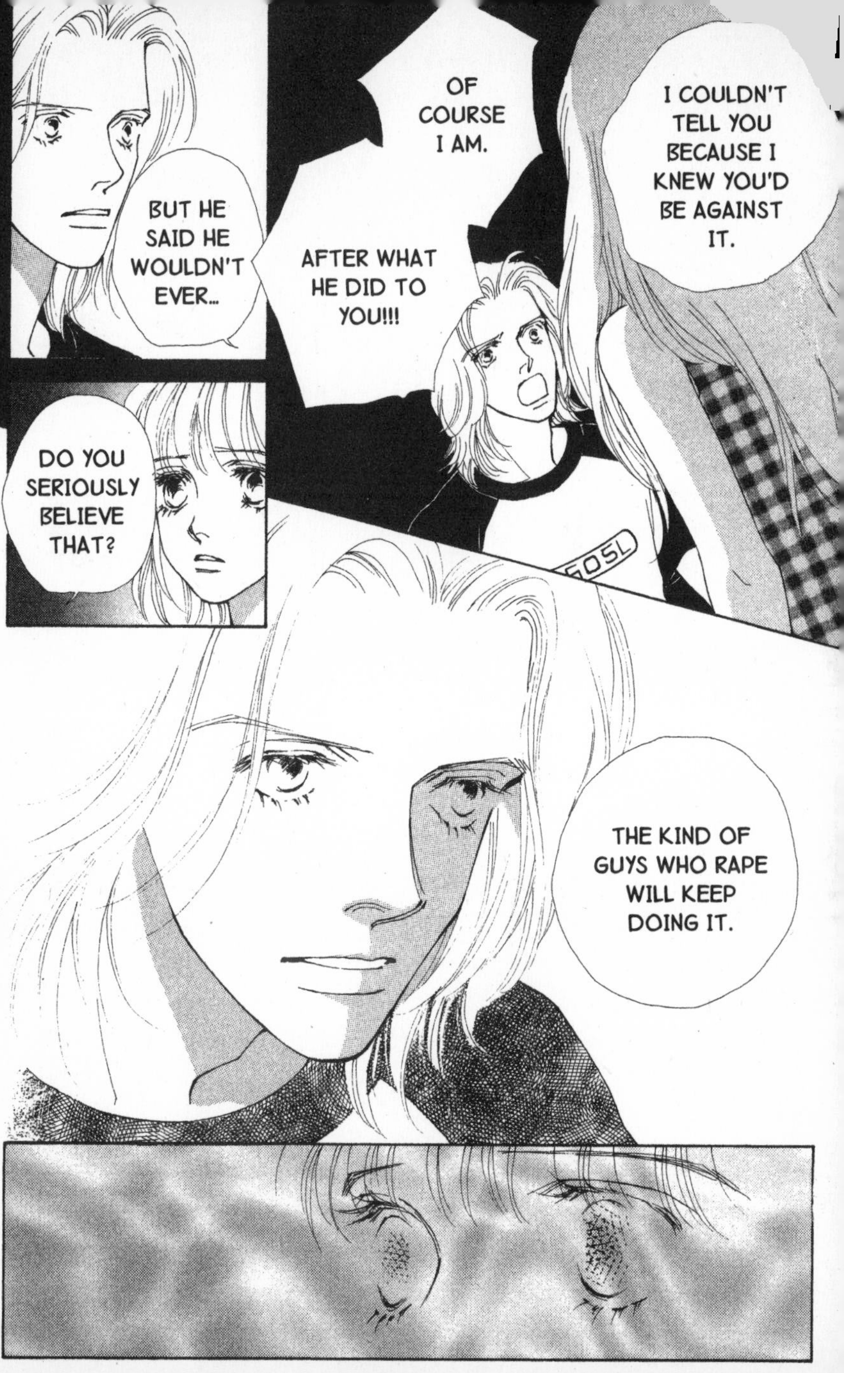
I COULDN'T TELL YOU BECAUSE I KNEW YOU'D BE AGAINST IT.
OF COURSE I AM.
AFTER WHAT HE DID TO YOU!!!
BUT HE SAID HE WOULDN'T EVER...
DO YOU SERIOUSLY BELIEVE THAT?
THE KIND OF GUYS WHO RAPE WILL KEEP DOING IT.

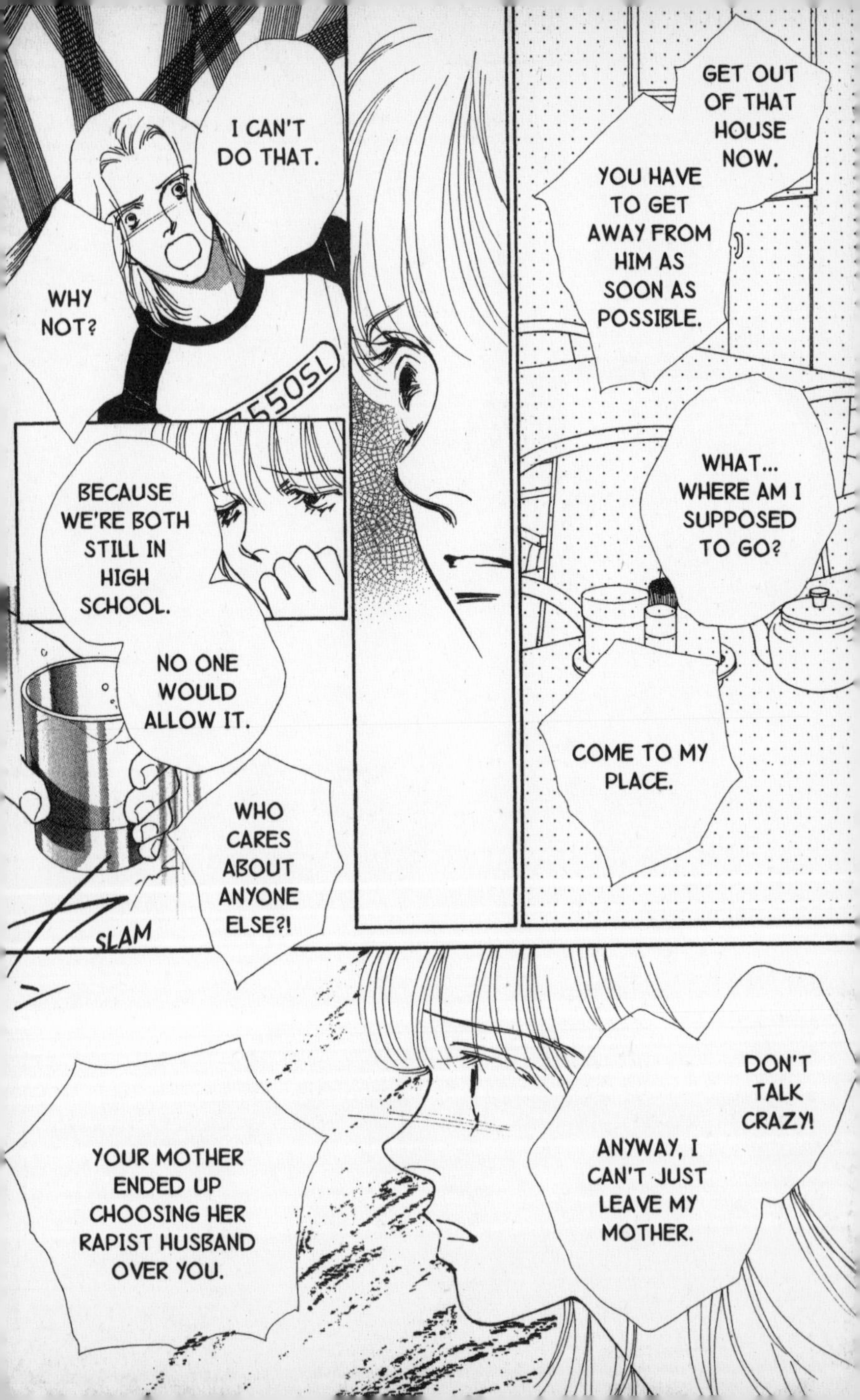
GET OUT OF THAT HOUSE NOW.
YOU HAVE TO GET AWAY FROM HIM AS SOON AS POSSIBLE.
WHAT... WHERE AM I SUPPOSED TO GO?
COME TO MY PLACE.
I CAN'T DO THAT.
WHY NOT?
BECAUSE WE'RE BOTH STILL IN HIGH SCHOOL.
NO ONE WOULD ALLOW IT.
WHO CARES ABOUT ANYONE ELSE?!
SLAM
DON'T TALK CRAZY!
ANYWAY, I CAN'T JUST LEAVE MY MOTHER.
YOUR MOTHER ENDED UP CHOOSING HER RAPIST HUSBAND OVER YOU.

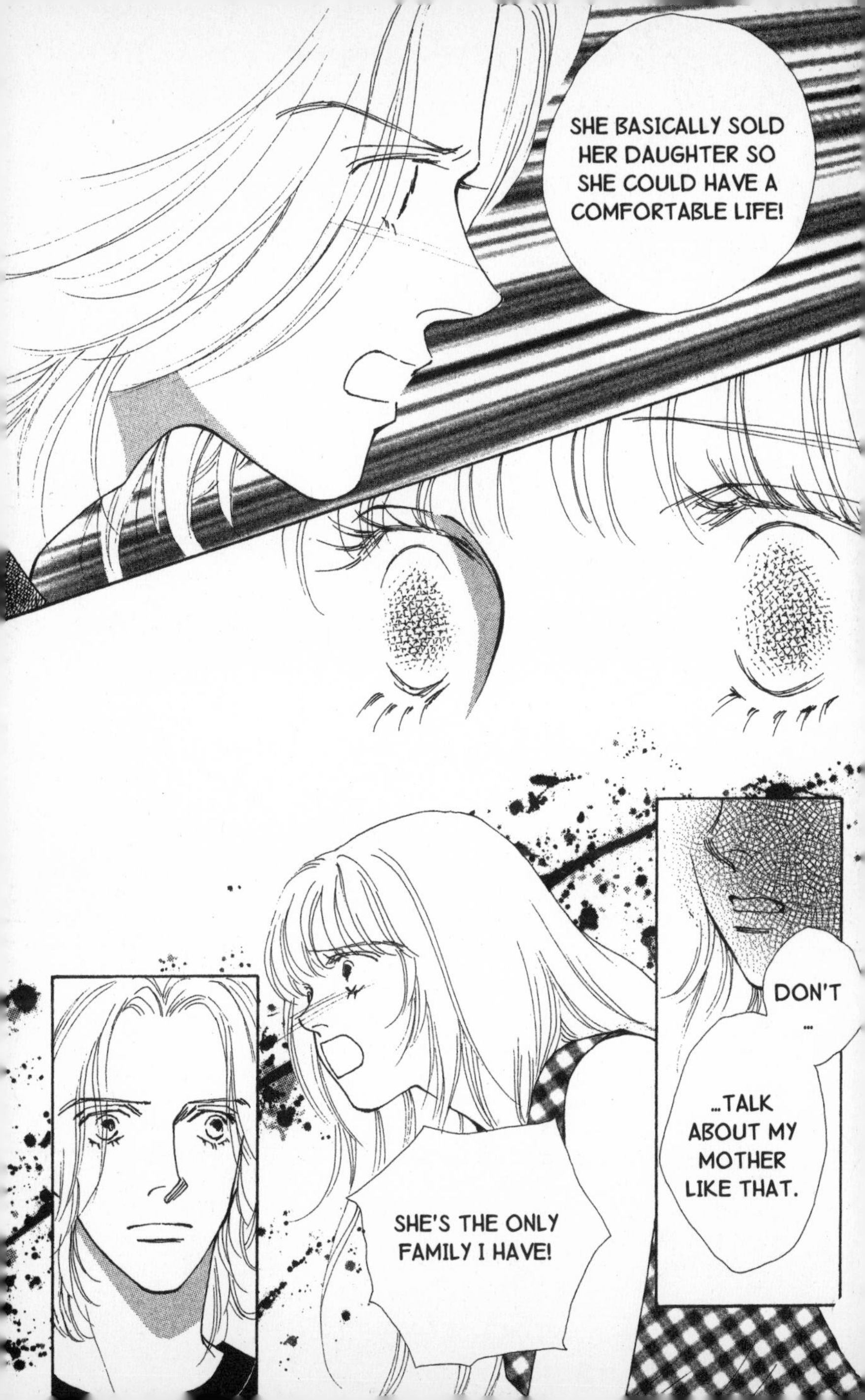
SHE BASICALLY SOLD HER DAUGHTER SO SHE COULD HAVE A COMFORTABLE LIFE!
DON'T ...
...TALK ABOUT MY MOTHER LIKE THAT.
SHE'S THE ONLY FAMILY I HAVE!

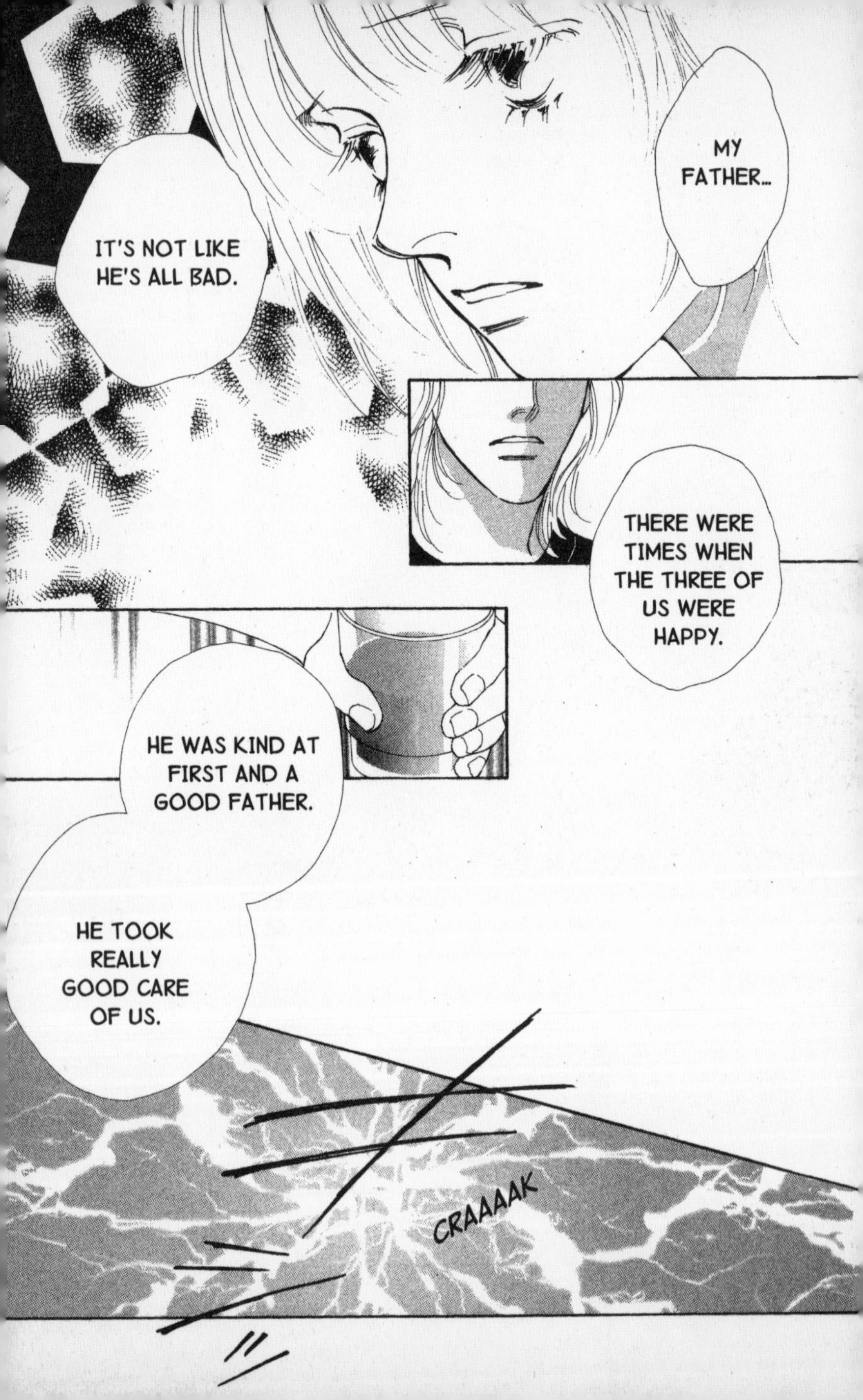
MY FATHER...
IT'S NOT LIKE HE'S ALL BAD.
THERE WERE TIMES WHEN THE THREE OF US WERE HAPPY.
HE WAS KIND AT FIRST AND A GOOD FATHER.
HE TOOK REALLY GOOD CARE OF US.
CRAAAK

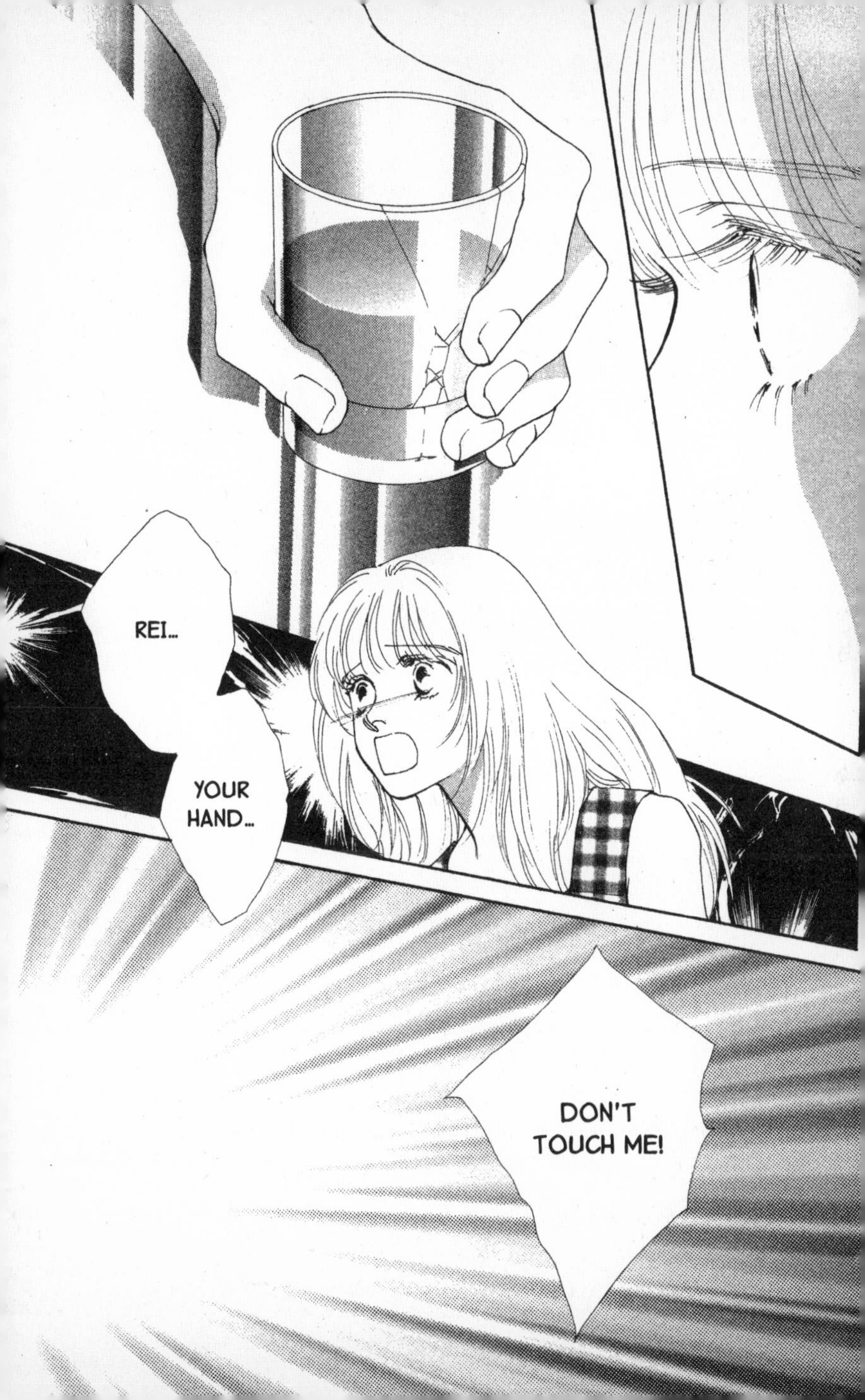
REI...
YOUR HAND...
DON'T TOUCH ME!

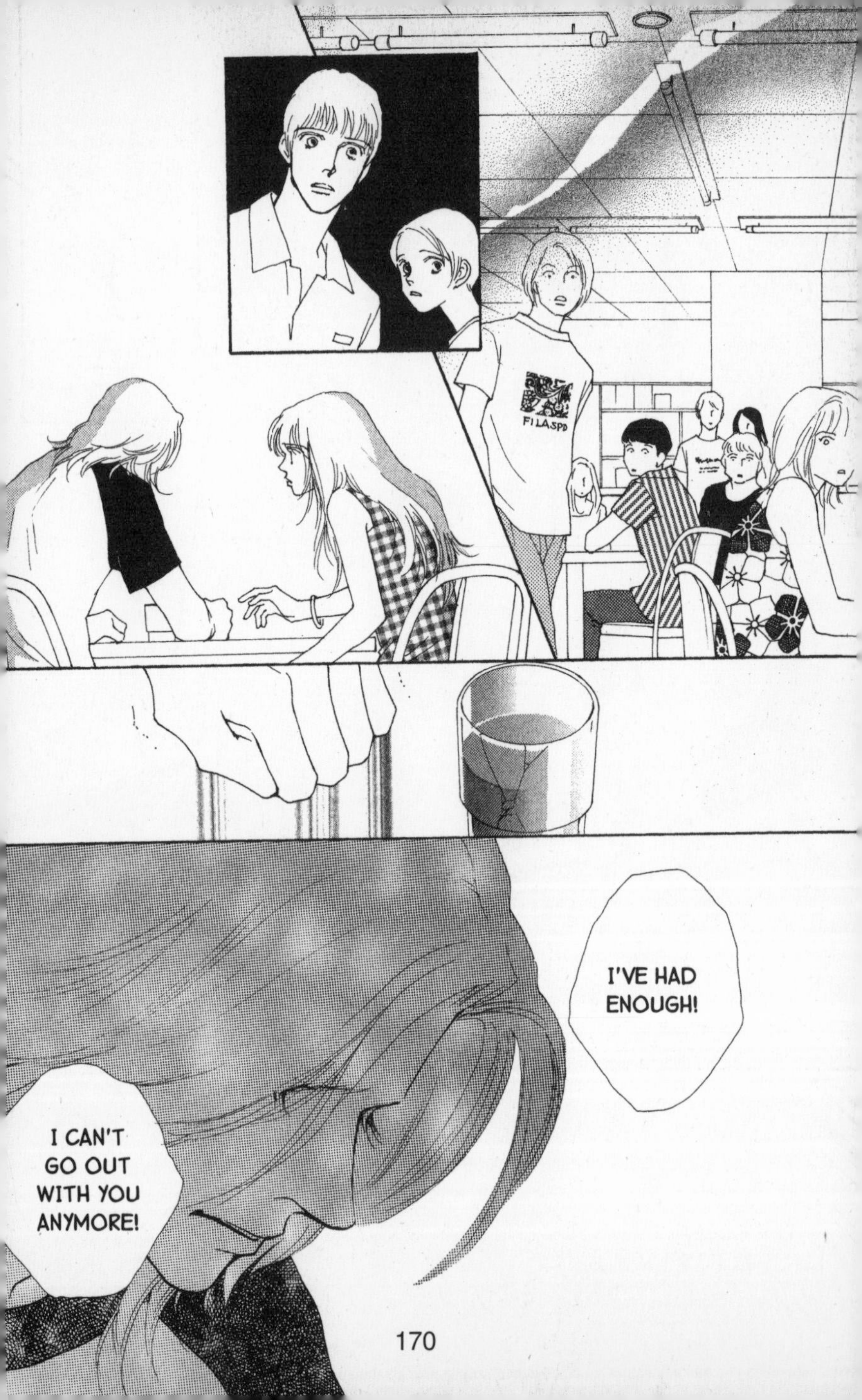
FILASPD
I'VE HAD ENOUGH!
I CAN'T GO OUT WITH YOU ANYMORE!

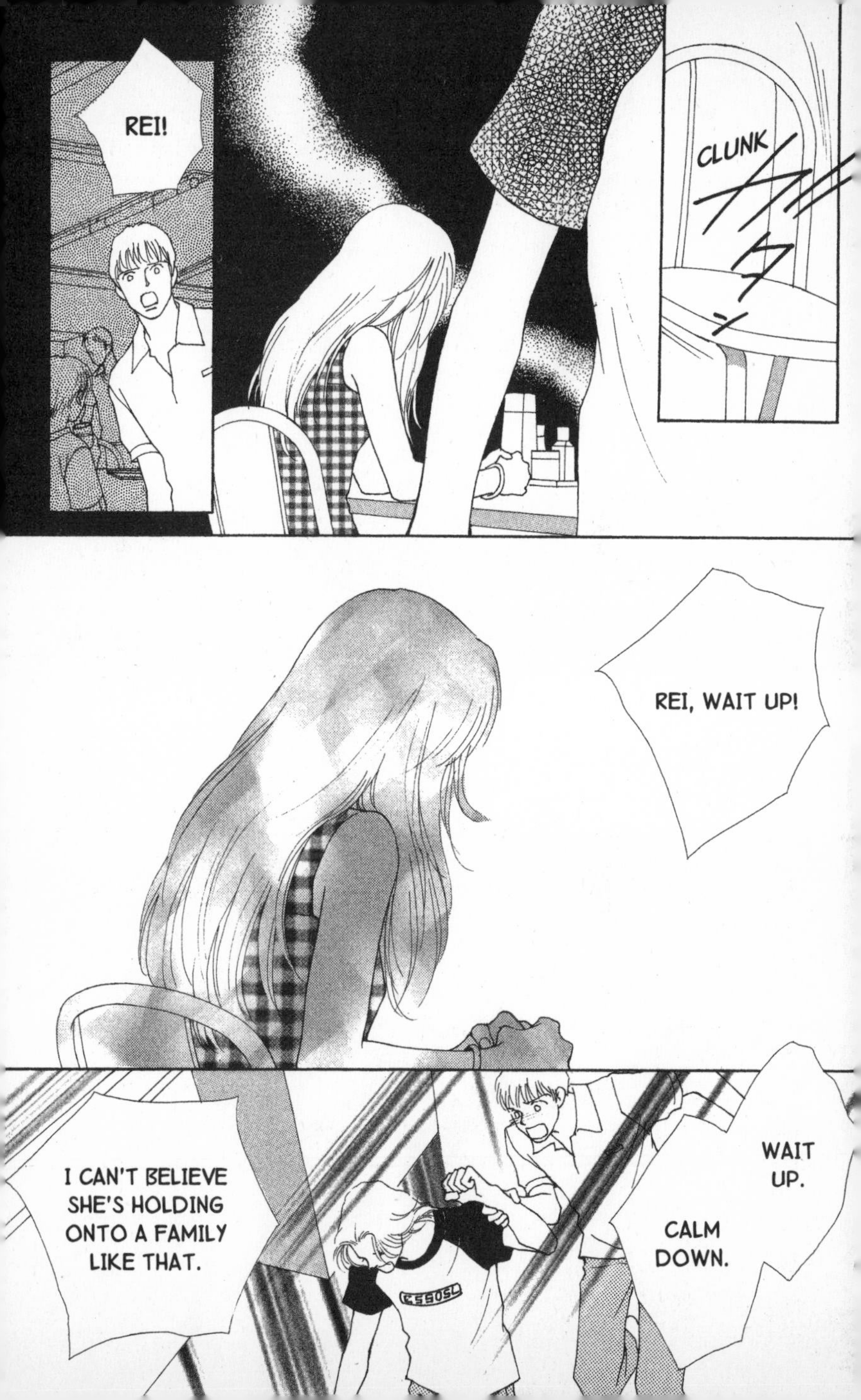
CLUNK
REI!
REI, WAIT UP!
WAIT UP.
CALM DOWN.
I CAN'T BELIEVE SHE'S HOLDING ONTO A FAMILY LIKE THAT.

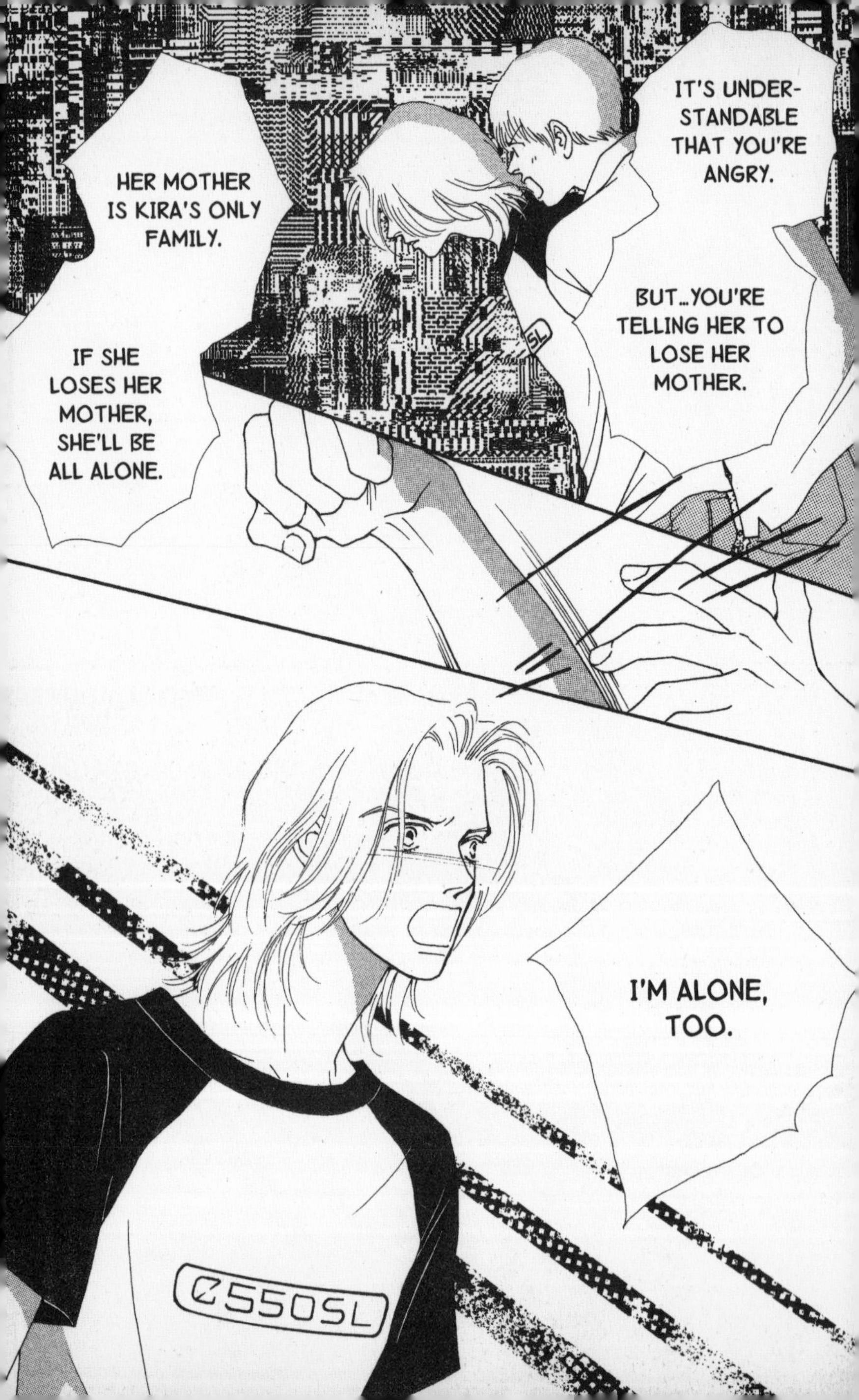
IT'S UNDER-STANDABLE THAT YOU'RE ANGRY.
BUT...YOU'RE TELLING HER TO LOSE HER MOTHER.
HER MOTHER IS KIRA'S ONLY FAMILY.
IF SHE LOSES HER MOTHER, SHE'LL BE ALL ALONE.
I'M ALONE, TOO.

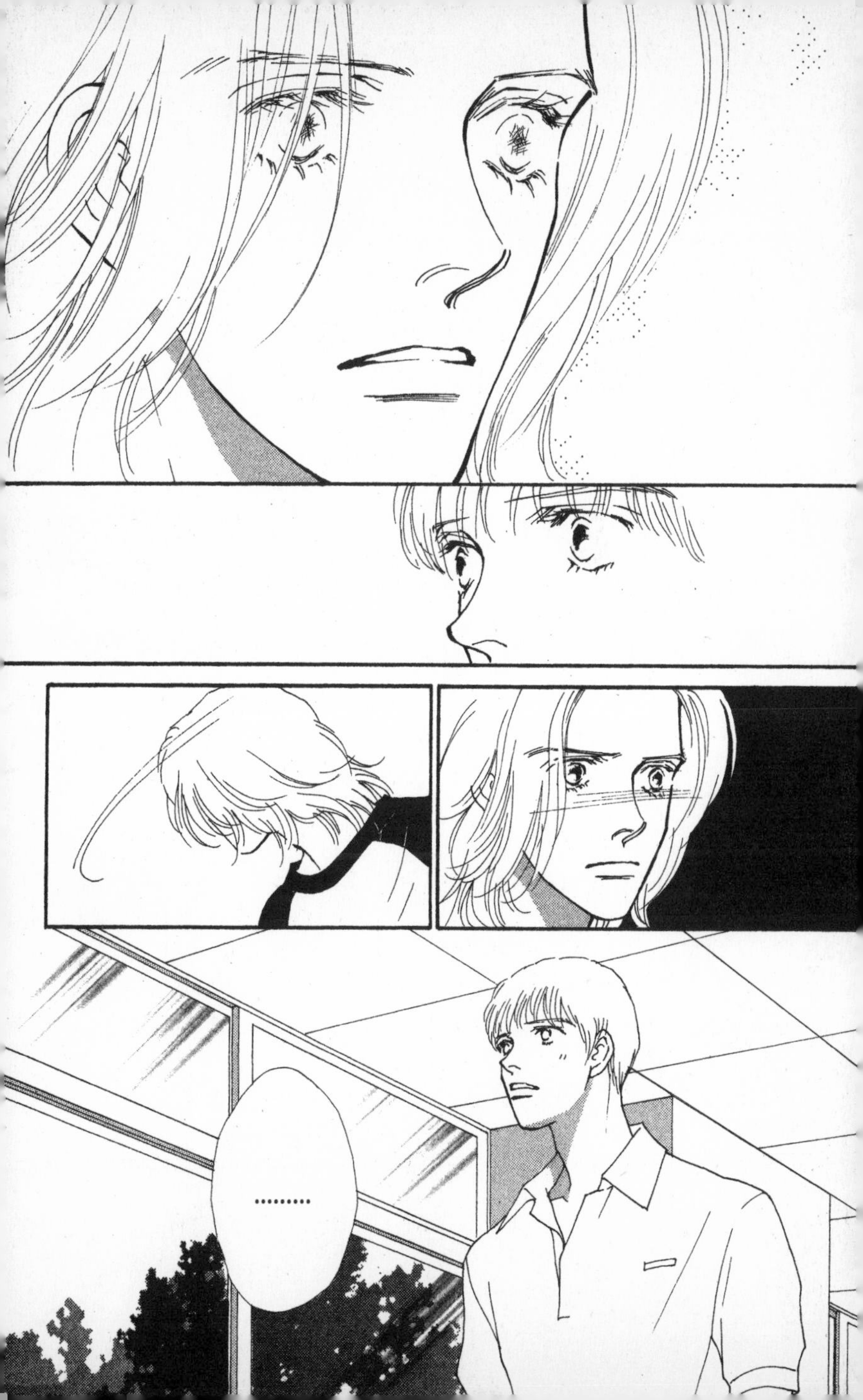
....

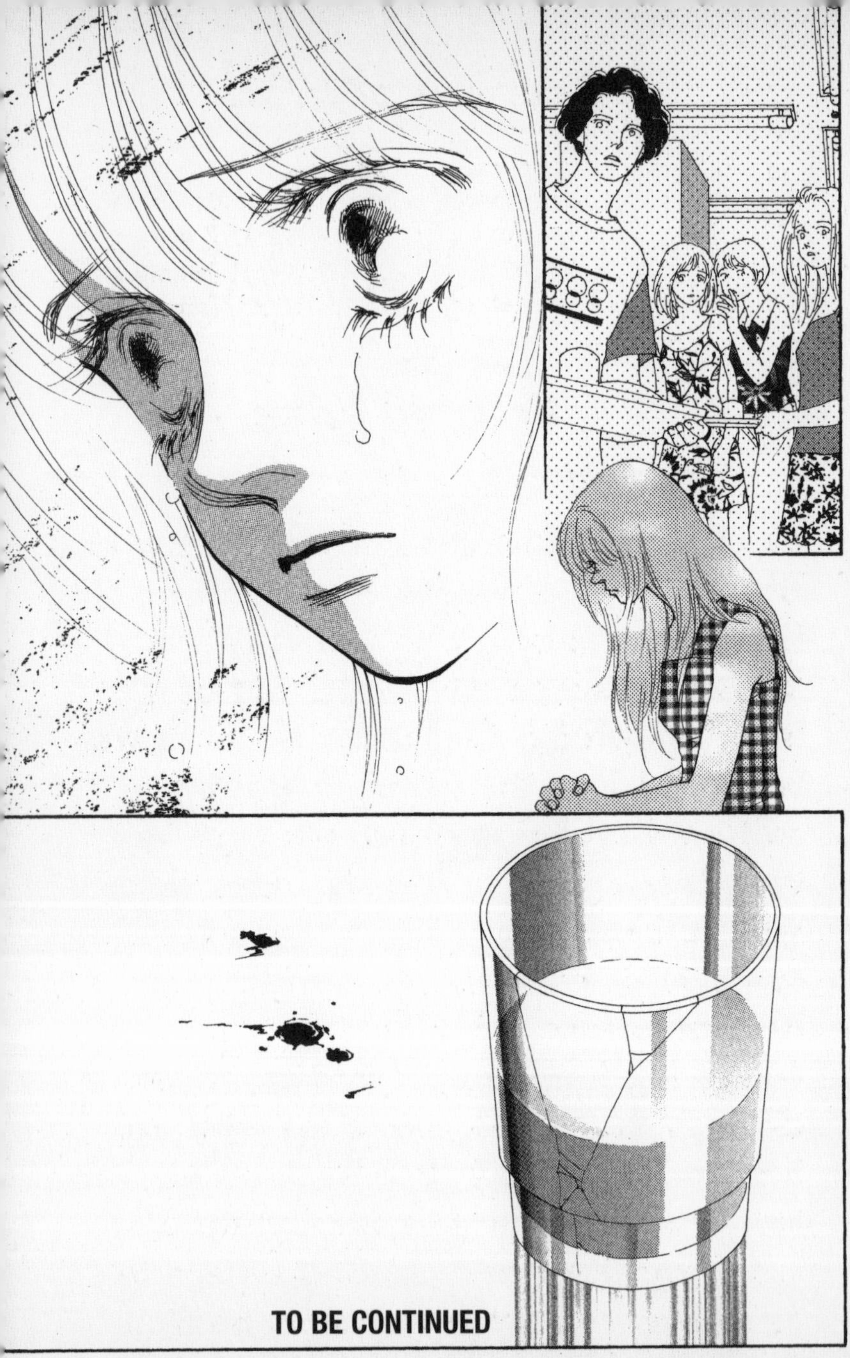
TO BE CONTINUED

Coming Soon...

Volume Nine

The unthinkable has happened! Rei and Kira have finally broken up and it's the talk of the town. Kira can only stand by helplessly as Rei walks out of her life. Though Rei feigns indifference as he walks into the arms of waiting suitors, he begins to realize that he may have been too hasty in his decision to break up. Kira struggles to come to grips with being alone and also questions what she has done. Following her friends' advice, Kira decides to try and make up with Rei before it's too late, but he is nowhere to be found. With her family life also suffering, Kira has no idea where to turn. Find out what happens next in this nail-biting volume of Mars!

Chobits

In the Future, Boys will be Boys and Girls will be Robots.

Graphic Novels Available Now

See TOKYOPOP.com for other CLAMP titles.

100% AUTHENTIC MANGA

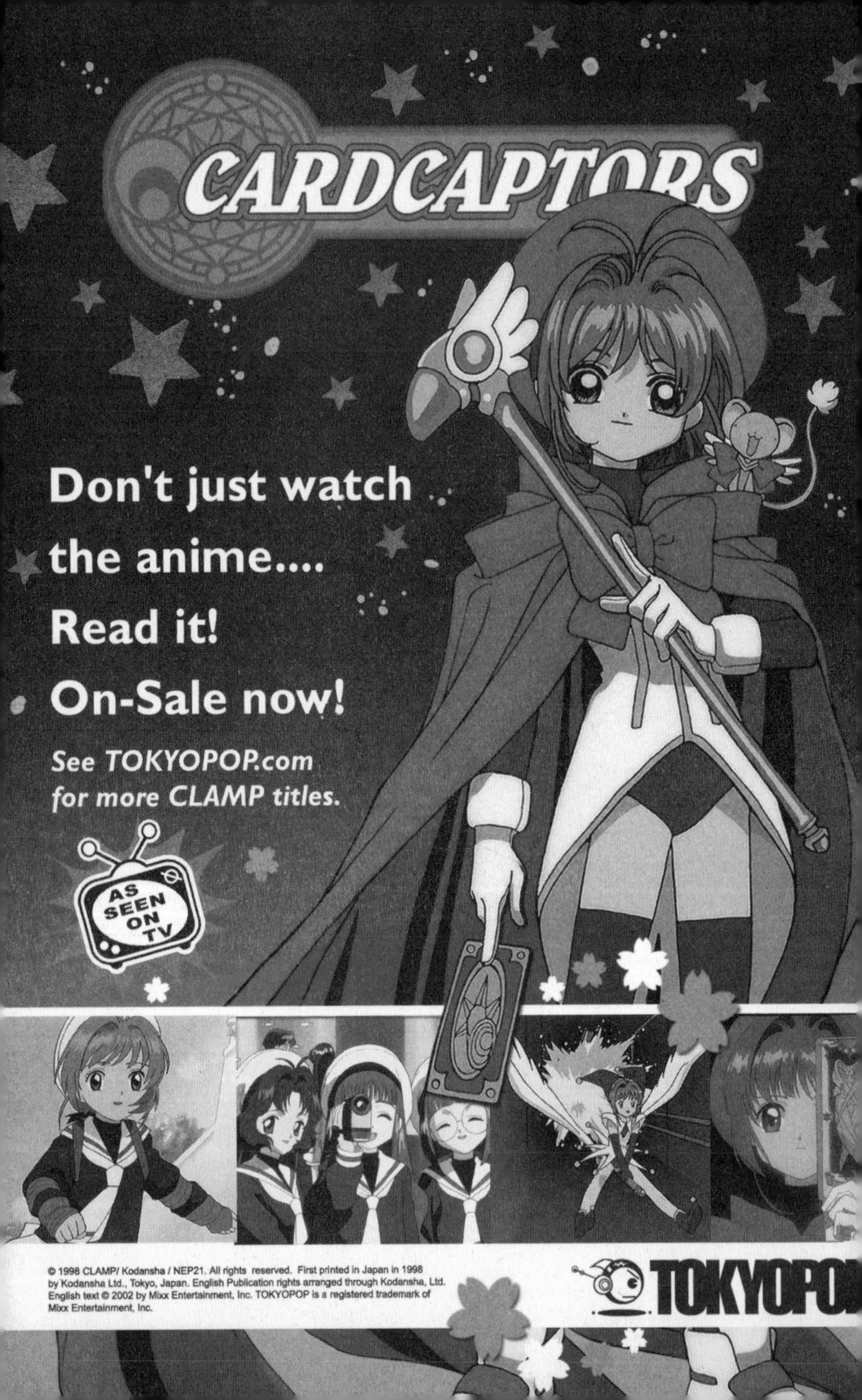
CARDCAPTORS
Don't just watch the anime....
Read it!
On-Sale now!
See TOKYOPOP.com for more CLAMP titles.
AS SEEN ON TV
© 1998 CLAMP/ Kodansha / NEP21. All rights reserved. First printed in Japan in 1998 by Kodansha Ltd., Tokyo, Japan. English Publication rights arranged through Kodansha, Ltd. English text © 2002 by Mixx Entertainment, Inc. TOKYOPOP is a registered trademark of Mixx Entertainment, Inc.
TOKYOPOP

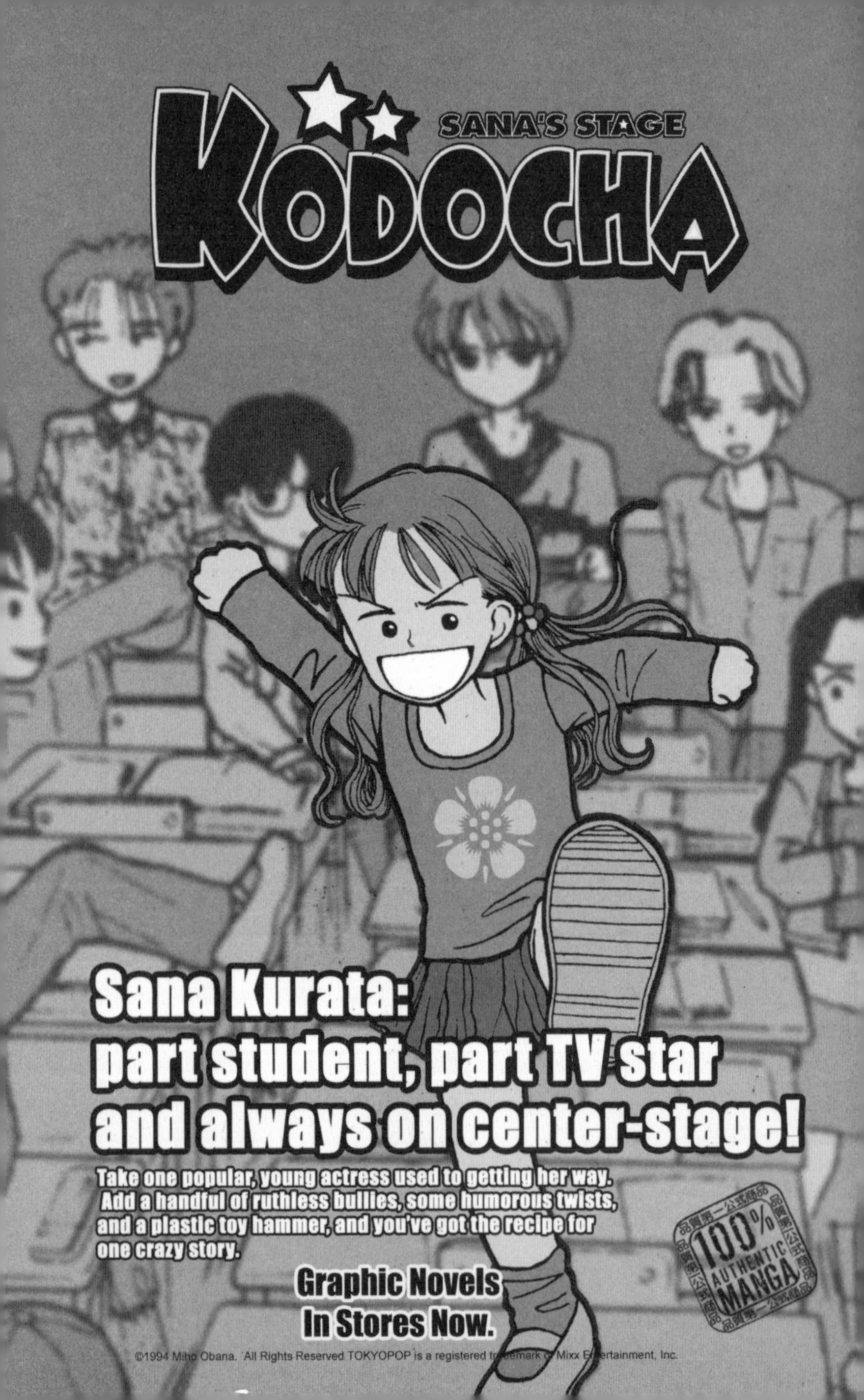
SANA'S STAGE
KODOCHA
Sana Kurata:
part student, part TV star
and always on center-stage!
Take one popular, young actress used to getting her way.
Add a handful of ruthless bullies, some humorous twists,
and a plastic toy hammer, and you've got the recipe for
one crazy story.
Graphic Novels
In Stores Now.
100% AUTHENTIC MANGA
©1994 Miho Obana. All Rights Reserved TOKYOPOP is a registered trademark of Mixx Entertainment, Inc.

Miki's a love struck young girl and Yuu's the perfect guy.

There's just one minor complication in

Marmalade Boy

A tangled teen romance for the new millennium

"Marmalade Boy
has a beguiling
comedic charm...and
the likable characters
make for a delightful
read."
- Andrew D. Arnold
Time.com

TOKYOPOP

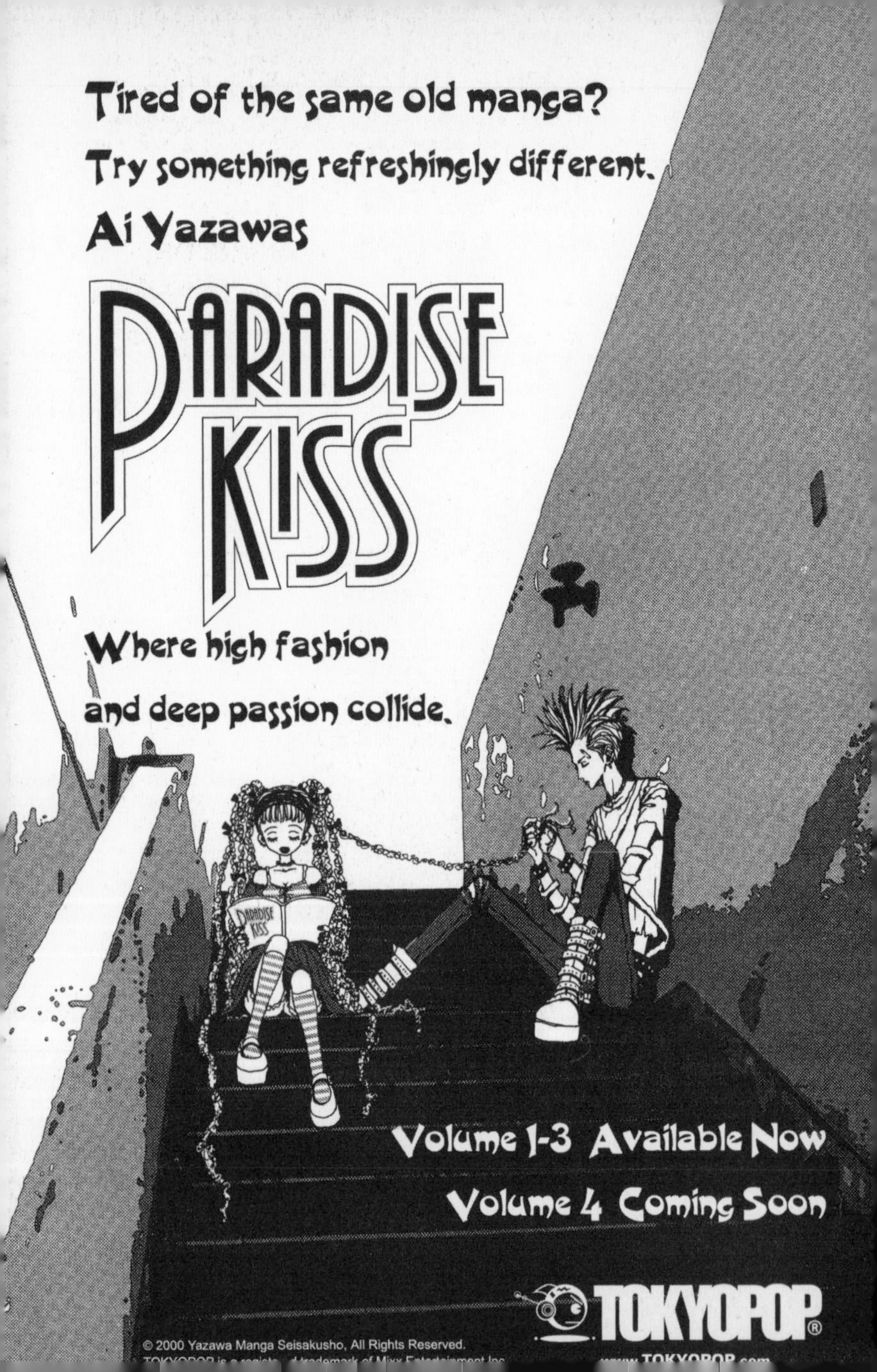
Tired of the same old manga?
Try something refreshingly different.
Ai Yazawas
PARADISE KISS
Where high fashion
and deep passion collide.
PARADISE KISS
Volume 1-3 Available Now
Volume 4 Coming Soon
TOKYOPOP®
© 2000 Yazawa Manga Seisakusho, All Rights Reserved.

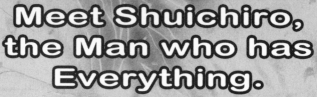

STOP!

This is the back of the book.
You wouldn't want to spoil a great ending!

This book is printed "manga-style," in the authentic Japanese right-to-left format. Since none of the artwork has been flipped or altered, readers get to experience the story just as the creator intended. You've been asking for it, so TOKYOPOP® delivered: authentic, hot-off-the-press, and far more fun!

DIRECTIONS

If this is your first time reading manga-style, here's a quick guide to help you understand how it works.

It's easy... just start in the top right panel and follow the numbers. Have fun, and look for more 100% authentic manga from TOKYOPOP®!